艺术类研究生英语教程
ART ENGLISH FOR GRADUATE STUDENTS

主编 倪 进
编著 赵彦阳 刘 丹 万国瑞
　　　樊晓玲 李美丽 王金凤

东南大学出版社
SOUTHEAST UNIVERSITY PRESS
·南京·

图书在版编目(CIP)数据

艺术类研究生英语教程 / 倪进主编. — 南京：东南大学出版社,2013.11

高等院校艺术专业系列精品教材

ISBN 978-7-5641-4621-4

Ⅰ.①艺… Ⅱ.①倪… Ⅲ.①艺术—英语—研究生—教材 Ⅳ.①H31

中国版本图书馆 CIP 数据核字(2013)第 267708 号

艺术类研究生英语教程

出版发行	东南大学出版社
社　　址	南京市四牌楼 2 号　邮　　编:210096
出 版 人	江建中
网　　址	http://www.seupress.com
经　　销	全国各地新华书店
印　　刷	常州市武进第三印刷有限公司
开　　本	787 mm×1092 mm　1/16
印　　张	23.25
字　　数	640 千字
版　　次	2013 年 11 月第 1 版
印　　次	2013 年 11 月第 1 次印刷
书　　号	ISBN 978-7-5641-4621-4
定　　价	58.00 元

本社图书若有印装质量问题,请直接与营销部联系,电话:025-83791830

序　言

　　课程是教学的基本单元,而教材则是这个单元的基本依据。东南大学艺术学院在长期的本科艺术专业人才培养过程中注重经验的积累,尤其是一部分中青年教师勤于钻研、勇于探索,在多年的课堂教学过程中逐步形成了自己的风格,也取得了良好的教学效果。在此基础上,我们决定组织撰写并出版本套教材。

　　本套教材主要针对工业艺术设计、美术学和动画三个本科专业的人才培养。

　　工业艺术设计是我院较早的本科专业,涉及平面、工业产品和环境艺术三大方面。随着国家的日益强大和国民的日益富裕,人们对自己所视、所用、所处都有了提升的愿望。因此,设计学已由艺术的边缘学科转化为集艺术与应用于一体的,可授予艺术学和工学两种学位的大学科。尤其是在国家经济转型的过程中,设计学的地位会显得越来越重要。十余年来,我院工业艺术设计培养了大批优秀人才,许多同学或在高等学校任教,或在设计公司任职,更为可喜的是,相当一部分同学凭借自身扎实的功底和设计能力独立组建设计公司,这些都体现出我院设计学的实力。

　　美术学专业是艺术类人才培养中的一个传统专业,我院针对本科生的从业形势和我院师资的基本特点,尝试凝练美术学的应用属性,一方面在传统的美术史论领域继续深入,另一方面在加强学生基本理论素养的同时探索美术学在艺术策划、艺术展览和艺术创作等方面的教学内容。我院美术学的毕业生一部分继续深造,另一部分在艺术管理或艺术创作领域从业,赢得了业界的广泛赞誉。

　　我院动画专业是新世纪以来随着国家对于动画人才的大量需求而设立的。在艺术专业当中,动画是一个特殊专业,因其综合性较强,故而对于人才的素质要求也相对较高。一位动画从业者不仅要关注艺术自身,而且要关心技术、关心市场。我院动画专业集中于影视动画创作与制作方向,在东南大学强大的艺术学、工学,优秀的管理学背景中成长,也取得了骄人的业绩。从目前的培养情形来看,我院动画专业学生在从业形势上也远远好于全国同类专业,绝大多数毕业生都以较高的薪资就职于知名动画企业,一部分同学继续深造,不少同学富有探索精神的风格化创作引起业界高度关注。

　　了解了我院三个本科专业的基本状况,对于理解本套教材的特点当有帮助。本套教材执笔者均为我院三个本科专业的一线教师。他们年富力强、乐观向上,在撰写本套教材的过程中付出了大量心血。

　　本教材适用于高等院校艺术类相关专业。鉴于各种条件限制,本套教材定当存在诸多不足,希望大学在使用的过程中提出宝贵意见。

东南大学艺术学院
2012 年 4 月

前　言

随着世界经济一体化进程速度的加快和我国市场经济改革的深入,我国艺术专业人士开始广泛与国际交流。培养高水平艺术类研究生、扩展研究生的艺术视野、迅速加强艺术类研究生的专业英语知识是目前研究生双语教学刻不容缓的任务。

由于历史的原因,目前,艺术类研究生外语水平不高影响了他们对艺术专业外文资料的理解和运用,导致一些研究难以深入,往往局限于"炒冷饭";另外,外语水平不高也妨碍了国内研究生在艺术研究领域与国际学术界之间的通畅交流。随着改革开放的深入,这一状况必须尽快得到改变。培养懂外语、懂艺术的研究型专业人才已迫在眉睫。

艺术专业研究生双语教学是扩大对外开放和实现教育面向世界、面向市场的需要。在艺术类研究生专业中实施双语教学,如何使研究生在有限的学时中,做到艺术专业知识与英语应用能力共同提高,这在很大程度上将依赖于教师的素质、研究生的英语水平和合适的教材。

进入21世纪以来,随着中国全方位地与国际接轨,各行各业对英语这一国际语言的需求与日俱增,而对目标能力的追求已从原来的单向接受国外信息,即读写能力,变为直接参与交际,即听说能力。原来的以结构主义为指导编写的教材已不能满足教学要求。近年来,国外各种新教学理论,如任务型语言教学理论、建构主义教学理论、认知心理学等被引入中国,从根本上改变了英语教材的面貌。然而,在新理论指导下编写的研究生英语教材多半是综合类基础课教材,而多数特殊用途英语(ESP)教材,则依然遵循结构主义的老路,方法上以语法翻译法为主。研究生ESP教材在编写上不同于综合类教材,有其自身的特点和原则,ESP教材的内容必须与既定的目标情景密切相关,教材的内容与研究生的专业相联系;ESP教材也不是专业教材,不能完全按该专业的体系来编写教材,而应该在结合专业的同时按语言、语言教学和语言学习的规律来编写。

合适的教材是实施双语教学的物质前提。目前国内可以用于艺术类研究生双语教学的ESP教材尚未见到,这就给艺术类专业研究生双语教学的正常开展带来极大的困难,艺术类专业研究生双语教材的编选也成了一个难题。即使对于国内较早实行双语教学的一些课程而言,在双语教材的选择上也一直存在分歧。我们认为,真正意义上的英汉双语教材的选择必须遵循"内容第一、语言第二"的原则,也就是说,在选择教材时,首先要考虑内容的完整性和领先性,在满足这个要求的前提下选择语言合适的版本。

本教材根据我国艺术专业研究生知识的要求,将新颖、前沿的专业内容编进教材。让研究生了解国内外艺术相关专业发展的最新动态,从中汲取艺术精华,丰富创作灵感,迅速跟上世界专业潮流。

本教材在特殊用途英语领域尝试运用最新语言教学理论,编写艺术类研究生专用的立体化教材,课堂教学与课后自主学习相结合,既满足艺术类研究生专业的特殊要求,又重点提升研究生的综合语言能力,特别是听说能力。在上述编写理念的指导下,本教材主要有如下特点:

一、合理把握难度,适应艺术类研究生的现有水平

依据教育部高教司制定的《非英语专业研究生英语(第一外语)教学大纲》来安排各单元的难度和词汇量,做到循序渐进,便于掌握。

二、选材方面,突出艺术学科的特殊用途

功能语言学认为,ESP实际上是一种语域变体,包含话语范围、话语基调、话语方式这三个变量。从教材层面上,主要体现在教材的语言组织和语言输入。

2011年3月,在国务院学位委员会、教育部新修订的《学位授予和人才培养学科目录(2011年)》中,艺术学成为第13个学科门类,下设艺术学理论、音乐与舞蹈、戏剧与影视学、美术学、设计学5个一级学科。

本教材的选材将充分考虑艺术学中的5个一级艺术学学科以及相近专业门类,兼顾各个门类艺术的研究生。所选课文绝大多数来自英美人士使用的相关话语以及英美报刊和各种出版物中的相关真实内容,努力为艺术类研究生营造逼真的情景语境。

三、教材编排适应艺术类研究生特点,多用图片等直观手段

心理学研究表明,在人的认知过程中,视觉信息占所有输入信息的90%以上,而视觉信息既是长时记忆的基础,其本身也是长时记忆的重要组成部分,人类语言能力中很大的一部分就是以视觉表象的形式存储于大脑中的。艺术类研究生的思维方式更倾向于形象思维,图片等直观手段更符合他们的认知习惯。视觉信息丰富是本教材的特色之一。

四、一个单元围绕同一个主题综合听、说、读、写、译五项技能,不再另设听说教程

格式塔心理学强调对心理活动的整体感知,提出整体大于部分之和的观点。语言的学习是一个认知心理过程,也应强调对各种能力的整体把握,以达到事半功倍的效果。以前的研究生英语教材一般分为《读写教程》和《听说教程》两大块,各自有自己的主题,彼此独立,缺乏统一性。本教材集听、说、读、写、译五项技能于一身,各部分围绕同一个主题展开,研究生可以对各种能力做到整体认知、整体把握,中英语言信息共享,五种技能综合,文化和人际、学术交流技能融为一体,从而激发艺术类研究生的英语学习积极性,真正提高研究生英语应用能力和交际能力。

五、以任务为主线,所有教学活动围绕任务展开,"做中学、学中做",研究生在教师的指导下做到自主学习

根据建构主义教学理论,教师的作用已从传统的传递知识的权威转变为研究生学习的辅导者,成为研究生学习的高级伙伴或合作者。教师是意义建构的帮助者、促进

者,而不是知识的提供者和灌输者。研究生是意义建构的主动者,而不是知识的被动接收者和被灌输的对象。甚至监控学习和探索的责任也可逐渐由以教师为主转向以研究生为主。使用本教材的研究生学习完全自主,变"以研究生为主体,教师为主导"为"以研究生为中心,教师为辅导",即:在教师的指导和帮助下,研究生自教自学,担当主要角色,班级设立评审委员会,由研究生轮流担任委员,点评研究生各项任务完成情况,教师退至幕后,仅提供组织、纠错、答疑等帮助,最终要使研究生达到自主学习的程度。

六、打破传统的课堂教学模式,教学场所跳出教室,直接进入真实的语境

在教学活动中可将研究生带至博物馆、美术馆、工厂、画廊等与教学主题有关的场所,克服在课堂上模拟语境带来的心理不真实感。一般情况下,日常教学活动不可能总是安排在有关场所,但为了营造学习环境和氛围,有必要借助于信息技术,将实际场景虚拟化。这是一个有效的解决办法。

七、教材框架

Highlight(学习重点)

包括 Topic area, Communication, Skills 三项。

以表的形式列出,让研究生清楚所要掌握的语言知识和交际内容。

Topic area	Communication	Skills
本课主题及各部分主要内容	本课重要词汇及重要句型、结构	与交际有关的话语功能

1. Starting-out Task

教师在网络平台上布置预习任务:由每组研究生就该课主题的一个方面拍摄 DV,或制作 PPT,上传至网络平台,然后由班级评审委员会评比,也可调动社会资源,邀请家长或专家参与评比,优胜者在课堂展示。

2. Listening Tasks

根据功能语言学情景语境理论,语言只有在一定的语境中才有意义,所以听力的学习也要放在情景语境中进行。本部分首先通过听写填词或听音辨析之类相对容易的题目让学生熟悉相关话题的关键词汇,然后是一篇对话或段落,配合相关练习,引导研究生进入情景语境。

3. Reading Tasks

图式阅读理论将阅读过程解释为读者所具备的背景知识与阅读材料互相作用的过程,经过以上背景知识的输入,研究生已经建立了自己的图式,为阅读和理解课文打下了基础。在充分理解的基础上,由研究生担任讲授者的角色,老师予以课前指导,课上纠错、补充,课后答疑,师生互换角色,研究生变被动为主动。练习部分以 Comprehension 为主,辅以 Vocabulary Expansion,让研究生既能提高语言应用能力,又能增长专业知识。

4. Interactive Tasks

这是一个输出过程,以上各部分的学习已对研究生进行了充分的语言输入,他们必然会产生语言输出的欲望,该部分以 Role-play 和 Group Work 等形式,让学生课后结对或组成小组来完成,课堂以展示为主。

5. Follow-up Task

本部分也属于输出过程,通过与本单元密切相关的主题句作文,重点训练学生的写作能力。

《艺术类研究生英语教程》是集体科研和智慧的结晶,它的编写和出版得益于众多专业院校的专家和教授的热情关心、真诚帮助和悉心指导,特别是全国外语协会会长李霄翔教授和东南大学艺术学院院长王廷信教授在本书的编写、出版等方面自始至终都给予编者以无私的帮助和指导,东南大学艺术学院为本书出版给予了经费资助。编者深知,如果没有他们的帮助和指导,要完成本套教材的编写是困难的。在此,编者向他们深表感谢!英国著名语言学家 Samuel Johnson 曾感慨,编写词典的人是"unhappy mortals(不幸的噍类)",而作者深深体会到要真正写好书,写书人又何尝不是"unhappy mortals"呢?

"梅雨润兼旬,暑月不知夏。"今夜,思绪在江南初夏的丝雨里徜徉,深深呼吸这江南初夏夜晚的清凉空气,提笔写完本书的最后几句话。可是,我却感觉不到多少轻松。这套书送给读者的是快意还是其他? 我说不好。也许就像李清照的词写的那样:"随意杯盘虽草草,酒美梅酸,恰称人怀抱。"

企盼使用者批评指正。

倪进
2013 年 6 月于东南大学梅庵

目录 Contents

上编

Unit 1　Oil Painting ………………………………………… 3

Unit 2　Performance Art …………………………………… 21

Unit 3　Drama ……………………………………………… 39

Unit 4　Pop Music ………………………………………… 56

Unit 5　Film ………………………………………………… 73

Unit 6　Comic and Animation …………………………… 90

Unit 7　Fashion …………………………………………… 108

Unit 8　Dancing …………………………………………… 125

Key and Script …………………………………………… 142

Translation of the Texts ………………………………… 166

下编

Unit 1　Chinese Painting ………………………………… 181

Unit 2　Sculpture ………………………………………… 199

Unit 3　Theatre …………………………………………… 216

Unit 4　Western Classical Music ……………………… 234

Unit 5　Graphic Designing ……………………………… 253

Unit 6　Landscaping ……………………………………… 270

Unit 7　Photography ……………………………………… 288

Unit 8　Chinese Traditional Folk Arts ………………… 305

Key and Script …………………………………………… 326

Translation of the Texts ………………………………… 348

上编

Unit 1 Oil Painting

Highlight

Topic area	Communication	Skills
Some famous western oil paintings; Spanish painter Diego Velázquez; Baroque style; Post-Impressionism and Post-Impressionists.	be well versed in in the hope of… legend has it that… universally acknowledged as… make…more accessible than…	Knowing some best-known paintings in the world; Knowing Spanish painter Diego Velázquez; Describing and discussing paintings.

Starting-out Task

1 **Look at these pictures and discuss the following questions with your partner.**

1. The following pictures show some best-known oil paintings in the world. Can you tell their names?

2. What else, such as the types, the styles and the names of the artists, do you know about these paintings?
3. How do you like these paintings and their creators?

Listening Tasks

Micro Listening Skills

2 **Listen to the following passage and try to fill in the missing words and expressions**.

Western painting is in general distinguished by its 1._____ on the representation of the human figure, whether in the 2._____ context of antiquity or the religious context of the early Christian and medieval world. The Renaissance 3._____ this tradition through a close examination of the natural world and an investigation of balance, 4._____, and perspective in the visible world, 5._____ painting to the developing sciences of anatomy and optics. The first real 6._____ from figurative painting came with the growth of landscape painting in the 17th and 18th centuries. Together they developed in the 19th century in a(n) 7._____ that was increasingly concerned with "painterly" qualities of the interaction of light and color and the 8._____ qualities of paint handling. In the 20th century these interests 9._____ to the development of a third major tradition in Western painting, abstract painting, which sought to 10._____ and express the true nature of paint and painting through action and form.

Unit 1 Oil Painting

Dialogue

Medieval and Renaissance Paintings

Ognissanti Madonna by Giotto

The Small Cowper Madonna by Raphael

Words & Phrases

medieval /ˌmedɪˈiːvl/ *adj.*	中世纪的
drab /dræb/ *adj.*	土褐色的；单调的
pigment /ˈpɪgmənt/ *n.*	颜料；涂料
yolk /jəʊk/ *n.*	蛋黄
halo /ˈheɪləʊ/ *n.*	晕轮，光圈

3 Listen to the dialogue and decide whether the following statements are true(T) or false(F).

1. ____ In medieval art, people are drawn in perspective instead of value of importance.
2. ____ Renaissance art gives an impression of being more colorful.
3. ____ Picture number one is a painting from the medieval era.
4. ____ In the third picture, there are angels in the background.
5. ____ Of all the pictures, the second one is the most realistic.

4 Listen to the dialogue again and complete the following sentences with the information you have heard.

1. Medieval art is more related to _____ than Renaissance art.
2. Colors in medieval art are mostly drab and _____ because the _____ are mixed with egg yolk.
3. The last painting compared to the others is _____ and there are no _____.
4. Picture number one is more _____ than the third picture but still not drawn very _____.
5. There is a _____ of green rolling hills in the second picture.

Reading Tasks

Focus Reading

Pre-reading Questions

1. Have you ever seen or heard of any Spanish paintings?
2. How do you like Spanish painter Diego Velázquez?
3. Why is Diego Velázquez regarded as one of the world's greatest artists?

Diego Velázquez: The Face of Spain[①]

Diego Velázquez, the most important Spanish painter of the 17th century, is universally acknowledged as one of the world greatest artists. The naturalistic style in which he was trained provided a language for the expression of his remarkable power of observation in portraying both the living model and still life. Stimulated by the study of 16th-century Venetian painting, he developed from a master of faithful likeness and characterization into the creator of masterpieces of visual impression unique in his time.

In 1599 Diego Velázquez was born in Seville to parents who belonged to the lesser nobility. When he was twelve he was apprenticed to Pacheco who was a painter of moderate talent, but well versed in the theory of art. Velázquez remained in Pacheco's school for five years, learning the technique of painting and being introduced to the history and theory of art. There he also came into contact with the intellectual society of Seville and with the works of the Spanish naturalist painters and the great Italian masters.

The Waterseller of Seville

Velázquez was exceptionally precocious and while he was still in his teens he painted pictures that display commanding presence and complete technical mastery. He followed his master's advice to "go to nature for everything", and in works such as the *Immaculate Conception* and the *Adoration of the Magi* he developed a more lifelike approach to religious art, in which the figures are treated like portraits rather than ideal types. In their strong chiaroscuro as well as their naturalism such pictures show an affinity with the work of Caravaggio, but the supple, clotted brushwork is already entirely Velázquez's own. His early work also included several *bodegones*—a type of genre scene to which he brought a new seriousness and dignity. The best known among them is *The Waterseller of Seville*, in

---

①This text is adapted from *Velázquez* from http://www.encyclopedia.com.

which the control of the composition, color, and light, the naturalness of the figures and their poses, and realistic still life already reveal his keen eye and prodigious facility with the brush. The water dripping down the jug shows his remarkable ability to create a sense of almost palpable reality.

In 1622, Velázquez visited Madrid for the first time, in the hope of obtaining royal patronage. He painted a portrait of the poet Góngora, but there was no opportunity of portraying the king or queen. In the following year he was recalled to the capital by Philip IV's chief minister, and painted a portrait of the king which pleased Philip so much that he appointed Velázquez his court painter. Thus, at the age of 24, he suddenly became the country's most prestigious painter, and he kept his position as the king's favorite for the rest of his life.

With his appointment as court painter, the direction of Velázquez's work changed. He entirely abandoned *bodegones*, and although he painted historical, mythological, and religious pictures intermittently throughout his career, he was from now on primarily a portraitist, chiefly occupied in portraying members of the royal family and their entourage. Technically, too, his work changed as a result of his move to Madrid, his palette lightening and his brushwork becoming broader and more fluid under the influence of the Venetian paintings in the royal collection. Although his portraits of the king and his courtiers are grand and dignified, he humanized the formal tradition of Spanish court portraiture, setting his models in more natural poses and giving them greater life and character.

In 1628 Peter Paul Rubens came to the court at Madrid on a diplomatic mission. Although the great Flemish master did not have a direct impact on the style of the younger painter, their conversations inspired Velázquez to visit the art collections in Italy that were so much admired by Rubens.

In August 1629 Velázquez departed from Barcelona for Genoa and spent most of the next two years traveling in Italy. From Genoa he proceeded to Milan, Venice, Florence, and Rome, returning to Spain from Naples in January 1631. In the course of his journey he closely studied both the art of the Renaissance and contemporaneous paintings and took copies of many famous works. Several of the works executed during his travels attest to his absorption of these styles; a notable example is *Joseph and His Brothers*, which combines a Michelangelesque sculptural quality with the chiaroscuro of Italian masters. As a result of his Italian studies, his development in the treatment of space, perspective, light, and color and his broader technique mark the beginning of a new phase in his lifelong pursuit of the truthful rendering of visual appearance.

After his return from Italy, Velázquez entered upon the most productive period of his career. For the decoration of the throne room of new palace in Madrid, Velázquez painted a series of royal equestrian portraits. His equestrian groups have a balance and poise closer to Titian's than to Rubens's Baroque compositions. He achieved a three-dimensional effect without detailed drawing or strong contrasts of light and shade but with a broad technique of brushwork and natural outdoor lighting.

The Surrender of Breda, Velázquez's famous contribution to the series of military triumphs painted for the same throne room, is his only surviving historical subject. It was inspired by Velázquez's first visit to Italy, in which he accompanied Ambrogio Spinola, who conquered the Dutch city of Breda in 1625. Though the elaborate composition was based on a pictorial formula of Rubens, he creates a vivid impression of actuality and of human drama by means of accurate topographical details and the lifelike portraiture of the principal figures.

The Surrender of Breda

Between 1648 and 1651 Velázquez paid another visit to Italy to purchase paintings and antiquities for the royal collection. In Rome he painted several portraits, including two of his most celebrated works—*Juan de Pareja* and *Pope Innocent X*. *Juan de Pareja* is an exceptional unofficial portrait, unusually boldly painted, which creates a powerful effect of familiar and living likeness. Velázquez made the portrait of his servant Juan de Pareja, before portraying the pope, as an exercise in painting a head from life. The *Innocent X* is by common consent one of the world's supreme masterpieces of portraiture, unsurpassed in its breathtaking handling of paint and incisiveness in characterization. Legend has it that when the pope saw the finished portrait, he exclaimed somewhat disconcerted "Troppo vero! (too truthful)". This portrait, which has long been Velázquez's most famous painting outside Spain, was copied innumerable times and won him immediate and lasting renown in Italy.

In his final years in Madrid, Velázquez continued to reach new heights as a painter. The effect of form, texture, and ornament is achieved in his late manner without any definition of detail, in a free "sketchy" technique. His last portraits are mainly of the new young queen, Mariana of Austria, and of the royal children. In these works his brushwork has become increasingly sparkling and free, and the gorgeous clothes the sitters wore allowed him to show his prowess as a colorist. Velázquez never ceased to base his work on scrutiny of nature, but his means grew increasingly subtle, so that detail is entirely subordinated to overall effect. Thus in his late works space and atmosphere are depicted with unprecedented vividness, but when the pictures are looked at closely the forms dissolve into what Kenneth Clark called "a fricassee of beautiful brushstrokes".

Pope Innocent X

The culmination of Velázquez's career is *Las Meninas*, also known as *The Royal Family*. It shows him at his easel, with various members of the royal family and their attendants in his studio, but it is not clear whether he has shown himself at work on a portrait of the king and queen when interrupted by the Infanta Margarita and her meninas or vice versa. The work's complex and enigmatic composition raises questions about reality and illusion, and creates an uncertain relationship between the viewer and the figures depicted. In this original figure compositions, the nearly life-size figures are painted in more or less detail according to their relation to the central figure of the infanta and to the source of light, creating a remarkable illusion of reality never surpassed by Velázquez or any other artist of his age. Because of these complexities, *Las Meninas* has been one of the most widely analyzed works in Western painting.

Velázquez died on August 6, 1660 and left few pupils or immediate followers at his time. As with most Spanish painters, Velázquez remained little known outside his own country until the Napoleonic Wars (1808 – 1814) brought Spain into the mainstream of European affairs. The opening of the Prado in 1819, with 44 of his paintings on display, made his work much more accessible than it had ever been before. From the mid-19th century his technical freedom was an inspiration to many progressive artists, above all Manet, who regarded him as the greatest of all painters.

(1,472 words)

Las Meninas

Vocabulary

portray /pɔːˈtreɪ/ vt. make a portrait of 画像；描绘
Venetian /vɪˈniːʃən/ adj. 威尼斯的
likeness /ˈlaɪknɪs/ n. similarity in appearance or character between persons or things 相像，相似
characterization /ˌkærɪktəraɪˈzeɪʃən/ n. the act of describing distinctive characteristics 刻画
apprentice /əˈprentɪs/ vt. be or work as an apprentice 使……当学徒
moderate /ˈmɒdəreɪt/ adj. being within reasonable or average limits 中等的
versed /vəsd/ adj. thoroughly acquainted through study or experience 精通的；熟练的
precocious /prɪˈkəʊʃəs/ adj. appearing or developing early 早熟的
commanding /kəˈmɑːndɪŋ/ adj. controlling because of a strong position 指挥的；居高临下的
lifelike /ˈlaɪflaɪk/ adj. evoking lifelike images within the mind 逼真的
chiaroscuro /kɪˌɑːrəˈskjʊərəʊ/ n. （绘画）明暗对照法
affinity /əˈfɪnɪtɪ/ n. inherent resemblance between persons or things 密切关系；类同
supple /ˈsʌpl/ adj. moving and bending with ease 柔软的；灵活的
clotted /ˈklɒtɪd/ adj. thickened 凝结的
genre /ˈʒɒŋrə/ adj. 风俗画的；以日常情景为主题的
prodigious /prəʊˈdɪdʒɪs/ adj. far beyond what is usual in magnitude or degree 惊人的，奇妙的
facility /fəˈsɪlɪtɪ/ n. ability to do or perform something easily 容易；灵巧
bodegone 西班牙静物画
drip /drɪp/ vi. fall in drops 滴下
palpable /ˈpælpəbl/ adj. capable of being handled, touched, or felt 摸得出的；可触知的
patronage /ˈpætrənɪdʒ/ n. the act of providing approval and support 庇护；赞助
prestigious /preˈstɪdʒəs/ adj. exerting influence by reason of high status or prestige 有名望的
mythological /ˌmɪθˈlɒdʒɪkəl/ adj. based on or told of in traditional stories 神话的
intermittently /ˌɪntəˈmɪtəntlɪ/ adv. in an intermittent manner 间断的；间歇的
entourage /ɒntʊˈrɑːʒ/ n. the group following and attending to some important person 随从
palette /ˈpælɪt/ n. the range of color characteristic of a particular artist 调色板；颜料
fluid /ˈfluːɪd/ adj. smooth and unconstrained in movement 流动的；流畅的
humanize /ˈhjuːmənaɪz/ vt. make more humane 赋予人性
courtier /ˈkɔːtjə/ n. an attendant at the court of a sovereign 朝臣
portraiture /ˈpɔːtrɪtʃə/ n. a picture of a person's appearance and character 肖像画

Unit 1 Oil Painting

Flemish /ˈflemɪʃ/ *adj.* 佛兰芒的

proceed /prəʊˈsiːd/ *vi.* move ahead 继续进行；行进

attest /əˈtest/ *vi.* provide evidence for 证明；作证

absorption /əbˈsɔːpʃən/ *n.* the condition of being absorbed. 吸收

execute /ˈeksɪkjuːt/ *vt.* make or produce especially by carrying out a design 制作（艺术品等）

render /ˈrendə/ *vt.* perform 实施

equestrian /ɪˈkwestrɪən/ *adj.* of or relating to or featuring horseback riding 骑马的

poise /pɔɪz/ *n.* a stably balanced state 平衡；姿势

pictorial /pɪkˈtɔːrɪəl/ *adj.* pertaining to or consisting of pictures 绘画的

formula /ˈfɔːmjʊlə/ *n.* a method of doing something that relies on a model 准则；方案

topographical /ˌtɒpəˈɡræfɪkəl/ *adj.* 地形的

antiquity /ænˈtɪkwɪtɪ/ *n.* an artifact surviving from the past 古物；古代文物

by common consent 大家都同意（公认）

breathtaking /ˈbreθˌteɪkɪŋ/ *adj.* inspiring awe, exciting 惊人的；激动人心的

unsurpassed /ˌʌnsəˈpɑːst/ *adj.* not capable of being improved on 非常卓越的；未被超越的

incisiveness /ɪnˈsaɪsɪvnɪs/ *n.* keenness and forcefulness of thought or expression 敏锐；深刻

sparkling /ˈspɑːklɪŋ/ *adj.* shining with brilliant points of light 闪闪发光的

gorgeous /ˈɡɔːdʒəs/ *adj.* dazzlingly beautiful 华丽的；极好的

prowess /ˈpraʊɪs/ *n.* a superior skill 超凡技术

scrutiny /ˈskruːtɪnɪ/ *n.* the act of examining something closely 详细审查；细看

subordinate /səˈbɔːdɪneɪt/ *vi.* rank or order as less important 居下位；服从

overall /ˈəʊvərɔːl/ *adj.* regarded as a whole 全部的

unprecedented /ˌʌnˈpresɪdəntɪd/ *adj.* having no precedent 空前的；无前例的

dissolve /dɪˈzɒlv/ *vi.* change gradually to 渐隐，使溶解

fricassee /frɪkəˈsiː/ *n.* 油焖原汁肉块

culmination /ˌkʌlmɪˈneɪʃən/ *n.* final climactic stage 顶点；高潮

easel /ˈiːzəl/ *n.* upright tripod for displaying something 画架；黑板架

sketchy /ˈsketʃɪ/ *adj.* giving only major points; lacking completeness 写生风格的

infanta /ɪnˈfæntə/ *n.* （西班牙）公主

meninas （西班牙）宫女

vice versa 反之亦然

enigmatic /ˌenɪɡˈmætɪk/ *adj.* not clear to the understanding 神秘的；谜一般的

complexity /kəmˈpleksɪtɪ/ *n.* the quality of being intricate and compounded 复杂，复杂性

Proper Names

Diego Velázquez	迭戈·委拉斯开兹
Seville	塞维利亚
Pacheco	帕切科
Immaculate Conception	《圣灵感孕》
The Adoration of the Magi	《贤士来拜》
Caravaggio	卡拉瓦乔(意大利画家)
The Waterseller of Seville	《塞维利亚卖水人》
Rubens	鲁本斯(佛兰芒画家)
Barcelona	巴塞罗那
Genoa	热那亚
Florence	佛罗伦萨
Naples	那不勒斯
Góngora	贡戈拉(西班牙诗人)
Philip IV	腓力四世
Joseph and His Brothers	《约瑟和他的兄弟》
Titian	提香(意大利画家)
The Surrender of Breda	《布雷达的投降》
Spinola	史宾诺拉(西班牙将领)
Juan de Pareja	《胡安·德·帕雷哈》
Pope Innocent X	《英诺森十世》
Mariana	玛丽安娜
Kenneth Clark	肯尼斯·克拉克(艺术史大师)
Las Meninas	《宫娥》
Napoleonic Wars	拿破仑战争
Manet	马奈(法国画家)

Text Exploration

5 Choose the best answer to each question with the information from the text.

1. Which of the following is true of Velázquez's early works?

    A. He didn't paint any portraits.

    B. He only produced traditional religious paintings.

    C. He followed Pacheco's style.

    D. He painted directly from life.

2. Which of the following is NOT true of Velázquez's *The Waterseller of Seville*?

    A. It depicts a moment of everyday life.

    B. Velázquez brought a new splendor to it.

    C. It shows Velázquez's great ability to create a sense of actuality.

    D. It is one of Velázquez's best genre paintings.

3. Velázquez was named official painter to the king because _____.
   A. he was recommended by the chief minister
   B. he was famous in Madrid
   C. he was well acquainted with the courtiers
   D. he succeeded in painting a portrait of the king
4. Velázquez spent most of his career at the court in Madrid executing _____.
   A. *bodegones*
   B. portraits
   C. historical paintings
   D. religious works
5. Velázquez went to Italy in 1629 mainly _____.
   A. to paint portraits for Italian nobles
   B. on a diplomatic mission
   C. to study Italian painting
   D. to accompany Ambrogio Spinola
6. Which of the following is true of *The Surrender of Breda*?
   A. It was painted when Velázquez was in Italy.
   B. Velázquez had never met the conqueror in the picture.
   C. It is a masterpiece of history painting.
   D. It depicts a fighting scene during the siege of Breda.
7. Velázquez painted *Juan de Pareja* because he _____.
   A. needed some practice before portraying the pope
   B. wanted to make a change in his style
   C. aimed to execute an unusually bold portrait
   D. needed an exercise in painting people's facial expressions
8. Which of the following is NOT true of the *Portrait of Pope Innocent X*?
   A. It is regarded as one of the world's best portraiture.
   B. It was painted with fluent technique.
   C. It has long been Velázquez's most famous painting in Spain.
   D. It brought Velázquez great prestige in Italy.
9. Which of the following scenes does "vice versa" (Line 2, Para 12) refer to?
   A. He was depicting himself in the mirror when interrupted by Margarita and her meninas.
   B. He was painting himself in the mirror when interrupted by the king and queen.
   C. He was painting the king and queen in the presence of Margarita and her meninas.
   D. He was portraying Margarita and her meninas when interrupted by the king and queen.
10. Velázquez's European fame dates from _____.
    A. the mid-19th century
    B. the beginning of the 19th century
    C. before the Napoleonic Wars
    D. the eighteenth century

6 Complete the following chart with the information from the text.

Periods	Time Span	Details
Sevillian Period	1611—1621	Velázquez was _____ Pacheco, studying the technique of painting and the works of _____; His early works included _____.
Early Years in Madrid	1621—_____	Velázquez was named _____ to the king and chiefly engaged in _____; His art was greatly influenced by _____.
First Italian Journey	_____—1631	Velázquez closely studied both _____; His development in painting skills marks _____.
Middle Years	1632—1647	Velázquez entered upon _____ of his career, during which he painted _____ and a great masterpiece of _____, *The Surrender of Breda*.
Second Italian Journey	_____	Velázquez paid another visit to Italy to _____; There he painted several portraits, including _____—*Juan de Pareja* and *Pope Innocent X*.
Last Years	1651—1660	Velázquez continued to _____ and the _____ provided new subjects for him to portray; *Las meninas* with its _____ marks _____ of Velázquez's career.

7 Discuss the following questions with the information from the text.

1. What type of art did Velázquez paint?

2. How did Velázquez's style of painting develop, and what were some of its influences?

3. What possibly makes *Las Meninas* one of the most widely analyzed works in Western painting?

4. Among the four paintings presented in the text, which one do you like best? Why?

5. What do you think makes a great painter?

Unit 1 Oil Painting

Vocabulary Expansion

8 Fill in the blanks with the right words given below. Change the form where necessary.

| apprentice | precocious | affinity | humanize | unprecedented |
| proceed | incisiveness | drip | prowess | absorption |

1. The milk _____ out of the bottle and down his shirt.
2. For all his _____ and experience, Herbert did not have a carefully written business plan for the girls.
3. The security expert praises Apple's marketing _____ and calls Steve Jobs a genius.
4. From 1641 to 1643, there had been a(n) _____ explosion of printing and publishing in England.
5. Childhood hardships matured in him a(n) _____ sense of responsibility.
6. We _____ by car on the mountainous roads.
7. These bamboos are treated as important space elements to _____ the scale of the yard and create poetic atmosphere.
8. The boy was _____ to a carpenter in the nearby village.
9. When it comes to healthy _____ of nutrients, taste matters.
10. Vermeer's work does show a(n) _____ with that of Fabritius, but their relationship remains uncertain.

9 Choose the word or phrase that best keeps the meaning of the sentence if it is substituted for the underlined word or phrase.

1. Ernest Hemingway was an eminent writer in America and a giant of modernist <u>well versed in</u> modern narrative art.
   A. come off well
   B. well out of
   C. well up in
   D. do well to
2. Anger rushed out in a <u>palpable</u> wave through his arms and legs.
   A. sensible
   B. perceptible
   C. audible
   D. visible
3. Diving need spatial awareness, coordination, flexibility, grace, <u>poise</u> and a sense of timing.
   A. agility
   B. balance
   C. softness
   D. sensitivity
4. His handling of the crisis <u>attests to</u> his strength of character.
   A. makes sure
   B. puts under oath
   C. certifies by signature
   D. gives proof for
5. He <u>came into contact with</u> a lot of new idea while working abroad.
   A. had contact with
   B. kept in contact with
   C. made contact with
   D. brought contact with
6. Time spun away when we were <u>occupied in</u> repairing the farm tools.
   A. worked on
   B. focused on
   C. dealt with
   D. engaged in

7. The firm is now in the course of moving the machines to a new factory.
   A. on course of	B. in process of
   C. by process of	D. running its course of
8. Art is sometimes subordinated to Science in these schools.
   A. more important than	B. regarded as superior to
   C. as important as	D. considered inferior to
9. He showed great facility in performing task.
   A. aptitude	B. power	C. skill	D. flexibility
10. The scene dissolves into a series of shots of the Morgan family.
    A. disintegrates gradually to	B. changes gradually to
    C. melts gradually into	D. breaks up to

10 Translate the Chinese sentences into English by simulating the sentences chosen from the text.

Chosen Sentences	Simulated Translations	Chinese Sentences
Diego Velázquez, the most important Spanish painter of the 17th century, is **universally acknowledged as** one of the world's greatest artists.		新首相是一位公认的有远见的政治家。(**farsighted**)
Velázquez visited Madrid for the first time, **in the hope of** obtaining royal patronage.		我们正在寄送样品，以期征求意见。
His development in the treatment of space, perspective, light, and color and his broader technique **mark the beginning of a new phase** in his lifelong pursuit of the truthful rendering of visual appearance.		该公司表示，这两种模式是里程碑式的产品，标志着其发展中的一个新阶段的开始。(**milestone product**)
Legend has it that when the pope saw the finished portrait, he exclaimed somewhat disconcerted "Troppo vero!"		传说这座寺庙建于明朝。(**monastery, Ming Dynasty**)
The opening of the Prado in 1819, with 44 of his paintings on display, **made** his work much **more accessible than** it had ever been before.		互联网的发展改变了世界，它使得信息的获取比以往任何时候都容易。

Unit 1 Oil Painting

Supplementary Readings

Passage One

Baroque is the term given to the art movement of the Counter-Reformation(反宗教改革运动) that began in the late 16th century and ended in the mid-18th century. As the dominant style of European art between Mannerism and Rococo, it originated in Rome and emerged mainly in Catholic countries. Not exclusively associated with religious art, however, the Baroque style can also be seen in certain Dutch still-life paintings.

Baroque art is characterized by dramatic scenes. As opposed to Renaissance art, which usually showed the moment before an event took place, Baroque artists chose the most dramatic point when the action was occurring. In comparison to the rationality and calm of the Renaissance, the Baroque art was meant to evoke passion and emotion. Moreover, Baroque paintings often tend to dramatize scenes by using chiaroscuro light effects. In the same way that Renaissance artists captured space by using perspective, Baroque artists captured light by using contrast effectively.

The leading figures of the Baroque style were Caravaggio and Annibale Carracci, who brought a new solidity and weightiness to Italian painting, which in the late 16th century had generally been artificial and often convoluted in style. In doing so they looked back to the dignified and harmonious art of the Renaissance. From the Mannerist style(风格主义) the Baroque inherited movement and fervent emotion, and from the Renaissance style solidity and grandeur, fusing the two influences into a new and dynamic whole. The supreme genius of Baroque art was Gianlorenzo Bernini, who dominated the High Baroque Period with his energetic and virtuous paintings. Slightly later, Andrea Pozzo marks the culmination in Italy of the Baroque tendency towards overwhelmingly grandiose display.

At the beginning of the 17th century, the Baroque style soon spread from Rome and migrated to varying countries, evolving as artists fused it with the traditions of their native countries. Spain and Latin America added extravagance to the style, while other countries made it more conservative. In Flanders it had one of its finest flowerings in the work of Rubens, but in Holland and England, the Baroque made comparatively slight inroads. In France the Baroque found its expression in the service of the monarchy rather than the Church. Louis XIV realized the importance of the arts as a medium in promoting his regal glory, and his palace at Versailles represents a great example of the Baroque fusion of the arts to create an overwhelmingly impressive whole.

1. Which of the following is true of Baroque movement?

   A. It flourished between Mannerism and Rococo eras.

   B. It was solely associated with religious art.

   C. It originated in Italy in the seventeenth century.

   D. It declined in the early eighteenth century.

2. Which of the following is NOT related to the features of Baroque style?
   A. using light and dark shadows to dramatize scenes
   B. depicting the moment before an event took place
   C. engaging the viewer emotionally
   D. showing the moment when the action was occurring
3. Baroque art inherited _____ from the Mannerist style.
   A. variety and grandeur   B. action and drama
   C. solidity and weightiness   D. movement and passion
4. Which Italian painter belongs to the High Baroque Period?
   A. Carracci.   B. Caravaggio.   C. Bernini.   D. Pozzo.
5. Outside Italy, the Baroque art _____.
   A. became more conservative in Spain and Latin America
   B. was successful in Flanders, supported by Peter Paul Rubens
   C. gained popularity in Holland or England
   D. was used by the French monarchy to express religious themes

Passage Two

According to literature, the stylistic innovation in painting known as Post-Impressionism began in the 1880's. Unlike the Impressionism, the Post-Impressionism did not concentrate on the play of light over objects, people and nature, breaking up seemingly solid surfaces, stressing vivid contrast between colors in sunlight and shade, and depiction reflected light in all of its possibilities. Instead, the new style wanted to depict what they saw in nature by pursuing a more personal and spiritual expression. The Post-Impressionists did not want to observe the world from indoors. Like earlier Impressionists, they abandoned the studio, painting in the open air and recording spontaneous impressions of their subjects instead of making outside sketches and then moving indoors to complete the work from memory.

Post-Impressionism was a movement in France that not only represented an extension of Impressionism, but also a rejection of that style's inherent limitations. Of all the painters in the Post-Impressionism, Paul Cezanne, Georges Seurat, Paul Gauguin, Vincent van Gogh, and Henri de Toulouse-Lautrec are the most famous ones.

The Post-Impressionists often presented their works together, but, unlike the Impressionists, who began as a close-knit group, they painted mainly alone. Cezanne painted in isolation in southern France; his solitude was matched by that of Paul Gauguin, who in 1891 took up residence in Tahiti, and of van Gogh, who painted in the countryside at Arles. Both Gauguin and van Gogh rejected the indifferent objectivity of Impressionism in favor of a more personal, spiritual expression. After exhibiting with the Impressionists in 1886, Gauguin renounced "the abominable(讨厌的) error of naturalism." Also, Gauguin sought a simpler truth and purer aesthetic in art. Turning away from the sophisticated, urban art world of Paris, he looked for inspiration in rural communities with more traditional values. The Dutch painter van Gogh quickly adapted Impressionist techniques and color to express his acutely felt emotions after his arrival in Paris. But later, he conveyed his emotionally charged and ecstatic(狂喜的) responses to the natural landscape by transforming the contrasting short brush strokes of Impressionism into curving, vibrant lines of color, exaggerated even beyond Impressionist brilliance.

　　The Post-Impressionism not only led away from a naturalistic approach but also developed the two major movements of early 20th-century: Cubism and Fauvism. Therefore, the works of the Post-Impressionists could be called as a basis for several contemporary trends and for early 20th-century modernism.

1. What view of painting in the nineteenth century does the passage mainly discuss?
   A. The impact of a new style of art on modern life.
   B. A new innovation in the materials used by artists.
   C. The differences between two major styles of art.
   D. A new style of art extended from Impressionism.
2. The word "depict" in line 5 is closest in meaning to _____.
   A. reorganize   B. represent
   C. deform   D. justify
3. Which of the following was one of the characteristics of Post-Impressionist painting?
   A. The depiction of the reflection of light and color.
   B. The pursuance of personal and spiritual expression.
   C. The focus on vivid contrast between colors in sunlight and in shade.
   D. The painters painted together.
4. The author mentions Gauguin in line 17 to give an example of an artist who _____.
   A. became as famous as Cézanne
   B. held exhibitions consistently in Paris
   C. adopted the contrasting short brushstrokes of Impressionism
   D. was in favor of a more personal, spiritual expression
5. Which of the following is true of Vincent van Gogh?
   A. He looked for inspiration in rural communities with more traditional values.
   B. He pursued the indifference objectivity in painting.
   C. He used curving, vibrant lines of color to express emotions.
   D. He focused on the play of light over objects.

Interactive Tasks

Role-play

13 Role-play the following situation with your partner.
Situation:
　　After visiting an art exhibition, Lucy and her friend David are talking about their favorite

painters. Lucy likes traditional painting while David prefers modern art.

You may begin like this:

Lucy: David, what's your favorite painter?

David: My favorite painter is Picasso. He often expresses such a strong feeling in his abstract paintings. I always get a strange sense of excitement when I see his work.

Lucy: Frankly speaking, I don't understand the point of his work. It's just too abstract for me. I prefer traditional paintings. They seem to be more representational than modern works.

David: Traditional paintings were always very detailed and delicate. Those Renaissance and Baroque painters certainly were skilled, but not as creative as Picasso. Since you like traditional painters, what do you think about Diego Velázquez?

Group Work

14 Work in groups to work out your own short drama.

1. Form groups of four or five students;
2. Each group chooses a topic concerning oil painting, e.g.

   A study of art movements at home or abroad;

   An introduction to a painter and his works.
3. Members of each group collect materials from library and the Internet to work out their PPT slides;
4. Based on the PPT slides, each member of the group gives oral presentation of his part.

Follow-up Task

Writing

15 Directions: For this part, you are going to write a composition on the topic: **How to Write an Artist's Statement.** You should write at least 120 words following the outline given below in Chinese:

1. 画展简介是现代画展不可或缺的一部分;
2. 画展简介是画家为画作撰写的简短说明,其作用有……
3. 最理想的简介应该具有易读性、信息性……

Unit 2　Performance Art

Highlight

Topic area	Communication	Skills
The concept of performance art; Marina Abramović and her performance pieces; Some performance events.	anything but... ensure against... collaboration in...with... with an emphasis on...	Understanding performance art; Describing and discussing performance events; Knowing some best-known performance artists and their works.

Starting-out Task

1 Look at the following pictures and share your opinions about performance art with your partner.

1. The following pictures show some best-known works of performance art. Can you tell their names?

2. What is the Chinese translation for performance art? Is it performing art like singing, dancing or theater?
3. How do you like performance art?

Listening Tasks

Micro Listening Skills

2 **Listen to the following passage and try to fill in the missing words and expressions.**

Performance art is art in which the 1._____ of an individual or a group at a particular place and in a particular time constitute the work. It can happen anywhere, at any time, or for any length of time. Performance art can be any situation that involves four basic elements: time, space, the performer's 2._____ and a relationship between performer and 3._____. It is opposed to painting or sculpture, for example, where a(n) 4._____ constitutes the work.

In performance art, usually one or more people perform in front of an audience. In contrast to the traditional performing arts, performance art is 5. _____. Performance artists often break conventions of traditional performing arts, and 6. _____ conventional ideas about "what art is," similar to the 7. _____ art movement. Thus, even though in most cases the performance is in front of an audience, in some cases, the audience becomes the 8. _____. The performance may be scripted, unscripted, or impromptu(即兴的). It may incorporate music, dance, song, or complete 9. _____. The audience may buy tickets for the performance; the performance may be 10. _____; or the performer may pay the audience to watch the performance.

Passage

Everybody Going Pillow Fighting

Pillow Fighting in London, 2012

Words & Phrases

Trafalgar /trəˈfælgə/ Square	特拉法尔加广场
Facebook /ˈfeɪsbʊk/ n.	脸谱(美国社会化网络站点)
track down	追查出
clear-up /ˈklɪə(r)ʌp/ n.	清理

❸ Listen to the passage and choose the best answer to the following questions.

1. When did the pillow fight in London start?
   A. On April Fool's Day.　　　　　B. On Valentine's Day.
   C. On Christmas Eve.　　　　　　D. On Halloween.
2. Where did Tom hear about the fighting?
   A. From the television.
   B. From the newspaper.
   C. From the radio.
   D. From the Internet.

3. How long did the pillow fight last?
   A. Ten minutes.
   B. Two hours.
   C. More than one hour.
   D. Thirty seconds.
4. How did the police treat the fighting?
   A. They arrested the organizer.
   B. They just watched it.
   C. They scattered the crowd.
   D. They blocked the square.

4 Listen to the passage again and complete the following sentences with the information you have heard.

1. People who came to take part in the pillow fight were dressed in _____, dressing gowns and _____ dress.
2. Towards the end, the wind blew the _____ into the sky.
3. The police said they would track down the _____ to pay for the _____.
4. Pillow fight took place in about _____ cities around the world.

Reading Tasks

Focus Reading

Pre-reading Questions
1. Do you often look into other people's eyes in communication?
2. What information can eyes convey?
3. How long can you lock eyes with other people? Please test it with your classmates.

"I Have to Be Like a Mountain"[①]

On March 14, 2010, the 63-year-old queen of performance art Marina Abramović[②], dressed in a flowing dark-blue dress, and looking extremely pale, sat down at a small table in the towering atrium of the Museum of Modern Art (MoMA) in New York. She would be there, motionless and silent, every day during museum opening hours for the next three months. This was the duration of her retrospective, *The Artist Is Present*—the first career survey MoMA had ever given to a performance artist—which was taking place concurrently up on the sixth floor. In the atrium, Abramović was making the title of her exhibition literal. And members of the public could share in her presence by sitting in the empty chair opposite her and engaging in silent eye contact for as long as they wanted, or as long as they could.

[①]This text is adapted from the article with the same title written by James Westcott at http://www.guardian.co.uk.
[②]Marina Abramović(1946-): a New York-based Yugoslavian performance artist who began her career in the early 1970s. Her work explores the relationship between performer and audience, and challenges the limits of the body.

"I have to be like a mountain." the artist told me a couple of days before going into her "big silence" for the performance. She would go home every evening when the museum closed, but, in order to sustain her meditative state, she would not speak until 31 May. "The atrium is such a restless place, full of people passing through. The acoustics are terrible—it's too big, too noisy. It's like a tornado. I try to play the stillness in the middle."

While I was talking to her, Abramović was anything but still. Her habitual anxiety and hyperactivity—so different from the formidable self-control and calmness she has demonstrated in 40 years of extreme acts of endurance—were in overdrive. "People don't realize it is pure hell sitting so long." she said in her thick Serbian accent, while fidgeting. Cramps would set in after an hour or so. Her bum would begin to hurt. But she would ride out the pain. "The concept of failure never enters my mind." she insisted. To ensure against it, a masseuse, a nutritionist and a personal trainer would visit her apartment before and after each day's work.

My meeting with the artist was the first time I had seen her in a year, in which time I had finished writing her biography. Her verdict on the book, now that it's finally out (after three years of intensive interviews and research, and four years before that spent working as her assistant, a position I quit in order to start writing) was this: "I will never let anyone write my biography again." We both laughed, even though she was deadly serious. I began dreading the inevitable moment when I would sit opposite her at the table a few days later.

Abramović's conclusion was also validating: the book was always meant to be both intimate and critical, and it was not written at her behest, or subject to her approval. However, it did rely on her total co-operation. I came to think that the process of writing the book was like her 1974 performance *Rhythm 0*, in which she stood totally passive for six hours while members of the public were allowed to do whatever they wanted to her. Chains, feathers, a Polaroid camera, olive oil, razor blades, an axe, a rose, a bullet and a gun were among the objects set out on a table nearby. She surrendered control of her biography to me without knowing what the result would be; she simply had to trust that I would not put the gun to her neck, as someone did in *Rhythm 0*.

Rhythm 0, 1974

Before queuing to sit opposite Abramović on the opening day of the retrospective, I checked out the exhibition. It opened with videos, photographs and objects relating to her first performances in the early 1970s. In these, the svelte and self-conscious young artist performed a string of acts such as stabbing knives repeatedly in the gaps between her splayed fingers, often missing and stabbing her hand instead (*Rhythm 10*, 1973); and, in 1976, brushing her hair with increasing violence while repeating the mantra:

"Art must be beautiful, artist must be beautiful." (*Art Must Be Beautiful*, *Artist Must Be Beautiful*)

Why did she do such things? I later came to think of them as the artist's revenge against the constraint of life. Growing up under the domestic regime of a lifer mother, Abramović used body art as a way to create rules even more extreme than the ones she found herself subjected to. In that way she could demonstrate a different kind of freedom.

At MoMA, most of Abramović's works (which includes live performance pieces as well as documentation) was taken from her 1976~1988 collaboration in love and art with the German artist Ulay①, here remade by some devoted young artists. A couple stared and pointed at each other without moving (*Point of Contact*, 1977), another motionless couple sat back-to-back with their hair braided together (*Relation in Time*, 1977), and another two stood and faced each other naked in a doorway (*Imponderabilia*, 1977). You could pass between them, but MoMA had modified the confrontation of the original by placing the performers so far apart that you barely brushed against them.

Imponderabilia, 1977

But there was a bigger problem than MoMA's institutional prudishness: these re-performances couldn't invoke the conditions—the audacity, trauma and charisma—of the original pieces. Abramović's work was inseparable from her and Ulay's history and magnetism. The pieces seen here seemed to sap the originals of their unpredictability and strangeness.

The Ulay phase of the retrospective included photos of *Nightsea Crossing*, which was Abramović's inspiration for this three-month-long sitting. In the 1980s, she and Ulay sat opposite each other, locked in eye contact and without moving, for a total of 90 days in museums around the world. If, in the first part of her career, she was masochistically confronting herself, and in the middle part she was confronting Ulay; since 1988, she had been directly confronting the public, though with an emphasis on physical presence rather than pain. *The House with Ocean View* (2002) was another prototype of her new performance in the atrium: the artist lived for 12 days without eating or speaking on three raised platforms in a gallery; her only nourishment was sustained eye contact with members of the audience.

So there was an irresistible force of historic logic behind what was going on in the atrium. And history revisited Abramović on the opening night, as a parade of fellow

---

①Ulay (1943-): real name Frank Uwe Laysiepen, an important performance artist of the late 60s and the 70s. From 1976 to 1989 he worked together with Marina Abramović. The performances of this period are the best known of Ulay's works.

performance artists sat with her: Tehching Hsieh (the undisputed king of endurance, legendary for his one-year performances in the 1980s), the Austrian feminist (and friend of Marina's) Valie Export, and Joan Jonas, perhaps the only artist of Abramović's generation to continue with performance art after the 1970s.

In between each of these sitters, Abramović looked down and closed her eyes, resetting her gaze and gathering energy. When she looked up again, sitting opposite her was none other than Ulay. A rapturous silence descended on the atrium. Abramović immediately dissolved into tears, and for the first few seconds had trouble meeting Ulay's calm gaze. She turned from superhero to little girl—smiling meekly; painfully vulnerable. When they did finally lock eyes, tears streaked down Abramović's cheeks; after a few minutes, she violated the rules of her own performance and reached across the table to take his hands. It was a moving reconciliation scene—22 years after they broke up.

Abramović - Ulay Reunion, 2010. Photo by Scott Rudd

As a steady stream of people sat down opposite Abramović, it became clear that she was being anything but a mountain—and her frailty made an already difficult performance even more exhausting. But the apparent spiritual support of the performance is: what could be better than three months of sustained eye contact with a public hungry for connection? What more profound human connection could there be?

After 90 minutes of queuing, it was finally my turn to sit opposite the artist. I was immediately stunned. Not by the strength of her gaze, but the weakness of it. She offered a Mona Lisa half-smile and started to cry, but somehow this served to strengthen my gaze; I had to be the mountain. After about 10 minutes, I started to relish our unspoken dialogue. Then, suddenly and involuntarily, my head dropped. It was as if Abramović had sent me a laser beam, and the moment was over.

(1,390 words)

Vocabulary

atrium /ˈeɪtrɪəm/ *n.* a hall or court at the center or entrance of a building, usually rising through more than one story 中庭

retrospective /ˌretrəˈspektɪv/ *n.* an exhibition of a representative selection of an artist's life work 回顾展

concurrently /kənˈkʌrəntlɪ/ *adv.* occurring at the same time 同时发生地

literal /ˈlɪtərəl/ *adj.* being or reflecting the essential or genuine character of something 照字面的；原义的

meditative /ˈmedɪtətɪv/ *adj.* showing deep and careful thought 沉思的；冥想的

acoustics /əˈkuːstɪks/ *n.* the physical properties of sound 音响效果

hyperactivity /ˌhaɪpə(r)ækˈtɪvɪtɪ/ *n.* a condition characterized by excessive restlessness and movement 极度兴奋

formidable /ˈfɔːmɪdəbl/ *adj.* strikingly impressive 令人惊叹（钦佩）的

overdrive /ˈəʊvəˌdraɪv/ *n.* a high gear used at high speeds to maintain the driving speed with less output power 高速挡位

Serbian /ˈsɜːbɪən/ *adj.* 塞尔维亚的；塞尔维亚人(语)的

fidget /ˈfɪdʒɪt/ *vi.* move restlessly 坐立不安，烦躁

cramp /kræmp/ *n.* a painful and involuntary muscular contraction 痉挛

ride out endure 经受得住

masseuse /mæˈsɜːz/ *n.* a female massager 女按摩师

nutritionist /njuːˈtrɪʃənɪst/ *n.* a specialist in the study of nutrition 营养学家

biography /baɪˈɒgrəfɪ/ *n.* an account of the series of events making up a person's life 传记

verdict /ˈvɜːdɪkt/ *n.* decision or judgment 论断；评语

validating /ˈvælɪdeɪtɪŋ/ *adj.* serving to support or corroborate 确认的；验证的

svelte /svelt/ *adj.* gracefully slender 苗条的

self-conscious /ˈselfˈkɒnʃəs/ *adj.* (*colloq*) shy (口) 羞涩的

splay /spleɪ/ *vt.* spread open or apart 张开

mantra /ˈmæntrə/ *n.* a commonly repeated word or phrase 咒语

lifer /ˈlaɪfə/ *n.* a person who spends the whole life serving in the army 职业军人

be subjected to undergo or experience 经受

collaboration /kəˌlæbəˈreɪʃən/ *n.* act of working jointly 合作，协作

prudishness /ˈpruːdɪʃnɪs/ *n.* excessive modesty 过分拘谨

audacity /ɔːˈdæsɪtɪ/ *n.* aggressive boldness 大胆

trauma /ˈtraʊmə/ *n.* any physical or emotional wound 创伤

charisma /kəˈrɪzmə/ *n.* a personal attractiveness that enables you to influence others 感召力

magnetism /ˈmægnɪˌtɪzəm/ *n.* power to attract 个人吸引力，个人魅力

sap /sæp/ *vt.* weaken 削弱

masochistically /ˌmæsəˈkɪstɪkəlɪ/ *adv.* in a way to get pleasure from one's own pain and

humiliation 受虐狂地
prototype /ˈprəʊtətaɪp/ *n.* a first or preliminary model of something 原型
feminist /ˈfemɪnɪst/ *n.* support of equal rights for women 女权主义者
rapturous /ˈræptʃərəs/ *adj.* feeling great delight 痴迷的；狂喜的
dissolve /dɪˈzɒlv/ *vi.* lose control emotionally 禁不住（笑起来或哭起来等）
meekly /ˈmiːklɪ/ *adv.* in a humble manner 温顺地，谦卑地
vulnerable /ˈvʌlnərəbl/ *adj.* susceptible to attack 易受伤的，脆弱的
violate /ˈvaɪəleɪt/ *vt.* fail to agree with 违反，违背
reconciliation /ˌrekənsɪlɪˈeɪʃən/ *n.* settling (a quarrel, difference of opinion, etc.) 和解，调和
frailty /ˈfreɪltɪ/ *n.* the state of being weak in health or body 虚弱
relish /ˈrelɪʃ/ *vt.* derive or receive pleasure from 享受
involuntarily /ɪnˈvɒləntərɪlɪ/ *adv.* against one's will 不由自主地
laser /ˈleɪzə/ *n.* an acronym for light amplification by stimulated emission of radiation 激光

Proper Names

Marina Abramović /məˈrinə ˌeɪbrəˈmɒvɪtʃ/   玛丽娜·阿布拉莫维奇
the Museum of Modern Art (MoMA)   现代艺术博物馆
Polaroid /ˈpəʊləˌrɔɪd/ camera   宝丽来一次成像照相机
Ulay /ʊˈleɪ/   乌雷
Imponderabilia /ɪmˌpɒndərəˈbɪlɪə/   《无法估量之物》
Tehching Hsieh /təˈtʃɪŋ ʃɪe/   谢德庆
Valie Export /vaˈliː ˈekspɔːt/   瓦莉·艾丝波尔
Joan Jonas /dʒəʊn ˈdʒəʊnəs/   琼·乔纳斯
Mona Lisa /ˈməʊnə ˈliːsə/   蒙娜·丽莎

Text Exploration

5 Choose the best answer to each question with the information from the text.

1. What would Abramović do at MoMA during the next three months?
   A. She would remake some of her previous performances.
   B. She would be there talking with some fellow performance artists.
   C. She would sit there still without saying a word.
   D. She would meet her former boyfriend.

2. The public could participate in her performance by _____.
   A. looking around in her exhibition
   B. looking into her eyes
   C. sitting with her
   D. acting in some performances

3. What is Abramović like in real life?
   A. She is overactive.

B. She is silent.
C. She is calm.
D. She is shy.

4. What happened to Abramović while she was performing in her performance *Rhythm 0*?
    A. A man gave her a rose.
    B. The public gathered to watch her.
    C. She was insulted.
    D. She was threatened by a gun.

5. Abramović kept stabbing knives in the gaps between her splayed fingers in her performance _____.
    A. *Rhythm 10*
    B. *Point of Contact*
    C. *Relation in Time*
    D. *Imponderabilia*

6. Which of the following is true of Abramović's early life?
    A. She was brought up in the army.
    B. She was subjected to very strict rules.
    C. She was a victim of family violence.
    D. She hated her mother.

7. Some of Abramović's previous performances, such as _____, were being remade at MoMA.
    A. *Point of Contact*, *Relation in Time* and *Imponderabilia*
    B. *The Artist Is Present*, *Point of Contact* and *Relation in Time*
    C. *Relation in Time*, *Imponderabilia* and *Nightsea Crossing*
    D. *Point of Contact*, *Imponderabilia* and *The House with Ocean View*

8. The origins of Abramović's three-month-long sitting could be traced back to her previous performances _____.
    A. *The House with Ocean View* and *Imponderabilia*
    B. *The House with Ocean View* and *Rhythm 10*
    C. *Nightsea Crossing* and *The House with Ocean View*
    D. *Nightsea Crossing* and *Point of Contact*

9. Abramović lost control of her emotion while she saw _____ sitting opposite her.
    A. Teching Hsieh   B. Ulay
    C. Valie Export   D. Joan Jonas

10. The author maintained eye contact with Abramović for _____.
    A. 7 hours   B. 3 hour
    C. 90 minutes   D. 10 minutes

Unit 2 Performance Art

6 Complete the following chart with the information from the text.

Time Periods	Typical Works	Details
The first part (in early 1970s) She was masochistically confronting _____.	Rhythm 0, 1974	She stood totally passive for _____ while members of the public were allowed to _____.
	Rhythm 10, 1973	She stabbed knives repeatedly in the gaps between _____ _____, often missing and stabbing her hand instead.
	Art Must Be Beautiful, Artist Must Be Beautiful, 1976	She brushed her hair with _____ while repeating the mantra: "Art must be beautiful, artist must be beautiful."
The middle part (1976~1988) She was confronting _____.	_____, 1977	She and Ulay stared and pointed at each other without moving.
	Relation in Time, 1977	She and Ulay sat back-to-back with their hair _____ _____.
	_____, 1977	She and Ulay stood and faced each other naked in a doorway.
	Nightsea Crossing (in the 1980s)	She and Ulay sat opposite each other, locked in eye contact and without moving, for a total of _____.
The present part (1988~present) She has been directly confronting _____.	The House with Ocean View, 2002	She lived for 12 days without eating or speaking on _____ _____ in a gallery.
	The Artist Is Present, 2010	She sat at the atrium of MoMA, motionless and _____, for three months.

7 Discuss the following questions with the information from the text.

1. How was the process of writing Abramović's biography like her 1974 performance *Rhythm 0*?

2. *Imponderabilia* was remade at MoMA as part of Abramović's retrospective while the original one was performed by Abramović and Ulay in 1977. What is the difference between this re-performance and its original?

3. How did Abramović respond while she saw Ulay sitting opposite her at the atrium MoMA?

4. What do you think might happen to Abramović and Ulay after the reunion? Would they kiss and make up?

5. Can you perform any of Abramović's works?

Vocabulary Expansion

8 Fill in the blanks with the right words given below. Change the form where necessary.

literal	formidable	fidget	biography	splay
sap	prototype	dissolve	vulnerable	violate

1. In this style of furniture, the feet of the chair legs are _____ out to provide balance.
2. They faced _____ difficulties in their attempt to reach the South Pole.
3. When the little girl saw the dead bird, she _____ into tears.
4. Had it not been for the bitter wind that _____ him of his remaining strength, he would have lived through the cold winter.
5. The boss of the insecticide factory was accused of _____ laws and regulations on environmental protection.
6. A _____ translation is not always the closest to the original meaning.
7. We're in a _____ position here, with the enemy on the hill above us.
8. After reading a _____ of George Washington he was able to tell many stories about the President.
9. Metal-wheeled chariots are the _____ of the tanks of modern warfare.
10. Children can't help _____ about if they're made to sit still for too long.

9 Choose the word or phrase that best keeps the meaning of the sentence if it is substituted for the underlined word or phrase.

1. State civil servants may not act concurrently as a company's director, supervisor or manager.
    A. simultaneously   B. jointly
    C. currently   D. consistently
2. Climbing up the mountain was anything but a pleasant trip.
    A. probably   B. really
    C. never   D. only
3. Albert Einstein was one of the most formidable intellects in the history of science.
    A. powerful   B. successful
    C. dreadful   D. amazing
4. I don't think the boat is strong enough to ride out the storms of the Cape of Good Hope.
    A. defeat   B. withstand
    C. survive   D. follow
5. The young girl tends to be self-conscious when talking with a young man.
    A. shy   B. unhappy
    C. painful   D. embarrassed
6. A man who has lost his position and wealth may be subjected to much indignity.
    A. obey   B. submit
    C. suffer   D. face

7. The Long March sapped many Red Army soldiers of their remaining strength.
   A. refreshed   B. exhausted
   C. kept   D. wiped

8. Richard dissolved into tears when he heard that he had lost all his savings in the scheme.
   A. cried bitter tears
   B. burst into a flood of tears
   C. held back his tears
   D. couldn't refrain from falling tears

9. The various military groups of the country have agreed to participate in the round-table meeting for national reconciliation.
   A. cooperation   B. compromise
   C. reformation   D. progress

10. Amy has been depressed since she broke up with her boyfriend.
    A. quarreled   B. disagreed
    C. separated   D. complied

10 Translate the Chinese sentences into English by simulating the sentences chosen from the text.

Chosen Sentences	Simulated Translations	Chinese Sentences
To insure against it, a masseuse, a nutritionist and a personal trainer would visit her apartment before and after each day's work.		为保证不致失败，敌人集中了优势兵力。（**concentrate, superior force**）
At MoMA, most of Abramović's works was taken from her *collaboration in* love and art *with* the German artist Ulay.		这家公司的多数新产品产生于它和一所国外大学在技术上的合作。（**technology**）
Abramović's work was *inseparable from* her and Ulay's history and magnetism.		中国的现代化离不开与世界各国的经济合作。（**modernization, cooperation**）
Since 1988, she had been directly confronting the public, though *with an emphasis on* physical presence rather than pain.		我在大学主修法律，重点是国际法。（**major in, international law**）
When she looked up again, sitting opposite her was *none other than* Ulay.		你在食堂里看到的那位高个子男子不是别人，正是我们经理。（**canteen**）

Supplementary Readings

Passage One

Trans-fixed 1974, by Chris Burden

Christopher "Chris" Burden (born in Boston, Massachusetts in 1946) is an American artist working in performance, sculpture, and installation art. Burden studied for his B. A. in visual arts, physics and architecture at Pomona College and received his MFA (Master of Fine Art) at the University of California from 1969 to 1971.

Burden began to work in performance art in the early 1970s, when he made a series of controversial performances in which the idea of personal danger as artistic expression was central. His most well-known act from that time is perhaps the 1971 performance piece *Shoot*, in which he was shot in his left arm by an assistant from a distance of about five meters. Originally, Chris Burden was to be grazed(擦伤) by the bullet. However, Burden was more than grazed; the copper head bullet penetrated his left arm.

Shoot was not the only performance piece in which Burden subjected himself to danger. Another "danger piece" was his 1974 performance called *Doomed*, performed in the Chicago Museum of Art. Very little has been found regarding this work; what is known is that Burden walked into the gallery space at midnight, set a clock on the wall, and laid underneath a piece of glass. The glass ran the length of his entire body. Burden laid there. He defecated, urinated and did whatever other bodily functions where necessary. People would walk by and observe Burden in this state. He was observed, but not interacted with. Unknown to the museum owners, Chris wasn't prepared to end the piece until someone interfered in some way. Forty-five hours later, a museum guard placed a pitcher of water within the grasp of Burden. Burden then stood up, broke the glass, and took a hammer to smash the clock, thus ending the piece.

Trans-Fixed, one of Burden's most reproduced and cited pieces, took place in 1974 at Speedway Avenue in Venice, California. For this performance, Burden lay face up on a Volkswagen Beetle and had nails hammered into both of his hands, as if he were being crucified on the car. The car was pushed out of the garage and the engine worked for two minutes before being pushed back into the garage.

In 1978 he became a professor at University of California, Los Angeles (UCLA), a position from which he resigned in 2005 following an incident involving a graduate student's performance piece. According to Burden, his resignation was "due to a decision made by UCLA for not suspending(停学) a graduate student who tried to reenact my *Shoot* piece in my class." The student pulled a revolving pistol from a paper bag, loaded it with a single bullet, spun the cylinder, aimed the pistol at his head and pulled the trigger. Since the student posed no threat to himself or others, the university allowed him to continue to attend classes while the investigation continued.

1. What happened to Chris Burden in his performance piece *Shoot*?
    A. He was almost killed.
    B. He was very seriously wounded.
    C. He was very slightly wounded.
    D. He was more seriously wounded than expected.
2. Which of the following is NOT true of Chris Burden's performance piece *Doomed*?
    A. He started at midnight.
    B. He was invisible under a piece of glass.
    C. He did all bodily functions under the glass.
    D. He was totally ignored for 45 hours.
3. Why did Burden end his piece when a museum guard gave him some water?
    A. The guard interfered with his performance.
    B. He was annoyed by the guard.
    C. He had run out of patience.
    D. He was very thirsty.
4. Which of the following is true of Burden's *Trans-fixed*?
    A. He had himself nailed to a car.
    B. He lay upside down on a car.
    C. He gave his performance at night.
    D. The car ran for two minutes.
5. Burden resigned his position as a professor because the university didn't suspend a student who _____.
    A. threatened to kill him in class
    B. remade his performance piece without his permission
    C. did dangerous things in class
    D. brought a pistol to class to threaten other people

Passage Two

Centurion Statue: living statue performed by Duncan Meadows

Living statues are street performers who stand around for a living. They show the audience something and are tipped. Today's living statues are actually part of a noble and historic tradition that dates back to the living pictures of the early medieval period. In the living picture, costumed actors would create a scene by remaining silent and motionless, as if they were in a picture. Over time, actors took the picture out onto the streets. It's now such a profitable business that there are "living statues" in every city around the world.

The traditionalists in the living-statues world still choose to look like a statue, specializing in stone, metal, glass or wood. But they have a problem. If they are too convincing, passers-by just pass them by and their takings suffer. So, these days, they move. If someone puts a few coins in their hat, they will blow a kiss, do a dance, hand over a flower—anything, as long as it attracts a crowd.

Living statues don't speak—which makes it difficult to ask them about their art. That difficulty is compounded by the fact that a lot of them are from overseas, meaning there's also a language barrier. The biggest problem, however, is that a lot of them don't want to be interviewed because it might mean identifying themselves to the authorities and paying tax on their cash-in-hand lifestyle.

For a living statue, make-up is the key. Natural hair looks wrong on a statue. Hats and wigs work well, so does a head wrap. So it helps if a living statue is bald. As to colors, non-metallic colors are water-based and are easy to remove, but metallic colors must be used sparingly—the less you have to put on, the easier it is to remove. Sometimes, they use sauna to clean the skin.

And then comes the standing still, which isn't as easy as it looks. For a start, it can go on for a considerable length of time. It's heavy on the body, and a single sway can ruin a performance. At this point, it's worth pointing out that living statues can't move their eyes. They are, after all, statues. So, they wear sunglasses (which the purists think of as cheating) or they focus on a fixed point until it's time to change position. All they can see clearly is what they focus on—everything else is peripheral.

1. How do living statues make a living?
   A. They are paid by the audience.
   B. They sell tickets for their performance.
   C. They make money by advertising on their bodies.
   D. They are wealthy people who perform living statue just for fun.
2. What is the origin of the living statue?
   A. Statues of ancient Greece.
   B. Street performance in modern time.
   C. Living picture of the medieval period.
   D. Noble manners in ancient Europe.
3. The living statues don't speak for all the following reasons EXCEPT _____.
   A. They speak foreign languages.
   B. Real statues never speak.
   C. They don't want to be identified.
   D. They don't want to pay the income tax.
4. Which of the following is NOT mentioned of their make-up?
   A. It's difficult for a living statue to conceal his natural hair.
   B. Water-based colors are easy to remove.
   C. Metallic colors are difficult to remove.
   D. Metallic colors are more expensive than non-metallic colors.
5. The living statues keep their eyes from moving by _____.
   A. closing their eyes
   B. lowering their heads
   C. focusing on a fixed point
   D. wearing masks

Interactive Tasks

Role-play

13 Role-play the following situation with your partner.
Situation:
   Two young students are talking over an event one of them saw on the street. It was a woman who put herself in a cage and barked like a dog, while a man was standing by, holding a sharp knife in his hand.
You may begin like this:
Lily: You can't believe what I saw yesterday.

Peter: What?

Lily: I went out for a walk, but I only saw on a street corner a woman who put herself in a cage and barked like a dog. A man was standing by, holding a sharp knife in his hand. What a scene!

Peter: Well, that's performance art from the West. It's part of postmodern art.

Group Work

14 Work in groups to work out your own performance art.

1. Form groups of four or five students;
2. Each group fills in the following chart first:

Names of participants:
Roles of participants:
Detailed Process:

3. Then, each group gives the performance in class and other groups discuss the theme;
4. After the discussion, a representative from each group gives a detailed report of the performance based on the chart they have filled in.

Follow-up Task

Writing

15 Directions: For this part, you are going to write a composition on the topic: **Aspects of Performance Art**. You should write at least 120 words following the outline given below in Chinese:

1. 行为艺术是20世纪五六十年代兴起于欧洲的现代艺术形态之一,指视觉艺术范畴中前卫派(avantgarde)或观念艺术(conceptual art)的一种;
2. 对行为艺术存在激烈的争论,有人认为它很深刻,有人认为它暴力、血腥;
3. 如何客观、公正地讨论这一艺术现象。

Unit 3　Drama

Highlight

Topic area	Communication	Skills
Concept of drama; Origins of western drama; Some external factors of drama; Athenian tragedy; Some well-known western dramas.	be intended to deprive...of... be approved for alternate with be furious at pay homage to	Grasping the concept of drama; Understanding the origins of western drama; Knowing some external factors of drama; Mastering Athenian tragedy; Being familiar with some well-known western dramas.

Starting-out Task

1　Discuss the following questions about Western drama with your partner.

1. Can you give "drama" a definition?
2. The two masks below are a laughing face and a weeping face. Do you know what they are used for?

3. The following pictures show two famous western dramas. How much do you know about the two dramas?

艺术类研究生英语教程

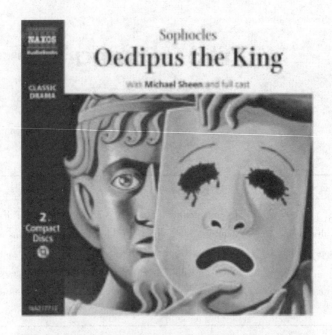

Listening Tasks

Micro Listening Skills

2 Listen to the following passage and try to fill in the missing words.

Western drama originates in classical Greece. The 1. _____ culture of the city-state of Athens produced three genres of drama: tragedy, comedy, and the 2. _____ play.

According to Aristotle, Greek drama, or, more explicitly, Greek tragedy, originated in the 3. _____. Tradition has it that at the Dionysia of 534 B.C., during the reign of Pisistratus, the lead singer Thespis of the dithyramb added to the chorus an actor with whom he carried on a dialogue, thus the 4. _____ possibility of dramatic action. Thespis is credited with the invention of tragedy.

Generally, the earlier Greek tragedies place more emphasis on the chorus than the later ones. In the 5. _____ plays of Aeschylus, the chorus serves to 6. _____ the personalities and situations of the characters and to provide ethical comment on the action. The increase in the number of actors resulted in less concern with 7. _____ problems and beliefs and more with dramatic conflict between individuals.

Greek comedy is divided by scholars into Old Comedy, Middle Comedy, and New Comedy. The sole literary remains of Old Comedy are the plays of Aristophanes, characterized by 8. _____, political satire, fantasy, and strong moral overtones. While there are no 9. _____ examples of Middle Comedy, it is 10. _____ that the satire, obscenity, and fantasy of the earlier plays were much mitigated during this transitional period. Most extant examples of New Comedy are from the works of Menander; these comedies are realistic and elegant, often revolving around a love-interest.

Passage

Some External Factors of Drama

Words & Phrases

elaborate /ɪˈlæbəreɪt/ adj.	精心制作的
exaggerate /ɪɡˈzædʒəreɪt/ vt.	夸大
distort /dɪsˈtɔːt/ vt.	使失真
reinforce /riːɪnˈfɔːs/ vt.	加强
ephemeral /ɪˈfemərəl/ adj.	短暂的
illuminate /ɪˈluːmɪneɪt/ vt.	照亮

3 **Listen to the passage and choose the best answer to the following questions.**

1. Which of the following about masks is wrong?
   A. Masks were rarely used in contemporary Western theaters.
   B. Masks are rarely used in African and Oriental theaters.
   C. Masks were essential in Greek and Roman dramas.
   D. Masks are used in most African and Oriental theaters.

2. Lighting design is _____.
   A. a long-history art
   B. to illuminate the stage and the spectators
   C. to create mood and control the focus of the performers
   D. a computerized control system in the most recent development

3. Which of the following belongs to the sound effect of theatrical performances?
   A. Music.
   B. Wind, rain and thunder.
   C. Animal noises.
   D. All the above.

4 **Listen to the passage again and complete the following sentences with the information you have heard.**

1. In Western theaters, makeup is used for two purposes: to _____ and _____ facial features that might otherwise be lost under bright lights or at a distance and to _____ signs of age, skin tone, or nose shape.

2. Setting design is the arrangement of _____; setting is the _____ environment in which a play is performed.

3. By pushing one button, all the lights will change _____ to the preprogrammed intensity and at the desired speed.

Reading Tasks

Focus Reading

Pre-reading Questions

1. Can you give "tragedy" a definition, according to your own understanding?
2. Do you know any western dramatists and their works?
3. To your way of thinking, does a tragedy always have a tragic and pessimistic ending?

Athenian Tragedy[①]

Tragedy refers to a specific tradition of drama that has played a unique and important role historically in the self-definition of Western civilization. It is a form of art based on human sufferings that offers its audience pleasure. Tragedy stresses the vulnerability of human beings whose suffering is brought on by a combination of human and divine actions, but is generally undeserved with regard to its harshness. It is not totally pessimistic in its outlook. Although many tragedies end

Mask of Dionysus. Greek, Myrina, 2nd century BCE

---

①This text is taken and adapted from *Introduction to Greek Tragedy* by Roger Dunkle at http://ablemedia.com/ctcweb/netshots/tragedy.htm

in misery for the characters, there are also tragedies in which a satisfactory solution of the tragic situation is attained.

Tragedy was a public genre from its earliest beginnings at Athens. Athenian tragedy, the oldest surviving form of tragedy, is a type of dance-drama that formed an important part of the theatrical culture of the city-state. Having emerged sometime during the 6th century BCE, it flowered during the 5th century BCE, and continued to be popular until the beginning of the Hellenistic period.

Tragedy was intended to be presented in a theater before an audience. Private reading of tragedy deprives us of the visual and aural effects. Our word "theater" is derived from the Greek word "theatron", which contains the meaning "to view as spectators". Drama is a Greek word meaning "action", related to the verb "to do". The author of a tragedy was not just a writer of a script. When his work was approved for presentation at the state religious festival in honor of the god Dionysus, the state assigned him actors and a chorus. The author then had to perform the additional tasks of training the actors and chorus and of composing the music for the various songs of the actors and chorus and providing choreography for the chorus.

Athenian tragedies were performed in late March/early April at an annual state religious festival. The presentations took the form of a contest between three playwrights chosen by a magistrate called an archon who had charge of the City Dionysia. They presented their works on three successive days. Each one of the tragedians presented a tetralogy, three tragedies and a satyr play, on one morning of the festival.

Performances were apparently open to all citizens, including women, but evidence is scant. The theater of Dionysus was, like all ancient Greek theaters, an open-air auditorium. Due to the lack of adequate artificial lighting, performances took place during the day. Scenes set at night had to be identified as such by the actors or the chorus; the audience, upon receiving these verbal clues, had to use its imagination. In general, the action of tragedy was well served by presentation in an open-air theater since interior scenes, which are common in our typically indoor theaters, are all but non-existent in tragedy. The action of a tragedy normally took place in front of palaces, temples and other outdoor settings. This seemed natural to the ancient audience because Greek public affairs, whether civic or religious, were conducted out of doors as was much of Greek private life due to the relatively mild climate of the Aegean area.

The theater of Dionysus in the earliest days of tragedy must have consisted of only the most basic elements. All that was required was a circular dancing area for the chorus at the base of a gently sloping hill, on which spectators could sit and watch the performance. On the other side of the orchestra facing the spectators there probably stood a tent in which the actors could change their costumes. It was suggested by the word "skene" which means "tent", and was used to refer to a wooden wall having doors and painted to represent a palace, temple or whatever setting was required. The wall, which eventually became a full-fledged stage building, probably acquired this name because it replaced the original tent. The construction of the wooden skene and of a formal seating area consisting of wooden benches on the slope, which had been hollowed out, probably took place some time toward the middle of the fifth century. The actors positioned themselves either in the orchestra with the chorus or on the steps leading to the doors of the skene. The plays of the three great tragedians Aeschylus, Sophocles, and Euripides in the earlier wooden theater were viewed by audiences of comparable numbers. The theater of Dionysus was as it survives today with the remains of an elaborate stone skene, paved orchestra and marble seats. This stone theater had a capacity of approximately fifteen thousand spectators.

Two mechanical devices which were part of the ancient Greek theater deserve mention. One device is a "wheeled-out thing", a platform on wheels rolled out through one of the doors of the skene, on which a tableau was displayed representing the result of an action indoors and therefore was unseen by the audience. The other device is called a "theatrical machine", a crane to which a cable with a harness for an actor was attached. This device allowed an actor portraying a god or goddess to arrive on scene in the most realistic way possible, from the sky. The machine deposited the actor on top of the skene so that he as a deity could address the human characters from an appropriately higher level. This device was not exclusively limited to use by divine characters, but was employed whenever the plot required any character to fly. On the other hand, not every god arrived on scene by means of this machine.

The actors in tragedy were hired and paid by the state and assigned to the tragedians probably by lot. By the middle of the fifth century three actors were required for the performance of a tragedy. In descending order of importance of the roles they assumed they were called the protagonist, deuteragonist and tritagonist. Since most plays have more than two or three characters, all three actors played multiple roles. The main duty of an actor was to speak the dialogue assigned to his characters. However, he occasionally had to sing songs solo or with the chorus or with other actors.

Since women were not allowed to take part in dramatic productions, male actors had to play female roles. The playing of multiple roles was made possible by the use of masks, which prevented the audience from identifying the face of any actor with one specific character in the play and helped eliminate the physical incongruity of men impersonating women. The masks also helped the audience identify the sex, age, and social rank of the characters. The fact that the chorus remained in the orchestra throughout the play and sang and danced choral songs between the episodes allowed the actors to exit after an episode in order to change mask and costume and assume a new role in the next episode.

The chorus was non-professionals who had a talent for singing and dancing and were trained by the tragedian in preparation for the performance. The standard number of members of a chorus was twelve throughout most of Aeschylus's career, but was raised to fifteen by Sophocles. The chorus, like the actors, wore costumes and masks. The first function of a tragic chorus was to chant an entrance song called a parodos as they marched into the orchestra. Once the chorus had taken its position in the orchestra, its duties were twofold. It engaged in dialogue with characters through its leader, the Coryphaeus, who alone spoke the lines of dialogue assigned to the chorus. The tragic chorus's most important function was to sing and dance choral songs called stasima. Choral songs in tragedy are often divided into three sections: strophe, antistrophe and epode.

Tragedy has a characteristic structure in which scenes of dialogue alternate with choral songs. This arrangement allows the chorus to comment in its song in a general way on what has been said and/or done in the preceding scene. Most tragedies begin with an opening scene of expository dialogue or monologue called a prologue. After the prologue the chorus marches into the orchestra chanting the parodos; then follows up with a scene of dialogue called an episode, which in turn is followed by the first stasimon. The alternation of episode and stasimon continues until the last stasimon, after which there is a final scene of dialogue called an exodos. The exodos is in general a scene of dialogue, but sometimes songs are included.

(1,400 words)

Vocabulary

vulnerability /ˌvʌlnərəˈbɪlɪtɪ/ *n.* susceptibility to injury or attack 易损性；弱点
undeserved /ˌʌndɪˈzɜːvd/ *adj.* not deserved or earned 不应得的，不该受的；冤枉的
harshness /ˈhɑːʃnɪs/ *n.* the quality of being cruel and causing tension or annoyance 严肃
theatrical /θɪˈætrɪkəl/ *adj.* of or relating to the theater 剧场的，戏剧的
Hellenistic /ˌhelɪˈnɪstɪk/ *adj.* relating to or characteristic of the classical Greek civilization 希腊文化的
deprive /dɪˈpraɪv/ *vt.* keep away from having, keeping, or obtaining 使丧失，剥夺
aural /ˈɔːrəl/ *adj.* of or pertaining to hearing or the ear 听觉的
choreography /ˌkɒrɪˈɒɡrəfɪ/ *n.* a show involving artistic dancing 编舞；舞艺
magistrate /ˈmædʒɪstreɪt/ *n.* a public official authorized to decide questions brought before a court of justice 地方法官
archon /ˈɑːkən/ *n.* governor 执政官（古代雅典九名统治者之一）
successive /səkˈsesɪv/ *adj.* in regular succession without gaps 连续的
tragedian /trəˈdʒiːdɪən/ *n.* a writer (especially a playwright) who writes tragedies 悲剧作家
tetralogy /teˈtrælədʒɪ/ *n.* a series of four related works (plays or novels) 四联剧；四部曲
satyr /ˈsætə/ *n.* one of a class of woodland deities 萨梯（希腊神话中森林之神）
scant /skænt/ *adj.* less than the correct or legal or full amount often deliberately so 不足的
auditorium /ˌɔːdɪˈtɔːrɪəm/ *n.* the area of a theater or concert hall where the audience sits 观众席；会堂
interior /ɪnˈtɪərɪə/ *adj.* situated within or suitable for inside a building 内部的
Aegean /iːˈdʒiːən/ *adj.* of or relating to or bordering the Aegean Sea 爱琴海的
skene /skiːn/ *n.* 永久性剧场背景建筑

full-fledged /ˈfulˈfledʒd/ *adj.* having reached full development 发育完全的
hollow /ˈhɒləʊ/ *vt.* remove the inner part or the core of 使成为空洞
comparable /ˈkɒmpərəbl/ *adj.* able to be compared or worthy of comparison 可比较的；比得上的
mechanical /mɪˈkænɪkəl/ *adj.* relating to or concerned with machinery or tools 机械的
tableau /ˈtæbləʊ/ *n.* any dramatic scene 戏剧性局面，画面
harness /ˈhɑːnɪs/ *n.* a support consisting of an arrangement of straps for holding something to the body 挽具状带子
deity /ˈdiːɪtɪ/ *n.* any supernatural being worshipped as controlling some part of the world or some aspect of life or who is the personification of a force 神
exclusively /ɪksˈkluːsɪvlɪ/ *adv.* without any others being included or involved 唯一地；专有地
protagonist /prəʊˈtægənɪst/ *n.* the principal character in a work of fiction 主演，主角
deuteragonist /ˌdjuːtəˈrægənɪst/ *n.* the second actor who plays the lesser important role in ancient Greek drama (古希腊戏剧中的)第二演员
tritagonist /traɪˈtægənɪst/ *n.* the third actor who plays the lesser important role in ancient Greek drama (古希腊戏剧中的)第三演员
incongruity /ˌɪnkɒŋˈgruːətɪ/ *n.* being unsuitable and inappropriate 不协调，不一致
impersonate /ɪmˈpɜːsəneɪt/ *vt.* assume or act the character of 模仿，扮演
parodos /ˈpærədɒs/ *n.* a song sung when the chorus comes on stage 合唱队登场时唱的歌
twofold /ˈtuːfəʊld/ *adj.* having more than one decidedly dissimilar aspects or qualities 双重的
Coryphaeus /ˌkɔːrɪˈfiːəs/ *n.* the leading singer of the choir 合唱团主唱
stasimon /ˈstæsəmɒn/ *n.* a song of the chorus without anapaests or trochees (古希腊戏剧尤指悲剧中的)合唱颂歌
strophe /ˈstrəʊfɪ/ *n.* one section of a choral ode in classical Greek drama 古希腊歌队唱的歌
antistrophe /ænˈtɪstrəfɪ/ *n.* the section of a choral ode answering a previous strophe in classical Greek drama 向右转时的回舞歌
epode /ˈepəʊd/ *n.* the third section of the Greek lyric ode 希腊抒情颂诗第三节
expository /ɪksˈpɒzɪtərɪ/ *adj.* serving to expound or set forth 说明的，解释的
episode /ˈepɪsəʊd/ *n.* a brief section of a literary or dramatic work that forms part of a connected series 插曲；插话
exodos /ˈeksəˌdɔs/ *n.* exit scene (古希腊悲剧的)结尾

Proper Names

Dionysus　　　　　　　　　　　　迪奥尼索司(希腊神话中的酒神)
Aeschylus　　　　　　　　　　　　埃斯库罗斯(古希腊悲剧诗人)
Sophocles　　　　　　　　　　　　索福克勒斯(古希腊悲剧诗人)
Euripides　　　　　　　　　　　　欧里庇得斯(古希腊悲剧诗人)

Text Exploration

5 Choose the best answer to each question with the information from the text.

1. Athenian tragedy _____.
   A. was the oldest surviving form of tragedy
   B. was popular until the end of the Hellenistic period
   C. was performed in late March or April at an annual state religious festival
   D. took the form of a contest between four playwrights

2. Performances in ancient Greek theatres were definitely open to _____.
   A. all citizens   B. male citizens
   C. female citizens   D. children

3. In ancient Greek theaters, _____.
   A. scenes were always set at the daytime
   B. performances took place both in the daytime and at night
   C. interior scenes were common in tragedy
   D. the action of a tragedy happened in outdoor settings

4. In the earlier Greek theatre, the skene referred to _____.
   A. a tent standing beside the spectators used as a kind of setting
   B. a wooden wall with doors just used for decoration
   C. a tent in which actors could get changed
   D. a wooden wall painted to represent required settings but without doors

5. Which of the following is incorrect about the two mechanical devices of the ancient Greek theatre?
   A. The "wheeled-out thing" is a platform on which a tableau was displayed representing the result of an action indoors.
   B. The "wheeled-out thing" rolled out through one of the doors of the skene.
   C. The "theatrical machine" is a crane to which a cable with a harness for an actor was attached.
   D. The "theatrical machine" was confined to divine characters.

6. The actors in tragedy were _____.
   A. hired and paid by the state
   B. assigned to the tragedian probably by lot
   C. increased to three by the middle of the fifth century
   D. all of the above

7. Why did the chorus remain in the orchestra between the episodes?
   A. Because they needed to sing and dance choral songs.
   B. Because they needed to help actors take the time to get ready for a new role.
   C. Because they didn't need to change costume.
   D. Because they needed to assume a new role in the next episode.

8. What is the most important function of the tragic chorus?

    A. Singing and dancing stasima.   B. Chanting a parodos.

    C. Engaging in dialogue with characters.   D. All of the above.

9. The standard number of members of a chorus was _____.

    A. twelve throughout Aeschylus's whole career

    B. more than fifteen by Sophocles

    C. twelve in most of Aeschylus's career

    D. not mentioned

10. What is the correct chronological order of a tragedy?

    A. A prologue, the parodos, an episode, a stasimon and an exodos.

    B. A prologue, the parodos, the alternation of episode and stasimon and an exodos.

    C. A prologue, the parodos, an exodos, the alternation of episode and stasimon.

    D. The parodos, a prologue, the alternation of episode and stasimon and an exodos.

6 Complete the following chart with the information from the text.

Athenian tragedy	Some Details
Origins	Having emerged sometime during the 6th century BCE, it flowered during the 5th century BCE, and continued to be popular until the beginning of _____.
Actors	The playing of multiple roles, both male and female, was made possible by _____ _____, which prevented the audience from identifying the face of any actor with one specific character in the play and helped _____ _____ of men impersonating women. The main duty of an actor was to speak the dialogue _____ _____. However, he occasionally had to sing songs solo or with the chorus or with other actors.
Chorus	The chorus was _____ who had a talent for singing and dancing and were trained by the tragedian in preparation for the performance. The chorus, like the actors, wore _____. Choral songs in tragedy are often divided into three sections: _____.
Structure	Tragedy has a characteristic structure in which scenes of dialogue _____ _____ choral songs. This arrangement allows the chorus to comment in its song in a general way on what has been said and/or done in _____.

7 Discuss the following questions with the information from the text.

1. According to the text, what is tragedy?

2. Was the author of a tragedy merely a writer of a script? Why or why not?

3. Which one do you prefer, tragedy or comedy? Please give your reasons.

4. What's the distinction between reading a drama script and watching a drama in the theatre?

5. Why were women not allowed to perform at the theatre in ancient Greece?

Vocabulary Expansion

8 Fill in the blanks with the right words given below. Change the form where necessary.

| theatrical | deprive | protagonist | stasimon | twofold |
| tragedian | tetralogy | interior | undeserved | tableau |

1. They were _____ of a normal childhood by the war.
2. *The Bacchae*, a play by the Greek _____ Euripides, shows a dramatic view of the confrontation between instincts and institutions.
3. New Shanghai Restaurant with elegant _____ decoration reopened yesterday.
4. _____ refer to the choral songs sung by the chorus in ancient Greek tragedies.
5. His father, Don Gregory, is a _____ and film producer in Newport Beach, California.
6. When the conspiracy was disclosed, they got the _____ punishment.
7. The Japanese author Yukio Mishima is the best-known for *The Sea of Fertility*, a _____ which explores the development of modern Japanese ideals.
8. New York's governor had appeared briefly on cable television with his wife in the traditional politician-and-spouse _____.
9. She has created a dashing young man as the _____ of her new novel.
10. The university library shoulders the _____ task which serves for the teaching and the scientific research.

9 Choose the word or phrase that best keeps the meaning of the sentence if it is substituted for the underlined word or phrase.

1. Outraged politicians rebuked them for their extravagance, and commentators noted the incongruity of travelling by luxury jet to ask for money.
    A. coordination   B. harmony
    C. discordance   D. excessiveness
2. The economic crisis has also exposed the vulnerability of commodity exporters to speculative activities.
    A. weakness   B. illegality
    C. opportunism   D. superiority
3. Continuity is ensured by using the same props in successive scenes
    A. on-again   B. discontinuous
    C. separate   D. continuing
4. However, Washington appears to have engaged in scant consultation with Europe before last week's announcement.
    A. adequate   B. insufficient   C. ample   D. divergent

5. Just a moment, feeling that his soul hollowed out, the hand with gun fell down beyond control.
   A. occupied   B. filled up   C. emptied   D. dominated
6. Although the mockingbirds superbly mimic the songs and calls of many birds, they can also be quickly identified as mockingbirds by certain aural clues.
   A. behavioral   B. visual   C. sensory   D. auditory
7. The Fed will also directly supervise any non-bank financial firms that reach a size and complexity comparable to these banks.
   A. superior to   B. commensurate with
   C. far behind   D. better than
8. Some argue that students should not be shunted off into exclusively vocational training but keep the option to go back into the academic stream.
   A. optionally   B. invariably   C. solely   D. urgently
9. On the web, anyone can impersonate an expert and anyone can open blog.
   A. imitate   B. become   C. ridicule   D. supplant
10. This type of expository writing deals with facts to give the reader information.
    A. argumentative   B. illustrative   C. narrative   D. expressive

10 **Translate the Chinese sentences into English by simulating the sentences chosen from the text.**

Chosen Sentences	Simulated Translations	Chinese Sentences
Tragedy *was intended to* be presented in a theater before an audience.		这座建筑原来是打算用作餐厅的。(**dinning hall**)
Private reading of tragedy *deprives* us *of* the visual and aural effects.		他们通常被视为是快节奏职场中被剥夺了学习时间的精神牺牲品。(**spiritual victims**)
When his work *was approved for* presentation at the state religious festival in honor of the god Dionysus, the state assigned him actors and a chorus.		人类生长荷尔蒙从未被批准使用在美容、抗老化上。(**human growth hormone**)
It *engaged in* dialogue with characters through its leader, the Coryphaeus, who alone spoke the lines of dialogue assigned to the chorus.		许多小朋友参加课外戏剧活动。(**extracurricular dramatics**)
Tragedy has a characteristic structure in which scenes of dialogue *alternate with* choral songs.		我有时头脑很不好使,而有时思维又灵到有很多创新的见解。(**mental dullness**)

Supplementary Readings

11 Passage One[①]

Oedipus at Colonus is one of the three Theban plays of the Athenian tragedian Sophocles. In the time order, the events of *Oedipus at Colonus* occur after *Oedipus the King* and before *Antigone*; however, it was chronologically the last to be written. The play describes the end of Oedipus' tragic life.

It is several years after Oedipus was banished from Thebes he once ruled. He is blind and hobbled, dressed in rags, led by his daughter Antigone. They stop in the grove of the Furies at Colonus, near Athens. A Colonus citizen passes by and tells them to move—they're on the sacred ground of the Furies. Oedipus, however, believes this grove was prophesied as the location of his life's final chapter. More citizens (the chorus) come, and Oedipus asks them to send for Theseus, king of Athens. When they learn who Oedipus is, they're frightened to let him leave.

Before Theseus arrives, his other daughter, Ismene, brings news from Thebes. Oedipus's two sons are fighting for control of the city. The leaders of Thebes want Oedipus to return, but merely at the border of Thebes, because the oracles say his presence would protect Thebes. Oedipus is furious at it. While they wait for Theseus, he reluctantly tells the chorus his deeds—killing his father and marrying his mother.

When Theseus arrives, Oedipus says if Theseus allows him to stay and be buried at Colonus, his tomb will bless Athens. Theseus promises him. Creon arrives from Thebes. He claims to have suffered at the thought of Oedipus's misfortunes and hopes Oedipus returns to Thebes. Oedipus states that he's being used as a pawn in the Theban power struggle. Creon's guards take his daughters as hostages trying to force Oedipus to come back. Theseus stops him and keeps Oedipus's daughters unharmed.

[①] This passage is adapted from *Oedipus at Colonus* at www.litcharts.com/files/pdf/printer/oedipusatcolonus-LitChart.pdf

Oedipus's son Polynices comes. He says the oracles have decreed that whichever side of the upcoming battle Oedipus supports will win, and asks for help. Oedipus curses him for failing to come to his aid when he was in exile and prophesy that Polynices's attack on Thebes will fail, and the two brothers will kill each other.

A thunderstorm begins, signaling Oedipus's death has arrived. After his daughters mourned him and received his blessing, he told everyone but Theseus to leave. When they look back, Oedipus has vanished, and Theseus is covering his eyes as if he's witnessed something supernatural. Although he won't tell Antigone and Ismenethe Oedipus's burial location, Theseus agrees to send them to Thebes, where they hope to stop the upcoming battle.

1. _____ is the correct performing timeline of the three Theban plays.
   A. *Oedipus at Colonus*, *Oedipus the King* and *Antigone*
   B. *Oedipus the King*, *Oedipus at Colonus* and *Antigone*
   C. *Antigone*, *Oedipus the King* and *Oedipus at Colonus*
   D. *Oedipus the King*, *Antigone* and *Oedipus at Colonus*

2. Why Oedipus doesn't want to leave when a citizen of Colonus asks them to move away from the grove?
   A. Because they're on the sacred ground of the Furies.
   B. Because they're too exhausted to move.
   C. Because Oedipus believes he will die there.
   D. Because Oedipus wants to meet the King of Athens.

3. The leaders of Thebes want Oedipus to return, for _____.
   A. Oedipus's appearance would protect their city
   B. they want to keep Oedipus at the border of the city
   C. they miss their King Oedipus
   D. they have forgiven Oedipus's evil deeds

4. Which statement is appropriate to Creon according to the passage?
   A. Creon feels truly sorry for Oedipus's misfortunes.
   B. Oedipus fiercely turns down Creon's requirement.
   C. Creon's guards protect Odipus's daughters to come back.
   D. Creon's guards take away Oedipus's daughters finally.

5. Which of the following expressions is right?
   A. Polynices receives his father's forgiveness.
   B. Oedipus gives his blessing to his daughters and sons.
   C. Only Theseus and Oedipus's daughters know his tomb.
   D. Oedipus's daughters are sent back to Thebes by Theseus.

12 Passage Two[①]

Macbeth is Shakespeare's shortest tragedy. It was probably written in 1606. *Macbeth* clearly reflects the playwright's close relationship with the sovereign. Shakespeare paid homage to his king's Scottish lineage. The theme of bad versus good kingship in *Macbeth* would have resonated at the royal court.

Scottish generals Macbeth and Banquo have defeated invading armies. When crossing a moor, they encounter three witches, who prophesy that Macbeth will be thane of Cawdor and King of Scotland, and Banquo will beget a line of Scottish kings but king. They treat the prophecies skeptically until King Duncan's men come and tell Macbeth that he has been named thane of Cawdor. Macbeth is intrigued by the prophecy, but uncertain. He visits King Duncan, and they will dine at Macbeth's castle at night. Lady Macbeth persuades Macbeth to kill him then.

Fearful that Banquo's heirs will seize the throne, Macbeth hires murderers to kill Banquo. Banquo's ghost visits Macbeth. Frightened, Macbeth goes to visit the witches, who prophesy: he must beware of Macduff; he is incapable of being harmed by any man born of woman; and he will be safe until Birnam Wood comes to his Dunsinane Castle. Macbeth is relieved because he knows all men are born of women and forests cannot move. When he learns that Macduff has fled to England to join Prince Malcolm to invade him, Macbeth orders that Macduff's castle be seized and Lady Macduff and her children be killed.

Lady Macbeth becomes plagued with sleepwalking and believes bloodstains are on her hands. Before Macbeth's opponents arrive, Macbeth learns that she has killed herself, causing him to a pessimistic despair. He is struck numb with fear, when learning the English

---

[①]This passage is adapted from http://www.sparknotes.com/shakespeare/macbeth/context.html

army is advancing on Dunsinane shielded with boughs cut from Birnam Wood.

The English forces overwhelm Macbeth's castle. Macduff declares that he was not "of woman born" but was "untimely ripped" from his mother's womb. Though he realizes that he is doomed, Macbeth continues to fight until Macduff beheads him. Malcolm, now the King of Scotland invites all to see him crowned at Scone.

Macbeth is not Shakespeare's most complex play, but its powerfulness has shocked audiences for years. There are accidents, even deaths taking place during runs of *Macbeth*. While many would say that any misfortune surrounding a production is mere coincidence, theatre people consider it misfortune to mention *Macbeth* by name inside a theatre, and refer to it as "the Scottish play", or "MacBee", or the character, "Mr. and Mrs. M". To say the name of the play inside a theatre is believed to doom the production to failure, and perhaps cause physical injury or death to cast members.

1. Which of the following events doesn't belong to the witches' prophecies?
   A. Macbeth will be made thane of Cawdor and then King of Scotland.
   B. Banquo will beget a line of Scottish kings, although he won't be king.
   C. Macduff will support Macbeth's accession to the throne.
   D. Macbeth will be safe until Birnam Wood comes to Dunsinane Castle.
2. According to Macbeth's psychological change, which of the statements is wrong?
   A. Macbeth treats the witches' prophecies skeptically in the very beginning.
   B. After knowing of being named thane of Cawdor, Macbeth is intrigued by the prophecy with certainty.
   C. Lady Macbeth's death causes him to sink into a pessimistic despair.
   D. At last, he is struck numb with fear, though he is doomed; Macbeth continues to fight to death.
3. What is not the aftermath of the characters in the play?
   A. Lady Macbeth commits suicide after the English forces overwhelm Macbeth's army.
   B. Lady Macduff and her children are murdered by Macbeth's men.
   C. The vengeful Macduff kills and beheads Macbeth.
   D. Prince Malcolm becomes the King of Scotland.
4. Which option is incorrect in the understanding of the tragedy of *Macbeth*?
   A. *Macbeth*, which may be written in 1606, is a play about a regicide.
   B. *Macbeth* is Shakespeare's shortest and most complex tragedy.
   C. *Macbeth* reflects Shakespeare's close relationship with the king.
   D. The theme of *Macbeth* is bad versus good kingship.
5. How do theater people think about the Play *Macbeth*?
   A. They consider it good luck to mention *Macbeth* by name while inside a theatre.
   B. They refer it directly, such as "the Scottish play", or "MacBee".
   C. They always refer to the character instead of the play itself.
   D. They believe that to say the name of the play inside a theatre is to doom the production to failure, and actors to misfortune.

Interactive Tasks

Role-play

13 **Role-play the following situation with your partner.**

Situation:

  Becky, an English major in her second year, comes across her friend Jack, who majors in Mathematics, on campus. They are talking about the coming drama performance competition.

You may begin like this:

Becky: Our department will hold a drama performance competition next week. I will perform the play "King Lear" with my partners.

Jack: Wow. That sounds cool. Is it Shakespeare's drama?

Becky: Right. It's one of Shakespeare's Four Great Tragedies. I will play the role of Cordelia.

Jack: Oh, who's Cordelia? Tell me more about this play.

Group Work

14 **Work in groups to work out your own presentation.**

1. Form groups of four or five students;
2. Each group chooses a topic concerning drama, e.g.
   A study of the history and development of drama in a certain period at home or abroad;
   An introduction to a dramatist and one of his works.
3. Members of each group collect materials from library and the Internet to work out their PPT slides;
4. Based on the PPT slides, each member of the group gives oral presentation of his part.

Follow-up Task

Writing

15 **Directions:** For this part, you are going to write a composition on the topic: **Drama or Movie**. You should write at least 120 words following the outline given below in Chinese:

1. 如今电影充斥着人们的闲暇生活,戏剧受到忽视;
2. 电影、戏剧各有好处,戏剧在人生中的作用不容忽视;
3. 两者兼顾,放松的同时,也不要忘了在感悟中前进。

Unit 4 Pop Music

Highlight

Topic area	Communication	Skills
Some well-known pop singers; Some well-known pop bands; The best-known music award in the world.	in response to evoke the attention of invoke the fury of in view of with respect of	Knowing some well-known celebrities in pop music; Knowing the story of Lady Gaga; Knowing the best-known music award in the world.

Starting-out Task

1 Look at these pictures and discuss the following questions with your partner.

1. What do you know about the Beatles, one of the best-known rock bands in history?

2. Who is your favorite pop singer? Share what you know about him or her with others.

3. What do you know about Grammy Award, which is usually called the Oscar in the music industry?

Listening Tasks

Micro Listening Skills

2 **Listen to the following passage and try to fill in the missing words.**

With 20th century music, there was a vast increase in music listening as the radio gained popularity and phonographs were used to replay and 1. _____ music. The focus of art music was characterized by exploration of new 2. _____, styles, and sounds. Jazz evolved and became a significant genre of music over the course of the 20th century, and during the second half of that century, rock music did the same. Jazz is an American musical art form that 3. _____ in the beginning of the 20th century in African American 4. _____ in the Southern United States from a confluence of African and European music 5. _____. From its early development until the present, jazz has also incorporated music from 19th and 20th century American 6. _____ music. Rock music is a genre of popular music that developed in the 1960s from 1950s rock and roll, rockabilly, blues, and 7. _____ music. The sound of rock often 8. _____ around the electric guitar or acoustic guitar, and it uses a strong back beat laid down by a rhythm section of electric bass guitar, drums, and keyboard 9. _____. Along with the guitar or keyboards, saxophone and blues-style harmonica are used as soloing instruments. In its "purest form", it has three chords, a strong, insistent back beat, and a catchy 10. _____.

Passage

Celine Dion

Unit 4 Pop Music

Words & Phrases

mortgage / ˈmɔːɡɪdʒ / n.	抵押贷款
album / ˈælbəm / n.	专辑
hiatus / haɪˈeɪtəs / n.	间断
diagnose / ˈdaɪəɡnəʊz / vt.	诊断

3 Listen to the passage and decide whether the following statements are true (T) or false (F).

1. ____ Dion's first record was financed by her future husband.
2. ____ In 1999, Dion announced a hiatus from entertainment because she got tired of show business.
3. ____ Dion returned to the top of music in 2002 and signed a contract to perform in Las Vegas.
4. ____ Dion's music has been mainly influenced by rock and country music.
5. ____ People have often had mixed remarks on Dion's music.

4 Listen to the passage again and complete the following sentences with the information you have heard.

1. Dion had first _____ in the 1980s.
2. During the 1990s, Dion _____ after signing with Epic Records and releasing several English albums along with additional French albums.
3. Dion is renowned for her _____ and powerful vocals.
4. In 2004, after _____ in album sales worldwide, Dion became the best-selling female artist of all time.

Reading Tasks

Focus Reading

Pre-reading Questions

1. Do you enjoy pop music? Can you give a brief introduction of an album that you love best?
2. Can you tell a tidbit about the pop singer that you love best?
3. What do you know about Lady Gaga?

Lady Gaga, a Star Surrounded by Controversy

Stefani Joanne Angelina Germanotta, better known by her stage name Lady Gaga, is an American pop singer and songwriter. Gaga has been influenced by rock artists such as David Bowie and Queen, as well as pop music artists such as Madonna, Britney Spears and Michael Jackson. The Queen's song "*Radio Ga Ga*" inspired her stage name, "Lady Gaga". She commented: "I adored Freddie Mercury and Queen had a hit called *Radio Ga Ga*. That's why I love the name...Freddie was unique—one of the biggest personalities in the whole of pop music." In response to the comparisons between herself and Madonna, Gaga stated: "I don't want to sound presumptuous, but I've made it my goal to revolutionize pop music. The last revolution was launched by Madonna 25 years ago."

Gaga has a vocal range of a contralto. Her vocals have drawn frequent comparison to those of Madonna and Gwen Stefani, while the structure of her music is said to echo classic 1980s pop and 1990s Euro pop. While reviewing her debut album *The Fame*, *The Sunday Times* asserted: "In combining music, fashion, art and technology, Gaga evokes Madonna, Gwen Stefani." Similarly, *The Boston Globe* commented that she draws "obvious inspirations from Madonna to Gwen Stefani…in her girlish but sturdy pipes and bubbly beats." Though her lyrics are said to lack intellectual stimulation, "she does manage to get you moving and grooving at an almost effortless pace." Music critic Simon Reynolds wrote.

Gaga has identified fashion as a major influence. She considers Donatella Versace her muse. Gaga has her own creative production team which she handles personally. The team creates many of her clothes, stage props, and hairdos. Her love of fashion came from her mother, who she stated was "always very well kept and beautiful." "When I'm writing music, I'm thinking about the clothes I want to wear on stage. It's all about everything altogether—performance art, pop performance art, and fashion. For me, it's everything coming together and being a real story that will bring back the super-fan. I want the imagery to be so strong that fans will want to taste and lick every part of it." The Global Language Monitor named "Lady Gaga" as the Top Fashion Buzzword with her trademark "no pants" coming in at No. 3. *Entertainment Weekly* put her outfits on its end of the decade "best-of" list, saying, "Gaga's outré ensembles brought performance art into the mainstream."

Unit 4 Pop Music

Critical reception of Gaga's music, fashion sense and persona are mixed. Her status as a role model, trailblazer and fashion icon is by turns affirmed and denied. Gaga's albums have received mostly positive reviews, with critics pointing out her unique place in pop music. Her role as a self-esteem booster for her fans is also lauded, as is her role in breathing life into the fashion industry. Her performances are described as "highly entertaining and innovative"; in particular, the blood-spurting performance of "*Paparazzi*" at the 2009 MTV Video Music Awards was described as "eye-popping" by MTV. She continued the "blood soaked" theme in *The Monster Ball Tour*, in which she wears a revealing leather corset and is "attacked" by a performer dressed in black who gnaws on her throat, causing "blood" to spurt down her chest, after which she lies "dying" in a pool of blood. Her performances of that scene in Manchester, England, triggered protests from family groups in the aftermath of a local tragedy, in which a taxi driver had murdered 12 people. "What happened in Bradford is very fresh in people's minds and given all the violence which happened in Cumbria just hours earlier, it was insensitive," said Lynn Costello of Mothers Against Violence. Chris Rock later defended her flamboyant, provocative behavior. "Well, she's Lady Gaga," he said. "She's not 'Lady Behave Yourself.' Do you want great behavior from a person named Gaga? Is this what you were expecting?" She later returned to the 2010 MTV Video Music Awards wearing a dress supplemented by boots, a purse and a hat—each fabricated from the flesh of a dead animal. The dress, named by *Time* magazine's Fashion Statement of 2010 and more widely known as the "meat dress", was made by an Argentinean designer and received divided opinions—evoking the attention of worldwide media but invoking the fury of animal rights organization. Gaga, however, later denied any intention of causing disrespect to any person or organization and wished for the dress to be interpreted as a statement of human rights.

Contrary to her outré style, *the New York Post* described her early look as like "a refugee from Jersey Shore" with "big black hair, heavy eye makeup and tight, revealing clothes." Gaga is a natural brunette; she bleached her hair blonde because she was often mistaken for Amy Winehouse. She often refers to her fans as her "little monsters" and has that inscription tattooed on the arm that holds her microphone. She has another six known tattoos, among them a peace symbol, which was inspired by John Lennon, who she stated was her hero, and a German script on her left arm quoting the poet Rainer Maria Rilke, her favorite philosopher, commenting that his "philosophy of solitude" spoke to her. Towards the end of 2008, comparisons were made between the fashions of Gaga and fellow recording artist Christina Aguilera that noted similarities in their styling, hair, and make-up. Aguilera stated that she was "completely unaware of Gaga" and "didn't know if it was a man or a woman." Gaga released a statement in which she welcomed the comparisons due to the attention providing useful publicity, saying, "She's such a huge star and if anything I should send her flowers, because a lot of people in America didn't know who I was until that whole thing happened. It really put me on the map in a way." Comparisons continued into 2010 when Aguilera released the music video of her single "*Not Myself Tonight*". Critics noted similarities between the song and its accompanying music video with Gaga's video for "*Bad Romance*". There have also been similar comparisons made between Gaga's style and that of fashion icon Dale from the band Missing Persons. Some have considered their respective images to be strikingly parallel although fans of Missing Persons note that Dale had pioneered the look more than thirty years earlier.

Besides her career in music, Gaga has enhanced her reputation as a philanthropist who has contributed to various charities and humanitarian works. Although declining an invitation to record a benefit song, Gaga held a concert of *The Monster Ball Tour* following the 2010 Haiti earthquake and dedicated it to the country's reconstruction relief fund. This concert, held at the Radio City Music Hall, New York, on January 24, 2010, donated any received revenue to the relief fund while, in addition, all profits from sales of products on Gaga's official online store on that same day were donated. Gaga announced that an estimated total of $500,000 was collected for the fund. After the earthquake and tsunami hit Japan on March 11, 2011, Gaga designed a bracelet, of which, all of the money generated went to Japanese relief efforts. The bracelets raised $1.5 million.

In view of Lady Gaga's influence on modern culture and her rise to global fame, sociologist of the University of South Carolina since the Spring of 2011 organizes a course titled "Lady Gaga and the Sociology of the Fame" with the objective of unraveling "sociologically relevant dimensions of the fame of Lady Gaga with respect to her music, videos, fashion, and other artistic endeavors".

(1,262 words)

Vocabulary

adore /əˈdɔː/ *vt.* love and respect deeply 敬爱；崇敬

presumptuous /prɪˈzʌmptʃuːəs/ *adj.* failing to observe the limits of what is permitted or appropriate 自以为是的

contralto /kənˈtræltəʊ/ *n.* the lowest female singing voice 女低音

echo /ˈekəʊ/ *vt.* have qualities or features in common with something 与……相似

evoke /ɪˈvəʊk/ *vt.* bring or recall to the conscious mind 唤起；使人想起

inspiration /ˌɪnspəˈreɪʃn/ *n.* the process of being mentally stimulated to do or feel something 灵感

sturdy /ˈstɜːdɪ/ *adj.* strong enough 结实的

bubbly /ˈbʌblɪ/ *adj.* full of vibrancy 生机勃勃的

lyric /ˈlɪrɪk/ *n.* the words of a song 歌词

groove /gruːv/ *vi.* dance with pop music 跟着流行乐跳舞

muse /mjuːz/ *n.* the process of being mentally stimulated to create art works 灵感

props /ˈprɒps/ *n.* stage properties 演出道具

hairdo /ˈheədu:/ *n.* the style of a woman's hair（女子）发式

lick /lɪk/ *vt.* pass the tongue over (something), typically in order to taste 舔尝

buzzword /ˈbʌzˌwɜːd/ *n.* a technical word or phrase that has become fashionable 时髦词语

outré /uːˈtreɪ/ *adj.* odd or eccentric 奇特的；怪异的

ensemble /ɑːnˈsɑːmbl/ *n.* a set of clothes chosen to harmonize when worn together 全套服装

persona /pəˈsəʊnə/ *n.* the aspect of someone's character that is presented to or perceived by others 表面形象

trailblazer /ˈtreɪlˌbleɪzə/ *n.* a pioneer; an innovator 先驱；创始人

booster /ˈbuːstə/ *n.* a thing or person that helps promote something 起推动作用的事或人

laud /lɔːd/ *vt.* praise highly 称赞，赞扬

revealing /rɪˈviːlɪŋ/ *adj.* allowing more of the wearer's body to be seen than is usual（服装）暴露的

corset /ˈkɔːsɪt/ *n.* tight outer bodice or dress 紧身胸衣（或外套）

gnaw /nɔː/ *vt.* bite at or nibble something persistently 咬；啃

trigger /ˈtrɪgə/ *vt.* cause an event or situation to happen 引发，引起

aftermath /ˈɑːftəmæθ/ *n.* the unpleasant consequences of an event（尤指不好的）后果

flamboyant /flæmˈbɔɪənt/ *adj.* tending to attract attention 抢眼的；惹人注目的

provocative /prəˈvɒkətɪv/ *adj.* causing another strong reaction 煽动的；刺激的

Argentinian /ˌɑːdʒənˈtɪnɪən/ *adj.* 阿根廷的

fury /ˈfjʊərɪ/ *n.* wild or violent anger 狂怒，暴怒
brunette /bruːˈnet/ *n.* a woman or girl with dark brown hair 深褐色头发的女人（或女孩）
bleach /bliːtʃ/ *vt.* become white or much lighter by a chemical process 漂白；使变成淡色
blonde /blɒnd/ *adj.* fair or pale yellow（多指毛发）金黄色的
inscription /ɪnˈskrɪpʃən/ *n.* a thing inscribed, as on a monument or in a book 铭文；题词
tattoo /tæˈtuː/ *vt.* mark a part of the body with an indelible design by inserting pigment into punctures in the skin 文身
solitude /ˈsɒlɪtjuːd/ *n.* the state or situation of being alone 独处；孤独
philanthropist /fɪˈlænθrəpɪst/ *n.* a person who seeks to promote the welfare of others 慈善家
humanitarian /hjuːˌmænɪˈteərɪən/ *adj.* concerned with or seeking to promote human welfare 人道主义的
tsunami /tsjuːˈnɑːmɪ/ *n.* a long high sea wave caused by an earthquake or other disturbance 海啸
unravel /ʌnˈrævəl/ *vt.* investigate and solve or explain 弄清；阐明
dimension /dɪˈmenʃən/ *n.* an aspect or feature of a situation, problem, or thing 方面；特征

Proper Names

Stefani Joanne Angelina Germanotta	斯蒂芬妮·乔安妮·安吉莉娜·杰尔马诺塔
David Bowie /ˈdeɪvɪd ˈbəʊɪ/	大卫·鲍伊
Madonna /məˈdɒnə/	麦当娜
Britney Spears	小甜甜布兰妮
Michael Jackson /ˈmaɪkl ˈdʒæksn/	迈克尔·杰克逊
Freddie Mercury /ˈfredɪ ˈmɜːkjurɪ/	弗雷迪·莫库里
Gwen Stefani	格温·史蒂芬尼
The Sunday Times	《星期日泰晤士报》
The Boston Globe	《波士顿环球报》
Simon Reynolds /ˈsaɪmən ˈrenəldz/	西蒙·雷诺兹
Donatella Versace	多那泰拉·范思哲
The Global Language Monitor	全球语言监测机构
Entertainment Weekly	《娱乐周刊》
Manchester /ˈmæntʃɪstə/	曼彻斯特
Bradford /ˈbrædfəd/	布莱德福特
Cumbria /ˈkʌmbrɪə/	坎布里亚
Lynn Costello /lɪz kɒsˈteləʊ/	林恩·科斯特洛
Chris Rock /krɪs rɒk/	克里斯·洛克
Time	《时代》
The New York Post	《纽约邮报》
Jersey /ˈdʒɜːzɪ/	泽西城
Amy Winehouse /ˈeɪmɪ ˈwaɪnhaʊs/	艾米·怀恩豪斯

John Lennon 约翰·列侬
Rainer Maria Rilke 勒内·马利亚·里尔克
Christina Aguilera 克里斯蒂娜·阿奎莱拉
Dale /deɪl/ 戴尔

Text Exploration

5 Choose the best answer to each question with the information from the text.

1. The stage name "Lady Gaga" was inspired by _____.
    A. Stefani Joanne Angelina Germanotta
    B. David Bowie
    C. Madonna
    D. Freddie Mercury

2. According to paragraph one, which of the following is NOT true?
    A. Madonna, Britney Spears and Michael Jackson did not influence Gaga as much as Freddie.
    B. Freddie was unique in Gaga's eye.
    C. "Radio Ga Ga" is a song by Queen.
    D. Gaga stated that Madonna failed to keep up with the trend in pop music.

3. Which of the following is NOT a feature of Gaga's music?
    A. Combining music, fashion, art and technology.
    B. Being able to make listeners move and groove easily.
    C. Sturdy pipes and bubbly beats.
    D. Intellectual stimulation.

4. Gaga identified fashion as a major influence for all the following reasons EXCEPT that _____.
    A. Gaga has her own creative production team called the Haus of Gaga
    B. Gaga believes a real story with everything together will bring back the super-fan
    C. Gaga wants audience to taste every component of her performance
    D. Gaga wants the imagery to be impressive

5. Who is the inspiration for Gaga's role of fashion trailblazer?
    A. Donatella Versace.
    B. Haus of Gaga.
    C. Her mother.
    D. Dale from the band Missing Persons.

6. Which of the following is true?
    A. Gaga received both positive and negative feedback for her public impression.
    B. Blood-spurting performance of "*Paparazzi*" received a great amount of positive feedback from public society.
    C. Chris Rock said that Gaga was expected to behave properly as a celebrity.
    D. A taxi driver murdered 12 people due to the influence of Gaga's blood-spurting performance.

7. How did Gaga address her intention behind "meat dress"?
   A. She wanted to attract public's attention.
   B. She wanted to attract public's concern about endangered animals.
   C. She wanted her performance to be more appealing.
   D. She wanted the dress to be interpreted as a statement of human rights.
8. Which of the following statements is NOT the description of Gaga's early look?
   A. Like a refugee from Jersey Shore.
   B. Big blond hair.
   C. Heavy eye makeup.
   D. In tight, revealing clothes.
9. Why did Gaga say she welcomed the comparisons between herself and Christina?
   A. They had great similarities in their styling, hair, and make-up.
   B. Aguilera was completely unaware of Gaga.
   C. Great publicity is provided through the comparison.
   D. Aguilera was a super star.
10. Which of the following is true about Gaga?
    A. Gaga has seldom paid any attention to the things outside her music career.
    B. Gaga has contributed to various charities and never turned down any benefit song recording.
    C. All the revenue of her concert held at the Radio City Music Hall after 2010 Haiti earthquake went to relief fund.
    D. Gaga earned one and half million for designing the Japan Prayer Bracelets.

6 Complete the following chart with the information from the text.

Music Style	1. The structure of Gaga's music is said to _____. 2. Gaga draws obvious inspirations from Madonna to Gwen Stefani and her music makes a feature of _____. 3. According to Music critic Simon Reynolds, Gaga does manage to make audience _____.
A Fashion Addict	1. Gaga has her own creative production team which _____. 2. Gaga wants to combine performance art, pop performance art and fashion together in order to _____. 3. Gaga wants her imagery to be so strong that _____. 4. The Global Language Monitor named "Lady Gaga" _____ with her trademark "no pants" coming in at No. 3.
Entertaining and Innovative Performances	1. In The Monster Ball Tour, she wears _____. 2. At the 2010 MTV Video Music Awards, Gaga wore _____.
A Philanthropist	1. After the 2010 Haiti earthquake, _____. 2. After the earthquake and tsunami hit Japan in 2011, _____.

Unit 4 Pop Music

7 Discuss the following questions with the information from the text.
1. What do you think of the role of fashion in pop music?

2. What is the controversy on Gaga's performance?

3. Do you appreciate Gaga's highly entertaining and innovative performance? Why?

4. What is the objective of the course organized by sociologist of the University of South Carolina?

5. Do you think that Lady Gaga can achieve her goal to revolutionize pop music? Why?

Vocabulary Expansion

8 Fill in the blanks with the right words given below. Change the form where necessary.

adore	echo	evoke	inspiration	trigger
provocative	inscription	humanitarian	dimension	unravel

1. This is the worst _____ disaster this country has ever seen.
2. The student and his teacher _____ each other in performing style.
3. The finding of the research suggests that stress or overwork can _____ an allergy.
4. People _____ him for his noble character.
5. The police are attempting _____ the cause of his death.
6. His _____ remarks on racial discrimination have received violent criticism.
7. There photo has brought that potent tang _____ nostalgic memories of childhood holidays.
8. These newly transplanted tropical flowers can add a new _____ to your garden.
9. There was a(n) _____ in Chinese characters over the arch.
10. The _____ from nature tend to help artists create magnificent works.

9 Choose the word or phrase that best keeps the meaning of the sentence if it is substituted for the underlined word or phrase.
1. People need a chance to reflect on spiritual matters in <u>solitude</u>.
   A. misery   B. hindrance   C. loneliness   D. peace
2. I hope I won't be considered <u>presumptuous</u> if I offer some advice.
   A. bold   B. offensive   C. conceited   D. intelligent
3. I need a bike that is <u>sturdy</u> enough to cope with bumpy tracks.
   A. solid   B. complex   C. expensive   D. sophisticated
4. His <u>muse</u> had deserted him, and he could no longer write.
   A. talent   B. intelligence   C. meditation   D. inspiration

5. Mail from home is a great morale booster for our soldiers.
   A. comfort   B. encouragement
   C. excitement   D. sympathy

6. He was a trailblazer for many ideas that are now standard fare.
   A. innovator   B. designer   C. critic   D. expert

7. His coat was adorned with a flamboyant bunch of flowers.
   A. noticeable   B. bright   C. colorful   D. magnificent

8. With respect to your other proposals, I am not yet able to tell you our decision.
   A. regardless of   B. in spite of
   C. based on   D. in terms of

9. In the aftermath of the hurricane, many people's homes were destroyed.
   A. influence   B. consequence   C. disaster   D. attack

10. He flew into a fury and said that the whole thing was disgusting.
    A. disappointment   B. excitement
    C. anger   D. violence

10 Translate the Chinese sentences into English by simulating the sentences chosen from the text.

Chosen Sentences	Simulated Translations	Chinese Sentences
Though her lyrics are said to lack intellectual stimulation, she **does** manage to get you moving and grooving at an almost effortless pace.		虽然在其他科目上成绩平平，但他的确在数学方面有极高的天分。
Her role as a self-esteem booster for her fans is also lauded, **as is** her role in breathing life into the fashion industry.		他面对媒体时的傲慢，就像他对妇女的歧视一样都受到了广泛的批评。（**arrogance, prejudice**）
The "meat dress" **received divided opinions**—**evoking** the attention of worldwide media **but invoking** the fury of animal rights organization.		关于"克隆人"一直以来饱受争议，它既给那些不育的妇女带来了希望，也引发了有关其是否符合伦理的争论。（**human cloning, infertile, ethical**）
In view of Lady Gaga's influence on modern culture, sociologist of the University of South Carolina organizes a course **with the objective of** unravelling sociologically relevant dimensions of the fame of Lady Gaga.		鉴于不断增加的失业人数，政府出台了一些新政策，旨在鼓励自主创业。（**unveil, self-employment**）

Unit 4 Pop Music

Supplementary Readings

Passage One

A Grammy Award is an accolade by NARAS (the National Academy of Recording Arts and Sciences of the United States) to recognize outstanding achievement in the music industry. The annual awards ceremony features performances by prominent artists, and some of the awards of more popular interest are presented in a widely viewed televised ceremony.

Record companies and individuals may submit recordings to be nominated. Nominations are made online and a physical copy of the work is sent to NARAS. Once a work is entered, reviewing sessions are held, by more than 150 experts from the recording industry, to determine whether the work is eligible and entered in the correct category for official nomination. The resulting list is circulated to all NARAS members, each of whom may vote to nominate in the general field (Record of the Year, Album of the Year, Song of the Year, and Best New Artist) and in no more than 9 out of 30 other fields on their ballots. The five recordings that earn the most votes in each category become the nominees.

After nominees have been determined, final voting ballots are sent to Recording Academy members, who may then vote in the general fields and in no more than 8 of the 30 fields. NARAS members are encouraged, but not required, to vote only in their fields of expertise. Ballots are tabulated secretly by the major independent accounting firm Deloitte Touche Tohmatsu. Following the tabulation of votes the winners are announced at the Grammy Awards. Winners are presented with the Grammy Award and those who do not win are given a medal for their nomination.

In both voting rounds, Academy members are required to vote based upon quality alone, and not to be influenced by sales, chart performance, personal friendships, regional preferences or company loyalty. The acceptance of gifts is prohibited. Members are urged to vote in a manner that preserves the integrity of the academy.

Because thousands of recordings appear each year and very few voting members have heard more than a relatively small number of them, it is likely that many individual votes will be cast by voters who are unfamiliar with all the recordings nominated in that category. Additionally, because of the small number of votes cast in many of the categories, a lobbying campaign for a particular recording may need only a few dozen votes for success. Large choruses have achieved Grammy awards after persuading many of their members to join NARAS.

1. Which of the following is NOT true?
   A. The Grammy is annually granted by NARAS.
   B. Famous artists are invited to perform on the awards ceremony.
   C. Viewers can watch some of the Grammy awards on television.
   D. Only record companies can submit recordings to be nominated.

2. Once a work to be nominated is entered, _____.
   A. A physical copy of the work should be sent to NARAS
   B. An application for its nomination should be prepared
   C. Experts will review it and decide whether it is qualified for official nomination
   D. NARAS members will discuss it officially
3. In the first voting round, _____.
   A. Each NARAS member votes in thirty-four fields
   B. Each NARAS member votes in his fields of expertise
   C. The five recordings earning the most in each category are nominated
   D. An independent accounting firm is responsible for collecting votes
4. In both voting rounds _____.
   A. NARAS members are required to vote only in their fields of expertise
   B. NARAS members are encouraged to exchange ideas
   C. Academy members are encouraged to take regional preferences into account
   D. Academy members are required to consider quality alone
5. What is the last paragraph mainly about?
   A. The increasing influence of the Grammy.
   B. The doubt the Grammy receives.
   C. The suggestion on how to ensure the integrity of votes.
   D. The prejudice held by a few voting members.

12 Passage Two

The Beatles' releases in the United States were initially delayed for nearly a year when Capitol Records, EMI's American subsidiary, declined to issue either "*Please Please Me*" or "*From Me to You*". Negotiations with independent US labels(唱片公司) led to the release of some singles, but issues with royalties and derision of the band's "moptop" hairstyle posed further obstacles. Once Capitol did start to issue the material, rather than releasing the LPs (唱片) in their original configuration, they compiled distinct US albums from an assortment of the band's recordings and issued songs of their own choice as singles. American chart(唱片销量) success came suddenly after a CBS news broadcast about British Beatlemania(披头士迷) triggered great demand, leading Capitol to rush-release "*I Want to Hold Your Hand*" in December 1963. The band's US debut was already scheduled to take place a few weeks later.

The Beatles left the United Kingdom with an estimated four thousand fans gathered at Heathrow, waving and screaming as the aircraft took off. "*I Want to Hold Your Hand*" had sold 2.6 million copies in the US over the previous two weeks, but the group were still nervous about how they would be received. At New York's John F. Kennedy Airport they were greeted by another vociferous crowd, estimated at about three thousand people. They gave their first live US television performance two days later on *The Ed Sullivan Show*, watched by approximately 74 million viewers—over 40 percent of the American population.

The next morning one newspaper wrote that they "could not carry a tune across the Atlantic", but a day later their first US concert saw Beatlemania erupt at Washington Coliseum. Back in New York the following day, they met with another strong reception at Carnegie Hall. The band appeared on the weekly *Ed Sullivan Show* a second time, before returning to the UK on 22 February. The Beatles held twelve positions on the Billboard Hot 100 singles chart during the week of 4 April, including the top five. That same week, a third American LP joined the two already in circulation; all three reached the first or second spot on the US album chart. The band's popularity generated unprecedented interest in British music, and a number of other UK acts subsequently made their own American debuts, successfully touring over the next three years in what was termed the British Invasion. The Beatles' hairstyle, unusually long for the era and mocked by many adults, was widely adopted and became an emblem of the burgeoning youth culture.

1. The Beatles' releases in the United State were initially delayed because _____.
   A. the problem of royalties was not solved
   B. the band's hairstyle seemed to be an obstacle
   C. Capitol Records declined to issue the band's album
   D. negotiations with independent US labels failed
2. Which of the following is NOT true according to paragraph one?
   A. The Beatles' releases in the United States began with singles.
   B. Their original configuration was kept when Capitol started to issue the Beatles' LPs.
   C. It was scheduled that the Beatles would visit US at the beginning of 1964.
   D. A CBS news broadcast promoted the sales of the Beatles' LPs.
3. When the Beatles left the United Kingdom, _____.
   A. the band was not so well-known in US
   B. the band had just achieved another chart success
   C. the members of it were not so confident of the visit to US
   D. Both B and C
4. Which of the following is NOT true of the Beatles' trip to US?
   A. The band was greeted by a huge number of fans at John F. Kennedy Airport.
   B. The band's US debut attracted about 74 million viewers.
   C. The band had to delay its return to UK.
   D. The band's first US concert triggered Beatlemania eruption.
5. The Beatle's success in US _____.
   A. generated Americans' great interest British culture
   B. gave rise to the following American debuts of other UK performing groups
   C. made the Beatles' hairstyle mocked by many adults
   D. reflected a burgeoning youth culture

Interactive Tasks

Role-play

13 **Role-play the following situation with your partner.**

Situation:

Two art students are talking about folk music and pop music.

You may begin like this:

Li Yang: What about the Chinese folk music concert you attended last night?

Lucy: It is so great! And some musical instruments are so impressive that I want to try playing them.

Li Yang: I am glad that you enjoy it so much. Actually, Chinese folk music is losing its young audience at home, but it seems that more and more foreigners are attracted by it.

Lucy: It is true that the young prefer pop music today. I find that most of my classmates know some pop singers very well while they are not interested in Chinese folk music.

Group Work

14 **Work in groups to work out your own project.**

1. Form groups of four or five students;
2. Each group chooses a topic concerning music, e.g.

   A study of jazz;

   An introduction to a favorite pop singer or band.
3. Members of each group collect materials from library and the Internet to work out their PPT slides;
4. Based on the PPT slides, each member of the group gives oral presentation of his part.

Follow-up Task

Writing

15 **Directions:** For this part, you are going to write a composition on the topic: **Listening to Music for Fun and Profit**. You should write at least 120 words following the outline given below in Chinese:

1. 音乐是生活中不可或缺的一个部分;
2. 听音乐带来的乐趣与好处;
3. 我对此的看法。

Unit 5　Film

Highlight

Topic area	Communication	Skills
Some well-known films; Some well-known film directors; The best-known film festivals in the world; Some well-known film stars.	it is best for somebody to do focus on be widely believed to do claim that at large	Knowing some well-known celebrities in cinema; Knowing the story of Bruce Lee; Knowing some best-known film festivals in the world.

Starting-out Task

1 Look at these pictures and discuss the following questions with your partner.

1. *Titanic* is a 1997 American epic romance and disaster film. What do you know about the film? Talk about your feelings on this film.

2. The following pictures show two well-known directors. Share with others what you know about them.

3. What do you know about the best-known film festivals in the world?

Listening Tasks

Micro Listening Skills

2 Listen to the following passage and try to fill in the missing words.

Universal Pictures (sometimes called Universal City Studios or Universal Studios for short), is one of the six major movie studios in the world. 1. _____ in 1912, it is one of the oldest American movie studios still in 2. _____ production. On May 11, 2004, the 3. _____ stake in the company was sold by Vivendi Universal to General Electric. The resulting media super-conglomerate was 4. _____ NBC Universal, while Universal Studios

Inc. remained the name of the production subsidiary. In addition to owning a sizable film library spanning the earliest 5. _____ of cinema to more contemporary works, it also owns a sizable 6. _____ of TV shows through its subsidiary NBC Universal Television Distribution. It also 7. _____ rights to several prominent filmmakers' works originally 8. _____ by other studios through its subsidiaries over the years. Its production studios are at 100 Universal City Plaza Drive in Universal City, California. Distribution and other 9. _____ offices are in New York City. Universal Pictures is the second-longest-lived Hollywood studio; Viacom-owned Paramount Pictures is the 10. _____ by a month.

Dialogue

Mike Invites Barbara to See a Movie

Words & Phrases

| blockbuster /ˈblɒkˌbʌstə/ n. | 大片 |
| ethical /ˈeθɪkəl/ adj. | 伦理的 |

3 Listen to the dialogue and decide whether the following statements are true (T) or false (F).

1. ____ Barbara would rather watch TV at home because she thinks present movies are disappointing.
2. ____ Barbara thinks that only a few blockbusters are worth the money paid for tickets.
3. ____ In Mike's eyes, watching movie is mainly for entertainment.
4. ____ Mike and Barbara are going to see a comic movie tonight.
5. ____ Mike and Barbara will meet at the cinema at seven o'clock.

4 Listen to the dialogue again and complete the following sentences with the information you have heard.

1. According to Barbara, the movies nowadays are simply the combination of money, stars, unrealistic plots and _____.
2. Barbara thinks that movies should _____ and mean something.
3. In Mike's eyes, as long as a viewer enjoys a movie's nice presentation and watches his _____, that would be worth it.
4. According to Mike, nowadays, more and more producers give priority to box office while _____ are given to artistic values.

Reading Tasks

Focus Reading

Pre-reading Questions

1. Do you enjoy martial arts films? Why?
2. Who is your favorite film star? Can you tell a story about him or her?

3. What do you know about Hollywood, the capital of film industry?

Martial Arts Hero—Bruce Lee[①]

In life, Bruce Lee didn't like to be called a "star". In death, Lee can't escape the word. Thirty years after he died, the first Asian American to star in a Hollywood film still is considered to be one of the greatest martial artists ever. His primal physicality and screen intensity exploded American interest in martial arts films, paving the way for later stars such as Jackie Chan, Chuck Norris and Steven Seagal.

In Seattle, where Lee lived for over four years and is buried, the new "Bruce Lee Collectors Exhibit 2003: The Beginning of a Legend, the Story of a Man," opens today with items from one of the biggest collectors of Bruce Lee memorabilia. "The thing that makes me the most happy to this day is that his image isn't diminishing," said Taky Kimura, one of Lee's closest friends and students. "It's still growing." Lee's image, resurrected digitally, will even star in a new film, *Dragon Warrior*, set for release next year. At the first major Bruce Lee Convention next month in Santa Monica, Calif., the Bruce Lee Foundation will award a scholarship in his honor. Schools around the world still teach Lee's innovative Jeet Kune Do, or "way of the intercepting fist." There are informal letter-writing campaigns to get a postage stamp and a posthumous Oscar granted to Lee.

So why is a man, who died before his first major movie hit the U.S., still larger than life? "He's the first Asian that broke a lot of stereotypes—that has a lot to do with it," said Doug Palmer, a Seattle attorney and former student of Lee. The first time Palmer, a high school boxer, saw Lee's moves, he was mesmerized. "I'd never seen anything like it before," said Palmer, who believes Lee's skill was without parallel. "The combination of the artistry and speed and power and grace were all wrapped up in one."

[①] This text is adapted from *The Way Of Bruce Lee Martial Arts Hero Is Still Larger Than Life 30 Years After His Death* from *Seattle Post-Intelligencer*

Born in San Francisco as Lee Jun Fan in 1940, "Bruce Lee" was coined by a hospital nurse for the first son of a Chinese opera star. Raised in Hong Kong, Lee was nicknamed "Never Sits Still." An average student who got into a lot of fights, Lee was also a child movie star, appearing in his first film at the age of three months, when he served as the stand-in for an American baby in *Golden Gate Girl*. Young Bruce Lee had made more than 20 films by age 18.

When he got in trouble for fighting with rival martial arts students, Lee and his mother decided it was best for him to return to his birth country and find his own way. The 19-year-old arrived in San Francisco in 1959 with $115 in his pocket.

Within a few months, Lee came to Seattle to stay with family friend Ruby Chow, and cleared tables at Ruby Chow's Restaurant. Later, Lee enrolled as a philosophy major at the University of Washington. He also got a job teaching the Wing Chung style of martial arts that he had learned in Hong Kong. By 1964, Lee had opened his own martial arts school in Seattle. He soon moved to California, where Lee opened two more schools in Los Angeles and Oakland. When he expanded his martial arts schools to Los Angeles, Lee attracted celebrity clients such as Steve McQueen, James Garner and James Coburn, who paid the sum of $250 an hour to study with the charismatic master. One of his students, Linda Emery, became his wife. At his schools, Lee taught mostly a style called Jeet Kune Do. He wowed crowds and attracted students with his demonstrations. That's how Taky Kimura first met the "little dragon".

"Bruce was a very gregarious, very popular guy," said Kimura, who was Lee's best man at his wedding in 1964. "He could be telling you the raunchiest joke one minute, then spouting Zen or Taoism the next."

"He was one of the strongest and the fastest martial artists," said Kimura, who still teaches Lee's Jeet Kune Do to about 70 students for free, as a way of giving back to Lee. He also tends Lee's grave, which an estimated 50 to 75 people visit each week.

The man who stood 5-foot-7 and weighed around 140 pounds was an awesome blur of cobra-fast fists and kicking heels to Perry Lee. It was 1964 and Perry Lee was a 14-year-old

Franklin High student watching a demonstration by the unknown martial artist. "He was able to do things you never saw anybody else do," said Perry Lee, 55, who was impressed with Lee's cool, confident demeanor. Perry Lee, became a martial arts enthusiast and began collecting Bruce Lee memorabilia. "Bruce Lee still sets the standard," said Lee, "Bruce Lee is to martial arts what Elvis was to rock 'n' roll or what Michael Jordan was to basketball or Muhammad Ali to boxing."

Bruce Lee started his first studio, while studying philosophy at the University of Washington. A plain-spoken iconoclast, Lee held little regard for traditional martial arts.

"To me 99 percent of the whole business of oriental self-defense is baloney," Lee once said. "It's fancy jazz. It looks good, but it doesn't work." Lee deemed that most martial arts full of unrealistic stances and mechanical moves. "A guy could be clobbered by while getting into his classical mess," Lee told reporters. Lee developed his own fighting system, June Keet Do, which focused on eliminating wasted motion and expressing one's individual talents.

Lee gained a measure of celebrity with his role in the television series *The Green Hornet*, which aired from 1966 to 1967. In the show, which was based on a 1930s radio program, Lee displayed his acrobatic and theatrical fighting style as the Hornet's loyal side-kick, Kato. He went on to make guest appearances in some TV shows, while his most notable role came in the 1969 film *Marlowe*, starring James Garner.

Lee developed the premise for film's "Kung Fu", though it stung when he wasn't considered for the leading role. Frustrated by the snail's pace of earning leading role in Hollywood, Lee left Los Angeles for Hong Kong in 1971, with his wife and two children.

Back in the city where he had grown up, Lee signed a two-film contract. *Fists of Fury* was released in 1971, featuring Lee as a vengeful fighter chasing the villains who had killed his kung-fu master. Combining his smooth Jeet Kune Do athleticism with the high-energy theatrics, Lee was the charismatic center of the film, which set new box office records in Hong Kong. Those records were broken by Lee's next film, *The Chinese Connection*(1972).

By the end of 1972, Lee was a major movie star in Asia. He had released his first directorial feature, *Way of the Dragon*. Soon, Warner Bros.① knocked on his door. Though he had not yet gained stardom in America, he was poised on the brink with his second directorial feature and first major Holly-wood project, *Enter the Dragon*.

On July 20, 1973, just one month before the premiere of *Enter the Dragon*, Bruce Lee died in Hong Kong at the age of 32. The official cause of his sudden and utterly unexpected death was a brain edema, found in an autopsy to have been caused by a strange reaction to a prescription painkiller he was reportedly taking for a back injury.

Controversy surrounded Lee's death from the beginning, as some claimed that he had been murdered. He was also widely believed to have been cursed because in 1993, his son, Brandon Lee was killed under similarly mysterious circumstances during the filming at the age of 28. The young actor was fatally shot with a gun that supposedly contained blanks.

With the posthumous release of *Enter the Dragon*, Lee's status as a film icon was confirmed. The movie went on to gross a total of over $200 million, and Lee's legacy created a whole new breed of action hero.

To the world at large, Lee has and continues to be simply the best martial artist ever in the films, giving audiences a psychologically complex and physically perfect Asian hero, who makes an everlasting impact in cinema. Much like other celebrities who die young—Marilyn Monroe, Elvis Presley, James Dean—there is the tantalizing thought of what could have been.

(1,389 words)

---

①Warner Bros. Entertainment, Inc., also known as Warner Bros. Pictures or simply Warner Bros. is an American producer of film and television entertainment.

Vocabulary

memorabilia /ˌmemərəˈbɪljə/ *n.* objects kept or collected because of their historical interest, especially those associated with memorable people or events 纪念物

diminish /dɪˈmɪnɪʃ/ *vt.* make or become less 减少；缩小

resurrect /ˌrezəˈrekt/ *vt.* restore (a dead person) to life 使复活

innovative /ˈɪnəʊveɪtɪv/ *adj.* (of a product, idea, etc.) featuring new methods 新发明的

intercept /ˌɪntəˈsept/ *vt.* obstruct (someone or something) so as to prevent them from continuing to a destination 拦截

posthumous /ˈpɒstʃəməs/ *adj.* occurring, awarded, or appearing after the death of the originator 死后发生的

stereotype /ˈstɪərɪətaɪp/ *n.* a widely held but fixed and oversimplified idea 老套的见解

mesmerize /ˈmezməˌraɪz/ *vt.* hold the attention of 使入迷

coin /kɔɪn/ *vt.* invent or devise (a new word or phrase) 创造(新词或短语)

stand-in /ˈstændˌɪn/ *n.* a person who stands in for another, especially in a match or performance 替身

enroll /ɪnˈrəʊl/ *vt.* officially register as a member of an institution or a student on a course 参加

celebrity /sɪˈlebrɪtɪ/ *n.* a famous person 名人

gregarious /grɪˈgeərɪəs/ *adj.* (of a person) fond of company; sociable 爱交际的；合群的

awesome /ˈɔːsəm/ *adj.* extremely good 棒极了的

demeanor /dɪˈmiːnə/ *n.* outward behavior or bearing 行为；举止

iconoclast /aɪˈkɒnəˌklæst/ *n.* a person who attacks cherished beliefs or institutions 攻击传统观念的人

oriental /ˌɔːrɪˈentəl/ *adj.* of, from, or characteristic of the East 东方的

baloney /bəˈləʊnɪ/ *n.* foolish or deceptive talk 瞎扯

clobber /ˈklɒbə/ *vt.* hit (someone) hard 猛打(某人)

eliminate /ɪˈlɪmɪneɪt/ *vt.* remove or get rid of 消除

acrobatic /ˌækrəˈbætɪk/ *adj.* performing, involving, or adept at spectacular gymnastic feats 杂技般的

theatrical /θiːˈætrɪkəl/ *adj.* of, for, or relating to acting, actors, or the theatre 戏剧性的

side-kick /ˈsaɪdˌkɪk/ *n.* a close friend 伙伴

vengeful /ˈvendʒfəl/ *adj.* seeking to harm someone in return for a perceived injury 图谋报复的

theatrics /θɪˈætrɪks/ *n.* dramatic performances 戏剧演出

charismatic /ˌkærɪzˈmætɪk/ *adj.* exercising a compelling charm which inspires devotion in others 有魅力的

premiere /prɪˈmɪə/ *n.* the first showing of a film (电影)首次公映

utterly /ˈʌtəlɪ/ *adv.* completely 完全地

edema /iː(ː)ˈdiːmə/ *n.* a condition characterized by an excess of watery fluid collecting in

the cavities or tissues of the body 水肿
autopsy /ˈɔːˌtɒpsɪ/ *n.* a post-mortem examination to discover the cause of death 验尸
painkiller /ˈpeɪnˌkɪlə/ *n.* medicine for lessening pain 止痛药
controversy /ˈkɒntrəvɜːsɪ/ *n.* disagreement, typically when prolonged, public, and heated（尤指长期、公开或激烈的）争论
icon /ˈaɪˌkɒn/ *n.* a person or thing regarded as a representative symbol of something 代表；典型
at large generally 总的说来
everlasting /ˌevəˈlɑːstɪŋ/ *adj.* lasting forever or a very long time 永久的；永恒的
tantalizing /ˈtæntəlaɪzɪŋ/ *adj.* exciting the senses or desires of someone 撩人的；煽情的

Proper Names

Jackie Chan	成龙
Chuck Norris /tʃʌk ˈnɔrɪs/	查克·诺里斯
Steven Seagal	史蒂文·西格尔
Taky Kimura	木村武之
Jeet Kune Do	截拳道
Doug Palme	道格·帕尔默
Golden Gate Girl	《金门女》
Steve McQueen	史蒂夫·迈奎恩
James Garner /dʒeɪmz ˈgɑːnə/	詹姆士·加纳
James Coburn	詹姆士·科本
Linda Emery	琳达·艾米莉
Zen	禅宗
Taoism	道教
Perry Lee /ˈperɪ lɪ/	李佩里
Michael Jordan /ˈmaɪkl ˈdʒɔːdn/	迈克尔·乔丹
Muhammad Ali	穆罕默德·阿里
The Green Hornet	《青蜂侠》
Marlowe	《丑闻喋血》
Fists of Fury	《唐山大兄》
The Chinese Connection	《精武门》
Way of the Dragon	《猛龙过江》
Warner Bros.	华纳兄弟娱乐公司
Enter the Dragon	《龙争虎斗》
Brandon Lee /ˈbrændən lɪ/	李国豪
Marilyn Monroe	玛丽莲·梦露
Elvis Presley	埃尔维斯·普雷斯利
James Dean /dʒeɪmz diːn/	詹姆斯·迪安

Text Exploration

5 Choose the best answer to each question with the information from the text.

1. The thing that makes Taky Kimura, one of Lee's closest friends and students the most happy to this day is that _____.
   A. "Bruce Lee Collectors Exhibit 2003: The Beginning of a Legend, the Story of a Man," opens today
   B. Lee's image, resurrected digitally, will even star in a new film
   C. Lee's impact is increasing
   D. Lee's impact is everlasting

2. When Palmer saw Lee's moves for the first time, he _____.
   A. thought it was so speedy
   B. was deeply fascinated
   C. was very excited
   D. thought it was so graceful

3. Which of the following is NOT true?
   A. "Bruce Lee" was coined by a hospital nurse.
   B. Lee's father was a Chinese opera star.
   C. Lee appeared in his first film at the age of three months, serving as the stand-in for an American baby.
   D. Lee used to be a shy student with average performance.

4. Lee's mother decided it was best for Lee to return to U.S. because _____.
   A. there would be more opportunities in Hollywood
   B. she wanted him to receive good education
   C. he got in trouble for fighting with rival martial arts students
   D. she wanted him to take a decent job

5. In Taky Kimura's eyes, Lee was very _____.
   A. talkative   B. reserved
   C. serious   D. energetic

6. What did Lee think of traditional martial arts?
   A. It looked good, but it was not so practical.
   B. It was full of unrealistic stances.
   C. It was full of mechanical moves.
   D. All of the above.

7. Jeet Kune Do, a style developed by Lee, laid emphasis on _____.
   A. combining traditional martial arts and western boxing skills
   B. removing wasted motions
   C. showing personal talents
   D. Both B and C

8. Why did Lee leave Los Angeles for Hong Kong in 1971?
   A. Because he got tired of the career in Hollywood.
   B. Because he lost his confidence in earning leading role in Hollywood.
   C. Because he wanted to meet new challenges.
   D. Because he wanted to direct a film by himself.
9. According to official report, Lee died of _____.
   A. heart attack
   B. brain edema
   C. murder
   D. curse
10. Which of the following is NOT true?
    A. *Enter the Dragon* was released after Lee's death.
    B. *Enter the Dragon* confirmed Lee's status as a film icon.
    C. *Enter the Dragon* achieved great success in box office.
    D. *Enter the Dragon* was Lee's first directorial feature and first major Hollywood project.

6 Complete the following chart with the information from the text.

Time	Details
1940	Bruce Lee was born _____.
1959	Bruce Lee had to _____ for he got in trouble for fighting with rival martial arts students.
1964	1. Bruce Lee _____ in Seattle. 2. Bruce Lee _____ Linda Emery.
1966	Bruce Lee _____ in the television series *The Green Hornet*.
1971	1. Frustrated by the snail's pace of earning leading role in Hollywood, Lee _____. 2. Back in Hongkong, Lee's first film, *Fists of Fury* was released and it _____.
1972	1. Lee's next film, *The Chinese Connection* _____. 2. By the end of 1972, Bruce Lee _____ in Asia.
1973	1. On July 20, Bruce Lee _____. 2. Lee's second directorial feature and first major Hollywood project, *Enter the Dragon* _____ and it went on to _____.

7 Discuss the following questions with the information from the text.
1. What is Lee's contribution to martial arts film?

2. Have you seen Lee's films? What do you think of them?

3. What is the controversy on Lee's death?

4. Can you tell a story of the martial arts hero who you like best?

5. What could have happened if Bruce Lee hadn't died young?

Vocabulary Expansion

8 Fill in the blanks with the right words given below. Change the form where necessary.

| diminish | stereotype | mesmerize | gregarious | spout |
| acrobatic | demeanor | vengeful | icon | everlasting |

1. Pursuing super excellence is our _____ aim.
2. He doesn't conform to the usual _____ of a businessman with a dark suit and rolled umbrella.
3. Films made by Hollywood aim at building this iron-jawed _____ of American manhood.
4. She was _____ by the blue eyes that stared so intently into her own.
5. The campers' food supplies gradually _____ as the days wore on.
6. His good _____ helped him a lot when he applied for the job.
7. She's very outgoing and _____, and this is why she is popular with her classmates.
8. He was _____ platitudes about his experiences during the war.
9. His chains now broken, the prisoner turned a _____ eye toward his former captors.
10. Inverted flight is a(n) _____ maneuver of the plane.

9 Choose the word or phrase that best keeps the meaning of the sentence if it is substituted for the underlined word or phrase.

1. It was he who coined the term "desktop publishing".
   A. made into coin   B. determined
   C. devised   D. stamped

2. A student wishing to enroll at this university must have a current passport.
   A. continue   B. register
   C. apply for   D. interview

3. It is best for you to cut the baloney on this subject.
   A. dispute   B. discussion
   C. nonsense   D. research

4. Lots of celebrities were at the film festival.
   A. famous people   B. journalists
   C. actors   D. directors

5. A gala dinner was held to celebrate the world premiere of the film.
   A. box office   B. release
   C. business success   D. first showing

6. He was utterly unscrupulous in his competition with rivals.
   A. completely   B. partly
   C. mostly   D. initially
7. The government will try to accord the controversy over the housing project.
   A. proposal   B. scheme
   C. disagreement   D. plan
8. The lecture is on how to eliminate eye exhaustion and pseudo myopia.
   A. remove   B. dissolve
   C. resolve   D. prevent
9. He was chosen as President because he was a fully qualified, charismatic statesman.
   A. inspiring   B. experienced
   C. appealing   D. persuasive
10. There is widespread agreement that the absence of fathers from households causes serious problems for children and, consequently for society at large.
    A. in general   B. with detail
    C. at freedom   D. at best

10 Translate the Chinese sentences into English by simulating the sentences chosen from the text.

Chosen Sentences	Simulated Translations	Chinese Sentences
The thing that makes me the most happy to this day **is that** his image isn't diminishing.		让影迷最兴奋的是他们可以获得成龙的亲笔签名。（**autograph**）
Lee and his mother decided **it was best for him to** return to his birth country and find his own way.		对他而言，最好的方法是多征求父母、老师的意见。（**seek**）
It's fancy jazz. **It looks good, but it doesn't work.**		与会双方提出的这些解决问题的办法听上去不错，可实际上并不管用。（**solution**）
Controversy surrounded Lee's death from the beginning, as **some claimed that** he had been murdered.		关于这个问题一直以来有争论，因为有些人声称大幅贬值货币以增加出口从长远来看是有风险的。（**devalue, dubious**）
He **was also widely believed to** have been cursed because in 1993, when Brandon Lee was killed under similarly mysterious circumstances during the filming at the age of 28.		人们普遍认为该政策将刺激经济增长，降低通货膨胀。（**stimulate, inflation**）

Supplementary Readings

11 Passage One

At the end of the 1930s, shocked by the interference of the fascist governments of Italy and Germany in the selection of films for the Mostra del cinema di Venezia, Jean Zay, the French Minister of National Education, decided to create an international cinematographic (电影的) festival in France, on the proposal of Philippe Erlanger and the support of the British and Americans. Many towns were proposed as candidates, as Vichy, Biarritz or Algiers, although finally Cannes was the chosen one; thus, Le Festival International de Cannes was born.

In June 1939, Louis Lumière agreed to be the president of the first festival, set to be held from 1 to 30 September 1939. The German attack on Poland on 1 September 1939, followed by the declaration of war against Germany by France and the United Kingdom on 3 September, ended the first edition of the festival before it started.

The festival was relaunched after World War II in 1946, in the old Casino of Cannes, financed by the French Foreign Affairs Ministry and the City of Cannes. The next year, in 1947, the festival was held again as the Festival du film de Cannes, dropping the international nature, but only in name, as films from sixteen countries were presented. Moreover, the principle of equality was introduced, so that the jury was to be made up only of one representative per country.

In 1955 the Golden Palm was created, replacing the Grand Prix du Festival which had been given until that year. In 1959 the Film Market was founded, giving the festival a commercial character and facilitating exchanges between sellers and buyers in the film industry. Today it has become the first international platform for film commerce.

During the 1970s, important changes occurred in the festival. In 1972 Robert Favre Le Bret was named the new President, and Maurice Bessy the Managing Director. He immediately introduced an important change in the selection of the participating films. Until that date, the different countries chose which films would represent them in the festival. Bessy created one committee to select French films, and another for foreign films. In 1978 Gilles Jacob assumed the President position, introducing new award and section. Other changes were the decrease of length of the festival down to thirteen days, reducing the number of selected films thus; also, until that point the jury was composed by Film Academics, and Jacob started to introduce celebrities and professionals from the film industry.

1. Which of the following is NOT true according to paragraph one?
   A. At the end of 1930s, film industry suffered interference of fascism.
   B. Jean Zay's decision to create a film festival in France was proposed by Philippe Erlanger.
   C. Jean Zay's decision to create a film festival in France received the support of the British and Americans.

D. Few towns bade for the host of the film festival.
2. In 1939, the first festival failed to be held because _____ ?
   A. the financial support wasn't settled.
   B. no one agreed to be the president of the festival.
   C. Germany invaded Poland.
   D. the old Casino of Cannes needed reconstruction.
3. What happened in 1947?
   A. The festival was relaunched.
   B. The French Foreign Affairs Ministry stopped financing the festival.
   C. The principle that each country only had one representative in the jury was introduced.
   D. Only French films were presented.
4. In 1959 the Film Market was founded in order to _____.
   A. add a commercial character to the festival
   B. contribute to film commerce
   C. make more films participate in the festival
   D. Both and A and B
5. Which of the following is NOT the change occurring in the festival during the 1970s?
   A. Two committees were created to select participating films.
   B. A new position, the Managing Director was introduced.
   C. Well-known persons and professionals from film industry started to enter the jury.
   D. The length of the festival was reduced.

12 Passage Two

Titanic is a 1997 American epic romance and disaster film directed, written, co-produced, and co-edited by James Cameron. It's a fictionalized account of the sinking of Titanic. Although the central roles and love story are fictitious, some characters are based on genuine historical figures. Cameron saw the love story as a way to engage the audience with the real-life tragedy.

Production on the film began in 1995, when Cameron shot footage of the actual Titanic wreck. The modern scenes were shot on board the Akademik Mstislav Keldysh, which Cameron had used as a base when filming the actual wreck. A reconstruction of the Titanic was built at Playas de Rosarito, Baja California, and scale models and computer-generated imagery were also used to recreate the sinking. The film was partially funded by Paramount Pictures and 20th Century Fox respectively, its American and international distributors. And at the time, it was the most expensive film ever made, with an estimated budget of US $ 200 million.

Paramount Pictures and 20th Century Fox expected Cameron to complete the film for a release on July 2, 1997. The film was to be released on this date in order to exploit the lucrative summer season ticket sales when blockbuster films usually do better. In April, Cameron said the film's special effects were too complicated and that releasing the film for summer would not be possible. With production delays, Paramount pushed back the release date to December 19, 1997. This fueled speculation that the film itself was a disaster. However, a preview screening in Minneapolis on July 14 generated positive reviews and hatter on the internet was responsible for more favorable word of mouth about the film. This eventually led to more positive media coverage. The film premiered on November 1, 1997, at the Tokyo International Film Festival, where reaction was described as "tepid" by *The New York Times*. However, positive reviews started to appear back in the United States; the official Hollywood premiere occurred on December 14, 1997, where the big movie stars who attended the opening were enthusiastically gushing about the film to the world media.

Titanic was an enormous critical and commercial success. It was nominated for fourteen Academy Awards, eventually winning eleven, including Best Picture and Best Director. It became the highest-grossing film of all time, with a worldwide gross of over \$1.8 billion—the first film to reach the billion dollar mark—and remained so for twelve years until Cameron's next directorial effort, *Avatar*, surpassed it in 2010. The film garnered mostly positive reviews from film critics. Review aggregate website Rotten Tomatoes reports the film as holding an overall 82% approval rating based on 97 reviews, with a rating average of 7.4 out of 10. The general consensus is that the film is a mostly unqualified triumph for Cameron, who offers a dizzying blend of spectacular visuals and melodrama.

1. According to paragraph one, which of the following is NOT true?
    A. *Titanic* is an epic romance and disaster film.
    B. *Titanic* was directed by James Cameron.
    C. The leading roles in Titanic originate from genuine history.
    D. The love story in *Titanic* is fictitious.

2. Why did the distributors of *Titanic* push back the release date to December 19, 1997?
    A. Because the post production was so complicated.
    B. Because tickets are usually well sold in this season.
    C. Because the preview screen was not successful.
    D. Because they were not so confident in the film.

3. The reaction to *Titanic* at the Tokyo International Film Festival was _____.
    A. positive   B. negative
    C. lukewarm   D. enthusiastic

4. Which of the following is NOT true of *Titanic*?
    A. The film received great success in box office.
    B. The film got positive reviews from most film critics.
    C. The film has kept the box office record so far.
    D. The film won eleven awards in Academy Awards.

5. It is generally agreed that _____.
    A. James Cameron merely achieves commercial success
    B. James Cameron fails to narrate the story entirely

C. James Cameron succeeds in delivering visual impacts
D. James Cameron combines visual impacts and narration successfully

Interactive Tasks

Role-play

13 **Role-play the following situation with your partner.**
Situation:
    Two art students are talking about Zhang Yimou's films.
You may begin like this:
Li Yang: Have you ever seen Zhang Yimou's films?
Lucy: Of course. I really enjoy the films he directed in the 1980s and 1990s like *Red Sorghum*, *Ju Dou*, and *Raise the Red Lantern*.
Li Yang: Why do you think Zhang Yimou's films are so popular abroad?
Lucy: In my opinion, there are some reasons for that.

Group Work

14 **Work in groups to work out your own project.**
1. Form groups of four or five students;
2. Each group chooses a topic concerning film, e. g.
   A study of movie history at home or abroad;
   An introduction to a best-liked film.
3. Members of each group collect materials from library and the Internet to work out their PPT slides;
4. Based on the PPT slides, each member of the group gives oral presentation of his part.

Follow-up Task

Writing

15 **Directions**: For this part, you are going to write a composition on the topic: **The Grading of Films**. You should write at least 120 words following the outline given below in Chinese:
1. 目前中国电影尚未实行分级制度;
2. 电影不分级可能带来的危害;
3. 我对此的看法。

Unit 6　Comic and Animation

Highlight

Topic area	Communication	Skills
Some best-known animators in the world; Walt Disney and his cartoons; The history of movie animation.	have an impact on so to speak be in place give birth to nothing more than go to great lengths to do call a halt to	Knowing some well-known cartoons in the world; Knowing the history of the movie animation; Learning to introduce animation productions.

Starting-out Task

1 Look at these pictures and discuss the following questions with your partner.

1. The following pictures show some well-known cartoon TV series or movies in the world. What do you know about them?

Unit 6 Comic and Animation

2. What are your favorite cartoon characters? Give reasons to support your answer.
3. How do you like these cartoons?

Listening Tasks

Micro Listening Skills

2 Listen to the following passage and try to fill in the missing words.

　　Japanese animation enjoys 1. _____ popularity in Asia where it has become a mainstream youth culture due to cultural and geographical proximity(亲近). Take Singapore for example. Japanese television cartoons are extremely popular among primary and secondary school students, who rushed home to watch this animation and bought *Macross* 2. _____, such as stickers and 3. _____. Following the global popularization of Japanese animation, it seems that the popularity of Japanese cartoons will continue to grow. In many ways, Japanese animation represents a popular form of 4. _____, consumer culture and youth culture, and its 5. _____ on Singapore society and culture is not yet very strong. To a certain extent, Japanese animation, together with other forms of Japanese popular culture, helps to 6. _____ the consumption of Japanese products and the interest in Japan among young Singaporeans. Through Japanese animation, Singapore viewers come to know more about 7. _____ Japan, although their understanding is usually 8. _____ and stereotyped. More importantly, unlike old-generation Singaporeans who have anti-Japanese 9. _____ due to their war experiences, young Singaporeans in general are 10. _____ about Japan out of their passion for Japanese popular culture.

艺术类研究生英语教程

Passage

Walt Disney

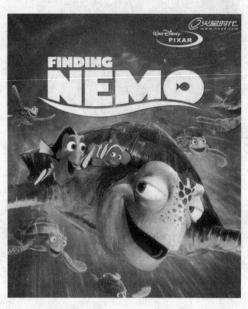

Words & Phrases

triumph /ˈtraɪəmf/ v.	获得胜利
ingenuity /ˌɪndʒɪˈnjuːɪtɪ/ n.	独创性
statuette /ˌstæjʊˈet/ n.	小雕像
flank /flæŋk/ v.	侧面与……相接
legacy /ˈlegəsɪ/ n.	遗产
thrive /θraɪv/ v.	兴旺
ground-breaking adj.	里程碑式的

❸ Listen to the passage and decide whether the following statements are true (T) or false (F).

1. ____ In Disney productions good triumphs over evil.
2. ____ The first sound cartoon starring Mickey Mouse was created in 1923.
3. ____ Walt Disney is universally recognized as the pioneer of modern American animation.
4. ____ One of the most notable innovations of Walt Disney is the advent of stereophonic sound.
5. ____ *Toy Story* is a feature length animated film released by Disney Company.

❹ Listen to the passage again and complete the following sentences with the information you have heard.

1. Disney has provided a(n) _____ amount of entertainment since the 1930s and has had a _____ many of our childhoods.

2. Snow White serves as an animation _____, marking the beginning of the Golden Age of animation.
3. During his lifetime, Disney remained personally involved with the _____ of all feature-length animated films.
4. Walt Disney Studios continues to pioneer and develop ground-breaking animation techniques _____ the latest in technology.

Reading Tasks

Focus Reading

Pre-reading Questions

1. Have you ever seen any early animated movies? If so, how do you feel about them?
2. What do you know about the history of movie animation?
3. Do you know any influential animators?

The History of Movie Animation

Animation is the rapid display of a sequence of images of 2-D artwork or model positions in order to simulate movement. The most common method of presenting animation is as a motion picture or video program. A series of drawings are linked together and photographed by a camera. Each drawing is slightly different from the one before, so when they are played back in rapid succession they create the illusion of movement.

The history of film animation began in the 1890s with the earliest days of silent films. The first animated film was created by Charles-Émile Reynaud①, who developed an animation system using loops of 12 pictures. He later exhibited animations consisting of loops of about 500 frames.

Early animations, which started appearing before 1910, consisted of simple drawings photographed one at a time. The development of celluloid around 1913 made the animation process easier to manage, as the animator could now have moving characters on a single stationary frame, making it unnecessary to repeatedly draw the background over and over again.

In 1914, after a full year of painstaking work, Winsor McCay② finished *Gertie the Dinosaur*. Ten

---

①Charles-Émile Reynaud (1844—1918): a French science teacher, responsible for the first projected animated cartoon films.
②Winsor McCay (1869—1934): an American cartoonist and animator.

thousand drawings, showing various stages of motion, had been individually inked on rice paper. Then each sheet was photographed, one frame at a time, with a motion picture camera. Not a very exciting process to be sure, but the result on the screen was a pure delight. When it was shown, the Chicago vaudeville audience sat on their edge of their seats, enthralled by the animated dinosaur leaping on the screen.

McCay's act was a winner and Gertie the Dinosaur became the first animated cartoon star. She was also the first cartoon character to show a personality all her own—now called character animation. As an outstanding representative of the early American animators, McCay's pioneering early animated films far outshone the work of his contemporaries, and set a standard followed by Walt Disney and others in later decades.

A lot of animation, so to speak, has been produced since then, but very little was created before Gertie. Films were almost 20 years old before the first pioneer efforts at animation were even attempted. The reason for the delay was simple economics. French film producer George Méliés[1] had used animation in his fantasy films as early as 1898, so the expertise was in place. But at the time, films were not rented to theaters. Rather they were sold outright—the standard price being ten-cents a foot. A 100-foot animated cartoon brought in the same $10 as a live-action film, but took a lot more time and money to produce.

James Stuart Blackton[2], a vaudeville "lightning sketch" artist, can be called the father of the animated film. The earliest surviving example of full animation is Blackton's *Humorous Phases of Funny Faces*, a three-minute film produced in 1906. Here Blackton draws various faces on a blackboard, which then came to life. A man blows smoke from a cigar, faces draw and un-draw themselves, a clown does a few tricks and his dog jumps through hoops. *Humorous Phases of Funny Faces* was an interesting novelty, but failed to make a real impact on the industry.

Even Winsor McCay—in two animated films before *Gertie the Dinosaur*—failed to arouse much interest in the animated cartoon. It was advertising that gave birth to the animated cartoon as a commercial enterprise—cartoons that were made to promote comic strips.

---

[1] Georges Méliés (1861—1938): a French filmmaker famous for leading many technical and narrative developments in the earliest cinema.
[2] James Stuart Blackton (1875—1941): an Anglo-American film producer of the Silent Era, the founder of Vitagraph Studios and among the first filmmakers to use the techniques of stop-motion and drawn animation.

Unit 6 Comic and Animation

The first comic strip, *The Little Bears and Tykes* by James Swinnerton①, appeared in *the San Francisco Examiner* in 1892. The next year Richard Outcault② published the famous *The Yellow Kid* in *the New York World*. In a few years the comic strip was well-established such as *Krazy Kat* and *Bringing up Father*. Some of these, featuring human characters, were adopted for live-action movies.

Newspaper publishers, notably William Randolph Hearst③, began making animated versions of the Sunday comics to promote circulation. At first animators used simple pen and ink drawings without backgrounds. No way had been discovered to include backgrounds unless they were individually drawn on each frame. And even if they were, like in *Gertie the Dinosaur*, they shimmered on the screen due to tiny variations in each drawing.

Storylines were practically nonexistent. Animated cartoons were nothing more than a few sight gags strung together to make a two- or three-minute film. When dialogue was needed, the animator simply drew a dialogue balloon as his newspaper counterpart did. The action would freeze for a moment until the audience had a chance to read the dialogue; then would continue.

At first the little cartoons were well received because they were a novelty, but audiences soon tired of them. Nickelodeon owners began using cartoons to clear the theater between performances, much like movies themselves had been used to clear vaudeville houses when audiences tired of the 30-second vignettes producers had been making for carnival peep show machines more than a decade earlier. Early animators tried to make their animation smoother and more lifelike by increasing the quality and number of drawings.

The first real breakthrough in animation technology came with cel animation, invented by Earl Hurd④ in 1915. This invention greatly relieved cartoonists' work and improved the efficiency of animation production since it eliminated the need to redraw background scenes.

Cartoons were then more pleasing to the eye. The skill of the animators improved and they would often go to great lengths to perfect a single effect. One time at the Bray Studio, for instance, Hurd attempted to realistically animate a flag waving in the breeze—something that

---

①James Swinnerton (1875—1974): an American cartoonist and a landscape painter of the Southwest deserts.
②Richard Outcault (1863—1928): an American comic strip writer-artist. He was the creator of the series *The Yellow Kid* and *Buster Brown*, and he is considered the inventor of the modern comic strip.
③William Randolph Hearst (1863—1951): an American newspaper magnate and leading newspaper publisher.
④Earl Hurd (1880—1940): a pioneering American animator and film director. He is noted for creating and producing the silent *Bobby Bumps* animated short subject series. Hurd and Bray are jointly responsible for developing the processes involved in cel animation.

had never been attempted before. The successful result so fired the imaginations of the other animators that they rushed to their desks to attempt similar effects. Bray's animators were spending so much time trying to imitate life that Bray finally had to call a halt to the experimenting.

Bray had a valid point. There wasn't much profit in animated cartoons as it was and wasting time on "art" cut profits down even more. More of an assembly line product was required. That, in itself, was difficult. In those days, a single animator was responsible for a single cartoon. He wrote the story, created the gags, painted the backgrounds and, at times, even operated the camera. He had to draw about 2,700 individual frames for each five-minute short. There was no time for experiments.

Early animators worked without a storyboard—that would come much later. They kept everything in their heads. The animator had to be a good draftsman, not only fast with a pencil but able to keep the character consistent from the beginning to the end of the movie. There are a number of films where the characters drawn by poor draftsmen changed their appearance to the point where they were almost unrecognizable by the end of the film.

1922 was a crucial year for animation. Cels were now being used by nearly everyone and animated cartoons were showing up frequently in film programs. The innovators were still at work. Tony Sarg and Herbert Dawley were reviving ancient "shadow plays," substituting rod puppets for animation. Not only that, they were adding color by tinting the film. This caused a dramatic change in animation production.

And a new star was rising in the firmament. In Kansas City, Missouri, a young commercial artist Walt Elias Disney① was fiddling with animation. His first movies were short

---

①Walter Elias Disney (1901—1966): an American film producer, director, screenwriter, voice actor, animator, entrepreneur, entertainer, international icon and philanthropist, well-known for his influence in the field of entertainment during the 20th century.

advertising films for local businesses, called *Laugh-O-Grams*. Then he had an idea. Why not combine live action with animation? Together with his friend Ub Iwerks①, the two youngsters began production of the *Alice and Cartoonland* films in which a live girl plays merrily with her animated friends. Alice was only the beginning for Walt Disney. Because of his innovations in the coming years, animated cartoons would never be the same again.

Walt Disney took animation to a new level. He was the first animator to add sound to his movie cartoons with the premiere of *Steamboat Willie* in 1928. In 1937, he produced the first full length animated feature film, *Snow White and the Seven Dwarfs*. It was also the first to both use Technicolor and become successful within the English-speaking world.

With the introduction of computers, animation took on a whole new meaning. Many feature films of today have animation incorporated into them for special effects. For example, *the Star Wars* series relies heavily on computer animation for many of its special effects. *Toy Story*, produced by Walt Disney Productions and Pixar Animation Studios, became the first full length feature film animated entirely by computer when it was released in 1995.

(1,442 words)

Vocabulary

simulate /ˈsɪmjuleɪt/ *v.* to make in imitation of 模拟
succession /səkˈseʃən/ *n.* the act or process of following in order or sequence 连续
illusion /ɪˈljuːʒən/ *n.* an erroneous perception of reality 幻想
loop /luːp/ *n.* something having a circular shape 循环
celluloid /ˈseljulɔɪd/ *n.* a colorless, flammable material made from nitrocellulose and camphor and used to make photographic film 赛璐珞
vaudeville /ˈvəʊdəvɪl/ *n.* stage entertainment offering a variety of short acts 歌舞杂耍
enthrall /ɪnˈθrɔːl/ *v.* captivate 迷住
leap /liːp/ *v.* jump 跳跃
outshine /aʊtˈʃaɪn/ *v.* to shine brighter than 胜过
contemporary /kənˈtempərərɪ/ *n.* belonging to the same period of time 同时代的人
fantasy /ˈfæntəsɪ/ *n.* the creative imagination 幻想
outright /ˈaʊtˈraɪt/ *adv.* completely 完全地
hoop /huːp/ *n.* a large wooden, plastic, or metal ring, especially one used as a plaything or for trained animals to jump through 箍；铁环
novelty /ˈnɒvəltɪ/ *n.* something new and unusual 新奇的事物
enterprise /ˈentəpraɪz/ *n.* an undertaking 事业
frame /freɪm/ *n.* a closed, often rectangular border of drawn or printed lines 框架
shimmer /ˈʃɪmə/ *v.* to shine with a flickering light 闪闪发光

---

①Ub Iwerks, (1901—1971): a two-time Academy Award winning American animator, cartoonist, character designer, inventor and special effects technician, who was famous for his work for Walt Disney.

storyline *n.* the plot of a film 故事情节

gag /gæg/ *n.* a comic effect or remark 插科打诨

counterpart /ˈkaʊtəpɑːt/ *n.* one that has the same functions and characteristics as another 对手

vignette /vɪˈnjet/ *n.* an unbordered picture, often a portrait, that shades off into the surrounding color at the edges 虚光照

carnival /ˈkɑːnɪvəl/ *n.* a festival marked by merrymaking and feasting 狂欢节

peep show 西洋景

breakthrough /ˈbreɪkˌθruː/ *n.* an act of overcoming an obstacle 突破

eliminate /ɪˈlɪmɪneɪt/ *v.* to get rid of 消除

halt /hɔːlt/ *n.* a suspension of movement or progress 停止

valid /ˈvælɪd/ *adj.* well grounded 正当的

storyboard *n.* (电影、电视节目或商业广告等的)情节串连图板

draftsman /ˈdrɑːftsmən/ *n.* a man who draws, especially an artist 画匠

crucial /ˈkruːʃəl/ *adj.* extremely significant or important 至关重要的

innovator /ˈɪnəʊveɪtə/ *n.* someone who helps to open up a new line of technology or art 革新者

revive /rɪˈvaɪv/ *v.* to restore to activity 使复兴

puppet /ˈpʌpɪt/ *n.* a small figure of a person or an animal designed to be manipulated by the hand 木偶

premiere /prɪˈmɪər/ *n.* the first public performance of a movie 初次公演

incorporate /ɪnˈkɔːpəreɪt/ *v.* to unite (one thing) with something else 使加入

Proper Names

Charles-Émile Reynaud /ˈreɪˌnən/	查尔斯·埃米尔·雷诺
Winsor McCay	温瑟·马凯
Gertie the Dinosaur	《恐龙葛蒂》
George Méliés	乔治·梅里
J. Stuart Blackton	詹姆斯·斯图尔特·布莱克顿
Humorous Phases of Funny Faces	《滑稽脸的幽默相》
The Little Bears and Tykes	《小熊和小淘气》
James Swinnerton /ˈswɪnətən/	詹姆士·斯温纳顿
The San Francisco Examiner	《旧金山观察家报》
Richard Outcault	理查德·奥特考特
The Yellow Kid	《黄孩子》
The New York World	《纽约世界》
Krazy Kat	《疯狂猫》
Bringing Up Father	《抚养老爸》
William Randolph Hearst /ˈrændɒlf ˈhɜːst/	威廉·兰道夫·赫斯特

Earl Hurd	厄尔·赫德
Tony Sarg	托尼·萨格
Herbert Dawley	赫伯·杜立
Walt Elias Disney	沃尔特·埃利亚斯·迪士尼
Laugh-O-Grams	《小欢乐》
Ub Iwerkes	乌伯·伊瓦克斯
Alice and Cartoonland	《爱丽丝在卡通国》
Steamboat Willie	《汽船威利》
Snow White and the Seven Dwarfs	《白雪公主和七个小矮人》
The Star Wars	《星球大战》
Toy Story	《玩具总动员》

Text Exploration

5 Choose the best answer to each question with the information from the text.

1. When did the early animation start?
   A. In the 1890s.
   B. In the 1990s.
   C. Before 1910.
   D. Not mentioned.

2. How did the audience feel about Winsor McCay's *Gertie the Dinosaur*?
   A. They felt fascinated by it.
   B. They felt bored with it.
   C. They felt touched by it.
   D. They were indifferent to it.

3. What's Winsor McCay's contribution to animation industry?
   A. He developed an animation system using loops of 12 pictures.
   B. He set a standard for other animators to follow in the following decades.
   C. He invented celluloid system which made the animation process easier to manage.
   D. He added sound to the movie for the first time.

4. What accounted for the delay of the appearance of animation compared with films?
   A. The fact that it was too boring to produce animation for animators.
   B. The fact that it's more difficult to produce animation.
   C. The fact that few people felt interested in seeing animation.
   D. The fact that it's less profitable to produce animation.

5. Why did newspaper publishers make animated versions of the Sunday comics?
   A. To compete with their opponents.
   B. To replace the traditional comics.
   C. To promote circulation.
   D. To reduce costs.

6. The invention of cel animation is viewed as a real breakthrough in animation technology because _____.

   A. it makes the images more eye-pleasing

   B. it eliminated the need to use a storyboard

   C. it enhances the efficiency of animation production

   D. it solves the problems of tinting the film

7. What do cartoons and movies have in common for Nickelodeon owners?

   A. Both of them were novelties for audience.

   B. Both of them were used to clear vaudeville houses.

   C. Both of them could attract more audience.

   D. Both of them could fascinate the audience.

8. Why was it difficult to have an assembly line product of animation in 1910s?

   A. Because an animator had too many tasks to fulfill to have time for experiments.

   B. Because there wasn't much profit in animated cartoons.

   C. Because the technology was not in place at that time.

   D. Because there were a serious lack of experienced animators.

9. What is the difficulty caused by the lack of a storyboard?

   A. Doing everything all by animators themselves.

   B. Animators being responsible for a single cartoon.

   C. Redrawing background scenes.

   D. Keeping the character consistent on the part of animators.

10. What is special about the *Alice and Cartoonland*?

    A. It's the first animation to combine live action with animation.

    B. It's the first animation to add sound to the movie cartoon.

    C. It's the first animation to add color to the animation.

    D. It's the first animation to rely heavily on computer animation.

6 Complete the following chart with the information from the text.

Periods		Representatives	What happened
Before 1910	1890s	Charles-Émile Reynaud	He developed a(n) _____ using loops of 12 pictures.
	1892	_____	He published *The Little Bears and Tykes*.
	1893	Richard Outcault	He published the famous *The Yellow Kid*.
	1898	George Méliés	He used animation in his _____ films.
	_____	J. Stuart Blackton	Produced a three-minute film *Humorous Phases of Funny Faces*.

(续表)

Periods		Representatives	What happened
After 1910	1914	Winsor McCay	He finished *Gertie the Dinosaur and* Gertie was the first cartoon character to _____ all her own.
	1915	Earl Hurd	He invented cel animation which is the first real _____ in animation technology.
	1922	Tony Sarg; Herbert Dawley	Cels were widely used; Animated cartoons showed up frequently in film programs; Ancient "shadow plays" were _____; Animators added color by tinting the film.
	1928	Walt Disney	He _____ to his movie cartoons *Steamboat Willie*.
	1937	_____	He produced the first full length animated feature film, *Snow White and the Seven Dwarfs*.
	1995	Walt Disney Productions and Pixar Animation Studios	The first full length feature film animated _____, *Toy Story*, was released.

7 Discuss the following questions with the information from the text.

1. How do animators simulate movement?

2. In what way does celluloid make the animation process easier?

3. Why was an assembly line product of animation very difficult in 1910s?

4. What do you know about life experience of Walt Disney?

5. Who are the most impressive cartoon characters for you?

Vocabulary Expansion

8 Fill in the blanks with the right words given below. Change the form where necessary.

simulate	fantasy	contemporary	counterpart	valid
breakthrough	halt	incorporate	painstaking	slightly

1. The young girl is living in a world of _____.
2. The scientists strive for a _____ in cancer research.
3. The only _____ imperfection in this painting is a scratch in the corner.

4. Due to the bribery scandal, his political career had come to a _____.
5. This novel explores the growth of the _____ teenagers.
6. These insects can _____ dead leaves.
7. As a result of many such _____ studies, our present knowledge of the oceans has accumulated.
8. The guy running the engineering department wasn't in constant touch with his _____ in manufacturing.
9. The _____ of the Internet by the Chinese news media is closely connected with the development of China's IT industry.
10. Oversleeping is not a _____ excuse for being late for school.

9 **Choose the word or phrase that best keeps the meaning of the sentence if it is substituted for the underlined word or phrase.**

1. Some driving teachers use computers to <u>simulate</u> different road conditions for learners to practice on.
   A. record   B. imitate
   C. duplicate   D. represent
2. Why does the story continue to <u>enthrall</u> generation after generation?
   A. inspire   B. terrify
   C. fascinate   D. capture
3. Ben Palmer easily <u>outshone</u> his rivals in the 200 meter freestyle.
   A. did better than   B. did as well as
   C. did poorer than   D. did quicker than
4. Those workers expected <u>nothing more than</u> a new-type machine.
   A. nothing but   B. other than
   C. anything but   D. except for
5. She could see her reflection in the water, <u>shimmering</u> in the moonlight.
   A. shining   B. splashing
   C. waving   D. shaking
6. During the past ten years there have been <u>dramatic</u> changes in the international situation.
   A. permanent   B. powerful
   C. striking   D. practical
7. The kids squealed with <u>delight</u> at the sight of the Christmas tree.
   A. grief   B. happiness
   C. anger   D. surprise
8. As to how to promote your products, do you have a plan <u>in place</u>?
   A. to consider   B. available
   C. to choose   D. to carry out
9. She had raised her voice to <u>bring in</u> the other two customers.
   A. attempt   B. persuade

C. attract   D. argue with

10. An astronaut will attempt to leave the <u>stationary</u> spaceship and then return to it.
     A. moving   B. operating
     C. flying   D. motionless

10 Translate the Chinese sentences into English by simulating the sentences chosen from the text.

Chosen Sentences	*Simulated Translations*	*Chinese Sentences*
A lot of animation, ***so to speak***, has been produced since then, but very little was created before Gertie.		他可谓是一部活字典。
It was advertising that ***gave birth to*** the animated cartoon as a commercial enterprise…		研究表明,接触污染空气的孕妇很可能生下患有心脏缺陷的孩子。(**expose**, **defect**)
Animated cartoons were ***nothing more than*** a few sight gags strung together to make a two-or three-minute film.		它只不过是杜撰的故事而已。(**make up**)
The skill of the animators improved and they would often ***go to great lengths*** to perfect a single effect.		他准备全力以赴实现他的计划。
Bray's animators were spending so much time trying to imitate life that Bray finally had to ***call a halt*** to the experimenting.		他们发现场地很滑时,决定停止比赛。(**slippery**)

Supplementary Readings

11 Passage One

    Animation has been a part of cinema history from the time motion pictures were created in the late 1800s. Early animated films were done by well-known newspaper cartoonists. Although three-dimensional animation techniques were attempted in the early years of filmmaking, major motion-picture studios decided that two-dimensional animation was the most efficient technique. Nowadays animated television shows have become great hits and animation has captured the hearts of individuals—young and old.

    In the decade or so since the first edition of TV cartoon shows, the industry has grown and expanded to previously unimagined heights, thanks in great part to the upsurge of cable TV services catering to animation fans. In the ten-year period from 1993 through 2003, nearly 450 new cartoon series have premiered in the U. S.

    Animation has had a global <u>renaissance</u> during the 1990s, and nowhere is this more evident than in Asia. With the exception of China and Japan, most Asian nations are relatively new to this art form. Over the last decade, areas such as Taiwan, South Korea, the Philippines, Thailand as well as China, have acted as major offshore production plants for North American and European studios. One of the spurs for this increase in activity has been the global growth of terrestrial, cable, satellite and video systems, all demanding large menus of programming, including animation. A second spur has been the exceptional popularity that Japanese anime has enjoyed across Asia, Europe and United States. For young people, Japanese cartoons have captivating plots, exquisite painting, beautiful characters, vivid dubbing, a strong visual sense, creative ideas, dynamic pictures as well as graceful accompaniment.

Despite these developments, there has not been corresponding growth of a serious literature covering industrial and aesthetic issues about Asian animation, and the small amount of work that has been produced has not been published in English. Animation in Asia and the Pacific provides the first continent-wide analysis. This kind of analysis in turn delves into issues of production, distribution, exhibition, aesthetics and regulation in this field. Animation in Asia and the Pacific also offers fascinating experiences for a group of animation pioneers. The historical and contemporary perspectives derive from various sources such as interviews, textual analysis and participation or observation data.

1. What's the reason for not using three-dimensional animation in the early filmmaking?

    A. Because it's less time-saving.

    B. Because it's less attempting.

    C. Because it's less eye-pleasing.

    D. Because it's less efficient.

2. What does the word "renaissance" in Para 3 mean?

    A. revival.   B. recession.

    C. depression.   D. success.

3. What's the result of the popularity of Japanese anime?

    A. A global renaissance of animation.

    B. Many Asian areas serving as production plants for North America and European studios.

    C. A rapid growth and expansion of animation industry in Asian countries.

    D. A more demanding demand for animation programming catering to animation fans.

4. According to the passage, what is the pity for Asian animation industry?

    A. It has not been recognized by many countries.

    B. It can't match animation production in America.

    C. There is not enough financial support from the governments.

    D. There is no corresponding growth of a serious literature in this field.

5. Which of the following statements is true according to the passage?

    A. Early animated films were done by experienced film makers.

    B. Nowadays animated TV shows are mainly enjoyed by young people.

C. The upsurge of cable TV in part leads to a quick growth and expansion of animation industry.
D. The historical and contemporary perspectives of Asian animation stem from the experience in producing animations in Asia.

12 Passage Two

There are a few things that transcend cultures. Often, countries and cultures are so different that what is accepted and loved in one country is not accepted and loved in another. As a result, the core value system or language is so different that it just never catches on. However, anime is one of those special things like music or some fashion choices that have managed to cross different cultures.

Anime, which is the shortened version of Japanese term animation, is huge in Japan. It is a genre that produces massive profits and it has been around for nearly 100 years. Anime is not only released in Japan but around the world. It is translated into multiple languages, bringing in billions of dollars every year.

Anime originated sometime around 1917. Japanese filmmakers began experimenting with animation techniques that were coming out of European countries; the oldest known anime clip consisted of a warrior testing a new sword that lasted 2 minutes. By 1933, companies released anime that had sound.

The manga boom of the 1970s also helped the industry grow. Mangas are Japanese comics, many of which ended up being turned into anime later on. This practice is still hugely popular in Japan where the most popular anime shows are actually adaptations of Japanese manga. By the 1980s, anime had become popular and accepted by the mainstream in Japan and that also caused production to increase.

Animes are defined by several unique things. These include things like very large eyes, very complex hairstyles and elongated limbs. Body proportion is directly related to the length of a head. For instance, almost all anime characters are drawn to a standard "eight heads" and then if they are taller, another "head" of height is added. The characters also have very large eyes that can be brilliantly colored in shades like silver or purple. This is done by shading the eye with a light color, the tone color and then a darker color.

An anime character's facial expression is also very important. Their faces are extremely expressive where Western cartoon characters are not. A variety of expressions that are never used in Western animation are commonplace in Japan. For instance, to express embarrassment, a sweat-drop is drawn on the character's head. If a character is particularly emotional, their eyes will actually seem to "waver."

1. What do anime, music and some fashion choices have in common?
   A. They can manage to cross different cultures.
   B. They can manage to convey complicated messages in simple ways.
   C. They can be viewed as national heritages.
   D. They can help people develop a sense of pride for their countries.

2. What is the major source of Japanese anime shows?

   A. Japanese folk tales.

   B. Chinese folk tales.

   C. Japanese comics.

   D. Foreign animation productions.

3. Why do Japanese anime characters have very big eyes?

   A. To make them more attracting.

   B. To make it easier to color them in shades.

   C. To help the characters more expressive.

   D. To strike a balance between Western animation and Japanese ones.

4. According to the passage, which of the following is NOT true about Japanese anime?

   A. It has existed for nearly 100 years.

   B. It is highly profitable in Japan.

   C. It led to the boom of manga in 1930s in Japan.

   D. By the late 20th century, it has been accepted by the mainstream in Japan.

5. What happened in the 1980s in Japan?

   A. Anime originated.

   B. Manga flourished.

   C. Anime was accepted by foreign countries.

   D. Animation production increased.

Interactive Tasks

Role-play

13 Role-play the following situation with your partner.

Situation:

   Lucy and David are talking about their favorite cartoon characters. Lucy is fond of Japanese cartoon characters while Jack likes those produced in America.

You may begin like this:

David: Hey, you have such a cute hat with DORAEMON!

Lucy: You think so? It's my favorite cartoon! I love all those produced in Japan!

David: Wow, you're nuts about them! I feel they are OK, but *Tom and Jerry* will be my love forever!

Lucy: It's absolutely classic.

Group Work

14 Work in groups to do an oral presentation.

1. Form groups of four or five students;

2. Each group chooses a topic concerning comic and animation, e.g.

A study of the current situation about Chinese animation industry;

An introduction to a well-known cartoon character or TV series.

3. Members of each group collect materials from library and the Internet to work out their PPT slides;
4. Based on the PPT slides, each member of the group gives oral presentation of his part.

Follow-up Task

Writing

15 Directions: For this part, you are going to write a composition on the topic: **Animation Industry in China**. You should write at least 120 words following the outline given below in Chinese:

1. 中国动画业的现状;
2. 中国动画行业存在的问题;
3. 应该如何解决现存的问题。

Unit 7　Fashion

Highlight

Topic area	Communication	Skills
Talking about fashion; Different opinions about beauty.	peer into be obsessed with range from … to… set one's eyes on make sense	Learn some new words and expressions about fashion; Know some basic knowledge about fashion industry and people's opinions about beauty.

Starting-out Task

1 **Look at the following pictures and share your opinions with your partner about fashion.**

1. What's your understanding of fashion? Is it the same as what is shown in these pictures?
2. What changes have taken place in the world of fashion in the past few decades?
3. What makes a person look fashionable? Give reasons to support your opinion.

Unit 7 Fashion

Listening Tasks

Micro Listening Skills

2 **Listen to the following passage and try to fill in the missing words.**

It's not enough for a designer to be 1. _____; you also have to have some business sense. As fashion gets more and more corporate driven, it's important to be 2. _____ of the business climate and understanding the 3. _____ behind it. By religiously reading trade papers like *Women's Wear Daily* you will get a lot of 4. _____ information. If you want to run your own company, you need to be 5. _____ organized and learn at least the basics of 6. _____. A lot of fashion schools are currently increasing business classes in their 7. _____. "Our students have to be smart enough to know how to 8. _____ a contract, or to pick a business partner," says Carol Mongo. It's perhaps telling that many of the designers that are really successful today, like Calvin Klein or Tom Ford, are 9. _____ in every aspect of the business—from licensing 10. _____ to ad campaigns to actually designing the clothes.

Passage

What Is Fashion?

Words & Phrases

refer to...as	将……称之为
apply to	应用
interior /ɪnˈtɪərɪə/ *adj.*	内部的
textile /ˈtekstaɪl/ *n.*	纺织品
garment /ˈɡɑːmənt/ *n.*	衣服
diversity /daɪˈvɜːsɪtɪ/ *n.*	多样性
pastel shades	清淡优美的色彩
fabric /ˈfæbrɪk/ *n.*	织物
nonverbal /ˌnɒnˈvɜːbəl/ *adj.*	不用语言的
conform to	符合

Unit 7 Fashion

3 Listen to the passage and decide whether the following statements are true (T) or false (F).
1. ____ The word "fashion" comes from Greek word, which means, "to make."
2. ____ Fashion is a way to celebrate the diversity and variety of the world in which we live.
3. ____ In winter, people prefer colors that are darker and brighter than those in summer.
4. ____ Fashion is important to people because it's a means to keep up with the latest trend.

4 Listen to the passage again and complete the following sentences with the information you have heard.
1. Fashion is commonly used to _____.
2. It is normal for the fashion trends _____.
3. For centuries individuals or societies have used clothes and other _____ _____ to indicate occupation, rank, gender, locality, class and wealth.
4. The clothes a person wears _____, as well as being a means of conforming to peer group expectations.

Reading Tasks

Pre-reading Questions
1. Have you ever tried to be on diet to become thinner? If so, why would you do that?
2. What's your understanding of beauty in your eyes?
3. What do you think of the use of super skinny models in fashion shows?

The Fashion Industry Imposes a Cruel Burden on Women[①]

The prison of the unachievable body shape has replaced the prison of the kitchen for millions of women fashion lovers in the world.

[①] This passage is slightly adapted from the article written by Johann Hari.

Another London Fashion Week① is to start this week, it will be another parade of the Emperor's Designer Clothes, made of tinfoil or feathers or rubber as usual. On its eve, a study was released which covers such a good story that it's for sure that all the economists and government officials would be desperately eager to read. According to the study, the direct value of the fashion industry to the British economy is nearly 21 billion pounds. If we take other induced and 'spill over' effects into consideration, the fashion industry's total contribution to the UK economy is estimated to stand at more than 37 billion pounds. And the fashion industry directly employs 816,000 people across a wide range of jobs and is the largest employer of all the creative industries. Everything seems perfectly all right. But what's behind the seemingly fabulous prosperity?

A few years ago, I was sent backstage to cover this event—and it took me a very long time to recover from what I saw. For the first time I was forced to peer into the industry that is making so many of my female friends ill.

What we saw on the runways was more or less the same: women so thin they not only made us gasp in disbelief, but also made us forget to look at the clothes. At the end of the catwalk, there stood a parade of young women who looked like they were about to collapse. On camera, fashion models look worryingly thin. In the flesh, they look so emaciated that the only other place I have ever seen people like them is reporting on African famines. Their eyes are glazed, shut-down because they have no fuel to run on. Smeared with cosmetics, these models were squeezed into a dress design that appeared to be made of rubbish bags and pushed out to shimmy down the catwalk, to be applauded by the likes of Kate Moss and Hugh Grant. When they stumbled back, they appeared faint and listless. Leaning against a wall, those models looked like they needed an IV drip.

The fashion world claims two sets of victims. The first are the women who it uses as models, for a brief window, before discarding them. They are, on average, 25 per cent below a normal, healthy woman's weight. We know how they achieve this, because many former models say so: they starve themselves. They live on water and lettuce for weeks. A model at 15 once admitted that she was so obsessed with food that she beat herself up over eating an

---

①London Fashion Week takes place in London twice a year, in February and September. It first took place in 1984 and currently ranks alongside New York, Paris and Milan as one of the "Big Four" fashion weeks.

apple. When they fall below a Body Mass Index① of 12 they start to consume their own muscles and tissues. In 2006, at least two models died from complications linked to eating disorders. Several other models have dropped dead from starvation after success at fashion shows in the past few years.

But there is a broader circle of victims, far beyond the catwalk's models. They are ordinary women who are bombarded with these highly manufactured images of "beauty" every day, and react either by feeling repulsive or trying out semi-starvation themselves. A Harvard University study found that 80 per cent of women are unhappy with their bodies and only one per cent are "completely happy". Men, by contrast, were broadly happy with how they look: the accepted idea of male hotness is so broad that it can range from 79-year-old Sean Connery to 20-stone James Corden. Another survey conducted by youth research firm Tru showed that almost nine in ten American teenage girls say they feel pressured by the fashion and media industries to be skinny. Thus an unrealistic, unattainable image of beauty has been created. We are now living through an epidemic of female anorexia, with over 50 million victims in Europe and the US. How many women do you know who are happy with the way they look?

The fashion industry tries every means to promote this sick vision. The recent documentary The September Issue—following the production of American *Vogue*② magazine's biggest edition of the year—had one great revelation. Anna Wintour③—the magazine's editor, and the most powerful woman in fashion—is a brittle, sullen woman who appears to take no pleasure in anything, and only seems to show any vigor when she is being cruel to those around her. Presented with a picture of a stick-thin woman, she announces she "looks pregnant". Presented with a man with a stomach, she reacts with incomprehension, as if fat is something that is revolting in the human body. She promotes the use of fur, indifferent to the cruelty to animals it involves. She promotes creepily thin models—is she indifferent to the cruelty to women it involves?

Her depression is infectious: it spreads out through the pages of *Vogue*. A study by the American Psychological Association found that after spending as short as three minutes looking at a fashion magazine, 70 per cent of women felt "depressed, guilty and ashamed." *Vogue* and its ilk are banned in most eating disorder clinics because they know that with very few exceptions it makes their readers lose their appetite quickly after they set their eyes on it. This magazine has done real harm to ordinary women in that it promotes the trend for bone-thin models for fashion industry.

But this raises the apparent paradox: if it makes women feel so unhappy, why do they

---

① Abbr. BMI: a measurement of the relative percentages of fat and muscle mass in the human body, in which weight in kilograms is divided by height in meters and the result used as an index of obesity.
体重指数:测量人体内脂肪和肌肉的相对百分比,用以米为单位的身高去除以千克为单位的体重,其结果用作肥胖症指标。
② *Vogue*: a fashion and lifestyle magazine that is published in 18 national and one regional edition. Each month, *Vogue* publishes a magazine addressing topics of fashion, life and design.
③ Anna Wintour, (1949—   ): British-born editor-in-chief of American *Vogue*, a position she has held since 1988.

buy it? If women are unwilling to see images of bony models in fashion magazines, how can we account for the fact that when fashion magazines consistently show normal women, their sales fall? There is a masochistic impulse among women that draws them to these sick images. What is it?

The best answer lies in *The Beauty Myth*[①], the 1991 classic by feminist Naomi Wolf[②]. She argues that it is wrong to believe there is one objective standard of "beauty". No. The Padung adore droopy breasts. Obese women were hot here in the 15th century. Our idea of beauty changes depending on how we want women to be.

Wolf points out something remarkable in the shifting tides of the fashion world. Whenever women become stronger in the real world, fashion models become weaker and thinner. In the 1910s, it was considered beautiful for women to have soft, rounded hips, thighs and bellies: most women's natural shape. In the 1920s, when women got the vote, the idea of what was beautiful changed. Suddenly models became bonier and feeble—and women started to starve themselves. In the 1950s, when women's rights receded, women could be curvy and eat again. With the 1960s and the rise of feminism, models became smaller and smaller—until today, when women are breaking glass ceilings, emaciated models are the norm.

Why would this happen? Women were kept down for thousands of years—and now, in a few generations, there have been incredible strides towards liberation. But the old, traditional beliefs are deep in our cultural DNA, for both men and women. Wolf believes women suffer from "guilt about our own liberation—latent fears that we may be going too far". The craze for skinny figure is a sort of distorted perception by both men and women who are stunned and disorientated by the rapid transformation of the gender relations. Women have replaced the

---

①*The Beauty Myth*, published in 1991, is a nonfiction book by Naomi Wolf. Its basic premise is that forced adherence to standards of physical beauty has grown stronger for women as they gained power in other societal arenas.
②Naomi Wolf (1962—): an US author and political consultant. With the publication of *The Beauty Myth*, she became a leading spokesperson of what was later described as the third wave of the feminist movement.

prison of the kitchen with the prison of an unachievable body shape, as if it doesn't make sense to be a woman without bearing a cruel burden. The more powerful a woman is, the more likely she is to be bulimic.

One day, we will look back on a time when women longed to be a walking corpse with the incomprehension we feel for Chinese foot-binding. But how do we get there? This is a problem that lies deep in our subconscious minds, and like all subconscious problems, it has to be dragged to the surface. Wolf says anorexic women "are walking question marks pleading with schools, universities, and the rest of us to tell them flatly: This is intolerable. This is unacceptable. We don't starve women here. We value women."

She's right. It's time to do away with our thinness obsessed culture which is destroying women. We need to start publicly scorning the people who promote sickness in women as if it was cool. Enough! Women should not be made to feel subconsciously bad about demanding equality; starvation is not the Siamese twin[①] of female success. It requires more of us—men and women—to say: No more. This industry is sick, and stupid, and wrong, and when we see it, we will show our contempt. Can't we have a vogue—and a *Vogue*—for that?

(1,476 words)

Vocabulary

impose /ɪmˈpəʊz/ *v.* to establish or apply as compulsory 强加于
parade /pəˈreɪd/ *n.* a ceremonial procession including people marching 游行
tinfoil /ˈtɪnˌfɔɪl/ *n.* a thin, pliable sheet of aluminum 锡箔
spill /spɪl/ *v.* to cause or allow (a substance) to run or fall out of a container 溢出
fabulous /ˈfæbjʊləs/ *adj.* barely credible 令人难以置信的
gasp /ɡɑːsp/ *v.* to draw in the breath sharply, as from shock 喘气
flesh /fleʃ/ *n.* the body as opposed to the mind or soul 肉体
emaciate /ɪˈmeɪʃieɪt/ *vi.* to become extremely thin, especially as a result of starvation 使消瘦
famine /ˈfæmɪn/ *n.* a drastic, wide-reaching food shortage 饥荒
smear /smɪə/ *v.* to spread with a sticky, greasy, or dirty substance 涂抹
shimmy /ˈʃɪmɪ/ *v.* to vibrate abnormally 晃动
stumble /ˈstʌmbl/ *v.* to proceed unsteadily 蹒跚
bombard /ˈbɒmbɑːd/ *v.* to attack with bombs, shells, or missiles 轰击
repulsive /rɪˈpʌlsɪv/ *adj.* disgusting 令人厌恶
epidemic /ˌepɪˈdemɪk/ *n.* an outbreak of a contagious disease that spreads rapidly and widely 流行病
anorexia /ˌænə(ʊ)ˈreksɪə/ *n.* loss of appetite, especially as a result of disease 厌食
revelation /ˌrevɪˈleɪʃən/ *n.* the act of revealing or disclosing 披露

---

① Siamese twin: one of a pair of identical twins born with their bodies joined at some point

brittle /ˈbrɪtl/ *adj.* lacking warmth of feeling; cold 冷淡的
sullen /ˈsʌlən/ *adj.* showing a silent resentment 闷闷不乐的
revolting /rɪˈvəʊtɪŋ/ *adj.* causing disgust 令人厌恶的
paradox /ˈpærədɒks/ *n.* one exhibiting contradictory aspects 自相矛盾
masochist /ˈmæsəʊkɪst/ *n.* someone who obtains pleasure from receiving punishment 受虐狂
feminist /ˈfemɪnɪst/ *n.* a person whose beliefs and behavior are based on feminism 女权主义者
adore /əˈdɔː/ *v.* to like very much 喜爱
feeble /ˈfiːbl/ *adj.* lacking strength; weak 虚弱的
recede /rɪˈsiːd/ *v.* to move back or away from a limit, point, or mark 后退
stride /straɪd/ *v.* to walk with long steps 大步走
latent /ˈleɪtənt/ *adj.* present in the unconscious mind but not consciously expressed 潜意识的
disorientate /dɪsˈɔːrɪənteɪt/ *v.* lose one's direction 失去方向
plead /pliːd/ *v.* to appeal earnestly 恳求
obsess /əbˈses/ *v.* to have the mind excessively preoccupied with a single topic 使困扰
scorn /skɔːn/ *v.* to express contempt 蔑视
the Siamese /saɪəˈmiːz/ **twin** 连体双胞胎
contempt /kənˈtempt/ *n.* open disrespect 轻视

Proper Names

Naomi Wolf /ˈneɪəmɪ wʊlf/   内奥米·沃尔夫(人名)
Kate Moss   凯特·莫斯(人名)
Hugh Grant /hjuː grɑːnt/   休·格兰特(人名)
Sean Connery /ʃɔːn ˈkɒnərɪ/   肖恩·康纳利(人名)
James Corden   詹姆士·柯登(人名)
Anna Wintour   安娜·温图尔(人名)

Text Exploration

5 Choose the best answer to each question with the information from the text.

1. According to Para. 1, what is suggested by the study released before another London Fashion Week?

    A. Fashion industry is a pillar industry in Britain.

    B. Fashion industry is the most profitable industry in Britain.

    C. Fashion industry is the one which makes the biggest contribution to British economy.

    D. Fashion industry is the largest employer of all industries in Britain.

2. Why did it take the author a long time to recover from what he saw in London Fashion Week?

    A. Because what he saw made him feel sick.

B. Because what he saw is the most uncomfortable experience for him.

C. Because what he saw made him worried about the industry.

D. Because what he saw changed his opinion about fashion industry.

3. According to Para. 4, what does it mean if a model falls below a Body Mass Index of 12?

   A. The model will be deprived of the right to any fashion shows.

   B. The model will have more chances to be invited to fashion shows.

   C. The model will suffer from diet disorders.

   D. The model will start to consume her own muscles or tissues.

4. What's the reason for the fact that men are generally happier with their bodies than women?

   A. Because men care less about their bodies than women.

   B. Because people feel a man's appearance makes no differences to his life.

   C. Because people are more tolerant of men's appearances.

   D. Because men don't have pressure caused by reading fashion magazines.

5. Which of the following is NOT true of Anna Wintour?

   A. She is the editor of American *Vogue*.

   B. She is indifferent to the welfare of animals.

   C. She takes pleasure in her fashion career.

   D. She feels that a man with a stomach is incomprehensible.

6. Why do most eating disorder clinics ban magazines like *Vogue*?

   A. Because doctors believe that reading those magazines will prolong the time for patients to recover.

   B. Because doctors believe that reading those magazines will directly lead to a loss of appetite.

   C. Because doctors believe that reading those magazines will stir women's desire for luxury items.

   D. Because doctors believe that those magazines are not marketed to patients with eating disorders.

7. According to Wolf, what is the root for women's craze for thinness?

   A. Women long to look more fashionable and beautiful.

   B. Women feel attracted by the images presented in fashion magazines.

   C. Women are generally unhappy with their bodies.

   D. Women feel guilty for what they have demanded.

8. What's the purpose for the author to mention Chinese foot-binding in Para. 12?

   A. The author aims to point out that both Chinese foot-binding and women's craze for thinness are incomprehensible.

   B. The author aims to criticize the practice of foot-binding in China.

   C. The author aims to point out that we should get rid of the old-fashioned ideas.

   D. The author aims to point out that our society is developing very quickly.

9. What is implied by the sentence "Can't we have a vogue—and a *Vogue*—for that?"
   A. It implies that we should stop reading *Vogue* Magazine.
   B. It implies that we should set up some new organizations other than *Vogue*.
   C. It implies that we should change our views about fashion and promote such a healthy view.
   D. It implies that *Vogue* Magazine plays a very bad role in fashion industry.
10. What's the author's attitude towards fashion industry?
    A. Supportive.
    B. Indifferent.
    C. Critical.
    D. Sarcastic.

6 Complete the following chart with the information from the text.

Fashion industry: sick, stupid and wrong. We should show our _____.	
Revealed from the study	The fashion industry plays an important _____ in Britain.
Seen by the author from the catwalk	Models _____ themselves to look thin enough; they appear faint and listless.
Presented by *Vogue* Magazine	An unrealistic, _____ image of beauty is created and _____; It is _____ by most eating disorder clinics because it leads to a loss of _____.
Discussed by the book *The Beauty Myth*	There is no _____ standard of beauty; Our idea of _____ changes depending on how we want women to be; Women suffer from "guilt about our _____".

7 Discuss the following questions with the information from the text.

1. What does fashion industry mean to British economy?

2. Who are the victims of fashion industry?

3. What do you know about model's lives?

4. Do you agree with Wolf's opinion that people's idea of beauty changes with how people want women to be?

5. What do you think of fashion industry?

Unit 7 Fashion

Vocabulary Expansion

8 Fill in the blanks with the right words given below. Change the form where necessary.

starve	release	range	collapse	impulse
consume	applaud	promote	prosperity	claim

1. When is the best moment to _____ the date of the election to the newspapers?
2. The new agreement raised hopes for conditions of _____ and harmony.
3. Due to the financial crisis, the country's economy is on the edge of _____.
4. The audience warmly _____ when the performance came to the end.
5. As a result, the Western industrialized nations undertook steps to limit oil _____.
6. The Olympic Games for the Disabled have been a great success in _____ international friendship and understanding.
7. I'm _____ very much now because I have had nothing at all today.
8. Though he is in his sixties, his interests _____ from reading to skiing.
9. A small terrorist group has _____ responsibility for the bombing in London.
10. I felt an irresistible _____ to approach Mary and seized her hands with sudden violence.

9 Choose the word or phrase that best keeps the meaning of the sentence if it is substituted for the underlined word or phrase.

1. Cheer up! You have <u>latent</u> force to develop in your studies.
   A. amazing   B. great
   C. potential   D. enough
2. The painful memories gradually <u>receded</u> in her mind.
   A. disappeared   B. faded
   C. became sweet   D. became unforgettable
3. Michael told us an <u>incredible</u> story about his grandmother catching a thief.
   A. disgusting   B. brave
   C. touching   D. unbelievable
4. Many girls in our school <u>adore</u> that famous football star.
   A. like   B. idolize
   C. love   D. respect
5. He is said to have been able to <u>peer into</u> the souls of his followers and tell them what sins they had on their conscience.
   A. probe into   B. get to know
   C. give guidance to   D. back up
6. Our country has been <u>obsessed with</u> those food safety incidents.
   A. troubled by   B. harmed by
   C. endangered by   D. fooled by

7. The <u>infectious</u> disease can be disseminated by the various ways.
   A. dangerous			B. deadly
   C. contagious			D. harmful
8. The new military government has <u>banned</u> strikes and demonstrations.
   A. legalized			B. advocated
   C. approved			D. prohibited
9. We will be able to <u>discard</u> those that seem totally irrelevant to our lives.
   A. throw away			B. put up with
   C. release			D. delete
10. The city has decided to <u>do away with</u> all the old buildings in its center.
    A. repair			B. set up
    C. get rid of			D. paint

10 Translate the Chinese sentences into English by simulating the sentences chosen from the text.

Chosen Sentences	Simulated Translations	Chinese Sentences
For the first time I was forced to **peer into** the industry that is making so many of my female friends ill.		那个过路人好奇地透过栅栏向庭院里窥视。(**passerby**, **railing**)
Is she **indifferent to** the cruelty to women it involves?		在大多数情况下，各国的政策对外国人的利益是漠不关心的。
With very few exceptions it makes their readers lose their appetite quickly after they **set their eyes on** it.		我第一眼就看出他不是一个值得信赖的人！
Wolf believes women suffer from "guilt and apprehension about our own liberation—latent fears that we may be **going too far**".		(这件事)别做得太过分了，否则你会招来麻烦的。
…as if it doesn't **make sense** to be a woman without bearing a cruel burden.		一项投资究竟有无意义最终取决于当前的市场状况。

Supplementary Readings

11 **Passage One**

In October 2009 a survey was conducted across eleven markets including Brazil, Canada, France, Hong Kong, India, Netherlands, Spain, Taiwan, the United Arab Emirates, Britain and the United States. The survey aimed to find out how people feel after they indulge themselves with some luxury items. The findings from the survey were quite out of people's expectations. While luxury goods are, in essence, supposed to make people feel good, the survey of respondents across Europe, Asia and the Americas revealed that 32 percent of luxury buyers flagellate(鞭打) themselves after making their purchase.

This was especially prominent in Britain, where 72 percent said they treated themselves to luxury, but then half—mostly women—reported feeling guilty about it. A majority in the United States also had the same conflicted relationship with luxury, the survey showed.

At the other end of the scale, a majority of respondents in India, Brazil and the Netherlands say they do not feel guilty after a luxury purchase, mainly because Indians and Dutch are "sensible" about spending their money while Brazilians tend to be more "hedonistic(快乐主义的)", the survey said.

A majority of luxury lovers also tend to love showing off their purchases. Nearly half of all respondents said they preferred to buy items with an obvious designer logo, especially in India, Hong Kong and the United Arab Emirates, where many people believe in the adage "if you've got it, flaunt it."

There are those who like a more subtle approach, with the survey showing that many Brazilians, French and British prefer luxury goods without a logo that screams in your face.

And the ultimate luxury item? Researchers asked people what was the one thing that they could buy, if money was no object, and would give them the most pleasure. The number one answer? A luxury car, followed by fine jewelry, designer clothes and gadgets.

1. What's the purpose of conducting such a survey?

    A. To find out how people feel after they buy some luxury items.

    B. To find out what luxury items are the most popular with people.

    C. To find out what determines people's purchasing decisions.

    D. To find out why people would buy luxuries.

2. Why are the survey findings out of people's expectations?

    A. Buying luxuries makes people feel pressure in terms of price.

    B. Many people feel happy with buying luxuries.

    C. Many people are sensible about buying luxuries.

    D. Buying luxuries makes many people feel guilty instead of feeling happy.

3. How do American people feel about buying luxuries?

    A. They feel good about buying luxuries.

    B. 72% of them feel guilty after making their purchase.

    C. About one third of them want to punish themselves after making their purchase.

    D. They tend to be very sensible about spending money.

4. People of which country love showing off their buying luxuries most?

    A. America.

    B. India.

    C. Brazil.

D. Britain.

5. Which of the following statements is true according to the passage?

   A. Luxury goods do not always make people feel good.
   B. A majority in Europe had a conflicted relationship with luxury.
   C. Luxury goods with obvious logo are more popular with British people than with Indians.
   D. If money was no object, jewelries would give people the most pleasure.

Passage Two

The fashion industry makes its mark by setting newer trends in clothing and by influencing the fashion conscious consumers through various means to make them fall in line with those trends. Change is constant and that is how this industry has turned out to be. Since modern day fashion is in a state of flux, one has to keep one's finger on the pulse to catch up with the pace. In fact, setting trends means inducing or luring the consumers to follow the latest in styles and trends. This process has led to a sea change in the popular concept leading the public to treat fashion clothing as a medium to express one's attitudes and status. These fashion goods will get replaced in accordance with the changes in fashion and trends. In other words, these designer clothes are not treated as durable goods that need to be thrown away only when they are unfit to be used.

The male and female models, images of men and women found in magazine covers are some of the images that usually come up when someone mentions the term "fashion". But, there are also people working behind the scenes in an effort to translate the ideas to create apparels that breathe life. Let it be in the creative, technical or business side of fashion industry, there are so many exciting career paths reserved for the creative minds in the world of fashion. Fashion industry is primarily concentrated in the cities of New York, London, Paris, and Italy. While the creative section offers career opportunities for people to work as illustrators, designers, costume designers and stylists, the business side of fashion opens up the future as fashion merchandisers, marketing personnel and trend analysts. And, coming up with brand new and exhilarating ways to design an item of clothing is the most challenging task faced by a fashion designer and the design team.

1. What is the nature of fashion industry?

   A. It intends to induce consumers to follow the latest trend.
   B. Change is constant.
   C. Fashion changes with the season.
   D. Catching up with fashion is a constant task for consumers.

2. Why are those designer clothes not treated as durable goods?

   A. Because fashion styles change constantly.
   B. Because designer clothes are unfit to be used in daily lives.
   C. Because those who can afford designer clothes can't bear using them for a long time.
   D. Because designer clothes are usually used for very special occasions.

3. What will people think of when someone mentions the term "fashion"?
   A. Designer clothes.
   B. Models presented in magazines.
   C. Superstars.
   D. Fashion designers.
4. Who will deal with the business side of fashion?
   A. They finally found Michelangelo the right person for the job.
   B. Models, designers and fashion merchandisers.
   C. Fashion merchandisers, marketing personnel and trend analysts.
   D. CEOs of fashion companies.
5. What is the most difficult task of fashion designers?
   A. To become the focus of mass media.
   B. To induce the consumers to follow the latest styles and trends.
   C. To find sponsorships from big fashion companies.
   D. To have brand new ideas in their designs.

Interactive Tasks

Role-play

13 **Role-play the following situation with your partner.**
Situation:
　　Lucy and Jack, two college students talked about "fashion" during the break. Lucy talked a lot about how to catch up with the latest fashion. Jack didn't agree with her opinions. He holds that to be oneself is the best way to be fashionable.
You may begin like this:
Lucy: Hey, I saw a wonderful movie last night. I enjoyed every minute of the story.
Jack: Oh, what's that?
Lucy: *The Devil Wears Prada*, it's about fashion.
Jack: Aha, I have seen that movie and I do love the ending...

Group Work

14 **Work in groups to do a role play.**
1. Form groups of four or five students;
2. Each group can be subdivided into two groups. The situation is that two or three guest speakers are invited in a talk show. The theme for the show is fashion. One student plays the role of the host or hostess and the other students play the role of guest speakers. In the program each expresses their own understanding of fashion or makes comments on some fashion phenomenon such as Lady Gaga.

Follow-up Task

Writing

15 Directions: For this part, you are going to write a composition on the topic: **What Is Fashion**? You should write at least 120 words following the outline given below in Chinese:

1. 时尚是什么?
2. 有些人认为时尚就是穿最流行的衣服;
3. 有些人不这么认为。

Unit 8　Dancing

Highlight

Topic area	Communication	Skills
Classification of Latin dancing; Benefits of Latin dancing; The Cha Cha dance; Latin dancing costumes; Latin dancing shoes.	coincide with in most cases with the addition of live up to in contrast to with the advent of It is advisable that	Mastering the general situation of Latin dancing; Being able to summarize and discuss the dance Cha Cha; Being familiar with the costumes and shoes for Latin dancing.

Starting-out Task

1 Look at these pictures and discuss the following questions with your partner.

1. Latin dancing belongs to one classification of Ballroom dancing. What category can Latin dancing be subdivided into?
2. The two pictures below are about the famous Blackpool Dance Festival. Have you ever heard of this well-known festival?

3. Are you familiar with the following excellent pair of dancers and their achievements?

Listening Tasks

Micro Listening Skills

2 **Listen to the following passage and try to fill in the missing words**.

Dance is an art form that generally refers to movement of the body, usually 1. _____ and to music, used as a form of expression, social interaction or presented in a spiritual or performance setting. 2. _____ dance refers to a set of partner dances, which are enjoyed both socially and competitively around the world. Because of its performance and entertainment aspects, ballroom dance is also widely enjoyed on stage, film and television. Ballroom dance is divided into two large 3. _____: Modern dance and Latin dance.

The term "Latin dance" may be used in two different ways: to 4. _____ dances that originated in Latin America and to name a category of International style ballroom dances. Many popular dances 5. _____ in Latin America, and so are referred to as Latin dances. International Latin is the name of a category of International style ballroom dances. International Latin 6. _____ of the following five dances: Cha-Cha, Rumba, Samba, Paso Doble and Jive. These dances are now performed all over the world as Latin-American dances in international dance sport competitions, as well as being danced socially.

Known for its 7. _____ hip action and sexy 8. _____, Latin dance is gaining popularity on dance floors everywhere. Movies about Latin dancing, ones that 9. _____ the beauty of the art of Latin dancing, seem to be favorites among dancers and non-dancers alike. Besides being a 10. _____ in the ballroom, many Latin dances are also being taken to country-western dance floors. Learning Latin dances is fairly easy, as most of the dances are made up of the same basic foot steps.

Dialogue

Benefits of Latin Dancing

Betty works in a big company and she often feels a bit stressed and tired. Just now she came across one of her friends Gerry, a dancing enthusiast. She told Betty a lot about the benefits of Latin Dancing and suggested she take Latin dancing lessons.

Words & Phrases

enthusiast /ɪnˈθjuːzɪæst/ *n.*	狂热者
unprecedented /ʌnˈpresɪˌdentɪd/ *adj.*	空前的
peerless /ˈpɪəlɪs/ *adj.*	无与伦比的
fantastic /fænˈtæstɪk/ *adj.*	极好的

3 **Listen to the dialogue and choose the best answer to the following questions.**

1. Which of the following expressions is consistent with the content?
   A. Latin dancing gets its popularity just because of the advent of the dancing shows.
   B. Smiling with your instructor and following students can bring you happiness.
   C. Socializing is not part of the dancing experience.
   D. Latin dancing cannot help you lose weight.

2. Which is more likely to be true according to the dialogue?
   A. Betty doesn't want to work in the big company because of the pressure.
   B. Betty is not satisfied with her present life and would like to change it.
   C. Gerry is a professional Latin dancer.
   D. Gerry is good at any kind of Latin dancing.

3. What does the word "wallflower" in the last sentence exactly mean?
   A. A kind of fragrant yellow or orange or brownish flower.
   B. A disgusting person.
   C. A neglected person.
   D. A sociable person.

4 **Listen to the dialogue again and complete the following sentences with the information you have heard.**

1. It can be a great way to get both _____ and _____ health benefits in a fun atmosphere.

2. Latin dancing is enjoying _____ popularity, with more and more people falling in love with the fast pace and _____.

3. In the Latin dancing lessons, you will be taught to extend your arms, legs and waist as you stretch to create beautiful body lines. This can increase your blood _____, range of motion in your joints and reduce muscle _____.

Reading Tasks

Focus Reading

Pre-reading Questions

1. Have you ever been a member of any dance association? If so, what kind of dance have you learned?
2. Cha Cha is a popular dance with popular music. Can you name any popular and classic Cha Cha music?
3. Do you know any great dancers in Cha Cha field?

Cha Cha Dance

Cha Cha is one of the five standard dances that constitute the Latin American program of international ballroom competitions. Cha Cha has the distinction of being one of the most dominant pop rhythms of the last 40 to 50 years and is characterized as having an upbeat, infectious rhythm, which creates a sense of playfulness and flirtation. Its dynamism towards passion gives the dance the flirtatious look, as well as the energy to sustain the dancers. Vivacious and resplendent, it renders a feeling of lightness and fun.

The dance Cha Cha has its roots in the religious ritual dances of the West Indies. In the islands of the West Indies, there are certain plants that produce seedpods known as cha-cha. These are used to make a small rattle also known as cha-cha. In Haiti the typical voodoo band consists of three drums, a bell and a cha-cha. The cha-cha is used by the leader as a guide instrument or "metronome" to set the time in secular dancing as well as in religious music and singing.

The modern style of dancing the cha-cha-chá comes from studies made by dance teacher Monsieur Pierre, who partnered Doris Lavelle. Pierre, then from London, visited Cuba in 1952 to find out how and what Cubans were dancing at the time. He noticed that this new dance had a split fourth beat, and to dance it one started on the second beat, not the first. The validity of his analysis was well established for that time. He brought this dance idea to England and with his partner eventually created what is now known as ballroom cha-cha-cha which has officially become known as "Cha-cha". Ballroom dancers and dance teachers throughout Europe took notice of it and its popularity rose steadily in Britain, France and Spain.

Rather than coming along as its own distinct dance form or being invented entirely by one founder, Cha Cha came into existence as the byproduct of another two dance forms. It is a derivative of the Mambo through its Latin music and it is also a stepchild of Swing (Lindy, as it is danced with a triple step and a break). Therefore, Cha Cha is a Cuban innovation of the old Latin form. Originally known as the Cha-Cha-Cha, the Cha Cha became popular about 1954. Several steps of Cha Cha coincide with the steps of Rumba and Mambo. The main difference between the dances is that the "slow" steps of the Rumba and the Mambo are replaced with a triple step known as the "Triple Mambo" in the Cha Cha. Typical figures of the cha cha include crossover breaks (also called New Yorkers), spot turns, the cross-body lead, fifth position breaks and the back spot turn also called the natural top.

Like any other Latin Dances, Cha Cha dance steps mainly consist of two simple movements namely: the Back Basic and the Forward Basic Movements. Each forward and backward basic can be considered to contain the following five steps: a break step, a replace step and a triple step chasse. The Cha Cha dance steps are created when the two movements are combined or used jointly and in most cases with slight variations of the body position. A Cha Cha move can be described loosely as a series involving eight steps. A full basic of the cha cha can be thought of as having a forward basic, which takes four beats of music and a backward basic, which takes four beats of music. So, eight beats of music are required to complete one full basic. The basic forward movement is supplemented with various turns, dips and slides. In the Cha Cha dance steps, it is sensible that the lady, who usually faces the man, performs steps that go together with those of the man or else the man will definitely step on her feet. For instance, when the man makes a forward movement with his left foot, the lady's right foot should move backwards and vice versa.

Steps in all directions should be taken first with the ball of the foot in contact with the floor and then with the heel lowering when the weight is fully transferred. When weight is released from a foot, the heel should release first, allowing the toe to maintain contact with the floor. The footwork is ball-flat, ball-flat for all steps. The dancers' hips are relaxed to allow free movement in the pelvic area as a result of the alternate bending and straightening of the knees. The upper body shifts over the supporting foot as the steps are taken (foot moves, body follows). This hip action is called Latin or Cuban motion, which is the essential element of the dance. In the International Latin style, the weighted leg should be straight; the free leg will bend, allowing the hips to naturally settle into the direction of the weighted leg. As a step is taken, a free leg will straighten the instant before it receives weight. It should then remain straight until it is completely free of weight again. Weight must be shifted carefully to make motions appear seamless. Basically, it's not just about the hip movements or the dips and spins; it is how the couple expresses themselves with perfect co-ordination. The beauty of this dance lies in co-ordination and display of graceful movements by the dancing couples.

Cha Cha is danced to the music of the same name introduced by Cuban composer and violinist Enrique Jorrín, who first referred to his music as the "cha-cha-cha". In 1953 the Cuban orchestra "America" started playing the time-honored "Danzon" with a new syncopated beat. This rhythm was developed from the Danzón by a syncopation of the fourth beat. It sounded like a slow Mambo and Cuban dancers used a slight triple hip undulation on the slow count. Gradually this was changed to a triple step on the slow count and the Cha Cha was born. Jorrín's North American tours introduced American Mambo dancers to its close relative, the cha-cha. The Cha Cha was introduced to the United States in 1954, and by 1959 Americans were "gaga over Cha Cha", with dance studios reporting it to be their most popular dance. It is such an "on the beat" dance that you can't help injecting your own feelings into it. By the end of the decade, the cha-cha had become a staple in American dance competitions, clubs and studios, sealing its place as one of the nation's favorite dances. Cha Cha is still the most popular of the Latin dances in the United States today.

It has also been suggested that the name Cha Cha is onomatopoeic and it is derived from the vocal imitation of the sound of the feet in the chasse, which included in many of the steps. This would account for it being called the "Cha Cha Cha" by some people whereas others call it the "Cha Cha". It is danced "Cha Cha" with the accent on the "1" beat. The tempo is fast, sassy and staccato.

Nowadays, Cha Cha dance music can be found in many music genres—from beach music, to hip hop, to rock and roll. In the music, the heavy beat is the one beat, the first beat of the measure. Cha Cha music is written in 4/4 time, with four beats to each measure. The music tempo is usually 110 to 130 beats per minute. For beginners, the best tempo range is 100~110 beats per minute. The music for the international ballroom cha-cha-cha is energetic and with a steady beat. Cha Cha may be danced to Cuban music with a more voluptuous style, because the Cuban cha-cha-chá is more sensual and may involve complex polyrhythms.

Cha Cha is known for its peppy and sensuous steps that weave magic on the floor. With the addition of the cha-cha-cha syncopation you can easily add multiple spins, fancy footwork, hand styling and Cuban Hip motion during the basic step. It helps then to utilize Cha Cha as a time to practice your technique but also your musicality. As you practice it more and more you can deviate from the restriction of doing the basic for a whole song.

Have you ever watched ABC's *Dancing with the Stars* and FOX's *So You Think You Can Dance* with those beautiful costumes, the romance and the infectious Cha Cha music and visualized yourself dancing to that mesmerizing beat? The reality television programs frequently feature Cha Cha and the dance remains one of the most popular Latin American dances in studios and dance halls worldwide. Play with the beat and accent polyrhythm as you dance. So put some cha cha on your iPod and ask the DJ to play some at the club and have fun.

(1,461 words)

Vocabulary

distinction /dɪsˈtɪŋkʃən/ *n.* a distinguishing quality 特质；特点
upbeat /ˈʌpbiːt/ *adj.* pleasantly (even unrealistically) optimistic 乐观的，欢乐的
infectious /ɪnˈfekʃəs/ *adj.* (figurative) easily spread 有感染力的
flirtation /flɜːˈteɪʃən/ *n.* behavior that shows you find someone sexually attractive but are not serious 调情；挑逗
flirtatious /flɜːˈteɪʃəs/ *adj.* behaving in a way that shows a sexual attraction to someone that is not serious 卖弄风情的
dynamism /ˈdaɪnəmɪzəm/ *n.* active strength of body or mind 活力，动态
vivacious /vɪˈveɪʃəs/ *adj.* vigorous and animated 快活的，有生机的
resplendent /rɪˈsplendənt/ *adj.* having great beauty and splendor 光辉的，华丽的
render /ˈrendə/ *vt.* give an interpretation or rendition of 呈现；渲染
ritual /ˈrɪtjuəl/ *adj.* of or relating to or employed in social rites or rituals 仪式的
seedpod /ˈsiːdpɒd/ *n.* a several-seeded dehiscent fruit as e. g. of a leguminous plant [植]心皮
rattle /ˈrætl/ *n.* an instrument that makes percussive noises when shaken 摇响器；拨浪鼓
voodoo /ˈvuːduː/ *n.* a religious cult practiced chiefly in Caribbean countries (especially Haiti)（尤指西印度群岛等地的）伏都教，巫术
metronome /ˈmetrənəʊm/ *n.* clicking pendulum indicates the exact tempo of a piece of music 节拍器
secular /ˈsekjʊlə/ *adj.* concerning those not members of the clergy 世俗的；现世的
validity /vəˈlɪdətɪ/ *n.* the quality of being logically valid 正确；正确性
compact /kəmˈpækt/ *adj.* closely and firmly united or packed together 紧凑的；紧密的
clasp /klɑːsp/ *n.* the act of grasping 紧握；紧攥
sturdy /ˈstɜːdɪ/ *adj.* having rugged physical strength 坚定的；强健的
derivative /dɪˈrɪvətɪv/ *n.* one thing that comes from another thing 派生物，衍生物
triple /ˈtrɪpl/ *adj.* having three units or components or elements 三倍的，三方的
crossover /ˈkrɒsˌəʊvə/ *n.* meeting and crossing 交叉
jointly /ˈdʒɔɪntlɪ/ *adv.* in conjunction with; combined 共同地；连带地
variation /ˌveərɪˈeɪʃən/ *n.* the act of changing or altering something slightly but noticeably from the norm or standard 变化
transfer /trænsˈfɜː/ *vt.* move from one place to another 使转移
footwork /ˈfʊtˌwɜːk/ *n.* the manner of using the feet 步法
pelvic /ˈpelvɪk/ *adj.* of or relating to the pelvis 骨盆的

seamless /ˈsiːmlɪs/ *adj.* perfectly consistent and coherent 天衣无缝的

dip /dɪp/ *n.* lowering briefly（降而复升的）一动

orchestra /ˈɔːkɪstrə/ *n.* a musical organization consisting of a group of instrumentalists including string players 管弦乐队

time-honored /taɪmˌɒnəd/ *adj.* honored because of age or long usage; acceptable for a long time 历史悠久的；久享盛名的

syncopated /ˌsɪŋkəpeɪtɪd/ *adj.* stressing a normally weak beat 切分音的

syncopation /ˌsɪŋkəˈpeɪʃən/ *n.* a musical rhythm accenting a normally weak beat 中略；省略；中间的音节

undulation /ˌʌndjʊˈleɪʃən/ *n.* a movement up and down or back and forth 波动；起伏

gaga /ˈɡɑːɡɑː/ *adj.* marked by foolish or unreasoning fondness 狂热的；疯疯癫癫的

onomatopoeic /ˌɒnəˌmætəˈpiːk/ *adj.* (of words) formed in imitation of a natural sound 拟声的

chasse /ʃæˈseɪ/ *n.* (ballet) quick gliding steps with one foot always leading 快滑步

tempo /ˈtempəʊ/ *n.* (music) the speed at which a composition is to be played 速度；拍子

sassy /ˈsæsɪ/ *adj.* improperly forward or bold 时髦的；活泼的

staccato /stəˈkɑːtəʊ/ *adj.* (music) marked by or composed of disconnected parts or sounds; cut short crisply 断奏的，断音的

polyrhythm /ˌpɒlɪˈrɪðəm/ *n.* having more than one rhythm 多旋律

voluptuous /vəˈlʌptjʊəs/ *adj.* having strong sexual appeal 撩人的

musicality /ˌmjuːzɪˈkælətɪ/ *n.* the property of sounding like music 音乐性；音感

deviate /ˈdiːvɪeɪt/ **from** be out of line with 偏离；脱离（常规等）

Proper Names

Monsieur Pierre	皮埃尔
Doris Lavelle	多丽丝·拉维尔
Mambo	曼波舞
Swing	摇摆舞
Rumba	伦巴舞
Enrique Jorrín	恩里克·乔恩（小提琴家）
Danzon	丹戎舞（古巴）

Text Exploration

5 Choose the best answer to each question with the information from the text.

1. Which of the following statements is right?

    A. The typical voodoo band consists of two drums, a bell and a cha-cha.

    B. The cha-cha is mainly used as a guide instrument in religious music and singing.

    C. Doris Lavelle from London visited Cuba in 1952.

    D. Lindy is danced with a triple step and a break.

Unit 8 Dancing

2. When the man makes a forwards movement with his left foot, the lady should _____?
   A. move backward with her right foot
   B. move backward with her left foot
   C. move forward with her right foot
   D. move forward with her right foot
3. It is also suggested that the name Cha Cha is derived from the vocal imitation of _____?
   A. the sound of the hands
   B. the sound of the feet
   C. the sound of the body
   D. the sound of the drum
4. The Cuban motion is _____.
   A. achieved through the alternate bending and straightening action of the knees
   B. the essential element of the dance
   C. also called as Latin motion
   D. All the above
5. Which of the following event matches the right character?
   A. Doris Lavelle visited Cuba in 1952 to find out how and what Cubans danced.
   B. Monsieur Pierre was a dancer who partnered with Doris Lavelle.
   C. Cuban dancer Enrique Jorrín first referred to his music as the "cha-cha-cha".
   D. In 1954 the Cuban orchestra "America" started playing "Danzon" with a new syncopated beat.
6. What typical figures does Cha Cha include?
   A. New Yorker, spot turns, the natural top.
   B. Crossover breaks, Jive Walk.
   C. Spot turns, the back spot, Samba Locks.
   D. Forward basic movement, back basic movement.
7. Which of the following two dances have much to do with the birth of Cha Cha?
   A. Rumba and Mambo.
   B. Manbo and Lindy.
   C. Rumba and Swing.
   D. Manbo and Samba.
8. According to the text, the beauty of Cha Cha dance mainly lies in _____.
   A. resplendent costumes
   B. experienced dancing skills
   C. flirtatious atmosphere
   D. seamless coordination
9. For beginners, the music tempo of dancing Cha Cha is _____.
   A. 110 ~ 130 beats per minute
   B. 100 ~ 120 beats per minute

C. 100~110 beats per minute

D. 120~130 beats per minute

10. What can you infer from your understanding toward the information provided in the text?

   A. Cha Cha is not as popular as before in the United States today compared with the other Latin dances.

   B. Modern Cha Cha has nothing in common with Cuban cha-cha-chá.

   C. *Dancing with the Stars* and *So You Think You Can Dance* are not dance competition programs.

   D. Both *Dancing with the Stars* and *So You Think You Can Dance* are American programs.

6 Complete the following chart with the information from the text.

Cha Cha	Details
Characteristics	Cha Cha is featured by a(n) _____ rhythm, with a sense of _____.
Origins	Cha Cha has its roots in _____ of the West Indies; Monsieur Pierre from London noticed that this new dance had _____, and to dance it one started on the second beat, not the first. He brought this dance idea to England, later the popularity of Cha Cha dance rose steadily in _____.
Dance steps	Just like the other Latin dances, Cha Cha dance mainly consists of two basic simple movements: _____ and _____. Steps in all directions should be taken first with _____ in contact with the floor, and then with the heel lowering when the weight is fully transferred.
Dance music	Cha Cha dance music can be found in _____ —from beach music to _____.

7 Discuss the following questions with the information from the text.

1. How do you understand that Cha Cha is considered to be one of the most popular among the social Latin-American dances?

2. What is called Latin or Cuban motion?

3. Cha Cha has much in common with Mambo and it is also been called "Triple Mambo". So how much do you know about Mambo?

4. What do you think makes a good dancer?

5. If you've got an opportunity to learn one of Latin Dances, which one will you choose? Try to state your reasons.

Unit 8 Dancing

Vocabulary Expansion

8 Fill in the blanks with the right words given below. Change the form where necessary.

| distinction | validity | undulation | flirtatious | derivative |
| transfer | secular | vivacious | seamless | musical |

1. The choir sings both sacred and _____ music.
2. Being somewhat isolated, the inhabitants of each region developed a _____ economic and cultural character.
3. The English language _____ mainly from the Germanic stock.
4. All elements fuse into a _____ organic whole.
5. We soon saw a field of wheat _____ in the breeze.
6. This statement was made in 1995, but indications are that it would still be _____ now.
7. Frank's efforts at _____ had become tiresome to her.
8. With his natural _____ and stunning technique, he sounded like a fully formed musician twice his age.
9. The patient was _____ to another hospital.
10. It has given me great consolation and delight to see such a _____ younger generation.

9 Choose the word or phrase that best keeps the meaning of the sentence if it is substituted for the underlined word or phrase.

1. The <u>upbeat</u> outlook for jobs and the economy has been seeping into consumer sentiment.
   A. negative   B. upward
   C. optimistic   D. gloomy
2. She had an <u>infectious</u> zest for living, and this remained with her until the very end.
   A. epidemic   B. appealing
   C. contagious   D. everlasting
3. Its <u>compact</u> appearance is a reflection of its inactivity.
   A. firm   B. loose
   C. flexible   D. slack
4. Any <u>sturdy</u> piece of wood or metal will make a lever.
   A. tender   B. brittle
   C. robust   D. healthy
5. It will host the European football championships in 2012, <u>jointly</u> with Ukraine.
   A. corporately   B. respectively
   C. severally   D. apart
6. Giving red envelop to children during Chinese New Year is a <u>time-honored</u> custom.
   A. tempting   B. praisable
   C. remarkable   D. old-line

7. Today, the political world was <u>gaga over</u> the reporting that Hillary Clinton will be secretary of state.

    A. fond of   B. crazy about

    C. scared of   D. concerned about

8. Dark reds and purples are bold colors that make me feel strong and <u>sassy</u>.

    A. modern   B. lively

    C. prevailing   D. fashionable

9. He used elaborate sentences, carefully balanced and <u>resplendent</u> words.

    A. gorgeous   B. obsolete

    C. complicated   D. sincere

10. And once you hit puberty, suddenly there's huge <u>variation</u> in the abilities you have to learn language.

    A. diversion   B. transformation

    C. change   D. conversion

10 Translate the Chinese sentences into English by simulating the sentences chosen from the text.

Chosen Sentences	Simulated Translations	Chinese Sentences
The dance Cha Cha **has its roots in** the religious ritual dances of the West Indies.		研究者说折磨可能根源于怨恨。(**grudge**)
The Cha Cha is very similar to the Rumba and Mambo, so several steps **coincide with** the steps of these dances.		市场有着不同的类型和规模，你的策略应与机遇保持一致。(**strategy**)
The Cha Cha dance steps are created when the two movements are combined or used jointly and **in most cases** with slight variations of the body position.		事实上，世界卫生组织说这是在大多数情况下婴儿在生命的前六个月得到的唯一食物。(**World Health Organization**)
With the addition of the cha-cha-cha syncopation you can easily add multiple spins, lots of shines, fancy footwork, hand styling and Cuban Hip motion during the basic step.		但分析人士表示，由于缺乏熟练工作人员，即使新机场投入使用，机场拥堵的老毛病仍将持续。(**chronic congestion**, **linger**)
As you practice it more and more you can **deviate from** the restriction of doing the basic for a whole song.		没什么可以阻挡我或使我脱离开早晨的送报路线。(**detain**)

Supplementary Readings

11 Passage One①

The Latin dance costumes are exactly similar to the dance form itself—sensual and vibrant. The Latin dance costumes are shiny, colorful and eye-catching. These dance costumes typically follow the shape of the dancers' bodies.

Latin dancewear options for women are just innumerable. The costumes generally have fitted bodices or even halter-tops. The length of the skirt or the dress depends on the style. Asymmetric skirts or dresses that have slits on the side are commonly worn. Colorful ruffles, ruches and bright colors help compliment the sensual dance moves and enhance the overall appearance of the dance. Women's ballroom dance costumes are often very elaborate, matching the attitude of the dance. Picking the perfect costume is all a matter of attitude— your own as well as the mood of the music you are dancing to and the style of the dance. For a waltz, for instance, a woman might wear a sweeping ball gown that flows to the floor, while the same woman would wear a short skirt covered with sequins to dance a Latin dance.

In competitive Latin dance, a man's outfit is simple and is less complicated than a woman's gown, which can include rhinestones, feathers, fringe and more. Latin dancewear for men usually comprises of sleek pants and buttoned or v-neck shirts. Satins and shimmering fabrics are more common, but if you are not comfortable with these, you can pick the fabric of your choice. Latin shirts can come in any color. However, typically used colors for competition are black, white or creme. Some prefer matching their partner's costume color. If the woman is wearing a light blue dress, for instance, the man might wear a blue vest, tie or even shirt. Shirts can come in different shapes and since they are often custom-

---

①This passage is adapted from *How to Learn Latin Dance* by Uttara Manohar at www. buzzle. com and *About Ballroom Dancing Costumes* by Sarah White at www. costumes. lovetoknow. com.

made, the mix-and-match options are endless. Options are zip-up, button-up or a solid top with no openings. They can have a mock turtleneck, V-neck opening or collar. Some have cuffs and rhinestones. Another style option is to place a dark vest over a white button-up Latin shirt for a refined look.

　　Pick out the right outfit based on aesthetic appeal but also the comfort. The most important thing when it comes to choosing a ballroom dance costume is that the dancer should be able to move around comfortably in the outfit. Some dances do not require as much freedom of movement, but when you get into the fast and fancy dances, you'll want to be able to move any way you need to.

1. Which of the following features can appropriately describe the Latin dance customs?
    A. Shiny and plain.
    B. Drab and sexy.
    C. Sensual and attractive.
    D. Colorful and shapeless.
2. Colorful ruffles, ruches, and bright colors cannot help _____.
    A. compliment the sensual dance moves
    B. change the dancer's bodily form
    C. strengthen the dancer's confidence
    D. enhance the overall appearance of the dance
3. "The attitude of the dance" in Para 2 refers to _____?
    A. dancer's own attitude toward the dance
    B. the style of the dance
    C. the mood of the dance music
    D. Dancer's attitude, the mood of dance music and the dance style
4. Which one of the following statements about a man's outfit is correct?
    A. Shirts are often custom-made; the mix-and-match options are endless.
    B. Latin shirts can come in any color, and typically used colors are blue, white or creme.
    C. Latin dancewear for men always comprises of sleek pants and buttoned or v-neck shirts.
    D. A man's outfit must match their partner's costume color.
5. What is the most important thing when one selects the costumes?
    A. The color.
    B. The style.
    C. The length.
    D. The comfortableness.

12 Passage Two[1]

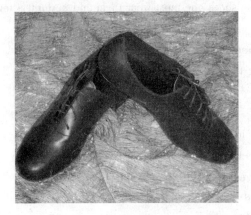

Be it the rumba, the samba, the salsa or the cha cha, Latin dances are known for their grace and sensuality. These dances are full of life and vigor and require the dancers to execute complex steps, while maintaining their balance. It is Latin dance shoes that gain their importance. Not only do they have to look bright and beautiful to live up to the spirit of the dance and the dress, they also have to be flexible and sturdy at the same time.

Dance shoes for women include pumps or sandals with heels within the specified height range (2~3 inches). Pumps are open at the sides, having a closed toe box and an ankle strap that secures the shoe firmly to the dancer's foot. Sandals have straps and are open around the toe area. Many women prefer to wear low heeled shoes initially. However, if one plans to give a public performance or go for formal dancing, casual footwear is an absolute no-no and it is always good to wear proper Latin dance shoes, as they accentuate the appearance of the dancer as well as her steps. These shoes are typically lightweight and have suede soles. They are flexible so that they easily blend with the dancer's feet and are sturdy enough to help her maintain balance as she moves across the floor.

Men wear shoes with Cuban heels that are 1.5 inches high. Like shoes for women, men's shoes are also lightweight with suede soles. They are flexible and provide a firm grip to the dancer. Men's Latin dance shoes can be made from leather, nubuck or patent leather. In contrast to women's shoes, Latin dance shoes for men are somber in color. They usually come in black, white, or brown leather or may have a combination of any of these colors.

It is important to take care of Latin dance shoes in order to keep them in good condition. They should be oiled and polished regularly to prevent them from cracking. The suede soles should be brushed regularly so that they are not ruined from stones, pebbles and dirt that get stuck to them. The best way to take care of one's Latin dance shoes is to avoid wearing them when not dancing.

With the advent of the Internet, the trend of buying shoes online has caught up with

---

[1] This passage is adapted from *Latin Dance Shoes* by Debopriya Bose at www.buzzle.com

people. However, it is always advisable that one buy Latin dance shoes in person. The shoes need to be a perfect fit. Before purchasing these shoes one must wear them and perform a few steps to be able to pick the right fit.

1. Can you figure out the significance of dancing shoes?

    A. They do no good to dancers maintaining their balance.

    B. They are flexible but not sturdy.

    C. They are bright and beautiful.

    D. They can help dancers get the elegance in the steps.

2. Which of the following statements is incorrect?

    A. The heels of dance shoes for women have no specific height range.

    B. Sandals have straps and are open around the toe area.

    C. Pumps have a closed toe box and an ankle strap.

    D. It's not advisable to wear casual footwear in formal dancing.

3. Compared with women's shoes, men's shoes are _____.

    A. heavyweight with suede sole

    B. somber in color

    C. a combination of black and white

    D. much cheaper

4. How to take care of your dance shoes?

    A. Oiling and polishing them regularly to avoid cracking.

    B. Brushing suede soles regularly to avoid getting stuck.

    C. Avoiding wearing them when not dancing.

    D. All the above.

5. Why should one buy the dance shoes in person?

    A. The dance shoes on-line are too expensive.

    B. It's unsafe to buy shoes in the Internet.

    C. Shoes bought in person are more suitable.

    D. Buying shoes online is inconvenient.

Interactive Tasks

Role-play

13 **Role-play the following situation with your partner.**

Situation:

　　Li Lan, a Chinese student in London, is at the dance party specially held for students abroad. Jack, an American boy, is asking her for a dance.

You may begin like this:

Jack: Hi, Li. How nice to see you here! May I have the favor to dance with you?

Li: Hi, Jack. I'm afraid I am not good at dancing.

Jack: It doesn't matter. I am a decent dancer. I can teach you.

Li: Wow! That will be cool!

Group Work

14 **Work in groups to work out your own presentation.**

1. Form groups of four or five students;
2. Each group chooses a topic concerning Latin dancing, e.g.

   A study of one of the five Latin dancing styles;

   An introduction to a couple of famous Latin dancers.
3. Members of each group collect materials from library and the Internet to work out their PPT slides;
4. Based on the PPT slides, each member of the group gives oral presentation of his part.

Follow-up Task

Writing

15 **Directions:** For this part, you are going to write a composition on the topic: **Dancing and Exercising.** You should write at least 120 words following the outline given below in Chinese:

1. 当今人们越来越重视健身,舞蹈则成为了一种时尚健身;
2. 舞蹈的好处;
3. 舞蹈有难度,但比起单调的健身房更有魅力。

Key and Script

Unit 1　Oil Painting

Starting-out Task

1 Look at these pictures and discuss the following questions with your partner.

1. They are *Boy with Basket of Fruit*《抱果篮的男孩》, *Rubens and Isabella Brant in the Honeysuckle Bower*《鲁本斯和伊莎贝拉·布兰特在金银花的凉亭》, *Poppies in Blooming*《罂粟花盛开》, and *Still Life with a Curtain*《静物与窗帘》.
2. *Boy with Basket of Fruit* was a portrait painting by Italian artist Caravaggio who had a formative influence on the Baroque school of painting. *Rubens and Isabella Brant in the Honeysuckle Bower* was created by Flemish Baroque painter Paul Rubens. *Poppies in Blooming* was a landscape painting by Claude Monet, a founder of French impressionist painting. *Still Life with a Curtain* was a still life painting by French artist and Post-Impressionist painter Paul Cézanne.
3. Open-ended.

Listening Tasks

2 Listen to the following passage and try to fill in the missing words and expressions.

1. concentration　2. heroic　3. extended　4. harmony　5. linking　6. break　7. atmosphere
8. expressive　9. contributed　10. uncover

3 Listen to the dialogue and decide whether the following statements are true(T) or false(F).

1. F　2. T　3. F　4. F　5. T

4 Listen to the dialogue again and complete the following sentences with the information you have heard.

1. religion　2. dull; pigments　3. flatter; dimensions　4. recent; realistically　5. landscape

Reading Tasks

Text Exploration

5 Choose the best answer to each question with the information from the text.

1. D　2. B　3. D　4. B　5. C　6. C　7. A　8. C　9. D　10. B

6 Complete the following chart with the information from the text.

Periods	Time Span	Details
Sevillian Period	1611—1621	Velázquez was apprenticed to Pacheco, studying the technique of painting and the work of the Spanish naturalist painters and the great Italian masters; His early works included religious art and bodegones.
Early Years in Madrid	1621—1628	Velázquez was named official painter to the king and chiefly engaged in portraying members of the royal family and their entourage; His art was greatly influenced by Venetian paintings in the royal collection.

(续表)

Periods	Time Span	Details
First Italian Journey	1629—1631	Velázquez closely studied both the art of the Renaissance and contemporaneous paintings; His development in painting skills marks the beginning of a new phase in his career.
Middle Years	1632—1647	Velázquez entered upon the most productive period of his career, during which he painted a series of royal equestrian portraits and a great masterpiece of historical subject, *The Surrender of Breda*.
Second Italian Journey	1648—1651	Velázquez paid another visit to Italy to purchase paintings and antiquities for the royal collection; There he painted several portraits, including two of his most celebrated works—*Juan de Pareja* and *Pope Innocent X*.
Last Years	1651—1660	Velázquez continued to reach new heights as a painter and the young queen Mariana of Austria with her children provided new subjects for him to portray; *Las Meninas* with its complex and enigmatic composition marks the culmination of Velázquez's career.

7 Discuss the following questions with the information from the text.

1. Velázquez's early works comprised *bodegones* and religious paintings, but as a court artist he was largely occupied in executing portraits, while also producing some historical, mythological and further religious works.
2. His painting was affected by the work of Rubens and by Venetian artists, especially Titian, as well as by the experience of two trips to Italy. Under these joint influences he developed a uniquely personal style characterized by very loose, expressive brushwork.
3. The work's complex and enigmatic composition raises questions about reality and illusion, and creates an uncertain relationship between the viewer and the figures depicted, which may result in many interpretations.
4. Open-ended.
5. Open-ended.

Vocabulary Expansion

8 Fill in the blanks with the right words given below. Change the form where necessary.

1. dripped   2. incisiveness   3. prowess   4. unprecedented   5. precocious   6. proceeded   7. humanize
8. apprenticed   9. absorption   10. affinity

9 Choose the word or phrase that best keeps the meaning of the sentence if it is substituted for the underlined word or phrase.

1. C   2. B   3. B   4. D   5. A   6. D   7. B   8. D   9. A   10. B

10 Translate the Chinese sentences into English by simulating the sentences chosen from the text.

1. The new prime minister is universally acknowledged as a farsighted statesman.
2. We are sending out samples in the hope of gaining comments.
3. The company says both models are milestone products that mark the beginning of a new phase in its development.
4. Local legend has it that the monastery was established in the Ming Dynasty.

5. The growth of the Internet has changed the world, making information more accessible than ever before in history.

11 Passage One

1. A   2. B   3. D   4. C   5. B

12 Passage Two

1. D   2. B   3. B   4. D   5. C

Unit 2   Performance Art

Starting-out Task

1 Look at the following pictures and share your opinions about performance art with your partner.

1. They are *Leap into the Void*《跃入虚空》by Yves Klein, *Theatre of Orgies and Mysteries*《纵欲神秘剧》by Hermann Nitsch, and *Relation in Time*《时间关系》by Marina Abramović and Ulay.
2. 行为艺术。
3. Open-ended.

Listening Tasks

2 Listen to the following passage and try to fill in the missing words and expressions.

1. actions   2. body   3. audience   4. object   5. unconventional   6. break down   7. postmodern
8. performer   9. silence   10. free

3 Listen to the passage and choose the best answer to the following questions.

1. A   2. D   3. C   4. B

4 Listen to the passage again and complete the following sentences with the information you have heard.

1. pajamas; fancy   2. feathers   3. organizers; clear-up   4. 130

Reading Tasks

Text Exploration

5 Choose the best answer to each question with the information from the text.

1. C   2. B   3. A   4. D   5. A   6. B   7. A   8. C   9. B   10. D

6 Complete the following chart with the information from the text.

Time Periods	Typical Works	Details
The first part (in early 1970s) She was masochistically confronting herself.	*Rhythm 0*, 1974	She stood totally passive for six hours while members of the public were allowed to do whatever they wanted to her.
	Rhythm 10, 1973	She stabbed knives repeatedly in the gaps between her splayed fingers, often missing and stabbing her hand instead.
	Art Must Be Beautiful, Artist Must Be Beautiful, 1976	She brushed her hair with increasing violence while repeating the mantra: "Art must be beautiful, artist must be beautiful."
The middle part (1976-1988) She was confronting Ulay.	*Point of Contact*, 1977	She and Ulay stared and pointed at each other without moving.
	Relation in Time, 1977	She and Ulay sat back-to-back with their hair braided together.
	Imponderabilia, 1977	She and Ulay stood and faced each other naked in a doorway.
	Nightsea Crossing (in the 1980s)	She and Ulay sat opposite each other, locked in eye contact and without moving, for a total of 90 days.

(续表)

Time Periods	Typical Works	Details
The present part (1988-present) She has been directly confronting the public.	*The House with Ocean View*, 2002	She lived for 12 days without eating or speaking on three raised platforms in a gallery.
	The Artist Is Present, 2010	She sat at the atrium of MoMA, motionless and silent, for three months.

7 **Discuss the following questions with the information from the text.**

1. Abramović surrendered control of her biography to the author without knowing what the result would be, just like her 1974 performance *Rhythm* 0, in which she stood totally passive for six hours without knowing what the public would do to her.
2. In the original, if visitors pass between the two performers they must brush against the two performers while in the re-performance, the performers were placed so far apart that you barely brush against them.
3. She lost control of her emotion and violated the rules of her own performance.
4. Open-ended.
5. Open-ended.

Vocabulary Expansion

8 **Fill in the blanks with the right words given below. Change the form where necessary.**

1. splayed 2. formidable 3. dissolved 4. sapped 5. violating 6. literal 7. vulnerable
8. biography 9. prototype 10. fidgeting

9 **Choose the word or phrase that best keeps the meaning of the sentence if it is substituted for the underlined word or phrase.**

1. A 2. C 3. D 4. B 5. A 6. C 7. B 8. D 9. B 10. C

10 **Translate the Chinese sentences into English by simulating the sentences chosen from the text.**

1. To ensure against defeat, the enemy concentrated a superior force.
2. Most of the new products of the company came out of its collaboration in technology with a foreign university.
3. China's modernization is inseparable from her economic cooperation with other nations.
4. I majored in law at university, with an emphasis on the international law.
5. The tall man that you saw in the canteen was none other than our manager.

11 **Passage One**

1. D 2. B 3. A 4. A 5. C

12 **Passage Two**

1. A 2. C 3. B 4. D 5. C

Unit 3 Drama

Starting-out Task

1 **Discuss the following questions about Western drama with your partner.**

1. Drama is the specific mode of fiction represented in stage performance. The term comes from a Greek word meaning "action", which is derived from "to do". The enactment of drama in theatre, performed by

actors on a stage before an audience, presupposes collaborative modes of production and a collective form of reception.

2. The two masks associated with drama represent the traditional generic division between comedy and tragedy. They are symbols of the ancient Greek Muses, Thalia and Melpomene. Thalia was the Muse of comedy (the laughing face), while Melpomene was the Muse of tragedy (the weeping face).

3. *Oedipus the King* is an Athenian tragedy by Sophocles. The play tells the King Oedipus was doomed to kill his biological father and marry his biological mother. It was the first play of Sophocles's three Theban plays to be performed.

Hamlet, is a tragedy by William Shakespeare. The play recounts how Denmark Prince Hamlet exacts revenge on his uncle Claudius for murdering the old King Hamlet and succeeding to the throne and marrying Gertrude (mother of Prince Hamlet).

Listening Tasks

2 Listen to the following passage and try to fill in the missing words.

1. theatrical   2. satyr   3. dithyramb   4. initiating   5. majestic   6. underscore   7. communal
8. obscenity   9. extant   10. conjectured

3 Listen to the passage and choose the best answer to the following questions.

1. B   2. D   3. D

4 Listen to the passage again and complete the following sentences with the information you have heard.

1. emphasize; reinforce; alter   2. theatrical space; visual   3. automatically

Reading Tasks

Text Exploration

5 Choose the best answer to each question with the information from the text.

1. A   2. B   3. D   4. C   5. D   6. D   7. B   8. A   9. C   10. B

6 Complete the following chart with the information from the text.

Athenian tragedy	Some Details
Origins	Having emerged sometime during the 6th century BCE, it flowered during the 5th century BCE, and continued to be popular until the beginning of the Hellenistic period.
Actors	The playing of multiple roles, both male and female, was made possible by the use of masks, which prevented the audience from identifying the face of any actor with one specific character in the play and helped eliminate the physical incongruity of men impersonating women. The main duty of an actor was to speak the dialogue assigned to his characters. However, he occasionally had to sing songs solo or with the chorus or with other actors.
Chorus	The chorus was non-professionals who had a talent for singing and dancing and were trained by the tragedian in preparation for the performance. The chorus, like the actors, wore costumes and masks. Choral songs in tragedy are often divided into three sections: strophe, antistrophe and epode.
Structure	Tragedy has a characteristic structure in which scenes of dialogue alternate with choral songs. This arrangement allows the chorus to comment in its song in a general way on what has been said and/or done in the preceding scene.

Key and Script

7 Discuss the following questions with the information from the text.
1. Tragedy is a form of art based on human sufferings that offers its audience pleasure.
2. No. When the author's work was approved for presentation at the state religious festival in honor of the god Dionysus, the state assigned him actors and a chorus. He then had to perform the additional tasks of training the actors and chorus and of composing the music for the various songs of the actors and chorus and providing choreography for the chorus.
3. Open-ended.
4. Open-ended.
5. Open-ended.

Vocabulary Expansion
8 Fill in the blanks with the right words given below. Change the form where necessary.
1. deprived   2. tragedian   3. interior   4. Stasima   5. theatrical   6. deserved   7. tetralogy   8. tableau
9. protagonist   10. twofold

9 Choose the word or phrase that best keeps the meaning of the sentence if it is substituted for the underlined word or phrase.
1. C   2. A   3. D   4. B   5. C   6. D   7. B   8. C   9. A   10. B

10 Translate the Chinese sentences into English by simulating the sentences chosen from the text.
1. This building was primarily intended to be a dinning hall.
2. They are usually regarded as spiritual victims of fast-paced jobs which deprive them of learning time.
3. Human growth hormone has never been approved for cosmetic or anti-aging uses.
4. Many children are engaged in extracurricular dramatics.
5. I have periods of mental dullness that alternate with periods of very creative thinking.

11 Passage One
1. B   2. C   3. A   4. B   5. D

12 Passage Two
1. C   2. B   3. A   4. B   5. D

Unit 4   Pop Music

Starting-out Task

1 Look at these pictures and discuss the following questions with your partner.
1. The Beatles were an English rock band, formed in Liverpool in 1960, and one of the most commercially successful and critically acclaimed acts in the history of popular music. From 1962, the group consisted of John Lennon (rhythm guitar, vocals), Paul McCartney (bass guitar, vocals), George Harrison (lead guitar, vocals) and Ringo Starr (drums, vocals). Rooted in skiffle and 1950s rock and roll, the group later worked in many genres ranging from pop ballads to psychedelic rock, often incorporating classical and other elements in innovative ways. The nature of their enormous popularity, which first emerged as "Beatlemania", transformed as their songwriting grew in sophistication. They came to be perceived as the embodiment of ideals of the social and cultural revolutions of the 1960s.
2. Open-ended.
3. Open-ended.

Listening Tasks

2 **Listen to the following passage and try to fill in the missing words.**

1. distribute 2. rhythms 3. originated 4. communities 5. traditions 6. popular 7. country
8. revolves 9. instruments 10. melody

3 **Listen to the passage and decide whether the following statements are true(T) or false(F).**

1. T 2. F 3. T 4. F 5. T

4 **Listen to the passage again and complete the following sentences with the information you have heard.**

1. gained international recognition
2. achieved worldwide fame
3. technically skilled
4. surpassing 175 million

Reading Tasks

Text Exploration

5 **Choose the best answer for each of the following questions.**

1. D 2. D 3. D 4. A 5. A 6. A 7. D 8. B 9. C 10. C

6 **Complete the following chart with the information from the text.**

Music Style	1. The structure of Gaga's music is said to echo classic 1980s pop and 1990s Euro pop music. 2. Gaga draws obvious inspirations from Madonna to Gwen Stefani and her music makes a feature of girlish but sturdy pipes and bubbly beats. 3. According to Music critic Simon Reynolds, Gaga does manage to make audience move and groove at an almost effortless pace.
A Fashion Addict	1. Gaga has her own creative production team which creates many of her clothes, stage props, and hairdos. 2. Gaga wants to combine performance art, pop performance art and fashion together in order to tell a real story that will bring back the super-fan. 3. Gaga wants her imagery to be so strong that fans will want to taste and lick every part of it. 4. The Global Language Monitor named "Lady Gaga" as the Top Fashion Buzzword with her trademark "no pants" coming in at No. 3.
Entertaining and Innovative Performances	1. In The Monster Ball Tour, she wears a revealing leather corset and is "attacked" by a performer in black who gnaws on her throat, causing "blood" to spurt down her chest, after which she lies "dying" in a pool of blood. 2. At the 2010 MTV Video Music Awards, Gaga wore a dress supplemented by boots, a purse and a hat—each fabricated from the flesh of a dead animal.
A Philanthropist	1. After the 2010 Haiti earthquake, Gaga held a concert of The Monster Ball Tour and dedicated it to the country's reconstruction relief fund. 2. After the earthquake and tsunami hit Japan in 2011, Gaga designed a bracelet and the money generated by it went to Japanese relief efforts.

7 **Discuss the following questions with the information from the text.**

1. Open-ended.
2. Open-ended.

3. Open-ended.
4. The objective is to unravel sociologically relevant dimensions of the fame of Lady Gaga with respect to her music, videos, fashion, and other artistic endeavors.
5. Open-ended.

Vocabulary Expansion

8 **Fill in the blanks with the right words given below. Change the form where necessary.**
1. humanitarian 2. echoed 3. trigger 4. adore 5. to unravel 6. provocative 7. evoking
8. dimension 9. inscription 10. inspiration

9 **Choose the word or phrase that best keeps the meaning of the sentence if it is substituted for the underlined word or phrase.**
1. C 2. C 3. A 4. D 5. B 6. A 7. A 8. D 9. B 10. C

10 **Translate the Chinese sentences into English by simulating the sentences chosen from the text.**
1. Though his grades on other subjects are ordinary, he does have great talent for mathematics.
2. His prejudice against women is widely criticized, as is his arrogance in front of media.
3. "Human cloning" has received divided opinions—bringing hopes to those infertile women but posing a dispute on whether it is ethical.
4. In view of the increasing number of unemployment, the government has unveiled some fresh policies with the objective of encouraging self-employment.

11 **Passage One**
1. D 2. C 3. C 4. D 5. B

12 **Passage Two**
1. C 2. B 3. D 4. C 5. B

Unit 5   Film

Starting-out Task

1 **Look at these pictures and discuss the following questions with your partner.**
1. Open-ended.
2. James Francis Cameron, born on August 16, 1954, is a Canadian film director, film producer, screenwriter, editor, and inventor. His writing and directing work includes: *The Spawning* (1981), *The Terminator* (1984), *Aliens* (1986), *The Abyss* (1989), *True Lies* (1994), *Titanic* (1997), and *Avatar* (2009).
   Zhang Yimou, born on November 14, 1950, is a Chinese film director, producer, writer and actor. He is counted amongst the Fifth Generation of Chinese filmmakers, having made his directorial debut in 1987 with *Red Sorghum*. Zhang has won numerous awards and recognitions, with Best Foreign Film nominations for *Ju Dou* in 1990 and *Raise the Red Lantern* in 1991, Silver Lion and Golden Lion prizes at the Venice Film Festival, Grand Jury Prize at the Cannes Film Festival, and the Golden Bear at the Berlin International Film Festival.
3. Venice Film Festival, Cannes Film Festival, Berlin International Film Festival.

Listening Tasks

2 **Listen to the following passage and try to fill in the missing words.**
1. Founded 2. continuous 3. controlling 4. renamed 5. decades 6. collection 7. acquired

8. released   9. corporate   10. oldest

3 **Listen to the dialogue and decide whether the following statements are true(T) or false(F).**

1. T   2. F   3. T   4. F   5. F

4 **Listen to the dialogue again and complete the following sentences with the information you have heard.**

1. highly technical devices
2. be close to real life
3. favorite movie stars
4. fewer and fewer considerations

Reading Tasks

Text Exploration

5 **Choose the best answer to each question with the information from the text.**

1. C   2. B   3. D   4. C   5. A   6. D   7. D   8. B   9. B   10. D

6 **Complete the following chart with the information from the text.**

Time	Details
1940	Bruce Lee was born in San Francisco.
1959	Bruce Lee had to return to his birth country U.S. and find his own way for he got in trouble for fighting with rival martial arts students.
1964	1. Bruce Lee opened his own martial arts school in Seattle. 2. Bruce Lee got married with Linda Emery.
1966	Bruce Lee gained a measure of celebrity with his role in the television series *The Green Hornet*.
1971	1. Frustrated by the snail's pace of earning leading role in Hollywood, Lee left Los Angeles for Hong Kong. 2. Back in Hong Kong, Lee's first film, *Fists of Fury* was released and it set new box office records in Hong Kong.
1972	1. Lee's next film, *The Chinese Connection* broke those records set by *Fists of Fury*. 2. By the end of 1972, Bruce Lee was a major movie star in Asia.
1973	1. On July 20, Bruce Lee died in Hong Kong at the age of 32. 2. Lee's second directorial feature and first major Hollywood project, *Enter the Dragon* was released and it went on to gross a total of over $200 million.

7 **Discuss the following questions with the information from the text.**

1. He exploded American interest in martial arts films, paving the way for later martial arts stars such as Jackie Chan, Chuck Norris and Steven Seagal.
2. Open-ended.
3. The official cause of his sudden and utterly unexpected death was a brain edema. Some claimed he had been murdered. He was also widely believed to have been cursed.
4. Open-ended.
5. Open-ended.

Vocabulary Expansion

8 **Fill in the blanks with the right words given below. Change the form where necessary.**

1. everlasting   2. stereotype   3. icon   4. mesmerize   5. diminish   6. demeanor   7. gregarious

Key and Script

8. spout   9. vengeful   10. acrobatic

9 Choose the word or phrase that best keeps the meaning of the sentence if it is substituted for the underlined word or phrase.

1. C   2. B   3. C   4. A   5. D   6. A   7. C   8. A   9. C   10. A

10 Translate the Chinese sentences into English by simulating the sentences chosen from the text.

1. The thing that made the fans the most excited was that they could get the autograph of Jackie Chan.
2. It is best for him to seek more advice from his parents and teachers.
3. The solutions put forward by the both parties at the meeting sounded good, but they didn't work in reality.
4. Controversy has been surrounding this issue, as some claim that devaluing currency greatly to increase export will be dubious in the long run.
5. The policy was widely believed to stimulate economic growth and decrease inflation.

11 Passage One

1. D   2. C   3. C   4. D   5. B

12 Passage Two

1. C   2. A   3. C   4. C   5. D

Unit 6   Comic and Animation

Starting-out Task

1 Look at these pictures and discuss the following questions with your partner.

1. *Tom and Jerry* is an American series of animated cartoon films, centering on a never-ending rivalry between a cat (Tom) and a mouse (Jerry) whose chases and battles often involved comic violence. *Tom and Jerry* has a worldwide audience that consists of children, teenagers and adults, and has also been recognized as one of the most famous and longest-lived rivalries in American cinema. In 2000, *Time* named the series one of the greatest television shows of all time.
2. *Kung Fu Panda* is a 2008 American computer-animated action comedy film produced by DreamWorks Animation. The computer animation in the film was more complex than anything DreamWorks had done before. *Kung Fu Panda* has received positive reviews from critics in America. It was also well-received in China.
3. Open-ended.

Listening Tasks

2 Listen to the following passage and try to fill in the missing words.

1. tremendous   2. merchandise   3. stationery   4. entertainment   5. impact   6. stimulate
7. contemporary   8. superficial   9. sentiments   10. positive

3 Listen to the passage and decide whether the following statements are true (T) or false (F).

1. T   2. F   3. F   4. T   5. T

4 Listen to the passage again and complete the following sentences with the information you have heard.

1. incredible; great impact on
2. milestone
3. conception and direction
4. utilizing

Reading Tasks

Text Exploration

5 Choose the best answer to each question with the information from the text.

1. C 2. A 3. B 4. D 5. C 6. C 7. B 8. A 9. D 10. A

6 Complete the following chart with the information from the text.

Periods		Representatives	What happened
Before 1910	1890s	Charles-Émile Reynaud	He developed a(n) animation system using loops of 12 pictures.
	1892	James Swinnerton	He published *The Little Bears and Tykes*.
	1893	Richard Outcault	He published the famous *The Yellow Kid*.
	1898	George Méliés	He used animation in his fantasy films.
	1906	J. Stuart Blackton	Produced a three-minute film *Humorous Phases of Funny Faces*.
After 1910	1914	Winsor McCay	He finished *Gertie the Dinosaur* and Gertie was the first cartoon character to show a personality all her own.
	1915	Earl Hurd	He invented cel animation which is the first real breakthrough in animation technology.
	1922	Tony Sarg; Herbert Dawley	Cels were widely used; Animated cartoons showed up frequently in film programs; Ancient "shadow plays" were revived; Animators added color by tinting the film.
	1928	Walt Disney	He added sound to his movie cartoons *Steamboat Willie*.
	1937	Walt Disney	He produced the first full length animated feature film, *Snow White and the Seven Dwarfs*.
	1995	Walt Disney Productions and Pixar Animation Studios	The first full length feature film animated entirely by computer, *Toy Story*, was released.

7 Discuss the following questions with the information from the text.

1. A series of drawings are linked together and photographed by a camera. Each drawing is slightly different to the one before, so when they are played back in rapid succession they create the illusion of movement.

2. With celluloid, the animator could have moving characters on a single stationary frame, making it unnecessary to repeatedly draw the background over and over again.

3. In those days, a single animator was responsible for a single cartoon. There was no time for experiments because an animator had to write the story, create the gags, paint the backgrounds and, at times, even operate the camera.

4. Open-ended.

5. Open-ended.

Vocabulary Expansion

8 Fill in the blanks with the right words given below. Change the form where necessary.

1. fantasy   2. breakthrough   3. slight   4. halt   5. contemporary   6. simulate   7. painstaking
8. counterpart   9. incorporation   10. valid

9 Choose the word or phrase that best keeps the meaning of the sentence if it is substituted for the underlined word or phrase.

1. B   2. C   3. A   4. A   5. A   6. C   7. B   8. B   9. C   10. D

10 Translate the Chinese sentences into English by simulating the sentences chosen from the text.

1. He is, so to speak, a walking dictionary.
2. It is revealed by a research that women exposed to air pollution during pregnancy are more likely to give birth to children with heart defects.
3. It is nothing more than a made-up story.
4. He is ready to go to great lengths to carry out his plan.
5. They decided to call a halt to the match when they found that the ground was very slippery.

11 Passage One

1. D   2. A   3. B   4. D   5. C

12 Passage Two

1. A   2. C   3. B   4. C   5. D

Unit 7   Fashion

Listening Tasks

2 Listen to the following passage and try to fill in the missing words.

1. creative   2. aware   3. mechanics   4. valuable   5. extremely   6. economics   7. curriculum
8. negotiate   9. involved   10. strategies

3 Listen to the passage and decide whether the following statements are true(T) or false(F).

1. F   2. T   3. T   4. F

4 Listen to the passage again and complete the following sentences with the information you have heard.

1. describe a style of clothing worn by most people of a country
2. to change according to the seasons
3. body decoration as a form of nonverbal communication
4. provide mental clues to a person's status and occupational role

Reading Tasks

Text Exploration

5 Choose the best answer to each question with the information from the text.

1. A   2. A   3. D   4. C   5. C   6. B   7. D   8. A   9. C   10. C

6 Complete the following chart with the information from the text.

Fashion industry: sick, stupid and wrong; We should show our contempt.	
Revealed from the study	The fashion industry plays an important role in Britain.
Seen by the author from the catwalk	Models starve themselves to look thin enough; they appear faint and listless;
Presented by Vogue Magazine	An unrealistic, unattainable image of beauty is created and promoted; It is banned by most eating disorder clinics because it leads to a loss of appetite.
Discussed by the book *The Beauty Myth*	There is no objective standard of beauty; Our idea of beauty changes depending on how we want women to be; Women suffer from "guilt about our liberation".

7 Discuss the following questions with the information from the text.

1. The fashion industry's total contribution to the UK economy is estimated to stand at more than 37 billion pounds. And it is the largest employer of all the creative industries in Britain.
2. There are two sets of victims. The first are the women who serve as models in fashion industry and the other are ordinary women.
3. They are the victims of fashion industry. They starve themselves in order to look thin, which in many cases leads to eating disorder or even death.
4. Open-ended.
5. Open-ended.

Vocabulary Expansion

8 Fill in the blanks with the right words given below. Change the form where necessary.

1. release 2. prosperity 3. collapse 4. applauded 5. consumption 6. promoting 7. starved
8. range 9. claimed 10. impulse

9 Choose the word or phrase that best keeps the meaning of the sentence if it is substituted for the underlined word or phrase.

1. C 2. B 3. D 4. B 5. A 6. A 7. C 8. D 9. A 10. C

10 Translate the Chinese sentences into English by simulating the sentences chosen from the text.

1. The passerby peered with curiosity through the railing into the courtyard.
2. In most cases national policies are simply indifferent to the interests of foreigners.
3. I knew he wasn't trustworthy the minute I set eyes on him.
4. Don't go too far in this matter; you may get into trouble if you do.
5. Whether an investment makes sense or not depends on the current market conditions.

11 Passage One

1. A 2. D 3. C 4. B 5. A

12 Passage Two

1. B 2. A 3. B 4. C 5. D

Unit 8 Dancing

Starting-out Task

1 Look at these pictures and discuss the following questions with your partner.

1. Latin dancing can be subdivided into five categories: Cha-Cha, Rumba, Samba, Paso Doble and Jive.

2. The 8-day Blackpool Dance Festival is the world's first and most famous annual ballroom dance competition of international significance, held in the Empress Ballroom at the Winter Gardens, Blackpool, England since 1920. It is also the largest ballroom competition: in 2003, 1,539 couples from 54 countries took part in the festival. As of the early 21st century the festival is held in May. It covers Ballroom and Latin American dancing.

3. Bryan Watson, a South African Latin American dancer and Carmen Vincelj, a German professional dancer formed a partnership from 1999. They are undefeated world champions in the professional category from then until their retirement in 2007, winning an incredible nine times on the trot. Meanwhile, they are also the seven-time Blackpool champions.

Listening Tasks

2 Listen to the following passage and try to fill in the missing words.

1. rhythmic   2. Ballroom   3. categories   4. denote   5. originated   6. consists   7. sensual   8. flair   9. portray   10. staple

3 Listen to the dialogue and choose the best answer to the following questions.

1. B   2. B   3. C

4 Listen to the dialogue again and complete the following sentences with the information you have heard.

1. physical; mental
2. unprecedented; peerless passion
3. circulation; tension

Reading Tasks

Text Exploration

5 Choose the best answer to each question with the information from the text.

1. D   2. A   3. B   4. D   5. B   6. A   7. B   8. D   9. C   10. D

6 Complete the following chart with the information from the text.

Cha Cha	Details
Characteristics	Cha Cha is featured by an <u>upbeat and infectious</u> rhythm, with a sense of <u>playfulness and flirtation</u>.
Origins	Cha Cha has its roots in <u>the religious ritual dances</u> of the West Indies; Monsieur Pierre from London noticed that this new dance had <u>a split fourth beat</u>, and to dance it one started on the second beat, not the first. He brought this dance idea to England, later the popularity of Cha Cha dance rose steadily in <u>Britain, France and Spain.</u>
Dance steps	Just like the other Latin dances, Cha Cha dance mainly consists of two basic simple movements: <u>Basic Back movement</u> and <u>Basic Forward movement</u>. Steps in all directions should be taken first with <u>the ball of the foot</u> in contact with the floor, and then with the heel lowering when the weight is fully transferred.
Dance music	Cha Cha dance music can be found in <u>many music genres</u>—from beach music to <u>hip-hop, rock and roll.</u>

7 Discuss the following questions with the information from the text.

1. Cha Cha is characterized as having an upbeat, infectious rhythm, which creates a sense of playfulness and flirtation. Its dynamism towards passion gives the dance the flirtatious look as well as the energy to sustain

the dancers. All of these features make it popular.
2. The dancers' hips are relaxed to allow free movement in the pelvic area as a result of the alternate bending and straightening of the knees. The upper body shifts over the supporting foot as the steps are taken (foot moves, body follows). This hip action is called Latin or Cuban motion, which is the essential element of the dance.
3. Open-ended.
4. Open-ended.
5. Open-ended.

8 Fill in the blanks with the right words given below. Change the form where necessary.
1. secular 2. distinctive 3. derives 4. seamless 5. undulating 6. valid 7. flirtation 8. musicality
9. transferred 10. vivacious

9 Choose the word or phrase that best keeps the meaning of the sentence if it is substituted for the underlined word or phrase.
1. C 2. B 3. A 4. C 5. A 6. D 7. B 8. B 9. A 10. C

10 Translate the Chinese sentences into English by simulating the sentences chosen from the text.
1. The researchers said the torture might have its roots in grudges.
2. Markets come in different forms and sizes and your strategy should coincide with the opportunity.
3. In fact, the World Health Organization says in most cases it is the only food babies should get during the first six months of life.
4. But analysts said chronic congestion will linger even with the addition of new airports, because of shortages in skilled personnel.
5. Nothing could detain me or make me deviate from my morning route.

11 Passage One
1. C 2. B 3. D 4. A 5. D

12 Passage Two
1. D 2. A 3. B 4. D 5. C

Unit 1 Oil painting

Listening Tasks

Micro Listening Skills

Western painting is in general distinguished by its concentration on the representation of the human figure, whether in the heroic context of antiquity or the religious context of the early Christian and medieval world. The Renaissance extended this tradition through a close examination of the natural world and an investigation of balance, harmony, and perspective in the visible world, linking painting to the developing sciences of anatomy and optics. The first real break from figurative painting came with the growth of landscape painting in the 17th and 18th centuries. Together they developed in the 19th century in a(n) atmosphere that was increasingly concerned with "painterly" qualities of the interaction of light and color and the expressive qualities of paint handling. In the 20th century these interests contributed to the development of a third major tradition in Western painting, abstract painting, which sought to uncover and express the true nature of paint and painting through action and form.

Dialogue

Medieval and Renaissance Paintings

Lucy and Jason are looking around at the local museum.

Lucy: Jason, here are some traditional paintings.

Jason: Really, these are Medieval and Renaissance art.

Lucy: They are different from each other, aren't they?

Jason: Yes, different periods with different styles.

Lucy: How are they different basically?

Jason: Generally speaking, Medieval art's colors are mostly drab and dull because the pigments are mixed with egg yolk. They also have more religious aspects to them. Renaissance art is more realistic and the colors are a lot richer. People are drawn in perspective instead of value of importance.

Lucy: The value of importance? What does it mean?

Jason: It means people are drawn bigger if they are considered more holy.

Lucy: Funny. Which one do you think is the oldest of all?

Jason: The last painting. I guess it's from the early medieval period. Look, everybody has gold halos. The colors are dull. Angels are in the background. Compared with the others, this painting is flatter and there are no dimensions.

Lucy: What about the third picture? The colors are still very simple and drab. Both the child and the adult have halos…

Jason: And the child is a lot bigger than he should be.

Lucy: It is also a medieval painting, isn't it?

Jason: Right. Picture No. 1 is more recent than this one.

Lucy: Yes. The colors are brighter and none of the people have halos.

Jason: It looks like a painting from the early renaissance period.

Lucy: How is that?

Jason: You see the picture is still not drawn very realistically. There is no landscape whatsoever in the painting.

Lucy: The second picture shows a woman in a red gown holding a baby. I like it best.

Jason: It is the most recent and most realistic of all the pictures. There is a landscape of green rolling hills which shows it is more modern than the others.

Unit 2 Performance Art

Listening Tasks

Micro Listening Skills

Performance art is art in which the actions of an individual or a group at a particular place and in a particular time constitute the work. It can happen anywhere, at any time, or for any length of time. Performance art can be any situation that involves four basic elements: time, space, the performer's body and a relationship between performer and audience. It is opposed to painting or sculpture, for example, where an object constitutes the work.

In performance art, usually one or more people perform in front of an audience. In contrast to the traditional performing arts, performance art is unconventional. Performance artists often break conventions of traditional performing arts, and break down conventional ideas about "what art is," similar to the postmodern art movement. Thus, even though in most cases the performance is in front of an audience, in some cases, the audience becomes the performer. The performance may be scripted, unscripted, or impromptu. It may incorporate music, dance, song, or complete silence. The audience may buy tickets for the performance, the performance may be free, or the performer may pay the audience to watch the performance.

Passage

Everybody Going Pillow Fighting

On April 1, 2012, hundreds of people flocked to Trafalgar Square in central London to beat one another over the head. They came dressed in pajamas, dressing gowns and fancy dress to take part in the pillow fight. Most of them carried feather-filled pillows that exploded as they fought.

Some had no sensible reason to be here. "I love this kind of fun," said Tom, surveying the gathering crowd in Trafalgar Square. "I heard about it on Facebook, and just thought, I've got to have some of this."

Others may have thought about it too much. "He's my main target," said Josie, glancing at her boyfriend Sam, "I don't normally get the opportunity to beat him."

The horn sounded. Trafalgar Square was immediately filled with hundreds of swinging pillows and innumerable flying feathers.

Ten minutes after the fighting began, a cheer went up, and the fighting stopped. Thirty seconds later everyone was at war again: they hadn't had enough and did not stop or slow for another hour. Towards the end, the feathers were lifted high into the air by the wind and fell down like snow on the strange crowd.

All this happened in front of smiling police officers who said that the event had been peaceful and they had no reports of any trouble. However, they later said they would attempt to track down the organizers to pay for the clear-up.

Similar scenes were organized in about 130 cities around the world.

Key and Script

Unit 3 Drama

Listening Tasks
Micro Listening Skills

Western drama originates in classical Greece. The theatrical culture of the city-state of Athens produced three genres of drama: tragedy, comedy, and the satyr play. According to Aristotle, Greek drama, or, more explicitly, Greek tragedy, originated in the dithyramb. Tradition has it that at the Dionysia of 534 B. C., during the reign of Pisistratus, the lead singer Thespis of the dithyramb added to the chorus an actor with whom he carried on a dialogue, thus the initiating possibility of dramatic action. Thespis is credited with the invention of tragedy.

Generally, the earlier Greek tragedies place more emphasis on the chorus than the later ones. In the majestic plays of Aeschylus, the chorus serves to underscore the personalities and situations of the characters and to provide ethical comment on the action. The increase in the number of actors resulted in less concern with communal problems and beliefs and more with dramatic conflict between individuals.

Greek comedy is divided by scholars into Old Comedy, Middle Comedy, and New Comedy. The sole literary remains of Old Comedy are the plays of Aristophanes, characterized by obscenity, political satire, fantasy, and strong moral overtones. While there are no extant examples of Middle Comedy, it is conjectured that the satire, obscenity, and fantasy of the earlier plays were much mitigated during this transitional period. Most extant examples of New Comedy are from the works of Menander; these comedies are realistic and elegant, often revolving around a love-interest.

Passage

Some External Factors of Drama

In Oriental theaters, as in classical Greek theaters, costume elements are formalized. A special element is the mask. Although rarely used in contemporary Western theaters, masks were essential in Greek and Roman dramas and are used in most African and Oriental theaters. Makeup may also function as a mask, especially in Oriental theaters, where faces may be painted with elaborate colors and images that exaggerate and distort facial features. In Western theaters, makeup is used for two purposes: to emphasize and reinforce facial features that might otherwise be lost under bright lights or at a distance and to alter signs of age, skin tone, or nose shape. Setting design is the arrangement of theatrical space; setting is the visual environment in which a play is performed. Its purpose is to suggest time and place and to create the proper mood or atmosphere. Lighting design, a more ephemeral art, has two functions: to illuminate the stage and the performers and to create mood and control the focus of the spectators. Until the Renaissance, almost all performances were outdoors and therefore lit by the sun, but with indoor performances came the need for lighting instruments. The most recent development in lighting technology is the memory board, a computerized control system that stores the information of each light cue or change of lights. By pushing one button, all the lights will change automatically to the preprogrammed intensity and at the desired speed. Sound, if required, is now generally recorded during the preproduction period. From earliest times, most theatrical performances were accompanied by music that, until recently, was produced by live musicians. Although music is still the most common sound effect, wind, rain, thunder, and animal noises have been essential since the earliest Greek tragedies.

Unit 4 Pop Music

Listening Tasks

Micro Listening Skills

With 20th century music, there was a vast increase in music listening as the radio gained popularity and phonographs were used to replay and distribute music. The focus of art music was characterized by exploration of new rhythms, styles, and sounds. Jazz evolved and became a significant genre of music over the course of the 20th century, and during the second half of that century, rock music did the same. Jazz is an American musical art form that originated in the beginning of the 20th century in African American communities in the Southern United States from a confluence of African and European music traditions. From its early development until the present, jazz has also incorporated music from 19th and 20th century American popular music. Rock music is a genre of popular music that developed in the 1960s from 1950s rock and roll, rockabilly, blues, and country music. The sound of rock often revolves around the electric guitar or acoustic guitar, and it uses a strong back beat laid down by a rhythm section of electric bass guitar, drums, and keyboard instruments. Along with the guitar or keyboards, saxophone and blues-style harmonica are used as soloing instruments. In its "purest form", it has three chords, a strong, insistent back beat, and a catchy melody.

Passage

Celine Dion

Celine Dion is a Canadian singer, songwriter, and actress. Growing up in a large family in the Province of Quebec, Canada, Dion emerged as a teen star in the French-speaking world after her manager and future husband René Angélil mortgaged his home to finance her first record. In 1990, she released the English-language album *Unison*, establishing herself as a well-known pop artist in North America and other English-speaking areas of the world.

Dion had first gained international recognition in the 1980s by winning both the 1982 Yamaha World Popular Song Festival and the 1988 Eurovision Song Contest. Following a series of French albums in the early 1980s, she signed on to CBS Records Canada in 1986. During the 1990s, with the help of Angélil, she achieved worldwide fame after signing with Epic Records and releasing several English albums along with additional French albums, becoming one of the most successful artists in pop music history. However, in 1999 at the height of her success, Dion announced a hiatus from entertainment in order to start a family and spend time with her husband, who had been diagnosed with cancer. She returned to the top of pop music in 2002 and signed a three-year contract to perform nightly in a five-star theatrical show at the Colosseum at Caesars Palace, Las Vegas.

Dion's music has been influenced by genres ranging from rock and R&B to gospel and classical. While her releases have often received mixed critical reception, she is renowned for her technically skilled and powerful vocals. Dion is the best-selling Canadian artist of all time and is the only female artist to have two singles that have sold more than a million copies in the United Kingdom. In addition, her 1995 album *D'eux*, is the best-selling French-language album of all time. In 2004, after surpassing 175 million in album sales worldwide, she was presented with the Chopard Diamond Award at the World Music Awards for becoming the best-selling female artist of all time. According to Sony Music Entertainment, Dion has sold over 200 million albums worldwide.

Unit 5　Film

Listening Tasks

Micro Listening Skills

Universal Pictures (sometimes called Universal City Studios or Universal Studios for short), is one of the six major movie studios in the world. Founded in 1912, it is one of the oldest American movie studios still in continuous production. On May 11, 2004, the controlling stake in the company was sold by Vivendi Universal to General Electric. The resulting media super-conglomerate was renamed NBC Universal, while Universal Studios Inc. remained the name of the production subsidiary. In addition to owning a sizable film library spanning the earliest decades of cinema to more contemporary works, it also owns a sizable collection of TV shows through its subsidiary NBC Universal Television Distribution. It also acquired rights to several prominent filmmakers' works originally released by other studios through its subsidiaries over the years. Its production studios are at 100 Universal City Plaza Drive in Universal City, California. Distribution and other corporate offices are in New York City. Universal Pictures is the second-longest-lived Hollywood studio; Viacom-owned Paramount Pictures is the oldest by a month.

Dialogue

Mike Invites Barbara to See a Movie

Mike: Hi, How is it doing?

Barbara: Not too bad, yourself?

Mike: Yeah good, I hear that there are heaps of new movies showing right now, you want to go to see movies with me tonight?

Barbara: Movies? Nah, I am not that into movies recently. To tell you the truth, I would rather watch TV at home.

Mike: Why?

Barbara: I reckon the movies nowadays are simply the combination of following things: money, stars, unrealistic plots and highly technical devices. Most movies today are extremely disappointing.

Mike: There is something in what you have said, but there are a few blockbusters which I think are worth watching.

Barbara: I did go to few of so called "blockbusters", but I really don't like them. They are not worth the money we pay for tickets. What was wrong with all those screenwriters and directors?

Mike: I get what you mean, but watching movies is mainly for relaxing, as long as you enjoy its nice presentation and watch your favorite movie stars, that would be worth it.

Barbara: I am afraid I can not agree with you. Movie should be close to real life and it should mean something. In other words, movies should have artistic and educational values besides entertainment values.

Mike: Perhaps we can not expect a movie to bring us so many things. Nowadays, more and more producers give priority to box office while fewer and fewer considerations are given to artistic values.

Barbara: It is so terrible! If the trend continues, the industry will go to a dead end. After all, a movie is expected to stir something in viewers' mind in addition to delivering its visual impact on viewers only.

Mike: It is true that many movies nowadays are too commercial, but there are still some movies which can satisfy your need. Why not go with me tonight to find a good movie?

Barbara: Anyway I will go through some movie with you tonight and see how it goes. We may encounter an impressive one if we are lucky enough.

Mike: What will you prefer tonight? Ethical movie, horror movie or comic movie?

Barbara: I'd like to see an ethical movie and I am hoping something in the movie will touch me. What about you?

Mike: I love ethical movie too. I am sure that we will be lucky enough tonight.

Barbara: What time and where shall we meet?

Mike: I will pick you up at seven.

Barbara: All right. Good-bye.

Unit 6   Comic and Animation

Listening Tasks

Micro Listening Skills

Japanese animation enjoys tremendous popularity in Asia where it has become a mainstream youth culture due to cultural and geographical proximity(亲近). Take Singapore for example. Japanese television cartoons are extremely popular among primary and secondary school students, who rushed home to watch this animation and bought *Macross* merchandise, such as stickers and stationery. Following the global popularization of Japanese animation, it seems that the popularity of Japanese cartoons will continue to grow. In many ways, Japanese animation represents a popular form of entertainment, consumer culture and youth culture, and its impact on Singapore society and culture is not yet very strong. To a certain extent, Japanese animation, together with other forms of Japanese popular culture, helps to stimulate the consumption of Japanese products and the interest in Japan among young Singaporeans. Through Japanese animation, Singapore viewers come to know more about contemporary Japan, although their understanding is usually superficial and stereotyped. More importantly, unlike old-generation Singaporeans who have anti-Japanese sentiments due to their war experiences, young Singaporeans in general are positive about Japan out of their passion for Japanese popular culture.

Passage

Walt Disney

Disney has provided an incredible amount of entertainment since the 1930s and has had a great impact on many of our childhoods. There are so many moments of humor, fear, tragedy and hope in the output of the studio, always pushing us to a noble ending, where good triumphs over evil.

Walt Disney is universally recognized as the pioneer of classic American animation. It began creating animated characters as early as 1923. The first sound cartoon starring Mickey Mouse, *Steamboat Willie*, followed later in 1928.

Talent, ingenuity and hard work allowed Disney and his legendary team to develop techniques which would define the future of animation. Disney's revolutionary animation accomplishment, *Snow White and the Seven Dwarfs* was recognized at the Academy Awards ceremony in 1937 when Shirley Temple presented Disney with a special Oscar: one large statuette flanked by seven smaller ones. Snow White serves as an animation milestone, marking the beginning of the Golden Age of animation.

For five decades, Disney continued to create new levels of animation achievements by introducing new techniques to the art of animation. The most notable innovations of this period include the use of live action and animated characters in the same scene, the advent of stereophonic sound and many others. More than twenty years after his death many of Walt's contributions to the field of animation are still used today—a fact which shows both his influence and his tremendous ingenuity.

During his lifetime, Disney remained personally involved with the conception and direction of all feature-length animated films. Walt's legacy and dreams continue to thrive to this day: With the release of feature length animated films such as *Toy Story*, Walt Disney Studios continues to pioneer and develop ground-breaking animation techniques utilizing the latest in technology.

Unit 7 Fashion

Listening Tasks

Micro Listening Skills

It's not enough for a designer to be creative; you also have to have some business sense. As fashion gets more and more corporate driven, it's important to be aware of the business climate and understanding the mechanics behind it. By religiously reading trade papers like *Women's Wear Daily* you will get a lot of valuable information. If you want to run your own company, you need to be extremely organized and learn at least the basics of economics. A lot of fashion schools are currently increasing business classes in their curriculum. "Our students have to be smart enough to know how to negotiate a contract, or to pick a business partner," says Carol Mongo. It's perhaps telling that many of the designers that are really successful today, like Calvin Klein or Tom Ford, are involved in every aspect of the business—from licensing strategies to ad campaigns to actually designing the clothes.

Passage

What Is Fashion?

Fashion is a term, which is referred to as a state of mind. This word comes from Latin word, which means, "to make." Fashion is most commonly associated with clothing, but it even applies to anything from interior architecture to models of toys.

However, fashion is commonly used to describe a style of clothing worn by most people of a country. Thus, as the word goes, fashion is generally associated with, textile, garments and trends. It is a way of celebrating the diversity and variety of the world in which we live. A fashion remains popular for the period of time that a large segment of society accepts it; that could be for a few months or years. However, it is normal for the fashion trends to change according to the seasons. For instance, during summers the common colors worn are the pastel shades and lighter fabric. In winter, the preferred color ranges are the darker and brighter ones and the fabric is heavier.

For centuries individuals or societies have used clothes and other body decoration as a form of nonverbal communication to indicate occupation, rank, gender, locality, class and wealth. Fashion not only embraces clothing, but also hairstyles. So body art, shoes, bags, jewelry and beauty products all constitute today's fashion trends.

What we wear and how and when we wear it, depicts our personality for changing situations. It is from the clothes a person wears that we get our first impression of personality. They provide mental clues to a person's status and occupational role, as well as being a means of conforming to peer group expectations. Fashion is important to us because it's a means of self-expression. It helps to identify ourselves with a group of others like us—whether it's a lifestyle, a religion, a profession, or an attitude. Thus, there are many reasons we wear what we wear.

Unit 8 Dancing

Listening Tasks

Micro Listening Skills

Dance is an art form that generally refers to movement of the body, usually rhythmic and to music, used as a form of expression, social interaction or presented in a spiritual or performance setting. Ballroom dance refers to a set of partner dances, which are enjoyed both socially and competitively around the world. Because of its performance and entertainment aspects, ballroom dance is also widely enjoyed on stage, film and television. Ballroom dance is divided into two large categories: Modern dance and Latin dance.

The term "Latin dance" may be used in two different ways: to denote dances that originated in Latin America and to name a category of International style ballroom dances. Many popular dances originated in Latin America, and so are referred to as Latin dances. International Latin is the name of a category of International style ballroom dances. International Latin consists of the following five dances: Cha-Cha, Rumba, Samba, Paso Doble and Jive. These dances are now performed all over the world as Latin-American dances in international dance sport competitions, as well as being danced socially.

Known for its sensual hip action and sexy flair, Latin dance is gaining popularity on dance floors everywhere. Movies about Latin dancing, ones that portray the beauty of the art of Latin dancing, seem to be favorites among dancers and non-dancers alike. Besides being a staple in the ballroom, many Latin dances are also being taken to country-western dance floors. Learning Latin dances is fairly easy, as most of the dances are made up of the same basic footsteps.

Dialogue

Benefits of Latin Dancing

Betty works in a big company, and she often feels a bit stressed and tired. Just now she came across one of her friends Gerry, a Latin dancing enthusiast. She told Betty a lot about the benefits of Latin Dancing and suggested her take Latin dancing lessons.

Gerry: Hi, Betty. How's everything going? You seem not to be in mood.

Betty: Hi, Gerry. Just so-so. I've been a lot tired and stressful these days.

Gerry: Well, You need more energy and passion in your life. I suggest you learn Latin dancing. It can be a great way to get both physical and mental health benefits in a fun atmosphere.

Key and Script

Betty: Sounds a good idea. Tell me more about it, OK?

Gerry: Well, Latin dancing is enjoying unprecedented popularity, with more and more people falling in love with the fast pace and peerless passion.

Betty: Why is Latin dance becoming so popular?

Gerry: Part of Latin dancing's popularity can be traced directly to the advent of competitive dance shows like *Dancing with the Stars* and *So You Think You Can Dance*. It is hard to miss the buzz around the television shows. They can be the best friends in your spare time.

Betty: Wow, I will try. So what exactly can I get through Latin dancing?

Gerry: In the Latin dancing lessons, you will be taught to extend your arms, legs and waist as you stretch to create beautiful body lines. This can increase your blood circulation, range of motion in your joints and reduce muscle tension.

Betty: Then I can release a whole day's exhaustion and get refreshed.

Gerry: Surely. Let go and forget one day's worries. Also sharing a smile with your teacher and fellow students can translate to a good mood in an instance.

Betty: That's great!

Gerry: Yes, meeting new people and socializing is part of the dancing experience!

Betty: But I am not so confident in dancing.

Gerry: Take it easy. It will start with basic moves. You just do it following your instructor.

Betty: Mm, but I am a little overweight.

Gerry: That's another benefit to learn Latin dancing. Latin dancing in particular can burn off extra calories. It can help you lose weight and make you more charming and confident.

Betty: Really? That's fantastic!

Gerry: Just imagine it: Listening to the beat of the music and dancing socially in public shows.

Betty: Cool! After learning Latin Dancing, I won't be a wallflower any more.

Translation of the Texts

Unit 1 Oil Painting

迭戈·委拉斯开兹——西班牙的面孔

西班牙17世纪最重要的画家迭戈·委拉斯开兹是举世公认的全世界最伟大艺术家之一。他所接受的自然主义风格的训练为他在描绘人物和静物时所显现的敏锐观察力提供了一种表达语言。对16世纪威尼斯绘画的研究使他从一个忠于真实再现与形象刻画的高手发展为当时独一无二的视觉印象杰作的创造大师。

委拉斯开兹出生于塞维利亚一个小贵族家庭,12岁时,他在帕切科处当学徒。帕切科是一位平庸的画家,但深谙艺术理论。委拉斯开兹在帕切科的学校度过了五年,学习绘画技巧,了解历史和艺术理论。在那里,他开始接触到塞维利亚文化界以及西班牙自然主义画家和意大利大师的作品。

委拉斯开兹格外早熟,十几岁时,他的绘画作品已显现出令人瞩目的气势和对技术的全面把握。他遵循了老师关于"向自然学习一切"的教导,在《圣灵感孕》、《贤士来拜》等宗教画作中他采用了更加生动的艺术手法,其中的人物没有塑造成理想化的类型,而是进行了肖像画般的处理。这些作品中强烈的明暗对比和自然主义风格显示出与卡拉瓦乔作品的相似之处,但柔顺、凝练的笔法则完全属于委拉斯开兹本人的特点。他的早期作品还包括一些风俗画,他赋予了它们庄重和尊严的新特点。其中最有名的是《塞维利亚卖水人》,作品对构图、色彩、光线的控制,对人物自然神态和静物写实的把握,已经显露出他敏锐的眼光和极熟练的用笔。画面中从水壶滴落下来的水滴,有着几乎触手可摸的真实感,显示了他非凡的创造力。

1622年,委拉斯开兹怀着获得王室赞助的希望第一次访问马德里。他画了诗人贡戈拉的肖像,但没有机会为国王或王后作像。次年,他被腓力四世的首相召到马德里,为腓力四世画了一幅肖像,腓力四世大为赞赏,任命他为宫廷画家。这样,在24岁时,他一跃成为西班牙最有名的画家,而且此后他一直受到国王的喜爱。

在成为宫廷画家之后,委拉斯开兹的创作方向发生了改变。他完全放弃了风俗画,尽管在整个绘画生涯中,他偶尔还会创造一些历史、神话、宗教题材的画作,但从现在起他基本是一名肖像画家,为王室和他们的随从画像。搬到马德里后他的绘画技术也有了变化,在王室收藏的威尼斯画派作品的影响下,他的用色变得明亮起来,笔触更加阔大流畅。虽然他的国王和大臣画像依然庄严尊贵,他却赋予这种拘谨刻板的传统西班牙宫廷肖像画以更多的人性,让模特摆出更自然的姿态,使他们更具活力和个性。

1628年彼得·保罗·鲁本斯因外交使命出访马德里的王宫。尽管这位伟大的佛兰芒画家没有直接影响年轻画家的风格,他们的谈话却激发了委拉斯开兹参观意大利艺术藏品的愿望,这些艺术藏品深受鲁本斯的推崇。

1629年8月,委拉斯开兹离开巴塞罗那前往热那亚,两年中的大部分时间都用于意大利之旅。从热那亚,他去了米兰、威尼斯、佛罗伦萨、罗马,于1631年1月从那不勒斯返回西班牙。在游历中,他仔细研究了文艺复兴时期的艺术和当时的绘画,临摹了许多著名作品。旅行中创作的一些作品证明了他对这些风格的吸收,其中有名的一幅作品《约瑟和他的兄弟们》就融合了米开朗基罗雕塑的特点与意大利大师的明暗对比绘画法。在意大利的访学,使他在处理空间、透视、光线和色彩方面有了进步,技法更加全面,这标示着他在追求真实再现视觉表象的终生事业中一个新阶段的开始。

从意大利返回后,委拉斯开兹进入了他艺术生涯中最多产的时期。为了装饰新的王宫御室,他画了一批王室成员的骑马像。委拉斯开兹的骑马群像有一种均衡感，在动态上更接近提香，而不是鲁本斯的巴洛克构图。他没有采用细节的刻画和光与影的强烈对比，而是运用阔大笔触和室外自然光，达到三维空间的效果。

《布雷达的投降》是委拉斯开兹唯一留存下来的历史题材作品，也是他献给同一御室记述军事胜利的著名绘画系列之一。该画的灵感来源于他第一次访问意大利与史宾诺拉结伴而行的经历，后者于1625年征服了荷兰小城布雷达。虽然复杂的构图是以鲁本斯的一种绘画样式为基础，但他透过精确描绘地形细节和逼真传神的主要人物创造出一种生动的真实感与人物的戏剧性效果。

1648～1651年委拉斯开兹进行了第二次意大利旅行，此行的目的是为国王购买油画和古董。在罗马他画了几幅画，其中有他最知名的两幅作品——《胡安·德·帕雷哈》和《英诺森十世》。《胡安·德·帕雷哈》是一幅绝无仅有的非正式肖像画，画得异常大胆，产生出一种亲密而又生动的强烈效果。在画教皇之前，为了练习头部写生，委拉斯开兹给他的仆人胡安·德·帕雷哈作了这幅肖像。《英诺森十世》被公认为全世界最出色的肖像杰作之一，它在油彩的处理和性格的深入刻画方面，令人惊叹、无可比拟。传闻当教皇看到已完成的画像时，有些不安地惊叫了一声"太真实了！"这幅画长期以来一直是委拉斯开兹在西班牙境外最著名的肖像画被无数次复制，很快他在意大利获得长久的声誉。

在马德里的最后几年中，委拉斯开兹继续创造了绘画的新高度。他晚期风格中的形式、质感和装饰物都在一种没有任何细节限制的自由"速写般的"技法中完成。他最后的肖像主要为年轻的新王后——奥地利的玛丽安娜和王室里的孩子所作。在这些作品中，他的笔触越来越灵动自由，模特穿着的华服使他有机会表现出作为一个色彩大师的实力。委拉斯开兹一直将创作植根于他对外部的仔细观察之上，但手段变得越发地微妙，细节完全服从于整体效果。因此，他的晚期作品对空间和氛围的表现有着前所未有的生动，但近距离观察时，画中有形的实体会渐渐消融变成肯尼斯·克拉克所说的"美丽笔触的大杂烩"。

委拉斯开兹职业生涯的巅峰是《宫娥》，又名《国王一家》。该作品显示他正在作画，王室成员及其随从都在他画室里的场景。但不清楚的地方在于，他表现的是为国王、王后画像时被玛格丽塔公主和她的宫女打断的情景，还是恰好相反的情景。这幅作品复杂、谜一般的画面提出了关于现实与虚幻的问题，在观者和画中人之间创建了一种不确定关系。在独特的人物构图中，几乎真人大小的人物需要多少细节是根据与中心人物小公主的关系及光源确定的，它所产生的一种非凡的真实世界的幻象再没有被委拉斯开兹本人或其他任何这个年纪的艺术家所超越。由于它的复杂性，《宫娥》一直是西方绘画中被广为分析的作品之一。

委拉斯开兹于1660年8月6日去世，当时他的学生或直接的追随者很少。像大多数西班牙画家一样，在拿破仑战争将西班牙带进欧洲事务主流之前，委拉斯开兹在本土之外很少为人知晓。1819年开放的普拉多博物馆展出了他的44件画作，使得了解他的创作比以往更加方便。自19世纪中叶开始，他在绘画技术上的自由风格成为许多前卫艺术家的灵感，特别是马奈，更视其为最伟大的画家。

Unit 2　Performance Art

"我要像一座山"

2010年3月14日，63岁的行为艺术女皇玛丽娜·阿布拉莫维奇身穿深蓝色拖地长裙，面色极其苍白，在纽约现代艺术博物馆高耸的中庭里的一张小桌子旁坐了下来。在接下来的3个月时间里，她会每天坐在那里，一动不动，一言不发，直到闭馆。这是她的名为《艺术家在场》的回顾展的延续，这也是现代艺术博物馆首次举办的行为艺术家的艺术生涯回顾展，这场展览同时在该馆六楼展出。在中庭里，阿布拉莫维奇让她的展览名称与事实相符。公众可通过坐在她对面的空椅子上来分享她的在场，他们和她面对面用眼神交流，想坐多久就坐多久，或者说能坐多久就坐多久。

艺术类研究生英语教程

"我要像一座山，"几天前，就在这位艺术家进入"完全安静"的表演状态前，她对我这样说。每天晚上闭馆之后她会回家，但为了维持沉思冥想的状态，她在5月31日前不会说话。"中央大厅是这样一个浮躁的地方，到处都是人，走来走去，声音嘈杂，太大、太吵。像龙卷风。我努力在其中表演安静。"

而在我和阿布拉莫维奇谈话时，她却一点也不安静。她习惯性的焦虑和亢奋——完全不同于她在40年的极端忍耐表演中所展现出的惊人自控力和平静——表现得特别明显。"人们意识不到，坐那么久实在是受罪。"她坐立不安，用浓浓的塞尔维亚口音说道。大约一个小时后痉挛开始，她的臀部开始感觉痛了，但是她能够忍受痛苦。"我从未有过失败的念头。"她坚持说。为确保克服这些困难，每天表演前和表演后，按摩师、营养师和私人教练都会造访她的公寓。

我和这位艺术家的会面是一年内和她的第一次见面，这一年里，我完成了她的传记。现在传记终于完成了（历经三年的广泛采访和研究，还有在这之前做了她四年助手，后来为了写作才放弃），她对书的评语是："我决不会再让任何人写我的传记了。"我们不禁哑然失笑，而她本人则是相当认真的。想到几天后不可避免地与她隔桌相对的那一刻，我开始有些畏缩了。

阿布拉莫维奇的结论也验证了（她以前的表演）：这本书始终应该是既亲密无间又挑剔批判，我并非是应她的要求或得到她的许可才写的，然而又的确依赖她的配合才能完成。我逐渐想到，这本书的写作过程就像她1974年名为《节奏0》的行为艺术作品，在那件作品中，她站立六个小时，其间观众可以任意摆布她的身体，旁边的桌子上摆放了很多物品供观众取用，包括锁链、羽毛、一部宝丽来一次成像照相机、橄榄油、剃须刀片、一把斧子、一枝玫瑰、一把枪和一颗子弹，等等。她完全任由我来写她的传记，却不知道结果会怎样。她只能相信我不会像《节奏0》中有位观众所做的那样，拿枪指着她的脖子。

回顾展开幕那天，在我排队去和阿布拉莫维奇对坐之前，先去看了看展览，有录像、照片和一些物品，都是关于她在20世纪70年代早期创作的第一批行为艺术作品。在这些展品中，纤弱而羞涩的年轻艺术家表演了一系列的作品，比如：摊开手指，用小刀在指缝间不断地扎刺，时而扎到手，时而扎不到。（《节奏10》，1973）还有，1976年，她一边用力梳着头发，一边口中念念有词："艺术必须是美丽的，艺术家必须是美丽的。"（《艺术必须是美丽的，艺术家必须是美丽的》）

她为什么要做这些表演呢？我后来逐渐认识到这些表演是艺术家对生活中压抑的一种报复。在军人母亲的严格家庭管制下长大，阿布拉莫维奇用身体艺术来创造出比她自己所遭受过的更为极端的规则。用这种办法，她可以宣示一种另类的自由。

在现代艺术博物馆中，阿布拉莫维奇的多数作品（包括现场表演片断和纪录片），都选自她1976～1988年间和德国艺术家乌雷在爱情和艺术上的合作。本次展览中，这些片断由一群热心的年轻艺术家来重现：一对夫妻四目相对，手指指向对方，一动不动（《触点》，1977）；另一对夫妻背靠背坐着，发辫结在一起（《时间关系》，1977）；另外还有两人在门口裸体面对面站着（《无法估量之物》，1977）。你可以从这两人中间穿过，但现代艺术博物馆对原作品进行了修改，两名表演者的距离较远，你在通过时几乎不会碰到他（她）们的身体。

然而，比起现代艺术博物馆习惯性的过度小心，更严重的问题是：这些重现无法再现原作品的大胆、创伤和感召力。阿布拉莫维奇的作品与她和乌雷两人的情史和个人魅力是分不开的。这里看到的片断似乎削弱了原作品的不可预见性和奇异性。

回顾展的乌雷时期包括《夜海穿越》的照片，这也是阿布拉莫维奇此次3个月久坐的灵感来源。20世纪80年代，她和乌雷相视对坐，一动不动，在全世界的博物馆总共表演了90天。如果说在她艺术生涯的前期，她以自虐的方式直面她自己，那么在中期，她则是直面乌雷。而自1988年起，她开始直面公众，虽然表演的重点由痛楚转为真实在场。《海景房》（2002）是她此次在中央大厅表演的另一个原型：在一家美术馆里吊起的三块平台上，艺术家生活了12天，期间不吃饭也不说话。唯一支持她的就是维持和观众的眼睛接触。

所以，在中央大厅所发生的事情背后，有不可抗拒的历史原因。在开幕那晚，历史重新拜访了阿布拉莫维奇，那天逐次坐在她对面的是一群行为艺术家同行：谢德庆（无可争议的忍耐之王，20世纪80年代时曾以长达一年的行为艺术表演闻名于世）、奥地利女权主义者（也是玛丽娜的朋友）瓦莉·艾丝波尔，还有琼·乔纳斯，在阿布拉莫维奇这一代艺术家中，也许只有她在20世纪70年代后还在从事行为艺术。

利用两名坐者之间的时间间隔，阿布拉莫维奇低下头，闭上眼，她要恢复眼神，重新积聚力量。当她再次抬头时，坐在她对面的不是别人，正是乌雷。整个大厅霎时因狂喜而陷入寂静。阿布拉莫维奇顿时潸然泪下，前几秒钟竟难以直视乌雷平静的目光。这时的她由超级英雄变成了小女孩——谦卑地笑着，痛楚而脆弱。当他们最终四目相对时，阿布拉莫维奇已泪流满面。几分钟后，她违背了她自己的表演规则，双手伸过桌子去握住乌雷的手。这是一幕感人的和解场面——在他们分手22年之后。

随着越来越多的人坐在阿布拉莫维奇对面，已经可以清楚地看出她绝不是一座山——原本就很困难的表演因她的虚弱而更令她疲惫不堪。但这场表演明显的精神支柱是：还有什么能比同渴望交流的公众对视3个月更好的吗？还有什么样的人际交流比这更深刻吗？

排了90分钟的队之后，终于轮到我坐在她对面。刚一坐下，我立刻感到震惊，不是因为她眼神的力量，而是因为她眼神的虚弱。她面带蒙娜·丽莎式的含蓄微笑，开始哭泣。不知为何，这却加强了我的眼神，我要做这座山。10分钟之后，我开始享受我们之间这种无声的交流了。然后，突然，我的头不由自主地垂了下去，仿佛阿布拉莫维奇向我发射了一束激光，于是这一刻结束了。

Unit 3　Drama

雅典悲剧

悲剧是戏剧中的一个特定传统，它在西方文明自我定位的历史长河中扮演着独特而重要的角色。它是一种取材于人类不幸遭遇而带给观众娱乐的艺术形式。悲剧强调的是人类的脆弱性，主人公的遭遇通常是由人、神共同导致的结果，但就其严重性而言，又是不该承受之重。悲剧的结局并不完全是悲观的。虽然许多悲剧是以主人公悲惨的结局收场，但是也有些深陷悲惨处境而最终得到善果。

悲剧是起源于早期雅典的公共题材。雅典悲剧是现存最古老的悲剧形式，是一种舞蹈戏剧，它是构成城邦戏剧文化的重要部分。悲剧出现于公元前6世纪的某个时期，盛行于公元前5世纪，并一直流行到希腊早期。

悲剧旨在剧院里呈现给观众。私下的阅读则剥夺了我们对悲剧的视觉和听觉效果。"剧院"一词是由希腊语演变而来的，它包含了"作为观众观看"之意。戏剧是一个希腊词汇，意为"动作"，和动词"做"有关。悲剧作家并不仅仅是脚本的写作者。当他的作品被批准在纪念酒神迪奥尼索司举行的国家宗教节日中演出时，国家就指派给他演员和合唱队。悲剧家就得开始训练演员和合唱队，为演员和合唱队的不同歌曲谱写音乐，并为合唱队编舞。

雅典悲剧在每年3月末、4月初的国家宗教节日中演出。演出以竞赛的形式举行，由掌管迪奥尼索司城的执政官选出3位剧作家。他们在接下来的3天中呈现自己的作品。每一位悲剧作家利用一个上午展现一部四联剧，包括三场悲剧和一场滑稽羊人剧。

演出似乎是向所有公民开放的，包括妇女，但是证据不足。迪奥尼索司剧院像所有的古希腊剧院一样，是一个露天剧场。由于缺乏足够的人工照明，演出在白天举行。夜间的场景只能通过演员和合唱队的表演来识别；观众得通过他们的话语暗示来想象。一般而言，悲剧情节可以在露天剧院很好地呈现，而当今室内剧场中很普遍的室内场景在悲剧中是不存在的。悲剧中的情节通常发生在宫殿和庙宇前以及其他的户外场景中。对于古时的观众来说，这似乎是很自然的事情，由于爱琴海地区有着

169

相对温和的气候，希腊的公共事务，不论是公众的还是宗教的，就同希腊人的大部分生活一样都是在户外进行。

在最早的悲剧中，迪奥尼索司剧院必须包括最基本的元素。其所需的只是一个位于缓坡底部的一个给合唱队的圆形舞池。观众可以坐在缓坡上观看演出。在乐队演奏处的另一边，正对着观众，有一个帐篷，演员可以在那里更换服饰。帐篷上面写着"背景建筑"字样，用来指有门的木墙，粉刷后用来象征宫殿、庙宇或任何需要的背景。这种墙最终成为了发展成熟的舞台建筑，来作为永久性剧场背景建筑，因为它取代了原始的帐篷。木帐篷和正式的座位场地的建设很可能开始于15世纪中期的某个时候，其中斜坡上的座位场地安置有中空长凳。演员或者与合唱队站在乐队演奏处，或者站在通往帐篷门口的台阶上。古希腊三大悲剧家埃斯库罗斯、索福克勒斯、欧里庇得斯的戏剧在早期的木质剧院中观众人数相当可观。保存至今的迪奥尼索司剧院有精致的石头棚，铺设好的乐队演奏处和大理石观众席。这种石头剧院可以容纳将近15 000名观众。

作为古希腊剧院的一部分，两种机械设备值得一提。一种是"用轮子出场的设备"，一个带轮子的平台，从背景建筑的门里推出，展示出一幅代表室内活动的画面，因此观众无法看到室内发生的情节。另一种设备叫做"戏剧机器"，是一种用绳索把演员吊起的吊车。这种设备使扮演神灵的演员以一种最逼真的方式从天而降。机器把演员停放在背景建筑的顶部，这样饰演神灵的演员就可以从一个比较合适的高度与凡人对话了。这种设备并不仅仅用于神灵角色，只要是需要飞翔的情节都可以用。反过来说，并不是每位神的出现都会用到。

国家雇佣悲剧演员并负担他们的酬劳，通过抽签分配给悲剧家。到15世纪中期时，悲剧的演出需要3个演员。按角色的重要性递减排序为主角、第二演员和第三演员。由于大部分戏剧都需要多于两三人的角色，因此3个演员都要饰演多个角色。演员的主要职责就是说出所扮演人物的台词。但是，偶尔他也需独唱，或是与合唱团同唱，再或是与其他演员合唱。

由于女性不允许参加戏剧演出，男演员就得扮演女性角色。多重角色的扮演都是通过面具来实现的。面具使观众识别不出扮演特定角色演员的真面孔，来帮助消除男扮女装的外在不协调。面具也可以帮助观众识别人物的性别、年龄和社会地位。在整部剧中，合唱队始终站在乐队演奏处，在情节交替时合唱歌曲和跳舞，这期间演员就可以退场，更换面具和服装，在下一场中继续扮演新角色。

合唱队是具有歌舞天赋的非专业演员，他们由悲剧家训练为演出作准备。在埃斯库罗斯的大部分戏剧中，合唱队的标准人数是12人，到索福克勒斯时增至15人。合唱队同演员一样，穿戏服、戴面具。合唱队的第一个功能就是，唱着入场歌走向乐队演奏处。合唱队准备就绪后，它的任务便是双重的了。它要通过主唱来和角色对话，主唱要先说出分配给合唱队的台词。合唱队最重要的功能是合唱颂歌。悲剧颂歌包括三部分：抒情颂歌第一节、向右转时的回舞歌和抒情颂歌第三节。

悲剧的典型结构是场景对话与合唱交替进行。这样的安排可以允许合唱队以歌唱的形式评论前一场景中的人物的话语或行为。大部分悲剧都是以说明性的对话或独白作为开场白。开场白之后，合唱队唱着颂歌走向乐队演奏处。接着便是一节对话场景，然后是第一次合唱颂歌。场景对话和合唱颂歌交替进行，最后一首颂歌后，便是最后一个场景对话，即悲剧结尾。结尾一般是场景对话的形式，但有时也包括歌唱。

Unit 4　Pop Music

一位饱受争议的明星——Lady Gaga

斯蒂芬妮·乔安妮·安吉莉娜·杰尔马诺塔，她的艺名"Lady Gaga"更为人所熟悉，是一名来自美国的流行歌手及创作人。Gaga深受摇滚乐手的影响，例如大卫·鲍伊、皇后乐队以及流行歌手麦当娜、小甜甜布兰妮和迈克尔·杰克逊。她的艺名"Lady Gaga"正是来自皇后乐队的歌"Radio Ga Ga"。

她说:"我当时崇拜的弗雷迪·莫库里和他的皇后乐队有一首主打歌叫做'Radio Ga Ga',这也是为什么我喜欢这个名字……弗雷迪是独一无二的——他是流行音乐界中最伟大的人物之一。"在被要求将自己和麦当娜进行比较的时候,Gaga说:"我并不想让人听起来觉得我自以为是,但是我给自己定了一个目标,要给流行音乐界带来一场革命,而上一次的革命是25年前由麦当娜引领的。"

Gaga有着女低音的音域。她的声音常被拿来和那些歌手诸如麦当娜和格温·史蒂芬尼相比较,而她音乐的整体结构据称与20世纪80年代的经典流行音乐和90年代的欧洲流行音乐十分相似。《星期日泰晤士报》对她的首张专辑《名望》评论道:"糅合了音乐、时尚、艺术和科技,Gaga使人想起了麦当娜和格温·史蒂芬尼。"《波士顿环球报》也评论说她"明显从麦当娜和格温·史蒂芬尼那里获取了灵感……来完善她既兼有少女特性又坚实的唱腔和充满活力的节拍"。尽管有人批评她的歌词没有内涵,但是"她的确能不费吹灰之力就让你舞动起来。"音乐评论家西蒙·雷诺兹写道。

Gaga认定时尚有着重要的影响。她将多那泰拉·范思哲视为自己的创作灵感。Gaga有由她亲自打理的创作队伍。这个队伍制作了许多她的服装、舞台道具以及发型。她对时尚的热爱源自于她的母亲,她说其"总是打扮体面并且漂亮"。"当我在创作音乐的时候,我会思考在舞台上应该穿什么衣服。重要的是把所有的东西糅合在一起——表演艺术、流行表演艺术和时尚。对我来说,只有当所有东西融合在一起形成一个真正的故事的时候,我才能赢得真正的支持者。我希望塑造的形象可以如此强烈以至于支持者们想仔细地品味其中的每一个部分。"全球语言监测机构将"Lady Gaga"评为时尚流行语第一位,而她的注册商标"no pants"位居第三。《娱乐周刊》将她的穿着列入了十年内最佳穿着名单,"Gaga的奇装异服无疑将表演艺术带入了主流"。

对于Gaga的音乐、时尚品位和个人形象的评价有好有坏。她作为一个榜样、一名开路先锋和时尚的标志有时被给予肯定,有时也被人否定。Gaga的专辑大多获得好评,评论家指出她在流行音乐中有着独一无二的地位。她对歌迷所产生的增强自尊的作用,将生活带入时尚界的作用都值得称赞。她的表演被称为"极具娱乐性和开拓性",特别是在2009年音乐电视视频音乐颁奖典礼上的《狗仔队》喷血表演,被音乐电视界称为"吸引眼球的表演"。在之后的"恶魔舞会巡演"中,她穿着一身暴露的皮革紧身胸衣,被一个穿着黑衣的人咬破了咽喉,导致"血"流淌到她的胸口,随后她倒在血泊中"离开了人世"。该场景在英国曼彻斯特的演出之后引起了当地家庭组织的抗议,特别是在发生了出租车司机杀害了12个人的惨剧之后。"发生在布莱德福特的事情仍让人记忆犹新,特别是在坎布里亚几小时前刚刚发生过另外一场,这样太麻木不仁了。"反暴力母亲组织成员林恩·科斯特洛说道。克里斯·洛克随后为她华丽且极具挑逗的表演辩护,"好吧,她是Lady Gaga,"他说道,"她不是'乖乖小姐'。你真的希望一个叫Gaga的人表现得很乖巧?这是你所希望的么?"Gaga之后在参加2010年音乐电视颁奖典礼时穿的裙子,包括配套的靴子、手袋和帽子,每件都是由死去的动物的肉制成的。《时代》杂志2010时尚宣言将其称为"肉裙",其广为人知,该裙是由一位阿根廷设计师所设计,并饱受争议——它引起了世界所有媒体的注意,但也激怒了动物权利组织。然而,Gaga随后否认自己想对任何组织或者个人表示不敬并且希望这件裙子被诠释为人权的宣言。

与她的奇装异服大相径庭,《纽约邮报》将她早期的样子比作是"来自泽西海滩的难民","深褐色的长发,厚重的眼妆以及紧身暴露的衣服。"Gaga天生黑发,她把头发漂染成金黄色是因为她总被错认为艾米·怀恩豪斯。她常把她的支持者称为"小怪物"并且将该词纹在"拿话筒的那只胳膊上"。她还有另外6个为人熟知的文身,其中之一是一个和平的符号,这是受到她眼中的英雄约翰·列侬所启发;还有一段德文引用了诗人勒内·马利亚·里尔克的诗,他也是Gaga最钟爱的哲学家,她认为他的"孤独哲学"在和她说话。在接近2008年底的时候,开始有人拿Gaga和克里斯蒂娜·阿奎莱拉在时尚造型方面作比较,指出她们的造型、发型以及化妆上的雷同。阿奎莱拉声称她"完全不知道Gaga这个人"同时也"不知道他是男是女"。Gaga发表了一篇声明说她欢迎这样的对比,因为这样引起了大众的注意同时也为她作了宣传,"她是这样一位巨星,总之我应该给她送花,因为很多美国人直到这件事发生才认识了我。这件事某种程度上真的使我出了名"。这样的比较一直持续到2010年当阿奎莱拉发布了她的新单曲《灵魂出窍夜》。评论家发现该歌曲及伴奏音乐歌曲中与 Gaga 的《邪恶传奇》有相似之处。也有人将 Gaga 的造型与来自"思念者"乐队的时尚标志戴尔进行比较。有些人觉得她们的形象非常类似,只不过戴尔的支持者觉得她在 30 年前就引领了这样的造型。

除了她的音乐事业外,作为一名慈善家,Gaga 也提升了她的声誉。她为各种慈善以及人道主义工作作出了贡献。尽管 Gaga 曾拒绝了一首慈善歌曲的录制,但在 2010 年海地地震之后,她举办了名为"恶魔舞会巡演"的演出为该国重建基金筹集资金。这场音乐会于 2010 年 1 月 24 日在纽约的瑞迪城市音乐厅举行,所有收入都捐赠给救济基金,与此同时,当天 Gaga 官方在线商店里所有的营业额也都被捐赠了出去。Gaga 宣布一共为基金筹得 50 万美金。在 2011 年 3 月 11 日地震及海啸袭击日本后,Gaga 设计了一个手镯,并将出售手镯所得的 150 万美元捐给日本用于救灾。

鉴于 Lady Gaga 对现代时尚文化的影响以及她在全球越来越大的名气,南卡罗莱纳州大学的社会学家在 2011 年春天开设了一门"Lady Gaga 和名人的社会学"的课程,旨在揭示"Lady Gaga 的成名以及她的音乐、音像制品、时尚和其他艺术活动的社会学特征"。

Unit 5 Film

功夫巨星——李小龙

在世的时候,李小龙不喜欢被人们称作"明星"。去世后,李小龙却无法回避这个称呼。虽然李小龙过世已有 30 年,但作为首位在好莱坞获得成功的亚裔美籍影星,至今他仍被视作是有史以来最伟大的功夫明星之一。凭借肌肉发达的形体和独具一格的银幕魅力,李小龙点燃了美国人对功夫电影的兴趣。这也为他之后的诸如成龙、查克·诺里斯以及史蒂文·西格尔等功夫明星的成功铺平了道路。

李小龙曾在西雅图居住了四年多,最终也长眠于此。今天,在西雅图,"一个传奇的开始,一个男儿的故事——2003 年度李小龙收藏品展览"开幕了。其展品来自于一位对李小龙生前物品收藏颇丰的藏家之手。作为李小龙最亲密的朋友之一,同时也是他的一位徒弟,木村武之说:"直到今天,李小龙的形象在人们心中没有消退,而是在不断增强。这让我感到特别高兴。"在明年上映的新片《龙武士》中,李小龙的风采将会通过数字技术再现出来。首届李小龙大会将于下个月在加利福尼亚的圣莫尼卡市举行。届时,李小龙基金会将以他的名义设立一项奖学金。如今,世界各地的学校仍然在向学生传授李小龙那套独创的"拦截对手拳头的方法"——截拳道。民众曾多次写信呼吁为李小龙专门发行一套邮票并且追授他奥斯卡奖。

李小龙还未等到其首部在美国大获成功的电影上映便去世了。但为什么他仍然具有如此大的影响力?"这很大程度上是因为他是第一个打破许多陈规的亚洲人。"李小龙的前弟子,如今在西雅图做律师的道格·帕尔默分析道。高中时帕尔默曾是一位拳击手,当他第一次看到李小龙的武术动作时,便被深深吸引了。他说:"此前,我从来没见过那样的动作,其融合了速度、力量、艺术与优雅。"在帕尔默眼里,李小龙的技艺无人能及。

李小龙原名"李振藩",1940 年出生于旧金山。他的父亲是一位中国戏剧名角。"布鲁斯·李"是医院的一位护士为这位父亲的第一个儿子起的名字。在香港长大的李小龙有一个绰号叫"坐不定"。作为学生,李小龙成绩一般,常常参与打架。李小龙儿时就是一位银幕童星。三个月大的时候就出演了自己的第一部影片《金门女》,在剧中为一个美国婴儿做替身。到 18 岁的时候,他已经参与了 20 多部电影的拍摄。

当李小龙因为与其他学武术的学生打架而惹上麻烦时,李小龙和他的母亲决定最好的办法就是返回其出生地美国去寻找出路。于是,19 岁的李小龙于 1959 年怀揣着 115 美元回到了旧金山。

接下来的几个月,李小龙来到西雅图,与家人的好友周鲁比住在一起,并且在周鲁比开的中餐馆里干一些擦桌子的活儿。后来,李小龙进入华盛顿大学学习哲学,并兼职教授他在香港学过的咏春拳。到了1964年，他已经在西雅图开办了自己的武术学校。不久李小龙搬到加利福尼亚，在洛杉矶和奥克兰也创办了两所武术学校。当李小龙将他的武术学校拓展到洛杉矶的时候，他吸引来了像史蒂夫·迈奎恩、詹姆士·加纳还有詹姆士·科本这样的名人弟子。他们每小时要支付250美元的学费，为的就是跟这位魅力超凡的大师学习武术。琳达·艾米莉，他的一位学生，后来成为了他的妻子。在他的学校里，李小龙主要教授一种被称之为截拳道的功夫。他通过作示范赢得人们的喝彩，同时吸引学生。木村武之就是这样第一次遇见了"小龙"。

1964年李小龙结婚，木村武之是伴郎。木村武之说："布鲁斯是一个非常合群，非常受欢迎的人。他可能一分钟前还在给你讲一个黄段子，紧接着却又跟你大谈禅宗或道教。"

木村说："李小龙是最强壮、最迅捷的武打演员之一。"如今木村武之仍然在免费教授70个学生学习李小龙的截拳道，将它看作是对李小龙的回报。另外，他也在照看着李小龙的墓地。每周大约有50～75人前来拜谒李小龙的墓。

对于李佩里而言，这个身高五英尺七，体重140磅的男人将快如眼镜蛇出击的拳术和腿功发挥得精妙莫测。那还是在1964年，当时还是富兰克林高中的14岁学生的李佩里正在观看一位不知名的武术演员作示范表演。现年55岁的李佩里说："他所能做到的事情你从未看到过别人能做到。"李小龙冷静、自信的风范给李佩里留下了深刻的印象。李佩里变成了一个武术的狂热爱好者，并且开始收集有关李小龙的各种纪念品。他说："李小龙仍然是标杆。他对于武术的影响，就如同'猫王'对于摇滚乐、迈克尔·乔丹对于篮球、穆罕默德·阿里对于拳击的影响一样。"

李小龙在华盛顿大学学习哲学的时候，开了第一个工作室。李小龙是个敢于直言的传统的叛逆者，他对传统武术有点不屑一顾。

李小龙曾说："在我看来，那些东方防身术99%都是在胡扯。它就像是花哨的爵士乐，看起来似乎不错，但根本不实用。"李小龙认为大多数武术充斥着不实用的姿势和呆板的动作。他告诉记者："即使一个人缩成一团，他也会被暴揍。"李小龙发展了一套自己的武打体系——截拳道。它强调去除多余的动作，展现个人的天赋。

李小龙因出演1966年～1967年间热播的电视剧《青蜂侠》而为人所知。该剧改编于20世纪30年代的一个广播节目。李小龙在剧中饰演青蜂侠忠实的伙伴——加藤，武打风格夸张滑稽。此后他继续在一些电视剧中客串表演。1969年他迎来了自己最重要的角色，扮演《丑闻喋血》中的詹姆斯·加纳。

尽管当自己无法成为主角的人选时，李小龙的心会隐隐作痛，但他已经为电影中的"功夫"定下了基调。迟迟无法在好莱坞获得出演主角的机会，李小龙深感灰心。1971年，他离开洛杉矶，带着妻子和两个孩子回到了香港。

回到他生长的城市后，李小龙签下了两部电影合同。1971年《唐山大兄》上映，李小龙饰演一个因为师父被杀而追踪歹徒的复仇者。拥有高超的截拳道功夫，加上充满活力的表演，李小龙成为影片中最受欢迎的角色。这部电影也创下了香港电影的票房纪录。1972年李小龙主演的《精武门》再次打破香港电影的票房纪录。

到1972年底，李小龙已经是亚洲顶级影星。他发行了自己导演的第一部电影《猛龙过江》。不久，华纳兄弟娱乐公司便找上门来。虽然他在美国还没有大红大紫，但他导演的第二部电影，也是他第一部好莱坞大片《龙争虎斗》已经将他带到了成功的门口。

1973年7月20号，距《龙争虎斗》的首映还有一个月，李小龙在香港去世，年仅32岁。对于他的意外死亡，官方的解释是死于脑水肿。此前有报道称李小龙背部有伤，为此正在服用一些止疼药。验尸的时候发现正是这种药的某些成分令李小龙产生奇怪的过敏反应并最终死亡。

有人声称李小龙是被谋杀的，由此关于李小龙死因的争论就开始了。有人声称李小龙死于诅咒，因为在1993年，李小龙之子李国豪在拍戏时也在类似的情况下离奇死亡，年仅28岁。这个年轻的演员不幸被原本应该是没有子弹的空枪射中而死亡。

艺术类研究生英语教程

李小龙去世后,《龙争虎斗》上映,李小龙的形象从此成为银幕的标志。该片后来的总票房收入超过 2 亿美元。李小龙之后也涌现了一批新的动作片明星。

对于整个世界而言,李小龙已经是而且将一直是电影史上最杰出的功夫演员。他留给观众的一个既有复杂心理又有完美身材的亚洲英雄的形象,持久地影响着电影界。玛丽莲·梦露、埃尔维斯·普雷斯利、詹姆斯·迪安……像这些英年早逝的名人一样,人们禁不住会想如果李小龙没有这么早地离开我们,那么情况又会如何呢?

Unit 6 Comic and Animation

电影动画的历史

动画是连续快速播放多张 2-D 图像或者模拟场景从而让画面动起来,其最常见的表现手法是电影或者电视。用摄影机将一系列图片衔接拍摄下来。每一张图片和上一张仅有细微的差别,所以当它们快速连续播放时,就会让人们产生一种画面在动的错觉。

电影动画的历史可以追溯到 1890 年的无声电影最早的时代。查尔斯·埃米尔·雷诺制作了首部动画电影,他运用 12 张图片一个循环开发了动画系统。接着他又展示了运用 500 帧一循环的动画。

1910 年前的早期动画是由一张一张拍摄的简单绘图组成。到 1913 年,由于赛璐珞片的发展,动画影片的制作过程更容易操作,动画绘制者可以在一帧(一个静止的画面)内使角色动起来,而无需重复地画背景了。

1914 年,动画家温瑟·马凯辛辛苦苦干了一整年才完成《恐龙葛蒂》。他画了一万幅呈现出动作的不同阶段的画,之后一幅幅地在米纸上着墨,然后用电影摄影机将每一张画作拍下来。这个过程当然不那么激动人心,但是呈现在屏幕上的结果实在让人惊喜。影片放映时,看杂耍的芝加哥观众坐在椅子边上,被屏幕上跳跃着的恐龙深深地吸引。

马凯的创作很成功,恐龙葛蒂也成了第一个动画明星。葛蒂也是第一个有自己个性的动画角色,如今我们称之为角色动画。作为美国早期动画家的杰出代表之一,马凯早期极富创意的影片使他的同代人黯然失色,也在之后的几十年里给包括华特·迪士尼和其他动画家树立了典范。

可以说在此之后有许多动画片制作出来,但在此之前创作的作品很少。仅出于经济的考虑,电影的制作要比动画早 20 年。法国电影制作人乔治·梅里爱在 1898 年就尝试着将动画应用于他的奇幻电影中,因此技术上已经不成问题。那时电影不是租借给剧院,而是直接出售给剧院方——标准价格是 1 英尺 10 美分。一部 100 英尺的动画片和一部真人出演的电影售价同样都是 10 美元,但是前者所花费的时间和金钱要多得多。

詹姆斯·斯图尔特·布莱克顿,一个杂耍素描艺术家,可以被称为动画片之父。保留下来的早期完整作品是布莱克顿在 1906 年制作的三分钟动画短片《滑稽脸的幽默相》,其中,他在黑板上画了不同的脸使画面变"活"。一个男人吐着雪茄烟圈,他的脸部出现又消失,一个小丑在变戏法,而他的狗在跳钢圈。《滑稽脸的幽默相》非常新奇有趣,但并没有对动画产生真正的影响。

就算是温瑟·马凯在《恐龙葛蒂》之前制作的两部动画片也没有能够激起公众对动画片多大的兴趣。是广告真正让动画以一种商业化的模式制作出来以促销连环画。

1892 年第一部连环漫画《小熊和小淘气》由詹姆士·斯温纳顿在《旧金山观察家报》上发表。第二年理查德·奥特考特在《纽约世界》上发表了著名的《黄孩子》。之后的几年里,像《疯狂猫》、《抚养老爸》等一些连环画大受欢迎。其中一些以人物为主角的漫画被改编为真人电影。

报纸出版商,特别是威廉·兰道夫·赫斯特,开始在报纸上开设星期日动画专栏来促进销量。最初动画家只是简单地用钢笔和墨水画画,连背景都没有。除非在每个框架中分别画不然没有办法来容纳背景。尽管如此,像温瑟·麦凯的《恐龙葛蒂》也因为在绘画上的细微变化而获得成功。

这些动画卡通几乎没有故事情节。它们只不过是把一些图片情景连在一起制作成两到三分钟的电影。如果需要对话,动画家会像报纸上那样简单地加上一些对话框。在播放的时候,动作会定格一会给观众阅读对话的时间,然后画面再继续。

最初这些新颖的小卡通漫画大受欢迎,但观众很快就对此感到厌倦。如同十多年前当观众对西洋镜30秒的虚像感到厌倦而在杂耍中播放影片一样,娱乐业主开始在演出中间播放卡通片来清场,告诉观众们节目结束了。一些早期的动画家都试图通过提高质量和绘画的数量来使得自己的动画变得更流畅、更逼真。

动画技术上真正的突破是1915年厄尔·赫德发明的赛璐珞片。这项发明极大地减轻了创作者的工作量,并使动画制作更加高效,因为他们不用重复画每一格的背景。

现在动画片更加悦目了。制作者们的技巧提高了,他们常常会用尽心力去追求完美的效果。像布赖工作室的赫德尝试着逼真地模拟一面在微风中飘扬的旗帜,要知道这在以前是从来没有人尝试过的。实验的结果大获成功,以至于其他的动画家都迫不及待地奔向自己的画桌去尝试制造类似的效果。布赖的动画师花费太多的时间力图模拟真实的生活,到最后公司不得不叫停这样的实验。

公司这样做是有理由的。做动画不如以前那样赚钱,再将时间浪费在"艺术"上就更没有利润。这需要一个流水线式的生产,而这一点,本身就很难做到。当时,一个动画师要负责一整部动画片。他们得自己写故事、想笑料、画背景,有时候还得亲自操作相机。一部5分钟的短片需要画上2 700帧图片。没有时间进行实验。

早期的动画师没有情节串联图板可以使用,它的出现是很久以后的事情了。他们得将所有的东西都记在脑子里。漫画家必须得是优秀的画匠,不仅要画得快,而且要从头到尾都要保持角色的一致性。有些画技拙劣的画师画出来的角色,外形的变化是如此之大以至于到影片结束时几乎无人能认出那是什么。

1922年是动画发展的关键年。几乎每一个人都使用赛璐珞片,而且动画卡通也经常在电影节目中出现。创新者前赴后继。托尼·萨格和赫伯·杜立将古老的"影子戏"复兴,取代了动画中的木偶,不仅如此,他们还通过给胶片渲染为动画加上颜色。这给动画制作带来了引人激动的改变。

同时一颗新星冉冉升起。在密苏里州的堪萨斯城,一个年轻的艺术家沃尔特·埃利亚斯·迪士尼投身于动画。他的第一部电影是宣传当地商业的广告,叫做《小欢乐》。接着他萌生了一个想法,为什么不将动画和真人结合在一起?于是他和朋友乌伯·伊瓦克斯一起开始制作第一部电影《爱丽丝在卡通国》,讲述了一个小女孩和她的卡通朋友的经历。爱丽丝是沃尔特·迪士尼的开始,他在未来日子里的不断创新使动画卡通变得与之前完全不同。

沃尔特·迪士尼将动画带入了一个新的高度。他在1928年的卡通片《汽船威利》中加入了声音,成为首位使卡通片有声的动画家。1937年,他制作了第一部真正的动画长片《白雪公主和七个小矮人》。这还是第一部使用染印法彩色技术的电影,并且在英语国家获得巨大成功。

电脑的出现赋予了动画全新的意义。如今很多动画片都利用电脑制作特效。比如:《星球大战》系列就运用了大量的电脑特效。1995年迪士尼公司和皮克斯公司制作的《玩具总动员》是第一部完全运用电脑技术制作的动画电影。

Unit 7 Fashion

时尚:套在女性身上沉重的枷锁

对全世界数以百万计时尚爱好者来说,束缚她们的不再是厨房,而是一种难以企及的苗条的体形。

又一个伦敦时装周即将开幕。跟往常一样,这又将是一场时尚盛宴,一场由锡纸、羽毛或是橡胶等材质制作的服饰的展览。在此之前,一项研究报告出炉了。报告的内容当然足以让所有的经济学家及政府官员迫不及待地要一睹为快。据调查,时尚产业对英国经济直接贡献的价值接近210亿英镑。如果将其衍生的价值以及外溢效应都算进来的话,这个数额高达370亿英镑以上。此外,直接受雇于这个行业的员工达到80多万人,这也使得时尚界成为所有的创意产业中雇佣人数最多的。一切看起来都近乎完美。不过,在繁华背后到底隐藏了什么?

几年前,我被派去后台报道伦敦时装周。亲眼目睹的一切让我在很长一段时间里都难以释怀。生平第一次,我窥见了这个让我众多的女性朋友"生病"的行业中不为人知的一幕。

在T台上大家见到的大抵差不多:瘦弱不堪的模特让人难以置信,甚至让人忘了看她们身上穿的是什么。在T台的尽头,站着一队年轻姑娘,她们看起来即将崩溃。在镜头前,她们瘦得让人不由得为她们担忧。当看到这些活生生的人时,我相信只有在报道非洲饥荒时才见过像她们那些弱不禁风的人。她们半闭着眼睛,眼神呆滞,因为她们的身体里面已经没有用来维持生命活动的能量了。这些脸上涂抹上化妆品的模特将自己的身体硬塞进那些看起来像是垃圾袋做成的时装里,之后又被别人推出去在T台上摇晃。而台下坐着的如凯特·摩丝、休·格兰特之流会鼓掌。当她们踉跄着走回后台,她们看上去虚弱而又倦怠。无力地倚靠在墙上的她们看起来需要打点滴。

有两种人成为了时尚的牺牲品。第一种是那些被用作模特的女性,在一次短暂的橱窗展示之后便被弃用。她们的体重与一个正常的健康女性相比,平均要低25%。我们知道这是如何做到的,因为许多当过模特的人都是这样说的:饿肚子。她们连续几周只喝水,吃生菜。一个15岁的模特曾坦言,她对进食如此之纠结以至于在吃了一个苹果后狠狠地揍了自己一顿。当这些模特的体重指数低于12时便开始消耗自身的肌肉和组织了。2006年至少有2位模特死于由进食障碍引发的并发症。在过去的几年中还有好几个模特在走秀成功后死于饥饿。

除了T台的模特,还有一个更为广泛的群体也成了时尚的牺牲品。她们就是普通的女性,每天不断地被迫面对那些人造美女的形象,要么感到排斥要么尝试着饿肚子来减肥。哈佛大学的一个研究发现,80%的女性对自己的身体不满意,仅仅只有1%的女性对自己的身体十分满意。相比之下,男性大多数满意于自身的形象。被人们认同的酷男范围极广,上至79岁的肖恩·康纳利,下至体重280磅的詹姆斯·柯登。另一个由年轻的调查公司Tru针对年轻人的一项研究表明,90%的美国少女感受到来自时尚界和媒体崇瘦的压力。由此一种完全不切实际并且几乎难以企及的美女形象得以创造出来。我们生活在一个女性厌食成为流行病的时代,在欧洲和美国这样的女性有5 000万之多。你认识的女性中有多少人对自己的容貌感到满意呢?

时尚界千方百计地将这种病态的形象加以推广。在美国《Vogue》杂志本年度最大制作推出之后,最近的一部纪录片"九月出品"中有一个大揭秘。安娜·温图尔,美国《Vogue》杂志主编,这个时尚圈最强势的女人,是一个冷淡而又整天闷闷不乐的人。除了对她身边的人表现冷酷时还能有点活力之外,她似乎对什么都提不起兴致。当她与一个骨瘦如柴的模特肖像合影时,她宣称那位女性看起来怀孕了;当她与一个有点小肚腩的男性合影时,她则表现得很不理解,仿佛人体里面的脂肪是令人厌恶的。她倡导使用毛皮,对其影响到的动物的残忍做法视若无睹。她喜欢用极瘦的模特,是否她对于所牵涉的女性所意味的残忍也视若无睹呢?

她的这种阴郁是有传染性的:它会随着《Vogue》杂志传播。美国心理协会的一个研究发现,70%的女性在浏览一份时尚杂志哪怕只有3分钟之后都会感到"沮丧,有负罪感,羞愧"。在大多数治疗饮食失调的诊所里都不允许阅读《Vogue》及其类似的杂志。医生们很清楚,只要读者看这本杂志,他们几乎毫无例外地会没有胃口。《Vogue》杂志这种推崇使用超瘦的模特的做法已经对普通女性造成了伤害。

不过,这看起来很矛盾:如果《Vogue》杂志让女士们感到如此不愉快,那她们为何要购买它呢?如果说女士们都不愿意在时尚杂志上看到瘦得皮包骨头的模特的话,那又如何解释这样的现象:一旦这些杂志不断地展示正常的女性,销量就会下降?看起来女性身体里有一种受虐的冲动去吸引她们喜欢那种病态的东西。这种冲动到底是什么呢?

在1991年的女权主义者内奥米·沃尔夫写的《美貌的神话》一书中有最好的解答。她认为,相信有一个关于美的客观标准是错误的。没有这样的标准。Padung人崇尚下垂的胸脯,肥胖的女性在15世纪大获青睐。人们关于美的看法随着人们对女性的要求而改变。

沃尔夫指出,在不断变换的时尚潮流里面有着非同寻常的东西。当女性在现实世界中变得强大时,模特们就会变得更加虚弱和瘦小。在20世纪初,大多数女性都有着柔软、圆润的臀部,大腿和腹部,人们认为这就是美。10年之后,女性们有了投票权,关于什么是美便发生了变化。突然之间,模特们变得更加骨感和瘦弱,而女士们呢,开始让自己饿肚子了。到了20世纪中叶,当女性们的权利缩水,她们又变得有曲线,又开始放开肚皮吃了。60年代,随着女权主义的兴起,模特们变得越来越瘦,越来越瘦。时至今日,女性们正在冲破种种无形的壁垒,憔悴的模特便成为了常态。

为什么会这样?数千年来女性一直被压制,反观现在,在几十年里,妇女们得到了极大的解放。但无论对于男性还是女性,那些传统的老观点是根深蒂固的。沃尔夫相信,女性对于自身的解放有一种负罪感——潜意识里害怕我们做得太过头了。性别关系的迅速转变让人们感到震惊和无所适从,由此才会有一种扭曲的对于骨感身材的狂热。给女性套上枷锁的不再是厨房,而是一种难以企及的苗条的体形。对她们来说,似乎身为女性竟然没有沉重的枷锁是不合理的。一个女性越强势,她就越有可能让自己饿肚子。

我们不理解为什么过去的中国妇女要缠脚,总有一天,当我们回顾这样一个女性们都想变得皮包骨头的时候,我们心里也会有同样的困惑。但是我们怎么会变成这样?这个问题深藏于我们的潜意识中,因此必须要让这样的问题浮出水面。沃尔夫说,那些患厌食症的女性就像是活生生的问号,在恳求我们的学校,大学以及其他人直截了当地告诉她们:"这是无法忍受的,也是无法接受的。我们不应该让妇女们饿肚子,我们要珍惜她们"。

伍尔夫说的是对的。是时候要去除这种正在毁灭女性的崇瘦的文化了。对于那些在女性中鼓吹病态是美丽的人,我们应公开表示蔑视。够了。女性不应该对要求平等潜意识里有罪恶感。女性的成功并不一定非得要伴随着饿肚子这样的责罚。这就需要更多的人——男人们和女人们——说:够了!我们应该对这个病态,愚蠢而又错误的行业表达我们的蔑视。难道我们不能有这样的一种时尚——和这样的一本《Vogue》杂志吗?

Unit 8   Dancing

恰恰舞

恰恰舞是国际标准舞比赛中拉丁舞系的五大舞种之一。四五十年来,恰恰舞始终列于最具主导地位的流行节奏中。它以欢快且具感染力的韵律为特色,营造出顽皮和挑逗感。它的动感与激情,赋予了舞蹈娇媚的姿色,也赐予了舞者无限的活力。活泼而又华丽,恰恰舞渲染出一种轻盈和快乐感。

恰恰舞起源于西印度群岛的宗教仪式舞蹈。在西印度群岛,有一种植物,生产着称为恰恰的心皮。这些心皮被用来做成一种同名的小拨浪鼓。海地典型的巫术乐队中包括三面鼓、一只钟铃和一个恰恰。指挥者用恰恰作为指挥乐器或"节拍器",为世俗的舞蹈及宗教音乐和歌唱设定时间。

恰恰舞的现代风格源自于舞蹈教师皮埃尔先生与其搭档多丽丝·拉维尔的研究。1952年,来自伦敦的皮埃尔访问了古巴,发现了那时的古巴人是如何跳舞的以及都跳些什么。他留意到,这种新的舞蹈第四节拍是分裂的,跳舞起于第二拍而非第一拍。他的正确分析在当时得到了很好的认可。他把这一新的想法带回了英国,最终与搭档创造了著名的恰恰恰,现在被正式称为"恰恰"。整个欧洲的舞者和舞蹈教师对此都很关注,其受欢迎程度在英国、法国和西班牙稳步上升。

恰恰舞并不是与众不同的舞蹈形式,也不是完全由一人独创的舞蹈,而是另外两种舞蹈的副产品。它是曼波舞在其拉丁音乐中的衍生,同时也是对摇摆舞的传承(林迪舞,一个三重步和一个断裂步)。因此,恰恰舞是在古老的拉丁舞蹈形式上的古巴式创新。原称"恰恰恰"的恰恰舞约在1954年开始流行。恰恰舞的一些舞步与伦巴舞和曼波舞的舞步一致。它们的主要区别是,在恰恰舞中,伦巴舞的节拍要放慢,而曼波舞则被三重步所取代,成为"三重曼波"。恰恰舞的典型动作包括交叉突破(亦称纽约步)、定点转、交叉领舞、第五位置断步以及背面点转(亦称右陀螺转)。

同其他的拉丁舞一样,恰恰舞步主要有两种基本动作,即:后退基本步和前进基本步。每个前进和后退基本步都包含了以下五个舞步:一个断裂步、一个替换步和三重步。当两种基本步结合在一起使用时,恰恰舞步就产生了,并且伴随着身体位置的轻微变化。一组恰恰舞步可宽泛地表述成包括八个舞步的系列动作。一个完整的恰恰基本步包括各占音乐四拍的前进基本步和后退基本步。因此,八个拍子完成一个完整的基本步。向前基本步可以添加各种旋转、屈膝和滑动。在跳恰恰舞时,女士面对男士,要紧随男士的步调,否则男士必然会踩到对方的脚。例如,当男士迈左脚做向前的基本步时,女士则应迈右脚向后做基本步,反之亦然。

各方位的舞步都应足掌先着地,然后随着重心的转移,脚后跟随之落下。当重心脱离一只脚时,脚后跟应先离地,脚尖保持着地。步法要脚掌平伏,并适用于所有舞步。舞者臀部放松,随着交替屈膝和伸直,胯部做自由运动。随着舞步的移动,上身移向支撑脚(身随脚动)。这种臀部运动称之为拉丁或古巴动作,它是恰恰舞的精华元素。在国际拉丁舞中,受重的腿要挺直;另一条腿弯曲使得臀部重心自然地落到受重的腿上。未受重的腿在承受重量的瞬间要伸直,直到重心再次完全脱离前要一直保持绷直。重心的转移必须要谨慎以使动作呈现得天衣无缝。恰恰舞不仅仅是要有胯部动作、屈膝和旋转,关键是舞者双方如何通过他们无懈可击的配合展现自我。恰恰舞的美就在于舞者双方的默契配合和优美舞姿的展现。

恰恰舞随着恰恰音乐起舞,恰恰音乐是由古巴作曲家和小提琴家恩里克·乔恩提出的,他首先称自己的音乐为"恰恰恰"。1953年,古巴乐队"美国"开始以一种新的切分音节拍演奏历史悠久的"丹戎舞"。这种旋律是通过对丹戎舞第四拍的切分发展而来的。听起来就像是慢节奏的曼波舞,古巴舞者随着慢节拍轻微地三重动臀部。这逐渐地演变成了慢节拍的三重步,于是恰恰舞诞生了。乔恩的北美之行向美国曼波舞者引入了它的近亲——恰恰。恰恰于1954年引入美国,1959年美国人便深深痴迷上了恰恰舞,舞蹈工作室都称恰恰舞成了他们最受欢迎的舞蹈。恰恰舞如此深入人心以至于人们情不自禁地倾情于它。10年后,恰恰已成为了美国舞蹈竞赛、俱乐部以及舞蹈工作室中的主导,确立了它成为全美最受欢迎的舞蹈之一的地位。如今恰恰舞在美国依然是最受欢迎的拉丁舞之一。

恰恰也被认为是拟声词,源自对快滑步中脚步的声音模仿,这种声音出现在许多这样的舞步中。这就是为什么一些人称之为"恰恰恰"或"恰恰"的原因。跳"恰恰"时,重拍落在第一拍。恰恰节奏轻快、活泼且短促。

如今,在恰恰舞曲中可以找到许多音乐流派——从海滨音乐到嘻哈再到摇滚乐。恰恰音乐中,强拍是一小节的第一拍。恰恰舞节奏为4/4拍,即四拍为一小节。音乐节奏为每分钟110~130拍。对于初学者来说,最好的节奏范围是每分钟100~110拍。国际标准舞中的恰恰恰音乐充满活力,节拍稳定。而伴着古巴音乐的恰恰则更具妩媚风格。因为古巴恰恰更加性感且包括了复杂的多旋律。

恰恰以其活力四射的性感舞步著称,舞池中尽显魅力。伴着恰恰恰切分音,舞者可以在基本步中轻松地添加多个旋转、花式步法、手造型和古巴胯动作。随着时间的推移,舞者不仅锻炼了自己的恰恰舞技巧也培养了音乐感。随着不断地练习,舞者可以不再拘泥于恰恰基本舞步。

你曾看过美国广播公司的《与星共舞》和福克斯电视台的《舞林争霸》节目吗?你曾想象过身着华美的服饰,浸着浪漫的气息,伴着那深具感染力的恰恰音乐,随着那迷人的节奏翩翩起舞吗?恰恰舞是这些真人秀节目的重头戏,而且它在世界范围内的工作室和舞厅中仍是最受欢迎的拉丁舞之一。伴着恰恰节拍和多旋律跳舞吧。在你的播放器中放些恰恰音乐或请舞厅的音乐人播放几曲,尽情地享受吧。

下编

Unit 1 Chinese Painting

Highlight

Topic area	Communication	Skills
Some best-known Chinese paintings in the world; Scholar-official painters and their works; Some outstanding modern and contemporary classical Chinese painters; Auction at Sotheby's.	more often than not lead…to the height of its glory distinguish…from have an immense impact on to very different ends	Knowing some best-known Chinese paintings and painters; Knowing how to appreciate the classical Chinese painting; Describing and discussing the Chinese paintings and painters.

Starting-out Task

1 **Look at these pictures and discuss the following questions with your partner.**
1. What categories, according to the contents, are classical Chinese paintings divided into?
2. The following pictures show some best-known works of ancient Chinese paintings. Can you tell their names?

3. What else, such as the names of the painters, the time of painting and the categories they belong to, do you know about these paintings?

Listening Tasks

Micro Listening Skills

2 **Listen to the following passage and try to fill in the missing words.**

   Chinese traditional painting is highly regarded throughout the world for its expression and 1. _____. According to the means of expression, Chinese painting can be divided into two categories: the *xieyi* school and the *gongbi* school. The *xieyi* school is marked by 2. _____ forms and freehand brush work. The *gongbi* school is characterized by close attention to 3. _____ and fine brush work.

Unit 1 Chinese Painting

Chinese painting and Chinese 4. _____ are closely related because lines are used in both. Lines are used not only to draw 5. _____ but to express the artist's concepts and feelings. For different subjects and different purposes a variety of lines are used. They may be straight or 6. _____, hard or soft, thick or thin, pale or dark, and the ink may be dry or 7. _____. The use of lines and strokes is one of the elements that give Chinese painting its 8. _____ qualities.

Traditional Chinese painting is a 9. _____ of the arts of poetry, calligraphy, painting, and seal engraving. In ancient times most artists were poets and calligraphers. Inscriptions and seal impressions help to explain the painter's ideas and sentiments and also add 10. _____ beauty to the painting.

Dialogue

Chinese Painting

Susan is an international student in China. She just visited an exhibition of classical Chinese paintings. Then she had a talk with her Chinese friend Ni Jin, who is fond of Chinese paintings.

Words & Phrases

Xuan paper	宣纸
texture /ˈtekstʃə/ *n.*	质地
stroke /strəʊk/ *n.*	笔画
landscape /ˈlændskeɪp/ *n.*	山水画
scenery /ˈsiːnərɪ/ *n.*	风景

3 Listen to the dialogue and choose the best answer to the following questions.

1. Why were many early Chinese paintings on silk?
   A. Paintings on silk look better.
   B. Painters could afford more expensive materials.
   C. They didn't have paper.
   D. They liked painting on silk.
2. What category of classical Chinese painting does Susan like best?
   A. Landscape.   B. Figure.
   C. Bird.   D. Flower.
3. What are reflected by bird & flower paintings?
   A. The natural beauty.
   B. The painters' love of nature.
   C. The society.
   D. The painters' own ideals and characters.
4. Which of the following are the most popular figures of the figure paintings?
   A. Emperor, officials and court ladies.

B. Emperors, philosophers and court ladies.
C. Emperors, farmers and court ladies.
D. Emperors, philosophers and children.

4 **Listen to the dialogue again and complete the following sentences with the information you have heard.**

1. It is believed that the _____ of *Xuan* paper is most suitable for Chinese painting. It allows the writing brush wet with Chinese ink, making _____ varying from dark to light.
2. Many Chinese painters were at the same time _____ and _____.
3. The classical Chinese painting is an art combining four Chinese arts: _____, _____, painting and _____.

Reading Tasks

Focus Reading

Pre-reading Questions

1. Can you name any of the most common subjects of the traditional Chinese painting?
2. Do you know any Chinese painters who were good at painting horses?
3. Why do Chinese painters always add inscriptions to their paintings?

"Reading" a Chinese Painting[①]

The Chinese way of appreciating a painting is often expressed by the words *du hua*, "to read a painting." How does one do that?

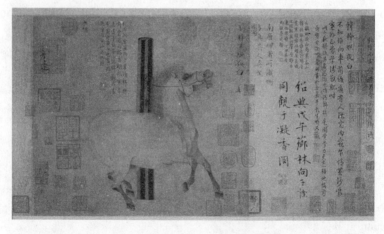

Night-Shining White, by Han Gan, Tang Dynasty (618—907)

[①]This text is taken and adapted from *Chinese Painting* by Maxwell Hearn at http://www.metmuseum.org/toah/hd/chin/hd_chin.htm; the pictures here are cited from the same website.

Unit 1 Chinese Painting

Consider *Night-Shining White* by Han Gan①, an image of a horse. Originally a little more than a foot square, it is now mounted as a handscroll that is twenty feet long as a result of the many inscriptions and seals that have been added over the centuries, so that the horse is all overwhelmed by this enthusiastic display of appreciation. Miraculously, the animal's energy shines through. It does so because the artist has managed to distill his observations of both living horses and earlier depictions to create an image that embodies the vitality and form of an iconic "dragon steed." He has achieved this with the most economical of means: brush and ink on paper.

This is the aim of the traditional Chinese painter: to capture not only the outer appearance of a subject but its inner essence as well—its energy, life force and spirit. To accomplish his goal, the Chinese painter more often than not rejected the use of color. Like the photographer who prefers to work in black and white, the Chinese artist regarded color as distraction. He also rejected the changeable qualities of light and shadow as a means of modeling, along with opaque pigments to conceal mistakes. Instead, he relied on line—the indelible mark of the inked brush.

The discipline that this kind of mastery requires derives from the practice of calligraphy. Traditionally, every literate person in China learned as a child to write by copying the standard forms of Chinese ideographs. The student was gradually exposed to different stylistic interpretations of these characters. He copied the great calligraphers' manuscripts, which were often preserved on carved stones so that rubbings could be made. Over time, the practitioner evolved his own personal style, one that was a distillation and reinterpretation of earlier models.

The practice of calligraphy became high art with the innovations of Wang Xizhi② in the fourth century. By the eleventh century, a good handwriting was one criterion—together with a command of history and literary classics—that determined who was recruited into the government through civil service examinations. Those who succeeded came to regard themselves as a new kind of elite, a group of "scholar-officials" responsible for establishing and maintaining the moral and aesthetic standards. It was their command of history that enabled them to influence current events. It was their interpretations of the past that established the strictures by which an emperor might be constrained. And it was their poetry, diaries, and commentaries that constituted the accounts by which a ruler would one day be judged.

These were the men who covered *Night-Shining White* with inscriptions and seals. Their knowledge of art enabled them to determine that the image was a portrait of an imperial

---

① Han Gan: a leading horse painter of the Tang Dynasty (618—907), known for portraying not only the physical likeness of a horse but also its spirit.
② Wang Xizhi (303—361): a Chinese calligrapher, traditionally referred to as the Sage of Calligraphy, who is considered by many to be one of the most esteemed Chinese calligraphers of all time, and a master of all forms of Chinese calligraphy, especially the running script.

stallion by a ruler of the eighth century. They recognized that the horse was meant as an emblem of China's military strength and, by extension, as a symbol of China itself. And they understood the poignancy of the image. "Night-Shining White" was the favorite steed of an emperor who led his dynasty to the height of its glory but who, tethered by his infatuation with a concubine, neglected his charge and eventually lost his throne.

The emperor's failure to put his stallion to good use may be understood as a metaphor for a ruler's failure to properly value his officials. This is undoubtedly how the retired scholar-official Zhao Mengfu① intended his image of a stallion, painted 600 years later, to be interpreted. Expertise in judging fine horses had long been a metaphor for the ability to recognize men of talent. Zhao's portrait of the horse and groom may be read as an admonition to those in power to heed the abilities of those in their command and to conscientiously employ their talents in the governance of their people.

Groom and Horse by Zhao Mengfu, Yuan Dynasty (1206—1368)

When an emperor neglected the advice of his officials, was unjust or immoral, scholar-officials not infrequently resigned from government and chose to live in retirement. Such an action had long been understood as a withdrawal of support, a kind of silent protest in circumstances deemed intolerable. Times of dynastic change were especially fraught, and loyalists of a fallen dynasty usually refused service under a new regime. Scholar-officials were at times also forced out of office, banished as a result of factionalism among those in power. In such cases, the alienated individual might turn to art to express his beliefs. Since these men acted as the moral conscience of society, their art was highly influential.

Scholar-official painters most often worked in ink on paper and chose subjects—bamboo, old trees, rocks—that could be drawn using the same kind of brush skills required for

---

①Zhao Mengfu (1254-1322): a great Chinese painter and calligrapher who, though occasionally condemned for having served in the foreign Mongol court, has been popularly remembered as a painter of horses in the manner of the Tang Dynasty master Han Gan. He also painted other animals, landscapes and bamboos.

calligraphy. This immediately distinguished their art from the colorful, realistic style of painting preferred by court artists and professionals. Proud of their status as amateurs, they created a new, distinctly personal form of painting in which expressive calligraphic brush lines were the chief means employed to animate their subjects.

Part of *Twin Pines*, *Level Distance*, by Zhao Mengfu, Yuan Dynasty (1206—1368)

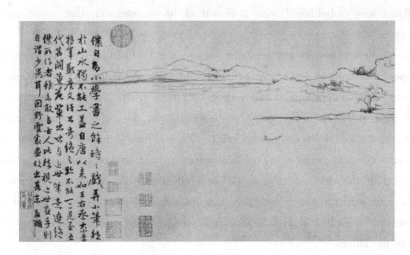

Inscription of *Twin Pines*, *Level Distance*, by Zhao Mengfu, Yuan Dynasty (1206—1368)

Zhao Mengfu epitomized the new artistic paradigm of the scholar-amateur. A scholar-official by training, he was also a brilliant calligrapher who applied his skill with a brush to painting. To distinguish his kind of scholar-painting from the work of professional craftsmen, Zhao defined his art by using the verb "to write" rather than "to paint." In so doing, he underscored not only its basis in calligraphy but also the fact that painting was not merely about representation—a point he emphasized in his *Twin Pines*, *Level Distance* by adding his inscription directly over the landscape. Zhao was a consummate scholar, and his choice of subject and painting style was carefully considered. Because the pine tree remains green through the winter, it is a symbol of survival. Because its outstretched boughs offer protection to the lesser trees of the forest, it is an emblem of the princely gentleman. Zhao, having recently withdrawn from government service under the Mongols, must have chosen to "write" pines as a way to express his innermost feelings to a friend. His painting may be read as a double portrait—a depiction of himself and also of the person to whom it was dedicated.

Since scholar-artists employed symbolism, style, and calligraphic brushwork to express their beliefs and feelings, they left the craft of formal portraiture to professional artisans. Such craftsmen might be skilled in capturing an individual's likeness, but they could never hope to convey the deeper aspects of a man's character.

Integrating calligraphy, poetry, and painting, scholar-artists for the first time combined the "three perfections" in a single work. In such paintings, poetic and pictorial imagery and energized calligraphic lines work in tandem to express the mind and emotions of the artist. Once poetic inscriptions had become an integral part of a composition, the recipient of the painting or a later appreciator would often add an inscription as his own "response." Thus, a painting was not finalized when an artist set down his brush, but it would continue to evolve as later owners and admirers appended their own inscriptions or seals. Most such inscriptions take the form of colophons placed on the borders of a painting or on the endpapers of a handscroll or album; others might be added directly on to the painting. In this way, *Night-Shining White* was embellished with a record of its transmission that spans more than a thousand years.

As the arbiters of history and aesthetic values, scholars had an immense impact on taste. Even emperors came to embrace scholarly ideals. Although some became talented calligraphers and painters, more often they recruited artists whose images magnified the virtues of their rule. Both the court professional and the scholar-amateur made use of symbolism, but often to very different ends. While Zhao Mengfu's pines may reflect the artist's determination to preserve his political integrity, a landscape painting by a court painter might be read as the celebration of a well-ordered empire. A scholar-painting of narcissus reflects the artist's identification with the pure fragrance of the flower, a symbol of loyalty, while a court painter's lush depiction of orchids was probably intended to evoke the sensuous pleasures of the harem.

To "read" a Chinese painting is to enter into a dialogue with the past; the act of unrolling a scroll or leafing through an album provides a further, physical connection to the work. An intimate experience, it is one that has been shared and repeated over the centuries. And it is through such readings, enjoyed alone or in the company of friends, that meaning is gradually revealed.

(1,444 words)

Vocabulary

mount /maʊnt/ *vt.* fix something on a support or in a frame 装裱
be overwhelmed by   be rendered powerless by 被……压倒

Unit 1 Chinese Painting

handscroll /hænd skrəʊl/ *n.* a continuous roll of paper or silk of varying length on which an image has been painted 中国画的卷轴（亦称手卷、手轴，横式装，只能平放案头，不便张挂）

inscription /ɪnˈskrɪpʃən/ *n.* a short message written on the surface of something as a lasting record 题跋

distill /dɪˈstɪl/ *vt.* remove impurities from 蒸馏；提炼

steed /stiːd/ *n.* (literary) a spirited horse for state or war 骏马

pigment /ˈpɪgmənt/ *n.* dry coloring matter 颜料

indelible /ɪnˈdeləbl/ *adj.* cannot be removed, washed away or erased（笔迹）无法消除的；擦不掉的

calligraphy /kəˈlɪgrəfi/ *n.* beautiful handwriting 书法

ideograph /ˈɪdɪəɡrɑːf/ *n.* a graphic character used in ideography 象形（表意）文字

manuscript /ˈmænjuskrɪpt/ *n.* handwritten book or document 手写本

rubbing /ˈrʌbɪŋ/ *n.* a copy (as of an engraving) made by laying paper over something and rubbing it with charcoal 拓本；拓印

recruit /rɪˈkruːt/ *vt.* register formally as a participant or member 录用

elite /eɪˈliːt/ *n.* a group or class of persons enjoying superior intellectual or social or economic status 社会精英

stricture /ˈstrɪktʃə/ *n.* severe criticism 约束

stallion /ˈstæljən/ *n.* adult male horse 公马

emblem /ˈembləm/ *n.* a visible symbol representing an abstract idea 象征；标记

poignancy /ˈpɔɪnjənsɪ/ *n.* a state of deeply felt distress or sorrow 辛酸

infatuation /ɪnˌfætʃuːˈeɪʃən/ *n.* foolish and usually extravagant passion or love 迷恋

concubine /ˈkɒŋkjəˌbaɪn/ *n.* a woman who cohabits with an important man 小妾

throne /θrəʊn/ *n.* the position and power of a ruler 王位，帝位

expertise /ˌekspəˈtiːz/ *n.* skillfulness gained by possessing special knowledge 专门知识或技能

groom /grʊm/ *n.* someone employed in a stable to take care of the horses 马夫

admonition /ˌædməˈnɪʃən/ *n.* a gentle warn to someone that they have done something wrong 轻责，（温和的）责备

heed /hiːd/ *vt.* pay close attention to 留心；注意

resign /rɪˈzaɪn/ *vi.* leave a job or position 辞职

fraught /frɔːt/ *adj.* marked by distress 充满着不愉快的事情的

regime /reɪˈʒiːm/ *n.* a particular type of government 政权

banish /ˈbænɪʃ/ *vt.* expel from a community or group 驱逐

factionalism /ˈfækʃənəlɪzəm/ *n.* quarrelling among groups 党派之争

turn to go or apply to 求助于

alienated /ˈeɪljəneɪtɪd/ *adj.* caused to be unloved 疏离的

epitomize /ɪˈpɪtəmaɪz/ *vt.* embody the essential characteristics of or be a typical example of

成为(某事物)的缩影
paradigm /ˈpærəˌdaɪm/ *n.* a standard or typical example 范例;模范
underscore /ˌʌndəˈskɔː/ *vt.* give extra weight to 强调
consummate /kənˈsʌmɪt/ *adj.* perfect and complete in every respect 完美的
Mongol /ˈmɒŋɡəl/ *n.* a member of the nomadic peoples of Mongolia 蒙古人
in tandem /ˈtændəm/ in agreement 同步地;一致地
colophon /ˈkɒləfən/ *n.* an inscription (usu. a page or more) placed usually on a painting or at the end of a book, giving facts or comments about its publication 画轴题记;书籍末页的版本记录
embellish /emˈbelɪʃ/ *vt.* add details to 美化;装饰
embrace /ɪmˈbreɪs/ *vt.* accept 接受
identification /aɪˌdentɪfɪˈkeɪʃən/ *n.* association 认同;视为同一
harem /ˈheərəm/ *n.* living quarters reserved for wives and concubines and female relatives in a Muslim household 后宫

Proper Names

Night-Shining White	《照夜白》
Han Gan	韩干(唐代画家)
Wang Xizhi	王羲之(东晋书法家)
civil service examination	科举考试;公务员考试
Zhao Mengfu	赵孟頫(元代书画家)
Groom and Horse	《人马图》
Twin Pines, Level Distance	《双松平远图》

Text Exploration

5 Choose the best answer to each question with the information from the text.

1. Over the centuries, *Night-Shining White* has grown from a painting of a foot square into a twenty-feet-long handscroll because _____.
   A. people have added new paintings to it
   B. ancient Chinese paintings tend to stretch over the ages
   C. people have decorated it with borders and endpapers
   D. many inscriptions and seals have been added to it

2. What methods did most traditional Chinese painters rely on in their paintings?
   A. Lines of the inked brush.
   B. Light and shadow.
   C. Bright colors.
   D. Opaque pigments.

3. Which of the following was NOT a skill required for the civil service examinations in the 11th century?
   A. Calligraphy.　　　　　　　　　　B. Painting.

C. History.　　　　　　　　　D. Literary classics.
4. What was Zhao Mengfu's purpose in painting *Groom and Horse*?
   A. To teach people how to recognize a good horse.
   B. To show the intimacy between the horse and the groom.
   C. To persuade the rulers to notice his talents.
   D. To reveal his own distress and sorrow.
5. Why did some scholar-officials leave their jobs?
   A. They refused to support an unjust or immoral emperor.
   B. They were loyal to a fallen dynasty.
   C. They became victims in the quarrelling among those in power.
   D. All of the above.
6. Most scholar-officials painters chose subjects like bamboo, old trees and rocks in their painting because _____.
   A. they could use their calligraphy skills to painting such things
   B. these subjects symbolized their integrity
   C. these things were easy to paint
   D. they liked natural things
7. Which of the following is NOT mentioned as a fact about Zhao Mengfu?
   A. He was a scholar-amateur painter.
   B. He was a brilliant calligrapher.
   C. He left his government job.
   D. He was the best painter of his time.
8. The "three perfections" in a classical Chinese painting refers to _____.
   A. calligraphy, painting and seal
   B. painting, poetry and paper
   C. calligraphy, poetry and painting
   D. poetry, painting and inscription
9. A painting was not finally finished until _____.
   A. the painter had stopped painting it
   B. no new inscriptions or seals were added to it
   C. it was mounted
   D. the painter died
10. To "read" a Chinese painting is to _____.
    A. understand the deeper aspects of both the painting and the painter
    B. read the inscriptions on the painting
    C. have a dialogue with the painter
    D. learn from it

6 Complete the following chart with the information from the text.

Paintings	Painters	Details
Night-Shining White	_____ Tang Dynasty (618—907)	"Night-Shining White" was the _____ of an emperor who led his dynasty to _____ but who, tethered by his infatuation with a _____, neglected his charge and eventually _____.
Groom and Horse	Zhao Mengfu, Yuan Dynasty (1206—1368)	Zhao's portrait of the horse and groom may be read as an admonition to those in power to _____ _____ and to conscientiously employ their talents in _____ _____.
Twin Pines, Level Distance	Zhao Mengfu, Yuan Dynasty (1206—1368)	The pine tree is a symbol of _____ and an emblem of _____. Zhao Mengfu's pines may reflect the artist's determination to preserve his _____.

7 Discuss the following questions with the information from the text.

1. What is the aim of the traditional Chinese painter?

2. What is the key distinction between the scholar-official paintings and the professional artisans' paintings?

3. Why did Zhao Mengfu define his art by using the verb "to write" rather than "to paint"?

4. What inscriptions would you add to the three famous paintings if you were their owner?

5. How do you "read" some famous Chinese paintings, say, *The Xiao and Xiang Rivers*(潇湘图) by Dong Yuan, *The Luoshen Appraisal*(洛神赋图) by Gu Kaizhi, etc?

Vocabulary Expansion

8 Fill in the blanks with the right words given below. Change the form where necessary.

distill	calligraphy	manuscript	elite	emblem
expertise	resign	regime	banish	paradigm

1. Jason _____ his directorship and left the firm.
2. Cambridge University only admits _____ students.
3. A foreign coach has special knowledge and _____ in raising the standard of the

Chinese football.
4. Chinese painting is an art combining poetry, _____, painting and seal cutting.
5. There is never any prevailing _____ in science that lasts forever.
6. The kangaroo is the national _____ of Australia.
7. Your kindness has _____ loneliness and fear from my mind.
8. Experience is _____ from suffering.
9. People suffered the fascist _____ during World War II.
10. The writer cancelled many unnecessary words in his _____.

9 Choose the word or phrase that best keeps the meaning of the sentence if it is substituted for the underlined word or phrase.

1. The enemy's defense was overwhelmed by our sudden attack.
   A. covered   B. overcome
   C. defeated   D. aroused
2. The party has recruited many new members from the middle class.
   A. registered   B. employed
   C. collected   D. enlisted
3. Thieves not infrequently resort to violence when they are discovered.
   A. occasionally   B. often
   C. finally   D. always
4. Faced with a shrinking job market, I turned to my old trade as a butcher.
   A. adapted to   B. referred to
   C. worked as   D. relied on
5. A high degree of autonomy has distinguished Hong Kong from other provinces or regions of China.
   A. differentiated   B. marked
   C. identified   D. placed
6. French philosophers and writers, whose works epitomized the Age of Enlightenment, often attacked injustice and intolerance.
   A. symbolized   B. stood for
   C. embodied   D. summarized
7. In China, education is developing in tandem with industrialization and economic progress
   A. in contrast   B. in order
   C. in step   D. in agreement
8. She bought a red dress embellished with lace and ribbons.
   A. improved   B. decorated
   C. added   D. glorified
9. For a long time, Hong Kong has embraced both the eastern and the western cultures.
   A. enjoyed   B. hugged
   C. accepted   D. covered

10. The identification with the traditional culture is no doubt the consensus among all Chinese people in the world.
   A. distinction   B. relation
   C. participation   D. recognition

10 Translate the Chinese sentences into English by simulating the sentences chosen from the text.

Chosen Sentences	Simulated Translations	Chinese Sentences
To accomplish his goal, the Chinese painter *more often than not* rejected the use of color.		每天晚上你多半能在附近的小酒店里找到伍德。(**Wood, local pub**)
"Night-Shining White" was the favorite steed of an emperor who *led* his dynasty *to the height of its glory*.		18世纪,维多利亚女王将英帝国带入煊赫的盛世。(**Queen Victoria**)
Most such inscriptions *take the form of* colophons placed on the borders of a painting or on the endpapers of a handscroll or album.		这门课是以讨论与讲课的形式进行的。(**seminar**)
As the arbiters of history and aesthetic values, scholars *had an immense impact on* taste.		技术已对社会产生重大的影响。(**technology**)
Both the court professional and the scholar-amateur made use of symbolism, but often *to very different ends*.		男人和女人都看足球赛,但目的往往大不一样。(**football games**)

Supplementary Readings

11 Passage One

Born in 1895, Xu Beihong began studying classic Chinese works and calligraphy with his father Xu Dazhang when he was six, and Chinese painting when he was nine. In 1915, he moved to Shanghai, where he made a living on commercial and private work. He traveled to Tokyo in 1917 to study arts. When he returned to China, he began to teach at Peking University's Arts School at the invitation of Cai Yuanpei. Beginning in 1919, Xu studied overseas in Paris, where he studied oil painting and drawing. His travels around Western Europe allowed him to observe and imitate Western art techniques. He came back to China in 1927 and, from 1927 to 1929,

Galloping Horse by Xu Beihong

Unit 1 Chinese Painting

gained a post teaching at National Central University in Nanjing.

In 1933, Xu organized an exhibition of modern Chinese paintings that traveled to France, Germany, Belgium, Italy, and the Soviet Union. During World War II, Xu traveled to Southeast Asia, holding exhibitions in Singapore and India. All the income from these exhibitions went to Chinese people who were suffering as a result of the war.

After the founding of the People's Republic of China in 1949, Xu became president of the Central Academy of Fine Arts and chairman of the Chinese Artists' Association.

Xu Beihong was a master of both oils and Chinese ink. Most of his works, however, were in the Chinese traditional style. In his efforts to create a new form of national art, he combined Chinese brush and ink techniques with Western perspective and methods of composition. As an art teacher, he emphasized the importance of the artist's experiences in life. Of all of the painters of the modern era, it can be safely said that Xu is the one painter most responsible for the direction taken in the modern Chinese art world.

Xu enjoyed massive support from art collectors across Asia. Between 1939 and 1941, he held solo exhibitions in Singapore, India and Malaya to help raise funds for the war relief effort in China. In one war benefit exhibition in March 1939, Xu held a group exhibition with Chinese ink painting masters Ren Bonian and Qi Baishi, and showcased 171 works of art at the Victoria Memorial Hall.

Xu constantly pushed the boundaries of visual art with new techniques and international aesthetics, in bid to reinvent Chinese art. He died of a stroke in 1953. After his death, a Xu Beihong Museum was established at his home in Beijing.

1. How old was Xu Beihong when he went abroad for the first time?
   A. 15.   B. 17.
   C. 20.   D. 22.
2. Where did he acquire his painting techniques?
   A. China, Japan and Europe.
   B. China, Singapore and France.
   C. China, India and Europe.
   D. China, Japan and Soviet Union.
3. Xu's purpose of holding exhibitions abroad was to _____.
   A. raise funds for arts' development
   B. relieve war victims in China
   C. make himself more famous
   D. push Chinese paintings to the world
4. Which of the following is NOT true of Xu Beihong's art career?
   A. He guided the direction of the modern Chinese art.
   B. He emphasized the artists' experiences in life.
   C. Half of his works were in the Western style.
   D. He combined Chinese techniques with Western methods.

5. What was done in honor of Xu Beihong after he died in 1953?

    A. A memorial was built.

    B. An art museum was established.

    C. A school was named after him.

    D. A prize was awarded in his name.

12 Passage Two①

HONG KONG, October 6, 2010—Yesterday's "Fine Chinese Paintings" auction at Sotheby's (苏富比拍卖行) proved once again that traditional painting challenges the imagination of Chinese art connoisseurs and the Chinese market. While sales results in other sectors, such as contemporary and modern Chinese art, have been uneven this season, the results for Chinese painting at this auction were so impressive that works reaching merely their high estimate seemed to be failures. Lot after lot, the hammer fell on prices that were several times of the high estimates.

The star painting of the day—Fu Baoshi's *Court Ladies*—was hammered down for HK $29 million ($3.7 million), four times its high

Court Ladies by Fu Baoshi, 1945

estimate of HK $7 million. 91% of the lots today were sold above the high estimate, and only 3 out of 270 works on offer were unable to find buyers. All of this added up to the best result ever achieved by Sotheby's sales, with a total haul of HK $407 million ($52 million).

The sale also installed 5 particular artists at the top of the market for traditional painting: Fu Baoshi, Qi Baishi, Wu Guanzhong, Xu Beihong, and Zhang Daqian. Of these five, four were represented in the auction's top ten lots.

Although Fu Baoshi's painting fetched the highest price, the undisputed star of the day was Zhang Daqian, who accounted for four of the top ten lots. An artist of prodigious and protean talent, he set the record this spring for the highest price ever paid for a Chinese work of modern or contemporary art when his *Ai Heng Lake* was knocked down at China Guardian Auctions (中国嘉德拍卖行) for 101 million yuan ($15 million). Today, Zhang was represented at auction by a range of works, from such masterpieces as *Sceneries of Jiangnan*—which was hammered for HK $25 million ($3.2 million)—to a simple nude study, *Nude*

---

①This passage is adapted from *$52 Million Sotheby's Sale of Traditional Chinese Paintings Hits Market's Sweet Spot* by Madeleine O'Dea at www.artinfo.com

Unit 1 Chinese Painting

No. 15(1990), which drew a winning bid of HK＄450,000 (＄58,000) against a high estimate of HK＄200,000. As an artist, Zhang appeals to a range of tastes. Even his calligraphy is admirable.

In theory, the sale was meant to offer something for every price range, but, as it turned out, even the most modest lots soared to high prices. More than once, the price jumped by more than HK＄1 million.

Chinese mainland buyers were utterly dominant. The saleroom hummed with Mandarin, and the Hong Kong buyers seemed lost in a sea of wealthy mainland buyers who always paid huge sums to acquire works.

1. How was the imagination of Chinese connoisseurs challenged at Sotheby's auction?
   A. They couldn't judge the real value of the works.
   B. They underestimated these works.
   C. They were puzzled by the final prices of the works.
   D. Most of the works reached much higher prices than their estimates.
2. Which of the following is true of the auction?
   A. All 270 lots were sold out.
   B. It achieved the best result of all Sotheby's sales.
   C. *Court Ladies* reached the highest price ever paid for any Chinese work of art.
   D. All the lots were sold above the high estimates.
3. Artists such as _____ are among the most popular of all Chinese painters at the traditional painting market.
   A. Wu Guanzhong, Xu Beihong, and Ren Bonian
   B. Fu Baoshi, Wu Guanzhong and Huang Yongyu
   C. Fu Baoshi, Qi Baishi and Zhang Daqian
   D. Xu Beihong, Wu Changshuo and Zhang Daqian
4. What made Zhang Daqian the undisputed star of the day?
   A. His works accounted for four of the top ten.
   B. He is the best of all modern and contemporary Chinese painters.
   C. Both his painting and calligraphy are admirable.
   D. Some of his masterpieces, like *Ai Heng Lake* and *Sceneries of Jiangnan* were among the lots of the day.
5. The dominant buyers of the day were from _____.
   A. Hong Kong
   B. Southeast Asia
   C. Taiwan
   D. Mainland China

Interactive Tasks

Role-play

13 **Role-play the following situation with your partner.**

Situation:

　　Zhang Hai, an art student of China, is at an exhibition of Chinese paintings with his foreign friend Richard. They are talking about a painting of shrimps by Qi Baishi.

You may begin like this:

Zhang: Come and look at this painting of shrimp! It is so simple yet so vivid!

Richard: Yeah. It's incredible! Is it the work of Qi Baishi?

Zhang: Yes, it is. How do you know that?

Richard: Well, Qi is famous all over the world, isn't he? Besides I am quite interested in Chinese paintings.

Group Work

14 **Work in groups to work out your own presentation.**

1. Form groups of four or five students;
2. Each group chooses a topic concerning Chinese paintings, e.g.

   A study of a famous Chinese painting preserved at home or abroad;

   An introduction of a painter and his works.
3. Members of each group collect materials from library and the Internet to work out their PPt slides;
4. Based on the PPt slides, each member of the group gives oral presentation of his part.

Follow-up Task

Writing

15 **Directions:** For this part, you are going to write a composition on the topic: **Traditional Chinese Landscape Painting and Internet**. You should write at least 120 words following the outline given below in Chinese:

1. 中国山水画历史悠久,有很强的生命力;
2. 互联网有助于山水画的新发展;
3. 互联网也给山水画发展带来问题。

Unit 2 Sculpture

Highlight

Topic area	Communication	Skills
Some best-known sculptures in the world; Seven periods of Greek sculpture; Roman and Greek sculpture; Michelangelo and his *Statue of David*.	attribute to in tribute to be more inclined to from the time...right up until... see the first time...	Knowing some best-known sculptures in the world; Knowing the history of the Greek sculpture; Describing and discussing statues.

Starting-out Task

1 **Look at these pictures and discuss the following questions with your partner.**

1. The following pictures show some best-known sculptures in the world. Can you tell their names?

2. What else, such as the materials, the time of creation and the names of the sculptors, do you know about these sculptures?
3. How do you like these sculptures?

Listening Tasks

Micro Listening Skills

2 Listen to the following passage and try to fill in the missing words.

Humans have created three 1. _____, sculptural objects throughout their history. A wide range of materials and techniques have been and continue to be used which reflect local practices and the 2. _____ available. Classical sculptors worked in both bronze and marble, but bronze was popular because its shiny gold color imitated oiled, 3. _____ skin. Sculpture is produced for numerous reasons and functions in a range of different ways. Many peoples produce sculptures that depict 4. _____ or cultural heroes in human or animal form which would have been used in a 5. _____ or ritual context. Other types of sculpture celebrate 6. _____ and power, commemorate ancestors or relate to beliefs about death and afterlife. Sculpture is found in a wide variety of contexts, both 7. _____ and secular. A work might be placed on a(n) 8. _____ located in the landscape or it could be applied to architecture. The works of 9. _____ sculptors can be found in both public and private contexts and explore a range of issues, both formal and 10. _____.

Unit 2 Sculpture

Dialogue

Sculptures in the British Museum

Bronze figurine of Hermes   Luohan

Jane and Richard are looking around in the British Museum.

Words & Phrases

bronze /brɒnz/ n.	青铜（铜与锡之合金）
Hermes /ˈhɜːmiːz/	赫耳墨斯（希腊神）
shrine /ʃraɪn/ n.	圣祠
Luohan	罗汉
Buddha /ˈbʊdə/ n.	佛陀
glaze /gleɪz/ n.	釉面

3 **Listen to the dialogue and decide whether the following statements are true(T) or false(F).**

1. ____ Hermes is a Greek god who carries messages for other gods.
2. ____ The statue of Hermes is nude because ancient Greeks viewed the nude man as the ideal man.
3. ____ Luohan is a disciple of Buddha.
4. ____ Luohan statues were usually placed in tombs.
5. ____ Western statues are more beautiful than eastern statues.

4 **Listen to the dialogue again and complete the following sentences with the information you have heard.**

1. The statue of Hermes might have been used to decorate household _____ or gardens or

as offerings to _____.
2. The statue of Luohan was made more than _____ years ago.
3. The glaze on the statue of Luohan does not rub off once _____.
4. Probably long ears indicated _____ in ancient China.

Reading Tasks

Focus Reading

Pre-reading Questions
1. Have you ever seen or heard of any Greek statues?
2. How do you like Greek sculptures?
3. Why did ancient Greeks sculpted so many naked human statues?

Seven Periods of Greek Sculpture①

Greek sculpture has had a profound effect throughout the ages. Many of the styles have been reproduced and copied by some of the finest artists to have ever lived e. g. Michelangelo. Actually, all of western art stem from ancient Greek sculpture. The Greeks used many different types of materials in their sculptures including bronze, marble and limestone as these were abundant in Greece. Other materials such as clay were also used; but due to their brittle nature very few have survived. Greek sculptures are very important as the vast majority of them tell us a story about gods, heroes, events, mythical creatures and Greek culture in general. Greek sculptures are mainly divided into 7 time periods—Mycenaean Art, Sub-Mycenaean or Dark Age, Proto-Geometric Art, Geometric Art, Archaic Age, Classical Art and Hellenistic Era.

Mycenaean Art is the first era in which we find surviving examples of Greek art. This era dates from around 1550 to 1200 BC on the Greek mainland. During this period there were two separate civilizations living on the mainland, the Greeks and the Mycenaeans. The Greeks at the time learned a lot from the Mycenaeans who were more technologically advanced. The Greeks learned how to build gates and tombs (such as Agamemnon's tomb) and how to use different metals in art, using Mycenaean techniques. The famous Cyclopean Wall of Mycenae before the lion gate is a good example of their masonry skills.

Around 1200 BC, attributed to the fall of Troy,② seems to be the downfall of Mycenaean art, this time period being known as the Sub-Mycenaean or the Dark Ages. This time period lasted from around 1200 to 1025 BC and very few examples of statues have been found. The few items that have been found show no new methods or innovation. This is probably due to the constant wars and invasions which crippled the growth of their civilization during that time.

---

①This text is adapted from *Sculpture and Art in Ancient Greece* at www. ancientgreece. com.
②The fall of Troy: in Greek mythology, the Trojan War was waged against the city of Troy by the Greeks, who besieged the city Troy for ten years before it fell to the trick of the Trojan Horse.

Unit 2 Sculpture

The next phase (1025—900 BC) is known as the Proto-Geometric art era. We begin to find pottery starting to be decorated with simple shapes, wavy lines and black bands. It is thought that this time period was the Greeks' first expression of reviving their civilization. With the invention of faster pottery wheels it is believed that experimenting with pottery began. Notable examples of this era have a broad horizontal band about the neck and belly, concentric circles applied with a compass and multiple brushes. They are mainly of abstract elements.

Geometric Art dates from around 900 to 700 BC and was a dramatic transformation that led to the establishment of primary Greek institutions such as the Greek city state (polis) and the Greek alphabet. Sculptures and carvings began to be made representing each city states' heroes and past legends including animals and humans. The growth of new trade routes and the opportunities for colonization permitted Greek art to flourish. Large temples and sanctuaries were built in tribute to the gods and were furnished with precious statues. The armed warrior, the chariot, and the horse are the most familiar symbols of the Geometric period.

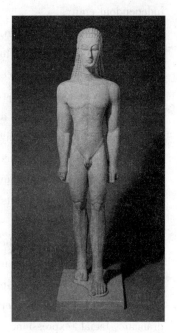

Statue of Kouros 590 BC

With the newly established trade routes in the Levant and the Nile Delta we begin to see an amalgamation of Greek and oriental art. This led to the Archaic Age (700—450 BC) which showed a more naturalistic style reflecting significant influence from the Near East and Egypt. Many Greek artists began to assimilate ideas from their Eastern counterparts, starting to use palmetto and lotus compositions, animal hunts and such composite beasts as griffins (part bird, part lion), sphinxes (part woman, part winged lion), and sirens (part woman, part bird). Competition between the Greek artists throughout the Greek mainland and colonies began to emerge to see who could produce the greatest and most innovative marvels. Sculptors in the Aegean islands, notably on Naxos and Samos, carved large-scale statues in marble. Goldsmiths on Rhodes specialized in fine jewelry, while bronze workers on Crete fashioned armor and plaques decorated with superb reliefs. The prominent artistic centers of mainland Greece, notably Sparta, Corinth, and Athens, also exhibited significant regional variation. Sparta and its neighbors in Laconia produced remarkable ivory carvings and distinctive bronzes. Corinthian potters invented a technique of silhouetted forms that focused on tapestry-like patterns of small animals and plant motifs on their vessels. By contrast, the vase painters of Athens were more inclined to illustrate mythological scenes. The Archaic age was best known for the emergence of stone statues of humans, such as the limestone *kouros* (male) and *kore* (female) statues.

These new statues showed young humans naked and always with a smile on their face. The main aim was to show perfection in human form; however, the majority of statues came across as rigid and unnatural. Despite these flaws it was the Greeks who first invented the free standing statues during this era.

Classical Art (480—323 BC) was created during a "golden age", from the time Athens rose to prominence and Greek expansion, right up until the death of Alexander the Great.① The Classical age could be seen as a turning point in art and produced some of the most exquisite sculptures known today. It was during this age that sculptors had mastered marble and began creating statues that showed joyous freedom of movement, while celebrating mankind as an independent entity.

Discobolos

The best example showing freedom of movement is the *Discobolos*(The Discus Thrower) by Myron. This is one of the most famous classic Greek statues from this period. The Classical age also saw the first time human anatomy was deemed worthy of being portrayed in a statue and for ever immortalized in stone and bronze. Portraying people in a static and stiff position had now been replaced with the more modern "snap-shot" three-dimensional movements, so that people could admire the human body for its aesthetic values. It was the first time that humans could be seen as almost God-Like, which meant that the human body became the subject of study for the first time and acquired the importance it deserved. From the Classical period all the Greek statues showed a lack of expression, whereas, the depiction of "barbarians" shows a dramatic facial expression. This was because the Greeks believed that suppression of the emotions was a noble characteristic of all civilized men, while the public display of human emotion was a sign of barbarism. Logic and reason was to dominate human expression even during the most dramatic situations.

Charioteer of Delphi

The greatest statues of this age were the *Statue of Zeus* at Olympia and the *Statue of*

---

①Alexander the Great(356—323 BC): a Greek king of Macedon(马其顿) who created one of the largest empires in ancient history.

Athena at the Parthenon, both of which were designed by Phidias. Smaller copies of these statues still exist but the originals unfortunately were destroyed in a fire. The sculptures of Greece more than any other art forms are the pure expression of freedom, self-consciousness and self-determination. These were the values that motivated the inhabitants of Ancient Greece to defeat mighty Persia and led them to the development of a model of society that ensured the dignity of every man within it.

The Hellenistic Era (323—31 BC) began around the death of Alexander the Great and ended with the Battle of Actium① in 31 BC. The Hellenistic period saw dramatic changes compared to previous logic. The artists of this period did not stick to classical conventions and rules but turned to a more experimental movement and a sense of freedom that allowed the artist to explore his subjects from different unique points of view.

Boy Jockey

The easiest way to explain this is to look at the *Charioteer of Delphi* and the *Boy Jockey* statues. The former is from the classical period and shows greatness and humility whereas the latter is from the Hellenistic Era which shows a greater expression of power and energy. Vast improvements in techniques and materials allowed one of the largest and most magnificent creations in human endeavor, the *Colossus of Rhodes* to be built. Unfortunately, the combined effects of looting and various earthquakes destroyed the statue, thought to have been as big as the *Statue of Liberty* in New York. Some of the best known Hellenistic sculptures are *Dying Gaul*, *Venus de Milo*, and the *Winged Victory of Samothrace*, all of which depict classical heroes but have a Hellenistic twist which shows a more sensuous and emotional taste.

(1,390 words)

---

①The Battle of Actium: the decisive confrontation between the forces of Octavian(屋大维) and the combined forces of Mark Antony and Cleopatra. Octavian's victory enabled him to consolidate his power over Rome.

Vocabulary

limestone /ˈlaɪmˌstəʊn/ *n.* 石灰石
brittle /ˈbrɪtl/ *adj.* hard but easily broken 硬但易碎的
geometric /ˌdʒiːəˈmetrɪk/ *adj.* 几何（学）的
archaic /ɑːˈkeɪɪk/ *adj.* of ancient times 古代的；古风的
Hellenistic /ˌheləˈnɪstɪk/ *adj.* relating to or characteristic of the classical Greek civilization 希腊风格的；希腊文化的
masonry /ˈmeɪsnrɪ/ *n.* stonework 石工
downfall /ˈdaʊnfɔːl/ *n.* fall from fortune or power 衰落
cripple /ˈkrɪpl/ *vt.* make useless or worthless 严重毁坏（或损害）
revive /rɪˈvaɪv/ *vt.* restore from a depressed, inactive, or unused state 使复苏
concentric /kənˈsentrɪk/ *adj.* having a common center 同一中心的，同轴的
institution /ˌɪnstɪˈtjuːʃən/ *n.* long-established law, custom, or group 惯例，习俗，制度
sanctuary /ˈsæŋktʃuːˌerɪ/ *n.* a consecrated place where sacred objects are kept 圣殿
in tribute /ˈtrɪbjuːt/ **to** 向……表示敬意
chariot /ˈtʃærɪət/ *n.* 敞篷双轮马车（古代用于战争或竞赛）
amalgamation /əˌmælgəˈmeɪʃən/ *n.* 融合
assimilate /əˈsɪmɪleɪt/ *vt.* take up mentally 吸收，接受（想法、态度等）
counterpart /ˈkaʊntəpɑːt/ *n.* a person or thing having the same function or characteristics as another 与对方地位相当的人或物
palmetto /pælˈmetəʊ/ *n.* kinds of small palm with fan-shaped leaves 小棕榈
marvel /ˈmɑːvəl/ *n.* wonder 不平凡的成果；成就；奇迹
plaque /plæk/ *n.* a memorial made of brass 匾额
relief /rɪˈliːf/ *n.* the feeling that comes when something burdensome is removed or reduced 减轻；解除
silhouette /ˌsɪluːˈet/ *vt.* (usu. passive) show, exhibit in black outline（常用被动态）现出……之轮廓
tapestry /ˈtæpɪstrɪ/ *n.* a wall hanging of heavy hand-woven fabric with pictorial designs 挂毯
motif /məʊˈtiːf/ *n.* a design that consists of recurring shapes or colors 装饰图案
vessel /ˈvesəl/ *n.* a craft designed for water transportation 容器
come across be perceived in a certain way 被理解；接受
flaw /flɔː/ *n.* imperfection 瑕疵
prominence /ˈprɒmɪnəns/ *n.* the state of being widely known or eminent 突出；显著
exquisite /ˈekskwɪsɪt/ *adj.* elegant and refined 精致的；精美的
anatomy /əˈnætəmɪ/ *n.* （生物体的）解剖结构
deem /diːm/ *vt.* (formal) consider（正式）认为
static /ˈstætɪk/ *adj.* not in physical motion 静态的
snap-shot /ˈsnæpʃɒt/ *n.* quickly taken photograph usually by an amateur 快照

barbarian /bɑːˈbeərɪən/ *n.* uncivilized people 野蛮人，蛮族
dominate /ˈdɒmɪneɪt/ *vt.* have control over 支配；控制
humility /hjʊˈmɪlɪtɪ/ *n.* humble condition or state of mind 谦恭
endeavor /enˈdevə/ *n.* (formal) effort, attempt（正式）努力
sensuous /ˈsenʃuːəs/ *adj.* taking delight in beauty 愉悦感官的

Proper Names

Michelangelo /ˌmɪtʃɪˈlændʒɪˌləʊ/	米开朗基罗
Mycenaean /ˌmaɪsəˈnɪən/	迈锡尼文明的
Agamemnon /ˌægəˈmemnən/	阿伽门农（特洛伊战争中希腊军队的统帅）
Troy /trɔɪ/	特洛伊
Levant /lɪˈvænt/	地中海东部地区
the Nile Delta /naɪl deltə/	尼罗河三角洲
Alexander the Great	亚历山大大帝
Zeus /zuːs/	宙斯（希腊神话中的主神）
Parthenon /ˈpɑːθəˌnɒn/	帕特农神庙
Phidias /ˈfɪdɪəs/	菲迪亚斯（古希腊的雕刻家）
Persia /ˈpɜːʃə/	波斯（西南亚国家，现在的伊朗）
Charioteer of Delphi	《德尔斐的驭手》
Boy Jockey	《男孩赛马》
The Colossus of Rhodes	《罗德岛太阳神巨像》
Dying Gaul	《垂死的高卢人》
Venus de Milo	《米洛的维纳斯》
Winged Victory of Samothrace	《萨莫色雷斯的胜利女神》

Text Exploration

5 Choose the best answer to each question with the information from the text.

1. The materials used by the Greeks in their sculptures included _____.
   A. bronze, marble and iron
   B. marble, limestone and clay
   C. limestone, clay and glass
   D. marble, clay and wood
2. Greek sculptures are mainly divided into _____ time periods.
   A. 5
   B. 6
   C. 7
   D. 8
3. Which of the following is NOT true of Mycenaean art?
   A. The earliest works of Greek art we have found today date back to this era.
   B. This era lasted about 350 years.
   C. The Mycenaeans were more technologically advanced than the Greeks.
   D. The Greeks learned how to build statues from the Mycenaeans.
4. What accounted for the downfall of Mycenaean art?
   A. The Trojan War.
   B. Lack of innovation.
   C. Natural disasters.
   D. Deadly diseases.

5. Works of the Proto-Geometric era have all the following features EXCEPT _____.
   A. concentric circles   B. broad horizontal band
   C. human forms   D. abstract elements

6. During the Geometric period, the most familiar symbols of statues include _____.
   A. the armed warrior   B. the chariot
   C. the horse   D. all of the above

7. Composite beasts such as griffins, sphinxes and sirens are used as examples of _____.
   A. the amalgamation of Greek and oriental art
   B. the conflict between Greek and oriental art
   C. a naturalistic style
   D. regional variations

8. Which of the following is true of the stone human statues of the Archaic age?
   A. They were made of marble.
   B. They were the earliest stone human statues of Greece.
   C. They showed naked people of all ages.
   D. They were free moving and natural.

9. Which of the following is true of the *Statue of Zeus* and the *Statue of Athena*?
   A. They were the greatest statues of the Hellenistic era.
   B. They were designed by Phidias.
   C. They were placed at Olympia.
   D. They were destroyed in natural disasters.

10. Which of the following are all Hellenistic sculptures?
    A. *Charioteer of Delphi*, *Colossus of Rhodes* and *Dying Gaul*.
    B. *Boy Jockey*, *Venus de Milo* and *Statue of Liberty*.
    C. *Dying Gaul*, *Boy Jockey* and *Colossus of Rhodes*.
    D. *Discobolos*, *Winged Victory of Samothrace* and *Venus de Milo*.

6 Complete the following chart with the information from the text.

Periods	Time Span	Details
Mycenaean Art	_____—1200 BC	During this period there were two separate civilizations on the mainland: _____; The Greeks learned _____ and _____.
Sub-Mycenaean or Dark Age	1200—1025 BC	The few items that have been found show _____.
Proto-Geometric Art	1025—900 BC	This time period was the Greeks' first expression of _____.

(续表)

Periods	Time Span	Details
Geometric Art	900—700 BC	This time period led to the establishment of primary Greek institutions such as _____ and _____; Large temples and sanctuaries were built in tribute to _____ and were furnished with precious _____.
Archaic Age	700—_____ BC	We begin to see an amalgamation of _____; The Archaic age was best known for the emergence of _____.
Classical Art	480—323 BC	It was during this age that sculptors had mastered _____ and began creating statues that showed _____, while celebrating mankind as _____.
Hellenistic Era	323—_____ BC	The artists of this period did not stick to _____ but turned to _____; One of the largest and most magnificent statues in human endeavor, the _____ was built during this period.

7 Discuss the following questions with the information from the text.

1. How did Greek sculpture influence western art?

2. What are the differences between the stone human statue of the Archaic Age and that of the classical period?

3. Why did the Greek statues of the classical period show no expression on the faces?

4. Can you tell the story of the Trojan War?

5. What kind of people would you like your statues to portray if you were a sculptor?

Vocabulary Expansion

8 Fill in the blanks with the right words given below. Change the form where necessary.

| downfall | cripple | revive | assimilate | counterpart |
| silhouette | prominence | exquisite | dominate | endeavor |

1. This flower vase was made with _____ workmanship.
2. He stood in front of the window, _____ against the evening sky.
3. Conflicts with neighboring countries would only _____ the economic growth of that country.
4. Many Asian nations are faced with recession and are looking to a growth in exports to _____ their economies.
5. The financial crisis led to the _____ of the government.
6. Maintaining a sustainable development is a long-term and arduous task that calls for persevering _____.
7. This insignificant athlete came into _____ as a result of his success in the Olympic Games.
8. The U.S. Congress is the _____ of the British Parliament.
9. We should critically _____ whatever is beneficial in literature and arts from other countries.
10. Her desire to _____ her husband has caused trouble in her family.

9 Choose the word or phrase that best keeps the meaning of the sentence if it is substituted for the underlined word or phrase.

1. The present wave of strikes <u>stems from</u> discontent among the lower-paid.
   A. is based on   B. starts from
   C. arises from   D. moves from
2. Our country is blessed with <u>abundant</u> natural resources.
   A. plentiful   B. excessive
   C. adequate   D. scarce
3. Steel with impurity substance in it would be too <u>brittle</u> to use.
   A. delicate   B. crisp
   C. soft   D. tender
4. The coach <u>attributed</u> the team's victory <u>to</u> training and practice.
   A. owed…to…   B. referred…to…
   C. assign…to…   D. connect…with…
5. A statue was erected <u>in tribute to</u> the founder of the university.
   A. in response to   B. in memory of
   C. for the sake of   D. to show admiration for
6. Founded in 1991, we <u>specialize in</u> import and export of electric appliances.
   A. deal with   B. concentrate on
   C. work on   D. care for
7. Due to the inflation, food prices <u>are inclined to</u> rise this year.
   A. are desired to   B. are willing to
   C. tend to   D. prefer to
8. The speaker spoke for a long time and his meaning <u>came across</u> in the end.

Unit 2 Sculpture

    A. was understood   B. was found

    C. was doubted   D. was enjoyed

9. Examinations can <u>motivate</u> students to seek more knowledge.

    A. urge   B. force

    C. coax   D. inspire

10. Having failed in all peace efforts, the two countries finally <u>turned to</u> force.

    A. complied with   B. resorted to

    C. adapted to   D. came to

10 Translate the Chinese sentences into English by simulating the sentences chosen from the text.

Chosen Sentences	Simulated Translations	Chinese Sentences
Many of the styles have been reproduced and copied by some of the finest artists *to have ever lived*.		罗丹是有史以来最著名的雕塑家之一。(**Rodin**)
The vase painters of Athens *were more inclined to* illustrate mythological scenes.		春天里人们更容易犯困。
Classical Art was created during a "golden age", *from the time* Athens rose to prominence and Greek expansion, *right up until* the death of Alexander the Great.		自公元前6世纪犹太人被驱逐,直到1948年以色列建国,犹太人一直散布在世界各地。(**Jews**, **exile**, **Israel**)
The Classical age also *saw the first time* human anatomy was deemed worthy of being portrayed in a statue.		2008年奥运会首次在中国举行。(**Olympic Games**)
The former is from the classical period and shows greatness and humility *whereas the latter* is from the Hellenistic era which shows a greater expression of power and energy.		人不同于野兽之处在于前者会说话而后者不会。(**in that**)

Supplementary Readings

11 Passage One

    The Roman style of sculpture was influenced strongly by Greek style. The Romans saw what the Greeks were doing, liked it and imitated it. Greek sculptors worked primarily with bronze, a metal that is a mixture of copper and tin, and with marble. The Romans also became accomplished in working with bronze and marble.

    Both Greeks and Romans used the lost-wax process to make bronze sculpture. In this technique the first version of the statue is molded from wax. This means that the statue can be modeled with enormous details because the wax is so easy to work on. This wax model is then enclosed in a clay mantle(外罩). When the clay shell has dried, molten bronze is poured in through small holes in the mold. The hot bronze melts the wax, and fills the mold. When the bronze has cooled the clay mantle is removed, revealing the bronze statue.

The Romans considered bronze sculpture to be more valuable than marble. They particularly liked statues of gods, leaders and heroes in action. They further increased the impact of bronze statues by making them life size or even larger than life. Large statues had to be cast in sections that were later attached to form a completed sculpture. Historians suspect that most ancient bronze sculptures have been lost because later generations melted the statues down and reused the metal for other purposes.

Marble is a very different medium than bronze. Since it is stone it cannot be easily re-used. While it is being sculpted, marble is relatively workable. It does not attain its full hardness until it is exposed to the air. This relative malleability(可塑性) explains the beauty and realistic detail of marble sculpture. Stone sculpture more successfully endured the wear and tear of centuries. Statues like the *Venus de Milo* may lose fingers, arms or other parts but much of their beauty survives today.

Sometimes it is hard to tell whether a statue is Greek or Roman. Roman statuary has some characteristics that make it quite distinctive. The Romans were realists and the Greeks, idealists. A Greek statue attempted to portray a perfect version of a god, goddess or hero. A Roman statue is more likely to portray an actual person. A sculpture with wrinkles that looks like a face you might see on the street is more likely to be Roman than Greek.

1. What are most of the Greek and Roman statues made of?
   A. Copper and stone.
   B. Bronze and marble.
   C. Tin and clay.
   D. Metal and wood.
2. Which of the following is NOT true of the lost-wax process?
   A. The first version of the statue is made of wax.
   B. This wax model is then covered by clay.
   C. When the clay shell has dried, the wax model is removed from the mold.
   D. Molten bronze is poured in through small holes in the mold and fills the mold.
3. Why, according to some historians, have most ancient bronze sculptures been lost?
   A. Later generations melted the statues down for other purposes.
   B. Most bronze statues have rotten away.
   C. Very few bronze statues were made.
   D. Bronze statues were too difficult to make.
4. The statue *Venus de Milo* is used as an example to show _____.
   A. Stone statues are less valuable than bronze statues.

B. Marble is relatively workable.

C. Stone statues are very beautiful.

D. Stone statues can endure the wear and tear of ages.

5. How to tell a Greek statue from a Roman statue?

A. A Greek statue is more beautiful than a Roman statue.

B. A Roman statue is more likely to be made of bronze.

C. A Greek statue portrays gods while a Roman statue portrays people in real life.

D. A Roman statue shows more details than a Greek statue.

Passage Two

The *Statue of David* was sculpted during a three year period beginning in 1501 by the artist Michelangelo. The subject of the work is the Biblical King David in the moment that he makes the decision to fight Goliath. The 17-foot tall statue became the symbol of defending the civic liberties of the Florentine Republic, an area surrounded by more powerful states.

Michelangelo wasn't the original artist of the sculpture. A group of officials sought to commission twelve sculptures based on the Old Testament to decorate a cathedral. The first two were completed by Donatello and Agostino di Duccio, his assistant. The buyers contacted di Duccio to create the work of *David*. He shaped the legs, feet and figure before he left the projects, possibly due to the death of Donatello.

The partially finished chunk of marble sat that way for the next twenty five years in the yard of a workshop. The deterioration of their expensive investment was enough for the group of buyers to restart the process of finding an artist. Various artists were interviewed for the task, including Leonardo da Vinci, but Michelangelo was finally hired in 1501.

David in the statue is thought to be preparing for a battle since the young man's body is tense and ready for action. There are bulging veins in his hand and a twisting in his body. His weight is shifted onto his right leg while the left leg is relaxed. To balance that out, his left arm is in motion (holding the rock) while his right arm hangs to his side. The pedestal of marble below him is treated as though it were something he just stepped up onto.

His proportions aren't realistic. The head and upper region of the body are larger than the lower parts of the body. The hands are also disproportionately large. The proportions are defended by experts as being proper for the originally intended home of the statue—high up on a church where the body's ratio would have looked accurate.

A vandal(故意毁坏文物者) attacked the statue in 1991, damaging some of the toes on the left foot with a hammer before he was restrained. The first serious cleaning of the statue since 1843 happened in 2003 with no damage done to the statue although there were concerns by many scholars before hand.

1. Which of the following is true of David?

A. David was king of the Florentine Republic.

B. David in the statue is ready to fight.

C. David was a very tall man.

D. David was remembered for defending the civil liberties.

2. What was the original purpose of creating the *statue of David*?
   A. It was created as part of ornaments on a big church.
   B. It was created in memory of King David.
   C. It was created to symbolize the civil liberties of the Florentine Republic.
   D. It was created to show the artistic beauty of sculpture.

3. Why did the group of officials restart the creation of the *Statue of David* in 1501?
   A. They finally found Michelangelo the right person for the job.
   B. The partially finished statue had stayed there for too long.
   C. They were under pressure from the people.
   D. They didn't want to waste the money they had invested in the statue.

4. The proportions of the *Statue of David* are not realistic because _____.
   A. David in the statue was preparing for a battle.
   B. Artists at that time were not concerned with the body ratio.
   C. It was originally intended to be placed high up on a church.
   D. That's what David was like.

5. What happened to the statue in 2003?
   A. It was slightly damaged.
   B. It was cleaned.
   C. It was repaired.
   D. It was attacked.

Interactive Tasks

Role-play

13 Role-play the following situation with your partner.
Situation:
   Two art students are talking about some world-famous sculptures exhibited at the Shanghai World Exposition. These sculptures include the *Peace Girl*(和平女孩) in front of the Luxembourg Pavilion, the *Bronze Age*(青铜时代) at the French Pavilion, the *Little Mermaid*(小美人鱼) at the Denmark Pavilion, etc.
You may begin like this:
David: Be sure not to miss the World Exposition held in Shanghai.
Lucy: Really? Why's that?
David: Well, the masterpieces of western sculpture will be on display at the exposition. It's a rare chance to see some of the world's greatest statues.
Lucy: No kidding. I've always wanted to see western sculptures.

Group Work

14 **Work in groups to work out your own project.**

1. Form groups of four or five students;
2. Each group chooses a topic concerning sculpture, e.g.
   A study of statues at home or abroad;
   An introduction of a sculptor and his works.
3. Members of each group collect materials from library and the Internet to work out their PPT slides;
4. Based on the PPT slides, each member of the group gives oral presentation of his part.

Follow-up Task

Writing

15 For this part, you are going to write a composition on the topic: **Modern Sculpture in China**. You should write at least 120 words following the outline given below in Chinese:

1. 20世纪以来,中国现代雕塑深受西方影响;
2. 五四运动以来,大批中国艺术家赴西方学习现代雕塑;
3. 90年代以来,中国现代雕塑取得重大突破,因为……

Unit 3 Theatre

Highlight

Topic area	Communication	Skills
Some well-known performing arts centres;	prior to	Knowing the Sydney Opera House;
Some well-known musicals;	beef up	Knowing the story of *Cats*;
The origin of opera;	launch into	Knowing the evolution of opera.
The history of Beijing Opera.	draw on	
	at will	

Starting-out Task

1 Look at these pictures and discuss the following questions with your partner.

1. What do you know about the Sydney Opera House, one of the most famous performing arts centers in the world? What do you know about other well-known opera houses or theatres?

2. What do you know about the Broadway theatre? Do you enjoy the style of Broadway musicals?

Unit 3 Theatre

3. Beijing Opera is the quintessence of Chinese culture. What do you know about its history?

Listening Tasks

Micro Listening Skills

2 **Listen to the following passage and try to fill in the missing words.**

　　Theatre is a branch of the performing arts. Any performance may be considered theatre; however, as a performing art, theatre focuses almost 1. _____ on live performers enacting a self-contained drama before an audience. A performance qualifies as dramatic by creating a representational 2. _____. The word "theatre" 3. _____ from the Ancient Greek Word *theatron* meaning "a place for viewing." A theatrical performance may include music, dance and various 4. _____ of stagecraft such as 5. _____, sets, lights, stage 6. _____ and sound engineering, among others.

Modern Western theatre derives in large measure from ancient Greek drama, from which it 7. _____ technical terminology, classification into genres, and many of its themes, stock 8. _____, and plot elements. Theatre scholar Patrice Pavis 9. _____ theatricality, theatrical language, stage writing, and the specificity of theatre as synonymous 10. _____ that differentiate theatre from the other performing arts, literature, and the arts in general.

Passage

The Evolution of Opera

Words & Phrases

opera seria /ˈɒpərəˈsɪərɪə/	主题严肃的歌剧
artificiality /ˌɑːtɪfɪʃˈælɪtɪ/ n.	不自然
grand opera /grænd ˈɒpərə/	大歌剧
verismo /veɪˈriːzməʊ/ n.	写实主义

3 Listen to the passage and decide whether the following statements are true (T) or false (F).

1. ____ The leading elements involved in opera are singing and acting.
2. ____ Opera originated from Italy at the beginning of the 16th century.
3. ____ The most prestigious form of Italian opera was opera seria before the 1760s.
4. ____ Mozart is best well-known for his Italian comic operas.
5. ____ In the 20th century, some opera singers had greater influence due to recording technology.

4 Listen to the passage again and complete the following sentences with the information you have heard.

1. Opera is usually performed in an opera house, _____.
2. The mid-to-late 19th century was _____, led and dominated by Wagner in Germany and Verdi in Italy.
3. During the 19th century, parallel operatic traditions emerged _____, particularly in Russia.
4. _____ on opera were done during the 20th century.

Unit 3 Theatre

Reading Tasks

Focus Reading

Pre-reading Questions

1. Why does theatre have fewer audiences than film has in China?
2. What musicals have you ever watched?
3. What do you think is the most attractive part of musical?

A Fantastic Visual Feast

Cats premiered in the West End at the New London Theatre on 11 May 1981. There was trouble initially as Judi Dench, one of the performers in the play, snapped a tendon during rehearsals prior to the London opening. The role was subsequently taken over by Elaine Paige. The role was beefed up for Paige and the song *Memory* was given to Paige. The musical was directed by Trevor Nunn, with associate director and choreography by Gillian Lynne. It played a total of 8,949 performances in London. Its final performance in London's West End was on its 21st birthday, 11 May 2002, and broadcast on a large screen in Covent Garden to the delight of fans who could not acquire a ticket for the final performance. It held the record as London's longest running musical until 8 October 2006, when it was surpassed by *Les Misérables*.

The show made its debut on Broadway on 8 October 1982, at the Winter Garden Theatre with the same production team. On 19 June 1997, *Cats* became the longest-running musical in Broadway history with 6,138 performances. It closed on 10 September 2000, after a total of 7,485 performances. Its Broadway record was surpassed on 9 January 2006 by *The Phantom of the Opera*. It remains Broadway's second longest-running show in history.

In 1998, a video version of *Cats* was produced, based upon the stage version, starring Elaine Paige, Ken Page, and Sir John with many of the dancers and singers drawn largely from various stage productions of the show. It was directed by David Mallet, with choreography and musical staging by the show's respected original creator Gillian Lynne in London's Adelphi Theatre, and was released on VHS and DVD, as well as broadcast on television worldwide.

Sir Andrew Lloyd Weber began setting music to T. S. Elliot's *Old Possum's Book of Practical Cats* in 1977. The songs were an experiment for Weber, to see if he could write music around lyrics. After performing the songs at a concert in 1980, Elliot's wife Valerie Elliot gave Weber some of her husband's unfinished verse, most notably "*Grizabella the Glamour Cat*". This verse inspired him to approach director Trevor Nunn, who joined forces with Weber to explore Elliot's works deeper, discovering many further references to *Cats*. Inspired by a rough draft of yet another poem given to the team by Valerie, the pair wrote the opening piece "*Jellicle Cats*".

At 83, original choreographer of the musical, Lynne still recalls those early days vividly. She was working on the musical *Oklahoma* when she received a call from British producer Cameron Mackintosh asking her to meet Webber, who had returned from a fruitless trip to the US trying to find support for the production.

"He took me straight to his home and he poured two glasses of white wine and launched into it. I was so thrilled and excited by what I heard that I talked all the time, and he talked all the time, so I don't think either of us ever heard what the other one said." she says.

Convinced by Weber that producing a large scale musical based on the Elliot poems was a good idea, Nunn began to visualize the staging and Lynne start working on the choreography. Nunn thought that the set should be an expression of what cats see, made to cat scale, including their version of wacky human behavior. In this way, the world of street cats in a junkyard was created. Lynne worked on the choreography for a month before the official rehearsal started, drawing on her experience of dancing in the West End musicals and getting help from a French mime artist. She began with studying her own cats to get a sense of their movement. Trying to capture the agility, sensuality, and mysterious emotions of cats, she put her dancers through strenuous exercises which eventually led to the physical capabilities she hoped for. Her vision was to "tell the story of each song, and not just interpret it at will."

When previews began, Lynne stayed late night after night refining the show. "It is an extraordinary show because it can look very childish if you're not careful," she says. "*Cats* works at its very best when it has enormous sensuality and a lot of spirituality. When those two things are combined with all the mime and the hard dance and the craziness and speed of it, it is superb."

However beside the choreography and staging, all the glitz and glamour of the lycra-clad coiffed felines would not be possible without the talents of costume supervisor Ron Morrison and wig maker Sharon Case. Morrison demanded that every costume in the production would be handmade, from the figure-hugging unitards to the striking yak hair wigs. He said that the costumes would have to be replaced every six to nine months because of the vigorous workout they got as the performers danced, leapt and frolicked around on stage. Case, whose credits include the likes of *The Matrix*, *Chicago* and *Titanic*, says the wigs are part of the actor, and not just something that's put onto their heads, as she "glues" the wig to the dancers' head just before show time. "It's a privilege to always come back and do the show as there are so many elements to it, there's always something new," she said. "There's a lot of love for the show and people who experience it for the first time are amazed at the depth of emotion they experience." There are about 60 wigs in the *Cats* inventory with each one valued at up to $4,000.

After its show on Broadway, *Cats* have been selling out shows across the world. 15 years ago, it wowed Sydney audiences and it is now returning home. The latest Australian production of *Cats*, which opened in Adelaide, has so far taken $14 million at the box office. Director Jo-Anne Robinson has been involved with *Cats* since its inception, helping original choreographer Gillian Lynne in creating the feline movements for Andrew Lloyd Webber's songs. "It was a collective thing. We thought 'This is either going to be a complete disaster or a phenomenal success.'" Robinson says. "The first time it was put in front of the public it was just an extraordinary reaction and we were thrilled." Robinson says Cats, which had its world premiere in 1981, was "as fresh as ever, a fantastic visual feast". But who could have imagined that most placid and domestic of creatures would inspire one of the most popular stage shows of all time?

In Australia, Queenslander Caleb Bartolo, 17, is the youngest of the new *Cats*. Bartolo warmed his feet in 2008 when he auditioned for *So You Think You Can Dance*. During rehearsals for *Cats*, he found picking up the movements challenging. "It's one thing to do the steps but to do it as a cat is a completely different thing." he says. "It was hard to find the felinity of moving like a cat. Everyone started off very dancer-like, but we learned about the anatomy of cats, how they move and how their anatomy helps them to do different things. We have to apply that to every moment, so there's a lot of back ripples and back work." The young cast bring as much energy and love to this *Cats* as any who went before them. They have the honour of introducing Grizabella, Rum Tum Tugger, Macavity and friends to a new generation of fans, and they really come together and grab their huge audience by the heart in large numbers.

Nearly thirty years after its London premiere, *Cats* has become more than a musical. It is a furry, feisty phenomenon far surpassing the average kitty's nine lives. If you love musical theatre and haven't seen a professional production of this show, don't let anything stop you seeing it. Just try to get seats near the front to enjoy the full experience of stage full of gorgeous furry kitties.

(1,344 words)

Vocabulary

snap /snæp/ *vt.* break or cause to break suddenly 折断
tendon /ˈtendən/ *n.* a flexible but inelastic cord of strong fibrous collagen tissue attaching a muscle to a bone 腱
rehearsal /rɪˈhɜːsəl/ *n.* a practice or trial performance of a play or other work for later public performance 排练
subsequently /ˈsʌbsɪkwəntlɪ/ *adv.* coming after something in time; following 随后的;紧接的
beef up　reinforce; supplement 增强;补充
associate /əˈsəʊʃɪeɪt/ *adj.* denoting shared function or membership but with a lesser status 副的
choreography /ˌkɒriːˈɒɡrəfɪ/ *n.* the sequence of steps and movements in dance, especially in staged dance 舞蹈动作编排
verse /vɜːs/ *n.* writing arranged with a metrical rhythm, typically having a rhyme 诗
choreographer /ˌkɔːriːˈɒɡrəfə/ *n.* the composer of performance of staged dance 编舞者
launch into　set about 着手开始做
visualize /ˈvɪʒʊəlaɪz/ *vt.* form a mental image of 想象
wacky /ˈwækɪ/ *adj.* funny or amusing in a slightly odd or peculiar way 滑稽古怪的
draw on　make use of 利用
mime /maɪm/ *n.* the theatrical technique of suggesting action, character, or emotion without words, using only gesture, expression, and movement 哑剧艺术
agility /əˈdʒɪlɪtɪ/ *n.* the ability to move quickly and easily 敏捷
sensuality /ˌsenʃuːˈælɪtɪ/ *n.* the condition of being pleasing or fulfilling to the senses 感官享受
strenuous /ˈstrenjʊəs/ *adj.* requiring or using great exertion 费力的
preview /ˌpriːˈvjuː/ *n.* a showing of play before its official opening (戏剧)预演
spirituality /ˌspɪrɪtjʊˈælɪtɪ/ *n.* affecting the human spirit or soul 精神上的影响
glitz /ɡlɪts/ *n.* extravagant but superficial display 浮华
glamour /ˈɡlæmə/ *n.* the attractive or exciting quality that makes certain people or things seem appealing 魅力
lycra-clad /ˈlaɪkrə klæd/ *adj.* in clothes made of an elastic polyurethane fiber or fabrics 身着由莱卡制作的衣服的

coif /kɔɪf/ *vt.* style or arrange the hair of someone 给……做发型
feline /ˈfiːˌlaɪn/ *n.* a cat or other member of the cat family 猫；猫科动物
wig /wɪg/ *n.* a covering for the head made of real or artificial hair 假发
unitard /ˈjuːnɪtɑːd/ *n.* a tight-fitting one-piece garment of stretchable fabric which covers the body from the neck to the knees or feet 弹力紧身连体衣
yak /jæk/ *n.* a large domesticated wild ox with shaggy hair, humped shoulders, and large horns 牦牛
vigorous /ˈvɪgərəs/ *adj.* strong, healthy, and full of energy 充满活力的
workout /ˈwɜːkˌaʊt/ *n.* vigorous physical exercise or training 训练
frolic /ˈfrɒlɪk/ *vi.* play and move about cheerfully, excitedly, or energetically 嬉戏
privilege /ˈprɪvɪlɪdʒ/ *n.* something regarded as a rare opportunity and bringing particular pleasure 特殊荣幸；特别待遇
inventory /ˈɪnvəntəri/ *n.* a complete list of items such as property or goods in stock 存货清单
inception /ɪnˈsepʃən/ *n.* the starting point of an activity 开始
phenomenal /fɪˈnɒmənəl/ *adj.* very remarkable; extraordinary 显著的；杰出的
placid /ˈplæsɪd/ *adj.* not easily upset or excited 温和的
audition /ɔːˈdɪʃən/ *vt.* perform an interview for a particular role or job as a singer, actor, dancer, or musician 面试演艺人员
anatomy /əˈnætəmi/ *n.* the bodily structure of an organism 机体结构
ripple /ˈrɪpl/ *n.* a thing resembling such a wave or series of waves in appearance or movement 波纹；波动
feisty /ˈfaɪsti/ *adj.* having or showing exuberance 生气勃勃的
kitty /ˈkɪti/ *n.* a pet name or a child's name for a kitten or cat（昵称或儿童用语）小猫
gorgeous /ˈgɔːdʒəs/ *adj.* beautiful; very attractive 美丽的；非常吸引人的

Proper Names

Judi Dench	朱迪·丹契
Elaine Paige	伊莲·佩姬
Trevor Nunn	特雷弗·纳恩
Gillian Lynne	吉莉安·林恩
Covent Garden /ˈkɒvənt ˈgɑːdn/	科文特公园
Les Misérables	《悲惨世界》
Broadway /ˈbrɔːdweɪ/	百老汇
Winter Garden Theatre	冬园剧院
The Phantom of the Opera	《歌剧魅影》
Ken Page /ken peɪdʒ/	肯·佩吉
Sir John	约翰爵士
David Mallet /ˈdeɪvɪd ˈmælɪt/	戴维·马利特

Adelphi Theatre	亚德菲剧院
Sir Andrew Lloyd Weber	安德鲁·劳伊德·韦伯爵士
T. S. Elliot	T. S. 艾略特
Old Possum's Book of Practical Cats	《老鼠讲讲世上的猫》
Valerie Elliot	瓦拉里·艾略特
Grizabella the Glamour Cat	《格瑞泽贝拉:魅力猫》
Jellicle Cats	《洁里柯的猫》
Oklahoma	《俄克拉荷马》
Cameron Mackintosh /ˈkæmərən ˈmækɪntɒʃ/	卡梅伦·麦金托什
Ron Morrison	罗恩·莫里森
Sharon Case	沙伦·凯斯
The Matrix	《骇客帝国》
Chicago	《芝加哥》
Titanic	《泰坦尼克号》
Adelaide /ˈædəleɪd/	阿得雷德
Jo-Anne Robinson	乔-安妮·罗宾逊
Queenslander	昆士兰人
Caleb Bartolo	卡莱布·巴特罗
So You Think You Can Dance	《你认为你可以跳舞》
Grizabella	葛丽兹贝拉
Rum Tum Tugger	罗腾塔格
Macavity	麦卡维弟

Text Exploration

5 Choose the best answer to each question with the information from the text.

1. When *Cats* premiered in the West End at the New London Theatre, _____.
   A. Judi Dench played a critical role in the premiere of Cats
   B. everything went smoothly
   C. Paige sang the song *Memory*
   D. it was directed by Gillian Lynne

2. Which of the following is NOT true?
   A. *Cats* had been running in London for over two decades.
   B. The final performance of *Cats* in London's West End London was broadcast.
   C. *Cats* remains Broadway's second longest-running show in history.
   D. *Cats* closed on Broadway due to *The Phantom of the Opera*.

3. The video version of *Cats* in 1998 _____.
   A. was based on the stage version
   B. was directed by David Mallet
   C. was released on VHS and DVD
   D. all of the above

4. In 1977, Andrew began setting music to Elliot's poem in order to _____.
   A. perform at a concert in 1980
   B. approach director Trevor Nunn
   C. see if he could write music around lyrics
   D. reproduce the video version of *Cats*

5. The verse given by Elliot's wife inspired Weber and Nunn to _____.
   A. read more references about cat
   B. join forces
   C. explore Elliot's works deeper
   D. write more music about lyrics

6. When Nunn began to visualize the staging, he thought _____.
   A. the set should humanize cats
   B. the set should reflect cats' perspective
   C. the set should express wacky human behavior
   D. the set should capture cats' anatomy

7. When Lynne worked on the choreography, _____.
   A. she encouraged her dancers to interpret each song at will
   B. she was inspired by ballet and French mime
   C. she asked her dancers to try to understand the story
   D. she made her dancers armed with demanded physical capabilities through strenuous exercises

8. The costumes need to be replaced regularly because _____.
   A. they tend to be damaged
   B. they have to be fit for new performers
   C. the director may have different requirements
   D. audience wants to have a fresh sense

9. Which of the following in NOT true about the latest Australian production of *Cats*?
   A. It has so far taken $14 million at the box office.
   B. It opened in Adelaide.
   C. It received an extraordinary reaction.
   D. The director attributed its success to the help from original choreographer Gillian Lynne.

10. According to Bartolo, which of the following is NOT the reason that make it challenging to pick up the movements for dancers?
    A. It was hard to find the felinity of moving like a cat.
    B. Cat is a placid and domestic creature.
    C. Everyone started off very dancer-like.
    D. A lot of back ripples and back work were involved.

Unit 3 Theatre

6 Complete the following chart with the information from the text.

Time	Details
1977	Sir Andrew Lloyd Weber began _____ T. S. Elliot's "*Old Possum's Book of Practical Cats*" to see _____.
1980	1. Elliot's wife gave Weber some of her husband's unfinished verse which _____ _____. 2. Inspired by a rough draft of yet another poem given to the team by Elliot's wife, Weber and Nunn _____.
1981	*Cats* _____ on 11 May.
1982	*Cats* _____ on 8 October.
1998	_____ based upon the stage version.
2000	*Cats* closed on Broadway on 10 September 2000, _____.
2002	_____ when its final performance in London's West End was on its 21st birthday, 11 May 2002.

7 Discuss the following questions with the information from the text.

1. What is the record held by *Cats*?

2. What did Lynne do when she worked on choreography?

3. What did Morrison demand on costume?

4. What factors do you think contribute to a musical's success?

5. Have you ever been to the theatre? If so, what is your feeling like?

Vocabulary Expansion

8 Fill in the blanks with the right words given below. Change the form where necessary.

| rehearsal | associate | sensuality | glamour | vigorous |
| privilege | inventory | inception | phenomenal | gorgeous |

1. The _____ showed that dairy products at the store were overstocked.
2. I've had a fortnight in _____ for the opera season which will start next week.
3. The program has been successful since its _____ due to both sides' efforts.
4. He was unanimously elected as the _____ director of the academy.
5. Scientific research shows tropical forests in Brazil are diminishing at a _____ rate.

6. Life can dazzle with its _____, its color.
7. What the young adore tends to be those drop-dead _____ Hollywood icons.
8. The _____ of the town lies in its peaceful and cozy life.
9. I had the _____ of giving a commencement speech at the best university in the world.
10. The old man is still _____ and lively by taking regular exercise.

9 **Choose the word or phrase that best keeps the meaning of the sentence if it is substituted for the underlined word or phrase.**

1. Nearly one hundred of them were subsequently tried, convicted and imprisoned.
   A. consequently   B. afterwards
   C. somehow   D. violently
2. It is difficult to visualize how the town must have looked years ago.
   A. neglect   B. discover
   C. imagine   D. rebuild
3. The government made strenuous efforts to upgrade the quality of the teaching profession.
   A. effective   B. hard
   C. regular   D. countless
4. Critics made mixed comments on the film when it began its sneak preview.
   A. publicity   B. inspection
   C. release   D. tryout
5. Children went on a picnic and frolicked in a field.
   A. played   B. danced
   C. chased   D. leapt
6. The team braced itself for the game by having a light workout this morning.
   A. break   B. training
   C. session   D. preparation
7. He may be the most suitable candidate for the job for his placid temperament.
   A. mild   B. aggressive
   C. brave   D. excitable
8. We must beef up our military forces to cope with deliberate provocation.
   A. transform   B. reform
   C. stabilize   D. reinforce
9. The marketing department launched into a two-hour sales pitch for the newly developed mobile phone.
   A. achieved   B. proposed
   C. began   D. refined
10. You'd better turn to Sue for she has a lot of past experience to draw on.
    A. depend on   B. make use of
    C. make up for   D. derive from

Unit 3　Theatre

10 Translate the Chinese sentences into English by simulating the sentences chosen from the text.

Chosen Sentences	Simulated Translations	Chinese Sentences
It held the record as London's longest running musical *until* 8 October 2006, *when* it was surpassed by *Les Misérables*.		他们被困在山顶直到十二日拂晓救援小组到达。(**dawn**)
Convinced by Weber **that** producing a large scale musical based on the Elliot poems was a good idea, Nunn began to visualize the staging and Lynne start working on the choreography.		被理查德说服此时是购房的最佳时机,他决定向银行申请抵押贷款。(**mortgage**)
All the glitz and glamour of the lycra-clad coiffed felines **would not be possible without** the talents of costume supervisor Ron Morrison and wig maker Sharon Case.		如果没有及时的人道主义救援,这些难民是不可能活下来的。(**humanitarian aid**)
Director Jo-Anne Robinson has been involved with Cats *since its inception*, *helping* original choreographer Gillian Lynne in creating the feline movements.		他从一开始就强烈地反对该计划,声称其完全不切实际。
Nearly thirty years after its London premiere, Cats has become **more than** a musical.		傅雷不仅是杰出的翻译家,也是了不起的美学家。(**esthetician**)

Supplementary Readings

11 Passage One

The Sydney Opera House is situated on Bennelong Point in Sydney Harbour, close to the Sydney Harbor Bridge. As one of the busiest performing arts centers in the world, hosting over 1,500 performances each year attended by some 1.2 million people, the Sydney Opera House provides a venue for many performing arts companies including the four key resident companies Opera Australia, the Australian Ballet, the Sydney Theatre Company and the Sydney Symphony Orchestra, and presents a wide range of productions on its own account. It is also one of the most popular visitor attractions in Australia, with more than 7 million people visiting the site each year.

Planning for the Sydney Opera House began in the late 1940s, when Eugene Goossens, the Director of the NSW State Conservatorium of Music, lobbied for a suitable venue for large theatrical productions. The normal venue for such productions, the Sydney Town Hall, was not considered large enough. By 1954, Goossens succeeded in gaining the support of NSW Premier Joseph Cahill, who called for designs for a dedicated opera house.

A design competition was launched by Cahill on 13 September 1955 and received 233 entries, representing architects from 32 countries. The criteria specified a large hall seating 3,000 and a small hall for 1,200 people, each to be designed for different uses, including full-scale operas, orchestral and choral concerts, mass meetings, lectures, ballet performances and other presentations. The winner, announced in 1957, was Jørn Utzon, a Danish architect. According to legend Utzon's design was rescued from a final cut of 30 "rejects" by the noted Finnish architect Eero Saarinen. Utzon visited Sydney in 1957 to help supervise the project. His office moved to Sydney in February 1963.

The Sydney Opera House opened the way for the immensely complex geometries of some modern architecture. The design was one of the first examples of the use of computer-aided design to design complex shapes. The design techniques developed by Utzon and Arup for the Sydney Opera House have been further developed and are now used for most reinforced concrete structures. The design is also one of the first in the world to use araldite to glue the precast structural elements together and proved the concept for future use.

The Opera House was formally opened by Elizabeth II, Queen of Australia, on 20 October 1973. A large crowd attended. The architect, Jørn Utzon, was not invited to the ceremony, nor was his name mentioned.

1. Which of the following is NOT true according paragraph one?
    A. The Sydney Opera House stands near the Sydney Harbour Bridge.
    B. The Sydney Opera House is a multi-venue performing arts centre.
    C. The Sydney Opera House attracts a huge number of tourists every year.
    D. The Sydney Opera House belongs to the four key resident performing companies.
2. Eugene Goossens wanted to build the Sydney Opera House because _____.
    A. he was backed up by NSW Premier Joseph Cahill
    B. the public enjoyed theatrical performance
    C. the seating capacity of the normal venue for large theatrical productions was not enough
    D. a dedicated opera house should be necessary in Sydney
3. What happened in the design competition for the Sydney Opera House?
    A. Jørn Utzon, a Danish architect was unanimously supported.
    B. Architects who entered for the competition must follow some criteria.
    C. Most of competitors came from Europe.
    D. Local architects were expected to have a telling advantage.
4. According to the passage, which of the following is true?
    A. A great deal of glue was used in constructing the Sydney Opera House.
    B. Jørn Utzon declined to attend the ceremony when the Opera House was formally opened.

C. The construction of the Opera House started in 1960.

D. It was said that the famous architect Eero Saarinen thought highly of Utzon's design.

5. What did the Sydney Opera House contribute to modern architecture?

   A. It advanced the theory of geometry.

   B. It firstly used araldite to glue the precast structural elements.

   C. It firstly used fantastic reinforced concrete structures.

   D. Its design was completely done by computer.

Passage Two

The word "opera" means "work" in Italian suggesting that it combines the arts of solo and choral singing, declamation, acting and dancing in a staged spectacle. *Dafne* by Jacopo Peri was the earliest composition considered opera, as understood today. It was written around 1597, largely under the inspiration of an elite circle of literate Florentine humanists. Significantly, *Dafne* was an attempt to revive the classical Greek drama, part of the wider revival of antiquity characteristic of the Renaissance. *Dafne* is unfortunately lost. A later work by Peri, *Euridice*, dating from 1600, is the first opera score to have survived to the present day. The honour of being the first opera still to be regularly performed, however, goes to Claudio Monteverdi's *L'Orfeo*, composed for the court of Mantua in 1607. The Mantua court of the Gonzagas, employers of Monteverdi, played a significant role in the origin of opera employing not only court singers of the concerto delle donne, but also one of the first actual opera singers, Madama Europa.

Opera did not remain confined to court audiences for long; in 1637 the idea of a season of publicly attended operas supported by ticket sales emerged in Venice. Monteverdi had moved to the city from Mantua and composed his last operas, *Il ritorno d'Ulisse in patria* and *L'incoronazione di Poppea*, for the Venetian theatre in the 1640s. His most important follower Francesco Cavalli helped spread opera throughout Italy. In these early Baroque operas, broad comedy was blended with tragic elements in a mix that jarred some educated sensibilities, sparking the first of opera's many reform movements, sponsored by Venice's Arcadian Academy which came to be associated with the poet Metastasio, whose librettist(歌剧剧本) helped crystallize the genre of opera seria, which became the leading form of Italian opera until the end of the 18th century. Once the Metastasian ideal had been firmly established, comedy in Baroque-era opera was reserved for what came to be called opera buffa.

1. Jacopo Peri composed *Dafne* to _____.

   A. inspire an elite circle of literate Florentine humanists

   B. entertain the Mantua court of the Gonzagas

   C. revive the classical Greek drama

   D. revive the drama of ancient Rome

2. Who made great contributions to the origin of opera?

   A. The Mantua court of the Gonzagas.

   B. Metastasio.

C. Claudio Monteverdi.

D. Madama Europa.

3. According to the passage, which of the following is true?

    A. *Euridice* is the first opera still to be regularly performed today.

    B. Operas were only watched by court audiences before the 1630s.

    C. The art of singing played the most significant role in opera performance.

    D. Opera initially remained confined to court audience due to its high costs.

4. Which of the following is true of early Baroque operas?

    A. They were sponsored by Venice's Arcadian Academy.

    B. Comedy was reserved for opera buffa.

    C. They were appreciated by the educated.

    D. tragic elements were mixed with broad comedy.

5. Which of the following is closest in meaning to the word "crystallize" (line 9, Para. 2)?

    A. Alter.

    B. Combine.

    C. Define.

    D. Promote.

Interactive Tasks

Role-play

13 **Role-play the following situation with your partner.**

Situation:

  Two art students are talking about Beijing Opera.

You may begin like this:

Li Yang: Susan, Have you ever seen a Beijing Opera?

Susan: Of course. Beijing Opera is regarded as the quintessence of Chinese culture. I think every foreigner interested in Chinese culture would manage to see one.

Li Yang: That's true. What do you think of Beijing Opera?

Susan: It is really so fascinating and amazing.

Group Work

14 **Work in groups to work out your own project.**

1. Form groups of four or five students;

2. Each group chooses a topic concerning theatre, e. g.

    A study of Beijing Opera;

    An introduction to Broadway.

3. Members of each group collect materials from library and the Internet to work out their PPT slides;

4. Based on the PPT slides, each member of the group gives oral presentation of his part.

Follow-up Task

Writing

15 Directions: For this part, you are going to write a composition on the topic: **How to Revive Beijing Opera**. You should write at least 120 words following the outline given below in Chinese:
1. 京剧是中国的国粹,有悠久的历史;
2. 如今京剧的观众减少了;
3. 就如何吸引观众、振兴京剧,我的建议。

Unit 4 Western Classical Music

Highlight

Topic area	Communication	Skills
Some important classical musical forms in the 19th century western world; Some important instruments and their respective makers; Some outstanding classical musicians, composers and makers; The development of the guitar and piano.	consist of with the rise of… the root cause of… have access to be replaced by	Knowing some best-known musical forms and musicians; Knowing how to appreciate the classical music; Describing and discussing the favorite musical forms.

Starting-out Task

1 Look at these pictures and discuss the following questions with your partner.

1. The classical music has many different musical forms. Can you give any examples and their respective outstanding musicians?
2. The following pictures show some best-known musical instruments of the western classical music. Can you tell their names?
3. Which type of music do you prefer? Can you play any musical instruments? Talk with your partner and have a detailed discussion on it.

Listening Tasks

Micro Listening Skills

2 **Listen to the following passage and try to fill in the missing words.**

George Shearing appeared on the American jazz scene in the early 1940s with a series of successful recordings that 1. _____ a fine-tuned rhythm section of guitar, bass, drums and vibraphone. He was already quite famous in England, but after the 2. _____ of his hit song *September in the Rain*, his quintet rose to new heights.

Shearing was born 3. _____ in London on August 13, 1919. He began playing piano at age three and soon fell in love with the music of Earl Hines, Fats Waller, and Art Tatum. At 19, he performed jazz accordion in Claude Bampton's all-blind band and got his first real taste of show business. Shearing won over American audiences with his own style of boogie-woogie, blues and jazz swing. One of his best-known 4. _____ is the jazz standard *Lullaby of Broadway*, 5. _____ with lyricist George David Weiss.

Shearing 6. _____ the trappings of jazz fusion, synthesizers and 7. _____ that arrived late in his career. He believed that more volume didn't 8. _____ mean better music. At the 9. _____ of his career, George Shearing was immortalized in Jack Kerouac's 1957 novel *On the Road*. Upon seeing Shearing in a Chicago nightclub, Kerouac wrote, "as always he 10. _____ his blind head on his pale hand, all ears opened like the ears of an elephant, listening to the American sounds and mastering them for his own English summer-night's use."

Passage

Piano

Words & Phrases

spinet /spɪˈnet/ n.	小型立式钢琴
dulcimer /ˈdʌlsɪmə/ n	洋琴
virginal /ˈvɜːdʒɪnl/ n.	维金琴
organ /ˈɔːgən/ n	风琴
clavichord /ˈklævɪkɔːd/ n	古钢琴
harpsichord /ˈhɑːpsɪkɔːd/ n	羽管键琴

3 Listen to the passage and choose the best answer to the following questions.

1. The ancestry of the piano can be traced to some early keyboard instruments of the fifteenth and sixteenth centuries. Which of the following is NOT true?
   A. Spinet.
   B. Guitar.
   C. Dulcimer.
   D. Virginal.

2. When did the piano supplant the organ, the clavichord, and the harpsichord?
   A. At the end of the seventeenth century.
   B. In the middle of the eighteenth century.
   C. In the middle of the seventeenth century.
   D. At the end of the eighteenth century.

3. What are the characteristics of the clavichord's tone?
   A. Metallic and powerful.
   B. Metallic but not powerful.
   C. Soft and not powerful.
   D. Soft but powerful.

4. In many composers' opinion, which instrument of the following is suitable for the chamber music?
   A. Harpsichord.
   B. Virginal.
   C. Dulcimer.
   D. Clavichord.

5. What is introduced to sustain or to soften the tone?
   A. Pedal.
   B. Roiling Hammer.
   C. Steel wire.
   D. Metal frame.

4 Listen to the passage again and complete the following sentences with the information you have heard.

1. The piano was _____ in the early eighteenth century by a harpsichord maker in _____.
2. This instrument was called a piano e forte (sort and loud), to indicate its dynamic _____;

its strings were _____ by a recoiling hammer with a felt-padded _____.
3. The mechanical improvements finally produced an instrument which can produce myriad tonal effects from the most _____ harmonies to an almost _____ fullness of sound, from a liquid, singing tone to a sharp, percussive _____.

Reading Tasks

Focus Reading

Pre-reading Questions

1. Can you name any of the most common instruments of the western classical music?
2. Can you name any outstanding musicians or composers?
3. Compared with other musical forms, do you think that classical music has some special characteristics?

Listen to the Nineteenth-Century Classical Music①

You must have heard the word "classical music". Have you ever pondered over the following questions: what is classical music? How to listen to this special kind of music? Here we will enter into the world of nineteenth-century classical music, where you may have a more comprehensive understanding of this special category of music.

The nineteenth century brought great upheaval to Western societies. Democratic ideals and the Industrial Revolution swept through Europe and changed the daily lives of citizens at all levels. Struggles between the old world order and the new were the root causes of conflicts from the Napoleonic Wars to the American Civil War. From New York, to London, to Vienna, the world was changing and the consequences can still be felt until today.

The lives of musicians, composers, and makers of musical instruments were greatly altered by these social changes. In earlier times, musicians were usually employed by either the church or the court and were merely servants to aristocratic circles. Composers wrote music for performances in these venues, and musical instrument makers produced instruments to be played by wealthy patrons or their servant musicians. In the 19th century, musical institutions emerged from the control of wealthy patrons, as composers and musicians could construct lives independent of the nobility.

A new artistic aesthetic, Romanticism②, replaced the ideals of order, symmetry, and form espoused by the classicists of the late eighteenth century. Romantics valued the natural world, idealized the life of the common man, rebelled against social conventions,

---

①This text is taken and adapted from *Nineteenth-Century Classical Music* by Iayson Kerr Dobney at http://www.metmuseum.org/toah/hd/amcm/hd_amcm.htm; the pictures here are cited from the same source.

②Romanticism: Resulting in part from the libertarian and egalitarian ideals of the French Revolution, the romantic movements had in common only a revolt against the prescribed rules of classicism. The basic aims of romanticism were various: a return to nature and to belief in the goodness of humanity; the rediscovery of the artist as a supremely individual creator; the development of nationalistic pride; and the exaltation of the senses and emotions over reason and intellect. In addition, romanticism was a philosophical revolt against rationalism.

and stressed the importance of the emotional in art. In music, Romanticism, along with new opportunities for earning a livelihood as a musician or composer, produced two seemingly opposite venues as the primary places for musical activity—the large theater and the parlor.

Theater Music

One result of the Industrial Revolution was the creation of the middle class. This new economic stratum consisted of a larger number of people with more expendable income and more leisure time than those had ever existed before. With the rise of the middle class, more people wanted access to music performances and music education. Increasing interest in music by the growing middle classes throughout Western Europe spurred the creation of organizations for the teaching, performance, and preservation of music. The musician or composer gained popularity with the masses of concertgoers. Beginning with Beethoven, composers began to arrange large concerts in order to introduce their works to the public. As audiences desired more, composers wrote larger musical works and demanded more of performers and their instruments.

The "bigger is better" mentality led to some new musical forms such as the tone poem and large-scale symphonic and operatic works. Orchestras grew, including larger string sections with a full complement of woodwinds, brass, and ever more percussion instruments. New types of orchestral winds and brass that allowed for greater facility and more accurate playing were introduced. The symphony came into its own as a musical form, and the concerto was developed as a vehicle for displays of virtuoso playing skill. Orchestras no longer required a harpsichord (which had been part of the traditional *continuo* in the Baroque style), and were often led by the lead violinist. Opera continued to develop, with regional styles in Italy, France, and German-speaking lands. The *opera buffa*, a form of comic opera, rose in popularity. The family of instruments used, especially in orchestras, grew. Composers such as Hector Berlioz, and later Johannes Brahms and Richard Wagner, continually pushed the limits of the available musical forms, performers, instruments, and performance spaces throughout the nineteenth century.

Musicians who could dazzle and amaze their audiences by their virtuosity became the first musical superstars. The two most famous nineteenth-century examples were the violinist Nicolò Paganini (1782—1840) and the pianist Franz Liszt (1811—1886). Both dazzled audiences throughout Europe with their performances, elevating the status of the musician from servant to demi-god. Their fame grew throughout Europe and their likenesses would be recorded in a variety of visual arts.

Nicolò Paganini (French, 1782—1840)　　　Violin: "The Antonius," 1717

In order to withstand the virtuosic and often bombastic playing of these soloists, as well as to provide the type of volume needed in large concert venues, more powerful instruments were needed. Larger and louder violins like those by Antonio Stradivari or Guarneri del Gesù (1698—1744)—preferred by Paganini[①]—replaced the quieter and subtler violins of earlier masters like Jacob Stainer or the Amati family. The demands of pianists like Franz Liszt pressed the technology and design of pianos to ever-larger instruments, eventually replacing the internal wooden structures of the eighteenth century with cast iron frames that could withstand thousands of pounds of pressure.

Parlor Music

Conversely, music gained popularity in the intimate nineteenth-century parlor. At the time, home life was centered in the salon, or parlor, where children played and learned with adult supervision, and where the family entertained company. Musical performances for small groups of people became popular events, and some composers/performers were able to support themselves financially by performing in these small venues and attracting wealthy patrons. Most famous among these was Frédéric Chopin (1810—1849).

Music in the parlor was of a very different sort than in the concert hall. Solo performances and chamber music were popular, and included everything from operatic and orchestral transcriptions to sentimental love songs and ballads. In the United States, hymns

---

①Niccolò (or Nicolò) Paganini (1782—1840): an Italian violinist, violist, guitarist and composer. He is one of the most famous violin virtuosi, and is considered one of the greatest violinists who ever lived, with perfect intonation and innovative techniques.

and folk songs by composers like Stephen Foster (1826—1864) supplemented the European repertoire.

With the rise of the parlor as the center of family life, music education became increasingly important. Children were often taught to play musical instruments as part of a well-rounded education; for girls, playing an instrument was more important than learning to read. When guests and potential suitors visited, the children and teenagers would entertain with performances of the latest popular works.

All sorts of musical instruments were used in the home, and at various times the guitar, harp, concertina, and banjo were extremely popular. However, the most important musical instrument in the home was the piano, because it was useful as both a solo instrument and as accompaniment to a group of singers or instrumentalists. To accommodate home use, smaller pianos were created, first square pianos and later uprights. Small pianos took up less space and, although they were not as powerful as larger types, they were also less expensive. With the technological advances of the Industrial Revolution, the mass manufacturing of musical instruments—especially pianos—provided a seemingly endless supply of musical instruments for the huge markets of both the United States and Europe. The piano would remain a central component of domestic life until it was replaced by the phonograph, radio, and television in the twentieth century.

Christian Frederick Martin (1796—1873)

Steinway & Sons, New York

Having a general knowledge of the nineteen-century classical music, it naturally comes to the conclusion that the development of the classic music, especially the two converse types of classical music forms, is indispensible from the changes of the society. Often perceived as opulent or signifying some aspect of upper-level society before, classical music had generally never been as popular with working-class society. However, the traditional perception that only upper-class society had access to and appreciation for classical music, or even that classical music represented the upper-class society, might not be true, given that many working classical musicians fall somewhere in the middle-class income range in the United States, and that classical concertgoers and CD buyers were not necessarily upper class. A case in point is that in the Classical era, Mozart's opere buffa such as *Così fan tutte* were popular with the general public. From this perspective, the development of different aspects of the culture is indispensible from the changes of the society.

(1,276 words)

Vocabulary

ponder over   think about something carefully (especially for a long time) 仔细思考;考虑
comprehensive /ˌkɒmprɪˈhensɪv/ *adj.* 全面的;广泛的
upheaval /ʌpˈhiːvl/ *n.* a big change that causes a lot of confusion, worry and problems 巨变,剧变
democratic /ˌdeməˈkrætɪk/ *adj.* based on the principle that all members of society are equal rather than divided by money or social class 民主的
sweep /swiːp/ *vi.* to move suddenly and/or with force over an area or in a particular direction 席卷
consequence /ˈkɒnsɪkwəns/ *n.* a result of something that has happened 结果
alter /ˈɔːltə/ *vt.* to become different; to make something different 改变;更改
aristocratic /ˌærɪstəˈkrætɪk/ *adj.* belonging to typical or the aristocracy 贵族的
circle /ˈsɜːkl/ *n.* a group of people who are connected because they have the same interests, jobs, etc. 圈子,集团,流派
instrument /ˈɪnstrəmənt/ *n.* a tool or device used for a particular task, especially for delicate or musical or scientific work 乐器;仪器,工具
institution /ˌɪnstɪˈtjuːʃn/ *n.* a large important organization that has a particular purpose 社会团体,机构
symmetry /ˈsɪmətrɪ/ *n.* the exact match in size and shape between two halves, parts or sides of something 对称;整齐
espouse /ɪˈspaʊz/ *vt.* to give your support to a belief, policy, etc. 支持,赞成,信奉
rebel /rɪˈbel/ *vi.* to fight against or refuse to obey an authority 反抗,反叛
venue /ˈvenjuː/ *n.* a place where people meet for an organized event, for example, a concert, sporting event or conference 地点,场地
strata /ˈstreɪtə/ *n.* a class in a society 层,阶层
consist of   be composed of; be made up of 由……组成
access /ˈækses/ *n.* the opportunity or right to use something or to see something or somebody (使用或见到的)机会,权利

preservation /ˌprezəˈveɪʃən/ *n.* the act of making sure that something is kept 保存，保持
percussion instruments 打击乐器
symphonic /sɪmˈfɒnɪk/ *adj.* related to a symphony, which is a long complicated piece of music for a large orchestra, in three or four main parts 交响乐的
operatic /ˌɒpəˈrætɪk/ *adj.* related to an opera 歌剧的，歌剧风格的
orchestral /ɔːˈkestrəl/ *adj.* related to an orchestra 管弦乐的
wind /waɪnd/ *n.* the group of musical instruments in an orchestra that produce sounds when you blow into them 管乐器
brass /brɑːs/ *n.* the musical instruments made of metal, such as trumpets or French horns, that form a band or section of an orchestra 铜管乐器
concerto /kənˈtʃɜːtəʊ/ *n.* a piece of music for one or more solo instruments playing with an orchestra 协奏曲
virtuoso /ˌvɜːtʃuˈəʊzəʊ/ *n.* a person who is extremely skilful at doing something, especially playing a musical instrument 技艺超群的人，尤指演奏家
harpsichord /ˈhɑːpsɪkɔːd/ *n.* an early type of musical instrument similar to a piano, but with strings that are plucked, not hit 大键琴，羽管弦琴
opera buffa 喜歌剧
dazzle /ˈdæzl/ *vt.* to impress sb. a lot with your beauty, skill, knowledge, etc. 使目眩
virtuosity /ˌvɜːtʃuˈɒsəti/ *n.* a very high degree of skill in performing or playing 精湛技巧
virtuosic /ˌvɜːtʃuˈɒsɪk/ *adj.* extremely skillful in doing something, especially playing an instrument 技艺精湛的
intimate /ˈɪntɪmət/ *adj.* private and personal, having a close and friendly relationship 私人的，亲密的
parlor /ˈpɑːlə/ *n.* a room in a private house for sitting in, entertaining visitors, etc. 客厅，会客室
entertain /entəˈteɪn/ *vt.* to invite people as your guests, especially in your home 款待
financial /faɪˈnænʃəl/ *adj.* connected with money and finance 财政的，财务的
solo /ˈsəʊləʊ/ *n.* a piece of music, dance, or entertainment performed by only one person 独奏曲；独奏
sentimental /ˌsentɪˈmentl/ *adj.* producing emotions such as pity, romantic love or sadness 感伤的
well-rounded *adj.* providing or showing a variety of experience, ability, etc. 全面的，面面俱到的
potential /pəˈtenʃl/ *adj.* that can develop into something or be developed in the future 潜在的，可能的
ballad /ˈbæləd/ *n.* a song that tells a story 歌谣；民谣
concertina /ˌkɒnsəˈtiːnə/ *n.* a musical instrument like a small accordion, that you hold in both hands, and you press the ends together and pull them apart to produce sounds 六角手风琴

banjo /ˈbændʒəʊ/ *n.* a musical instrument like a guitar, with a long neck, a round body and four or more strings 班卓琴

accompaniment /əˈkʌmpənɪmənt/ *n.* music that is played to support singing or another instrument（音乐）伴奏

accommodate /əˈkɒmədeɪt/ *vt.* to change your behavior so that you can deal with a new situation better 适应

square piano 方形钢琴

opulent /ˈɒpjələnt/ *adj.* made or decorated using expensive materials 富丽堂皇的；华丽的

appreciation /əpriːʃɪˈeɪʃn/ *n.* pleasure that you have when you recognize and enjoy the good qualities of something 评价，评定

represent /ˌreprɪˈzent/ *vt.* to be a symbol of something 象征

perspective /pəˈspektɪv/ *n.* a particular attitude toward something; a way of thinking about something 判断事物的方法；眼力；观点

Proper Names

Romanticism	浪漫主义（运动）
Ludwig van Beethoven	路德维希·冯·贝多芬
Nicolò Paganini	尼科洛·帕格尼尼（意大利著名小提琴家）
Franz Liszt	弗朗茨·李斯特（匈牙利作曲家、钢琴家、指挥家）
Antonio Stradivari	安东尼奥·斯特拉迪瓦里（小提琴制琴师）
Guarneri del Gesù	瓜奈里家族（小提琴制琴师）
Jacob Stainer	雅克·斯内特尔（小提琴制琴师）
Amati family	阿玛蒂家族（小提琴制琴师）
Frédéric Chopin	弗雷德里克·肖邦（波兰裔法国作曲家、钢琴家）
Wolfgang Amadeus Mozart	沃尔夫冈·阿玛多伊斯·莫扎特（奥地利作曲家）
Così fan tutte	《女人心》（莫扎特作品）

Text Exploration

5 Choose the best answer to each question with the information from the text

1. What were the root causes of conflicts from the Napoleonic Wars to the American Civil War?
   A. Industrial Revolution.
   B. Romanticism.
   C. Struggles between the old world order and the new.
   D. Both A and B.

2. In the earlier times, what were the usual identities of the musicians, composers as well as the makers of musical instruments?
   A. Counterparts to the nobility.
   B. Employees of either the church or the court.
   C. Merely servants to aristocratic circles.

D. Both B and C.

3. The classicists of the late eighteenth century advocated some typical ideals. Which of the following is not correct?

   A. Symmetry.   B. Order.
   C. Democracy.   D. Form.

4. What were the possible actions and ideals of the Romanticists?

   A. Romantics valued the natural world.
   B. Romantics idealized the life of the common man.
   C. Romantics rebelled against social conventions, and stressed the importance of the emotional in art.
   D. All of the above.

5. As far as the development of classical music is concerned, what is the author's attitude toward the newly emerging middle class?

   A. Indifferent.   B. Positive.
   C. Negative.   D. Satirical.

6. According to the passage, two musicians in the nineteen century dazzled audiences throughout Europe with their performances, elevating the status of the musician from servant to demi-god. Who are they?

   A. Nicolò Paganini and Franz Liszt.
   B. Nicolò Paganini and Wolfgang Amadeus Mozart.
   C. Franz Liszt and Hector Berlioz.
   D. Richard Wagner and Hector Berlioz.

7. The violins made by which one is quieter and subtler than those of the others?

   A. Antonio Stradivari.
   B. Amati family.
   C. Guarneri del Gesù.
   D. Jacob Stainer and the Amati family.

8. According to the text, some composers/performers were able to support themselves financially by performing in these small venues and attracting wealthy patrons. Which musician of the following was one typical example of them?

   A. Franz Liszt.   B. Johannes Brahms.
   C. Frédéric Chopin.   D. Hector Berlioz.

9. As far as the parlor music is concerned, why the most important musical instrument was the piano?

   A. Because it was inexpensive at that time and it was easy to perform.
   B. Because the sound it made was the most pleasurable and would attract a large number of audience.
   C. Because it was useful as both a solo instrument and as accompaniment to a group of singers or instrumentalists.

D. All of the above answers are correct.
10. The piano would remain a central component of domestic life until it was replaced by some new inventions in the twentieth century. Which of the following is not belonging to the new ones?
   A. Phonograph.
   B. Television.
   C. Computer.
   D. Radio.

6 Complete the following chart with the information from the text.

Musical Instruments or Musical forms	Representative Musicians	Details
Violin	A famous violinist: (1782—1840) Name: _____	He preferred the larger and _____ violins like those by Antonio Stradivari or Guarneri del Gesù
Piano	A famous pianist: (1811—1886) Name: _____	He and Paganini dazzled audiences throughout Europe with their performances, elevating the status of the musician from _____ to _____.
Opera buffa	Name: Wolfgang Amadeus Mozart	His opere buffa such as _____ were popular with the general public

7 Discuss the following questions with the information from the text.

1. In some sense, a new economic stratum pushed the development of the classical music. Which economic stratum is it?

2. According to which standard does the author divide the nineteen century classical music into theater music and parlor music?

3. The "bigger is better" mentality led to some new musical forms. Can you give some examples?

4. What musical instrument do you like most? Can you give some reasons why you preferred it to others?

5. In some people's opinions, music has some positive effects on people's mind. For instance, it can pacify people's emotions. Can you say something about your understanding? Your real experience is preferred here in combination with your understanding.

Vocabulary Expansion

8 **Fill in the blanks with the right words given below. Change the form where necessary.**

| comprehensive | consequence | symmetry | espouse | rebel |
| access | preservation | virtuosity | entertain | financial |

1. Students must have _____ to good resources in order to broaden their knowledge and enhance their abilities.
2. They _____ the notion of equal opportunity for all in education, which is supported especially by women.
3. She is still _____ dependent on her parents although she has graduated from her university for nearly two years.
4. The matter has been _____ discussed because of the shortage of time.
5. People's bodies are never quite _____.
6. The _____ of the orchestra dazzled the audience.
7. The north of the country rose in _____ against the government which was corrupted.
8. Barbecues are a favorite way of _____ friends, especially in the western world.
9. The child was born deformed in _____ of an injury to its mother.
10. The central issue in the strike was the _____ of jobs.

9 **Choose the word or phrase that best keeps the meaning of the sentence if it is substituted for the underlined word or phrase.**

1. His talents are not fully appreciated in that company.
   A. valued   B. estimated
   C. known   D. appointed
2. They were left to ponder over the implications of the announcement.
   A. think about   B. make out
   C. figure out   D. distinguish
3. She is well known in the theatrical circles.
   A. round   B. family
   C. department   D. group or stratum
4. We still remember the latest upheavals in the educational system.
   A. great changes   B. modification
   C. progress   D. increases
5. Each color on the chart represents a different department.
   A. symbolizes   B. expresses
   C. demonstrates   D. distinguishes
6. It is a report that looks at the education system from the perspective of the deaf people.
   A. attitude or opinion   B. circumstance
   C. stance   D. need

Unit 4 Western Classical Music

7. First and foremost, we need to identify actual and potential problems of this project.

   A. existing   B. latent

   C. past   D. virtual

8. Rumors of his resignation swept through the company.

   A. spread in   B. brushed through

   C. moved in   D. cleaned in

9. They espoused the notion of equality between men and women in the work.

   A. supported   B. called

   C. raised   D. clarified

10. I quickly accommodated to the new schedule.

    A. changed   B. accustomed to

    C. entered into   D. finished up

10 Translate the Chinese sentences into English by simulating the sentences chosen from the text.

Chosen Sentences	Simulated Translations	Chinese Sentences
Have you ever **pondered over** the following questions: what is classical music? How to listen to this special kind of music?		老师让学生们仔细琢磨这段文字中谚语的含义。(**proverbs**)
Struggles between the old world order and the new were **the root causes of** conflicts from the Napoleonic Wars to the American Civil War.		贫富差距是导致这次罢工的根本原因。(**disparity, strike**)
This new economic stratum **consisted of** a larger number of people with more expendable income and more leisure time than those had ever existed before.		现场工作多半为进行磁带录音。(**fieldwork**)
With the rise of the middle class, more people wanted **access to** music performances and music education.		随着职业学校的兴起,越来越多的年轻人可以接受专业教育。(**vocational school**)
The piano would remain a central component of domestic life until it was **replaced by** the phonograph, radio, and television in the twentieth century.		所有现有的型号都终将被新的设计所取代。(**eventually**)

Supplementary Readings

11 Passage One

The Viennese school of piano making produced one of the two distinctive types of piano to develop in the eighteenth century. Like its counterpart, the English piano, the so-called Viennese piano began as a regional tradition and was first built by makers and players mostly in Austria and southern Germany. Through the enormous influence of Vienna, which was then the center of the musical world, these pianos would become known throughout Europe and used by most of the great composers of the classical music period.

Grand piano

The basic form of the Viennese piano was invented in Augsburg by the organist and keyboard maker Johann Andreas Stein (1728—1792). The composer and musician Wolfgang Amadeus Mozart (1756—1791) visited Stein in Augsburg in 1777. His purpose was to organize a concert and at the same time to look at the instruments of the Augsburg maker. Stein helped Mozart to produce the concert, which proved to be a great success and included a performance of the composer's triple-clavier concerto (K. 242) using three of Stein's pianos, with both of the men playing solo parts. During his stay, Mozart penned a famous letter to his father describing Stein's pianos and giving them much praise. It is believed that Mozart returned to Augsburg in 1781, where he played a duo piano concert with his sister Maria Anna (nicknamed Nannerl).

The rising popularity of the piano in Vienna caused a great demand for the instrument, which manufacturers were only too pleased to fill. By 1800, there were approximately sixty known makers building pianos in Vienna. The new musical styles of the time, which we now call "classical music", were well suited for the Viennese action piano and composers were beginning to write a great deal of music for the instrument. Musicians such as Mozart, Joseph Haydn, Johann Nepomuk Hummel, and the young Ludwig van Beethoven played these early Viennese instruments and helped drive the demand for them.

In the nineteenth century, musical trends changed as professional music moved out of the small chamber ensembles of the aristocracy and into the more democratized public auditoriums. As concert halls grew and the audience's appetite for spectacle increased, orchestras expanded and musical instrument makers of all types manufactured louder instruments with larger ranges. Piano makers were perhaps at the forefront of this movement, greatly expanding the compass of the instrument from the somewhat standard five octaves (sixty-one keys) of the late eighteenth century, through the first decades of the nineteenth century, until there were a full seven octaves (eighty-five keys) by the middle of the century. Composers and pianists in Vienna and beyond continued to use the Viennese piano through the middle of the century, with such famous musicians as Schubert, Mendelssohn, Chopin, Schumann, Kalkbrenner, Liszt, and Brahms all playing or owning instruments of the Viennese style.

1. Which of the following about the Viennese piano is NOT correct?
   A. It was one of the two distinctive types of piano to develop in the eighteenth century.
   B. Its counterpart was the English piano.
   C. It began as a regional tradition.
   D. It was first built by makers and players mostly in Britain and southern Germany.
2. What is Wolfgang Amadeus Mozart's purpose of visiting Johann Andreas Stein in Augsburg in 1777?
   A. To help the latter to make a better piano.
   B. To organize a concert.
   C. To look at the instruments of the Augsburg maker.
   D. Both B and C.
3. By 1800, there were approximately _____ known piano makers in Vienna.
   A. 50   B. 60
   C. 55   D. 65
4. What was Wolfgang Amadeus Mozart's attitude toward Johann Andreas Stein?
   A. Appreciative.   B. Confused.
   C. Jealous.   D. Admired.
5. What's the purpose of the author's writing this passage?
   A. To tell us the differences between the English piano and the Viennese piano.
   B. To help common people to learn how to play piano.
   C. To enable us to have a basic understanding of Viennese piano in the 18th and 19th century.
   D. To tell us the famous pianists in the world during the classical music period.

Passage Two

The beginnings of the European guitar are unknown. Scholars disagree as to whether the guitar, like the lute, was introduced to medieval Europe from the Middle East, or if it was indigenous to Europe. It is impossible to establish the history of the guitar before the Renaissance, but there are some much earlier plucked-string instruments which are related to later guitars either in physical form or playing technique.

During the medieval and Renaissance periods, a wide variety of plucked-string instruments could be found in both literature and art. The first instruments that modern audiences would recognize as guitars were built in the fifteenth century. At that time, the guitar was much smaller than its modern counterpart, and it was made with four double courses of gut strings (occasionally the top string was single). The guitar also had tied gut frets, friction tuning pegs, a decorative rose, a bridge set near the bottom of the instrument, and sometimes a round rather than a flat back. Its courses of double strings were tuned in the intervals of fourth, major third, fourth (for example, g'/g-c'/c'-e'/e'-a'), often with the lowest course in octave rather than unison doubling.

One of the typical guitars is the Baroque guitar. The Baroque guitar is similar in shape and body to earlier guitars, but is typified by five double courses of strings (which appeared as early as the late fifteenth century). From about 1600 until the mid-eighteenth century, its popularity supplanted both the four-course guitar and the six- or seven-course vihuela. The five-course Baroque guitar was a bit larger than the earlier model, averaging approximately 92 centimeters long, with string lengths of 63-70 centimeters. Guitars used by players were probably relatively plain, perhaps typified by many Spanish guitars of the period.

The repertory of the Baroque guitar required a mixture of techniques, including strummed or *eado* chords, *punteado* (the characteristic *pizzicato* lute technique), and the ringing melodic passage-work called *campanelas*. Five-course guitars featured a variety of tunings; one typical tuning was a/a-d'/d'-g/g-b/b-e'. The third course is the lowest, a system called "re-entrant" tuning, so that two fingers could more easily combine the low fifth and third courses with higher courses in scale passages. Also, without true bass strings, the instrument has a higher, brighter sound than the modern guitar.

The five-course guitar was a Spanish favorite, but spread to Italy and then to France, England, Germany, and the Low Countries in the seventeenth and eighteenth centuries.

1. According to the text information, which of the following about the origins of guitar is correct?
   A. We have clear idea of when and where it began.
   B. The historians have unanimous conclusion of the origin of guitar.
   C. Not all the historians and scientists agree with each other in this issue.
   D. No one has ever thought about this problem till now.
2. The first instruments that modern audiences would recognize as guitars were built in the _____ century.
   A. 15th B. 16th C. mid-16th D. mid-15th
3. The guitar in the beginning had some characteristics. Which of the following is NOT true?
   A. The guitar had tied gut frets, friction tuning pegs, a decorative rose as well as a bridge set near the bottom of the instrument.
   B. Sometimes it had a round back.
   C. The guitar was much larger than its modern counterpart.
   D. Its courses of double strings were tuned in the intervals of fourth, major third, fourth.
4. Compared with earlier guitars, the Baroque has some similarities and differences with them. Which of the following is inconsistent with the original information of the text?
   A. Baroque guitar is similar in shape and body to earlier guitars.
   B. Baroque guitar is typified by four double courses of strings.
   C. From about 1600 until the mid-eighteenth century, its popularity supplanted both the six- or seven-course vihuela.
   D. Baroque guitar was a bit larger than the earlier model.
5. Which of the following about the various tunings of the five-course guitars is consistent with the text information?
   A. The third course is the highest.
   B. Without true bass strings, the instrument has a lower, brighter sound than the modern guitar.
   C. Baroque guitar does not belong to this group.
   D. One typical tuning was a/a-d'/d'-g/g-b/b-e'.

Interactive Tasks

Role-play

13 **Role-play the following situation with your partner.**
Situation:
Li Lei, a Chinese student in Beijing University, is invited by his foreign friend Jack to

go to a concert. On the way to the concert, they have a heated discussion about the western classical music.

You may begin like this:

Li: I am greatly impressed by the virtuosity of the famous musicians, such as Beethoven, Liszt, Mozart and many others.

Jack: They are all extraordinary musicians in the classical music period.

Li: Yes, and as far as music is concerned, I like classical music best. What about you?

Jack: I cannot agree more. To our joy, the concert we are going to listen to is the classical music.

Group Work

14 **Work in groups to work out your own presentation.**

1. Form groups of four or five students;
2. Each group chooses a topic concerning classical music, e.g.

   An introduction to a classical musical form, such as piano;

   A demonstration of the music career of a musician and his representative works.
3. Members of each group collect materials from library and the Internet to work out their PPT slides;
4. Based on the PPt slides, each member of the group gives oral presentation of his part.

Follow-up Task

Writing

15 **Directions:** For this part, you are going to write a composition on the topic: **Classical Music and Emotions**. You should write at least 120 words following the outline given below in Chinese:

1. 古典音乐的演奏乐器种类繁多,可以满足不同听众的需要;
2. 人的情绪很容易受到环境的影响;
3. 古典音乐的音律可以影响人的情绪状态,如:可以起到安抚情绪和缓和情绪的作用。

Unit 5 Graphic Designing

Highlight

Topic area	Communication	Skills
American Designer Saul Bass; Graphic design in the 19th century; Graphic design in the early 20th century; The IBM Logos.	cost half as much as touch off last well into actively involved in deeply concerned with	Knowing some well-known graphic works in the early 20th century; Knowing graphic design in the 19th century; Describing and discussing logos.

Starting-out Task

1 Look at these pictures and discuss the following questions with your partner.

1. The following pictures show some famous graphic works in the early 20th century. Do you know where they come from and what they were used for?

2. What are the elements of design used in these works?
3. How do you like the styles of these graphic designs? Which one do you like best?

Listening Tasks

Micro Listening Skills

2 Listen to the following passage and try to fill in the missing words.

Graphic design is a creative process that 1. _____ art and technology to communicate ideas. Graphic designers work with a variety of communication tools in order to 2. _____ a message from a client to a 3. _____ audience. They handle drawn, painted, photographed, or 4. _____ images, but they also design the letterforms that 5. _____ various typefaces found in books, menus, movie credits and even on computer 6. _____. They create or choose these elements—the typography, images, and the so-called "white space"—and then 7. _____ them into one piece of artwork. Graphic design is a part of your daily life. From 8. _____ things like gum wrappers to huge things like 9. _____ to the T-shirt you're wearing, graphic design informs, persuades, 10. _____, attracts attention and provides pleasure.

Unit 5 Graphic Designing

Passage

American Designer Saul Bass

Logos designed by Saul Bass   Vertigo

Words & Phrases

Saul Bass /sɔːl ˈbɑːs/	索尔·巴斯
geometric /ˌdʒɪəˈmetrɪkl/ *adj.*	几何线条的
uncanny /ʌnˈkænɪ/ *adj.*	不寻常的
title sequences	片头序列
opening credits	片头字幕
top off	结束，完成
Why Man Creates	《人为何要创造》
Academy Awards	学院奖（奥斯卡金像奖）

3 **Listen to the passage and decide whether the following statements are true (T) or false (F).**

1. ____ In his early years Bass studied designing in California.
2. ____ Bass began his work designing logos for big companies.
3. ____ In 1964 Bass won an Oscar for his short film *Why Man Creates*.
4. ____ Bass applied animated graphic design to opening credits for horror films.
5. ____ Bass designed the posters for several Academy Awards shows.

4 **Listen to the passage again and complete the following sentences with the information you have heard.**

1. Bass developed a unique style that is both _____ and _____.

2. Bass was able to use _____ shapes to deliver a _____.
3. Bass started his career in the _____ doing _____.
4. Bass created _____ for companies, many of which _____.

Reading Tasks

Focus Reading

Pre-reading Questions
1. What do you think of the Industrial Revolution?
2. How much do you know about William Morris and the English Arts and Crafts Movement?
3. Have you ever heard of any artist who is related to Art Nouveau?

Graphic Design in the 19th Century①

The Industrial Revolution was a dynamic process that began in the late 18th century and lasted well into the 19th century. The agricultural and handicraft economies of the West evolved into industrial manufacturing economies powered by steam engines, electricity, and internal-combustion motors. Many aspects of human activity were irrevocably changed. Society found new ways to use graphic designs and developed new technologies to produce them. Industrial technology lowered the cost of printing and paper, thus allowing a designer's work to reach a wider audience than ever before.

One popular medium for the graphic designer became the poster. Posters printed with large wood types were used extensively to advertise new modes of transportation, entertainment, and manufactured goods throughout the 19th century. This was possible in part because type founders developed larger sizes of types and innovated new typefaces including sans serif and decorative designs. An American printer, Darius Wells, invented a router that enabled the economical manufacture of abundant quantities of large wooden types, which cost less than half as much as large metal types.

The poster became even more popular as a result of advances in lithography, invented in 1798 by Alois Senefelder of Bavaria. Building upon this discovery, chromolithographs were widely used in the second half of the 19th century. Designers created increasingly colorful posters that decorated the walls of cities, publicizing events, entertainment shows, and household products. Designers of chromolithographic prints drew the text and image as one piece of artwork; freed from the technical restraints of letterpress printing, they could invent fanciful ornaments and lettering styles at will.

Momentum for this poster-design approach began in France, where poster designer Jules Chéret was a pioneer of the movement. Beginning his career in 1867, he created large-scale lithographic posters that featured vibrant color, animated figures, and textured areas

---

①This text is adapted from *Graphic Design* at http://www.britannica.com

juxtaposed against flat shapes, capturing *la belle époque* of turn-of-the-century Paris. Chéret designed more than one thousand posters during his career.

During the 19th century, one by-product of industrialism was a decline in the quality of book design and production. Cheap, thin paper, shoddy presswork, drab, gray inks, and anemic text typefaces were often the order of the day. Near the end of the century, a book-design renaissance began as a direct result of the English Arts and Crafts Movement. William Morris, the leader of the movement, was a major figure in the evolution of design. Morris was actively involved in designing furniture, stained glass, textiles, wallpapers, and tapestries from the 1860s through the 1890s. Deeply concerned with the problems of industrialization and the factory system, Morris believed that a return to the craftsmanship and spiritual values of the Gothic period could restore balance to modern life. He rejected tasteless mass-produced goods and poor craftsmanship in favor of the beautiful, well-crafted objects he designed.

A page from *The Works of Geoffrey Chaucer*

In 1888 Morris decided to establish a printing press to recapture the quality of books from the early decades of printing. His Kelmscott Press began to print books in 1891, using an old handpress, rich dense inks, and handmade paper. It recaptured the beauty and high standards of incunabula, and the book again became an art form. The press's masterwork is the 556-page *The Works of Geoffrey Chaucer*, which took four years in the making.

The influence of William Morris and the Kelmscott Press upon graphic design was remarkable. Morris's concept of the well-designed page, his beautiful typefaces, and his sense of design unity inspired a new generation of graphic designers. Morris's searching and reexamination of earlier type styles also touched off an energetic redesign process that resulted in a major improvement in the quality and variety of fonts available for design and printing; many designers directly imitated the style of the Kelmscott borders, initials, and type styles. More commercial areas of graphic design, such as printing and advertising, were similarly revitalized by the success of Morris.

Also inspired by the Arts and Crafts Movement, American book designer Bruce Rogers played a significant role in upgrading book design. By applying the ideals of the beautifully designed book to commercial production, Rogers set the standard for well-designed books in the early 20th century. Rogers possessed a fine sense of visual proportion. He also saw design as a decision-making process, feeling that subtle choices about margins, paper, type styles and sizes, and spatial position combine to create a unity and harmony.

Art Nouveau was an international design movement that emerged and touched all of the design arts during the 1890s and the early 20th century. Its defining characteristic was a sinuous curvilinear line. Art Nouveau graphic designs often utilized stylized abstract shapes, contoured lines, and flat space inspired by Japanese ukiyo-e woodblock prints. Building upon the example of the Japanese, Art Nouveau designers made color, rather than tonal modeling, the primary visual attribute of their graphics.

One of the most innovative posters of the Art Nouveau movement was Henri de Toulouse-Lautrec's 1891 poster of the dancer La Goulue, who was then performing at the Moulin Rouge. Toulouse-Lautrec captured the atmosphere and activity of the dance by reducing imagery to simple, flat shapes that convey an expression of the performance and environment. Although Toulouse-Lautrec only produced about three dozen posters, his early application of the ukiyo-e influence propelled graphic design toward more reductive imagery. He often integrated lettering with his imagery by drawing it in the same casual technique as the pictorial elements.

La Goulue, poster designed by Toulouse-Lautrec

Alphonse Mucha, a young Czech artist who worked in Paris, is widely regarded as the graphic designer who took Art Nouveau to its ultimate visual expression. Beginning in the 1890s, he created designs—usually featuring beautiful young women whose hair and clothing swirl in rhythmic patterns—that achieved an idealized perfection. He organized into tight compositions lavish decorative elements, stylized lettering, and sinuous female forms. Like many other designers at the time, Mucha first captured public notice for poster designs, but he also received commissions for magazine covers, packages, book designs, publicity materials, and even postage stamps. In this way, the role and scope of graphic-design activity steadily expanded throughout the period.

Job, poster designed by Alphonse Mucha

Will Bradley, a self-taught American designer, emerged as another early practitioner of

Art Nouveau. His magazine covers, lettering styles, and posters displayed a wide range of techniques and design approaches. Bradley synthesized inspiration from the European Art Nouveau and Arts and Crafts movements into a personal approach to visual imagery. By the 1890s, photoengraving processes had been perfected. These allowed much more accurate reproduction of original artwork than hand engraving. Bradley's work, in which he integrated words and picture into a dynamic whole, was printed from plates using this new technology.

Art Nouveau rejected historicism and emphasized formal invention, and so it became a transitional movement from Victorian design to the modern art movements of the early 20th century. This sense of transition is quite evident in the work of the Belgian artist and designer Henry van de Velde. After turning from Post-Impressionist painting to furniture and graphic design in the 1890s, he used lines and shapes inspired by the natural world and abstracted them to the point that they appeared as "pure form"; that is, they appeared as abstract forms invented by the designer rather than as forms from nature. In works such as his poster for Tropon food concentrate (1899), undulating linear movements, organic shapes, and warm-hued colors combine into a nonobjective graphic expression. Although this poster has been interpreted as signifying the process of separating egg yolks and whites, the typical viewer perceives it as pure form.

poster for Tropon food concentrate

Similarly exploring issues of form, architects Charles Rennie Mackintosh and Herbert McNair joined artists (and sisters) Margaret and Frances Macdonald in a revolutionary period of creativity beginning in the 1890s. This group in Glasgow (the Glasgow Four) developed a rectilinear structure held together by a geometric composition combined with floral and curvilinear elements. The work used bold, simple lines to define flat planes of color. They synthesized rectangular structure with romantic and religious imagery in their unorthodox furniture, crafts, and graphic designs. In a poster it made for the Glasgow Institute of Fine Arts, for example, the group's emphasis upon rising vertical composition is evident.

(1382words)

Vocabulary

handicraft /ˈhændɪkrɑːft/ *n.* craft that requires skillful hands 手工艺
internal-combustion /ɪnˈtɜːnəl kəmˈbʌstʃən/ *n.* 内燃机
irrevocably /ɪˈrevəkəblɪ/ *adv.* in an irrevocable manner 不能取消地
typeface /taɪpfeɪs/ *n.* a specific size and style of type within a type family 字体

san serif 无衬线字体
router /ruːtə/ n. 木版切割机
lithography /lɪˈθəgæfɪ/ n. 平版印刷术
chromolithograph /krəʊməˈlɪθəgæf/ n. 彩色平版印刷
publicize /pʌblɪsaɪz/ vt. make public 宣传；推广
letterpress /ˈletəpres/ n. 凸版印刷
fanciful /ˈfænsɪfʊl/ adj. having a curiously intricate quality 式样奇特的
lettering /ˈletərɪŋ/ n. letters inscribed on something 书写的文字
at will 随意；任意
momentum /məʊˈmentəm/ n. an impelling force or strength 势头
vibrant /ˈvaɪbrənt/ adj. of colors that are bright and striking (色彩)鲜明的
juxtapose /ˌdʒʌkstəˈpəʊz/ vt. place side by side 并置，并列
la belle époque 美好年代（泛指欧洲19世纪末期到一战之间的历史阶段）
shoddy /ˈʃɒdɪ/ adj. of inferior workmanship and materials 粗制滥造的；劣质的
anemic /əˈniːmɪk/ adj. lacking vigor or energy 贫血的
order of the day 议事日程；流行的事物
textile /ˈtekstaɪl/ n. artifact made by weaving or knitting natural or synthetic fibers 纺织品
tapestry /ˈtæpɪstrɪ/ n. a wall hanging of heavy hand-woven fabric with pictorial designs 挂毯
craftsmanship /ˈkrɑːftsmənʃɪp/ n. skill in an occupation or trade 技术；技艺
Gothic /ˈgɒθɪk/ adj. 哥特式的
recapture /ˌriːˈkæptʃə/ vt. capture again 取回
incunabula /ˌɪnkjʊˈnæbjʊlə/ n. 古版书
exhaustive /ɪgˈzɔːstɪv/ adj. very thorough 详尽的；彻底的
touch off 触发，激起
font /fɒnt/ n. a specific size and style of type within a type family 字体；字形
border /ˈbɔːdə/ n. the boundary line or the area immediately inside the boundary 镶边；包边
initial /ɪˈnɪʃəl/ n. the first letter of a word 首字母
revitalize /riːˈvaɪtəlaɪz/ vt. give new life or vigor to 使具有新的活力
upgrade /ˈʌpgreɪd/ vt. improve what was old or outdated 升级；提高品级(或标准)
sinuous /ˈsɪnjʊəs/ adj. curving in and out 弯弯曲曲的
curvilinear /kəːvɪˈlɪnɪə/ adj. characterized by or following a curved line 曲线的
contoured /ˈkɒntʊəd/ adj. 波状外形的
ukiyo-e 浮世绘
woodblock /ˈwʊdblɒk/ adj. 木版印刷的
propel /prəʊˈpel/ vt. cause to move forward with force 推动；推进
reductive /rɪˈdʌktɪv/ adj. characterized by or causing diminution or curtailment 还原的；减少的
swirl /swɜːl/ vi. turn in a twisting or spinning motion 盘绕，打旋

rhythmic /ˈrɪðmɪk/ *adj.* recurring with measured regularity 有节奏的
lavish /ˈlævɪʃ/ *adj.* characterized by extravagance and profusion 极其丰富的
practitioner /prækˈtɪʃənə/ *n.* someone who practices a learned profession 实践者
synthesize /ˈsɪnθəsaɪz/ *vt.* combine so as to form a more complex product 合成,综合
photoengraving 照相制版
engraving /ɪnˈgreɪvɪŋ/ *n.* a block or plate that has been engraved 雕版
abstract /ˈæbstrækt/ *vt.* remove by drawing out gently 提取,抽取
undulating /ˈʌndjʊleɪtɪŋ/ *adj.* 波状的;波浪起伏的
nonobjective /ˌnɒnəbˈjektɪv/ *adj.* not representing or imitating external reality or the objects of nature 抽象的;非写实的
signify /ˈsɪgnɪfaɪ/ *vt.* represent or denote 表示;意味
rectilinear /rektɪˈlɪnɪə/ *adj.* characterized by a straight line or lines 直线的
flora /ˈflɒrə/ *n.* all the plant life in a particular region or period 植物系;植物群
unorthodox /ʌnˈɔːθəˌdɒks/ *adj.* breaking with convention or tradition 非正统的
rectangular /ˈrektæŋgjʊlə/ *adj.* having four right angles 矩形的

Proper Names

Darius Wells	达留斯·威尔斯(美国发明家)
Alois Senefelder	阿罗斯·塞菲尔德(德国发明家)
Bavaria	巴伐利亚(德国地名)
Jules Chéret	儒勒·舍雷(法国艺术家)
William Morris	威廉·莫里斯(英国设计师)
Arts and Crafts Movement	英国工艺美术运动
Kelmscott Press	凯尔姆斯科特出版社
The Works of Geoffrey Chaucer	《杰弗里·乔叟作品集》
Bruce Rogers	布鲁斯·罗杰斯(美国设计师)
Art Nouveau	新艺术运动
Henri de Toulouse-Lautrec	亨利·德·图卢兹·罗特列克(法国艺术家)
La Goulue	拉·古留(法国人名)
the Moulin Rouge	红磨坊(巴黎)
Alphonse Mucha	阿尔丰斯·穆夏(捷克艺术家)
Will Bradley	威尔·布拉德利(美国设计师)
Henry van de Velde	亨利·凡德·威尔德(比利时艺术家)
Tropon food concentrate	Tropon 浓缩食品
Charles Rennie Mackintosh	查尔斯·雷尼·麦金托希(苏格兰建筑师)
Herbert McNair	赫伯特·麦克内尔(苏格兰建筑师)
Margaret Macdonald	玛格丽特·麦克唐纳(苏格兰艺术家)
Frances Macdonald	弗朗西斯·麦克唐纳(苏格兰艺术家)
the Glasgow Institute of Fine Arts	格拉斯哥美术学院

Text Exploration

5 **Choose the best answer to each question with the information from the text.**

1. Which of the following items was invented by Darius Wells?
   A. A large metal type used in book designs.
   B. A decorative typeface used in posters.
   C. A machine to produce large wooden types.
   D. A device to manufacture large metal types.

2. Which of the following is NOT true of chromolithograpy?
   A. It was developed from lithography.
   B. It was invented by Alois Senefelder in 1798.
   C. It brought more technical freedom to graphic design.
   D. It was widely used in the second half of the 19th century.

3. Jules Chéret's lithographic posters had the following features EXCEPT _____.
   A. bright and striking colors   B. realistic figures
   C. textured areas   D. two dimensional shapes

4. Which of the following is NOT true of William Morris?
   A. He established the Kelmscott Press.
   B. He believed in the spiritual values of the ancient Greek.
   C. He was successful in promoting the craftsmanship.
   D. He designed furniture and stained glass.

5. Which of the following does not represent Bruce Rogers's idea about designing?
   A. Design is a decision-making process.
   B. Standards should be set for well-designed books.
   C. Good design should not be applied to commercial production.
   D. The unity and harmony come from careful choices about details.

6. How did Toulouse-Lautrec integrate lettering with the imagery in his work?
   A. He utilized contoured lines inspired by the ukiyo-e woodblock prints.
   B. He reduced the imagery to simple shapes to match with lettering.
   C. He drew lettering in the same delicate way as he handled the pictorial elements.
   D. He handled lettering in the same casual way as he did with the pictorial elements.

7. Much of Mucha's early fame can be attributed to his designs for _____.
   A. posters   B. books
   C. postage stamps   D. packages

8. Bradley's work was printed from plates using _____.
   A. hand engraving which was more efficient than photoengraving
   B. hand engraving which was as accurate as photoengraving
   C. photoengraving which was more precise than hand engraving
   D. photoengraving which was as efficient as hand engraving

9. The work of Henry van de Velde _____.
   A. used forms copied directly from nature
   B. utilized "pure forms" abstracted from nature
   C. applied Post-Impressionist techniques to designing
   D. only focused on furniture design
10. Which of the following is NOT true of the Glasgow Four?
   A. Their works are characterized by rectilinear structures.
   B. They applied romantic and religious imagery in their design.
   C. They came from four families.
   D. They focused on probing new forms of art.

6 Complete the following chart with the information from the text.

Paragraphs	Aspects	Details
1	The Industrial Revolution	The Industrial Revolution has changed _____ of the West into _____; It also changed the _____ and provided _____.
2—4	Poster as a popular medium	Posters were used widely to _____; The poster became a popular medium for graphic designing, partly due to _____ and _____; It became even more popular as a result of _____ and the _____.
5—8	William Morris and the Kelmscott Press	Morris believed that a return to _____ _____ could restore balance to modern life; Morris' Kelmscott Press recaptured _____ of incunabula, and the book again became _____; The Kelmscott Press had a great impact on _____.
9—14	Art Nouveau	Art Nouveau was an _____ that touched all of the design arts; Its graphic designs were inspired by _____ and characterized by _____; It became a transitional movement from _____ to the _____.

7 Discuss the following questions with the information from the text.

1. What technology could possibly make the poster a popular medium for graphic designing in the 19th century?

2. How did William Morris and the Kelmscott Press influence the graphic design at that time?

3. What is Art Nouveau and its defining characteristic?

4. Which designer mentioned in the above text do you like best?

5. Which common use of graphic design are you interested in, posters, book designs, or packages?

Vocabulary Expansion

8 Fill in the blanks with the right words given below. Change the form where necessary.

| publicize | craftsmanship | vibrant | practitioner | upgrade |
| revitalize | momentum | abstract | rhythmic | signify |

1. They began to lose _____ in the second half of the game.
2. It is not right to _____ science and religion from their historical context.
3. This old art form needs to be _____ and promoted to a new generation.
4. It will take a month for the company to _____ their security systems.
5. He always uses _____ colors in his paintings.
6. The artist's work shows the perfect union of _____ and imagination.
7. I love the _____ melody as well as the soft and fresh style of the music.
8. As an advocator and _____ of the public library, he bought and collected books and provided reading chances for each person.
9. Red blooms _____ romance and passion and yellow denotes friendship.
10. We are trying to _____ our products by advertisement on buses.

9 Choose the word or phrase that best keeps the meaning of the sentence if it is substituted for the underlined word or phrase.

1. If you drop one of these plates, it will be irrevocably scuffed, marked, damaged or even broken into pieces.
   A. finally　　B. incurably　　C. permanently　　D. unalterably
2. Edward Jenner's discovery of the first effective vaccine against smallpox set the pace for modern medicine to evolve into what it is today.
   A. get into　　B. enter into　　C. develop into　　D. extend into
3. Engineers are forever seeking more economical methods of solving old problems.
   A. thrifty　　B. economic　　C. generous　　D. careful
4. She is making a desperate bid to free herself from a loveless marriage.
   A. take…off　　B. set…from　　C. rid…of　　D. release…of
5. They will impose a fine on anyone who should pick flowers at will.
   A. at one's best　　　　　　　　B. at any moment
   C. at one's option　　　　　　　D. at arm's length
6. Our new washing-machine keeps breaking down; it's entirely due to its shoddy workmanship.

A. confused   B. casual   C. irregular   D. inferior

7. Students are required to do **exhaustive** research prior to writing the term paper.

A. superficial   B. sketchy   C. thorough   D. casual

8. The fatal accident **touched off** a renewed debate about Metro safety.

A. set off   B. turned off   C. let off   D. gave off

9. His works **synthesize** photography, painting and linguistic devices.

A. analyze   B. dissect   C. produce   D. combine

10. He couldn't **recapture** the form he'd shown in getting to the semi-final.

A. reach   B. regain   C. recognize   D. enter

10 Translate the Chinese sentences into English by simulating the sentences chosen from the text.

Chosen Sentences	Simulated Translations	Chinese Sentences
Industrial technology lowered the cost of printing and paper, thus allowing a designer's work to **reach a wider audience than ever before**.		互联网使自由设计师可以拥有比以往更广泛的受众。（**freelance designer**）
An American printer, Darius Wells, invented a router that enabled the economical manufacture of abundant quantities of large wooden types, which **cost less than half as much as** large metal types.		据报道，规划好的高速列车系统的耗资不到兴建高速公路和机场跑道的一半。（**high-speed**, **freeway lane**）
The Industrial Revolution was a dynamic process that began in the late 18th century and **lasted well into** the 19th century.		一些气象学家担心干旱可能会一直持续到2012年。（**meteorologist**）
Morris was **actively involved in** designing furniture, stained glass, textiles, wallpapers, and tapestries from the 1860s through the 1890s.		她曾积极参与到人力资源管理的实践中去，管理了公司大约200名员工。（**HR practices**）
Deeply concerned with the problems of industrialization and the factory system, Morris believed that a return to the craftsmanship and spiritual values of the Gothic period could restore balance to modern life.		很多人深切关注着这场地震，他们将灾难变成了爱的火炬接力赛。（**torch relay**）

Supplementary Readings

Passage One

In the first decade of the 20th century, the experiments with pure form begun in the 1890s continued and evolved. In Austria, a group of young artists led by Gustav Klimt formed the Vienna Secession(维也纳分离派). These artists and architects rejected academic traditions and sought new modes of expression. In their exhibition posters and layouts for the Secession magazine, *Ver Sacrum* (*Sacred Spring*), members pushed graphic design in uncharted aesthetic directions. Koloman Moser's poster for the 13th Secession exhibition (1902) blends three figures, lettering, and geometric ornament into a modular whole. The work is composed of horizontal, vertical, and circular lines that define flat shapes of red, blue, and white. Moser and architect Josef Hoffmann were instrumental in establishing the "Vienna Workshops", which produced furniture and design objects.

The German school of poster design called Plakatstil ("Poster Style") similarly continued the exploration of pure form. Initiated by Lucian Bernhard with his first poster in 1905, Plakatstil was characterized by a simple visual language of sign and shape. Designers reduced images of products to elemental, symbolic shapes that were placed over a flat background color, and they lettered the product name in bold shapes.

In Germany, Peter Behrens played an important role in graphic design. Behrens helped to develop a philosophy of "New Objectivity" in design, which emphasized technology, manufacturing processes, and function, with style subordinated to purpose. For AEG (a German company), Behrens developed what may be considered the first cohesive "visual identity system"; he consistently used the same logo, roman typeface styles, and geometric grids to create product catalogs, magazines, posters, other printed matter, and architectural graphics. Behrens's work for AEG was a harbinger of a major area of graphic design in the second half of the 20th century: the creation of the corporate identity.

Graphic design also played an important political role in the early 20th century. Color printing had advanced to a high level, and governments used poster designs to raise funds for the war effort, encourage productivity at home, present negative images of the enemy, encourage enlistment in the armed forces, and shore up citizens' morale. Plakatstil was used for many Axis(轴心国) posters, while the Allies(同盟国) primarily used magazine illustrators versed in realistic narrative images for their own propaganda posters. The contrast can be seen in a comparison of German designer Gipkens's poster for an exhibition of captured Allied aircraft with American illustrator James Montgomery Flagg's army recruiting poster (both 1917). Gipkens expressed his subject through signs and symbols reduced to flat color planes within a unified visual composition. In contrast, Flagg used bold lettering and naturalistic portraiture of an allegorical person appealing directly to the potential recruit.

1. Which of the following is NOT true of Koloman Moser?

   A. He is a member of the Vienna Secession.

B. He designed a poster for the 13th Secession exhibition.

   C. He used figures, lettering, and geometric ornament in all his posters.

   D. He helped to establish the "Vienna Workshops".

2. Who created the first Plakatstil poster?

   A. Josef Hoffmann.　　　　　　　B. Lucian Bernhard.

   C. Gipkens.　　　　　　　　　　D. Peter Behrens.

3. Which of the following element is closest in meaning to "harbinger" (Line 7, Para3)?

   A. Follower.　　　　　　　　　　B. Forerunner.

   C. Advocate.　　　　　　　　　　D. Practitioner.

4. Which of the following are mentioned as purposes of Graphic design in the early 20th century?

   A. Aesthetic, educational, commercial, and corporate purposes.

   B. Educational, commercial, corporate and political purposes.

   C. Aesthetic, commercial, corporate and political purposes.

   D. Aesthetic, educational, commercial, and corporate purposes.

5. The poster produced by Gipkens for an exhibition of captured Allied aircraft has all the following features EXCEPT _____.

   A. a realistic narrative image

   B. simple signs and shapes

   C. flat color planes

   D. a unified visual composition

12 Passage Two

IBM has one of the world's most recognizable logos. In the 96 years of the Company's existence, the IBM logo has been changed and improved many times. Over the years, the Company has used a series of IBM logos on products, stationery, vehicles, service packs, flags etc. to promote immediate recognition of the brand throughout the world.

The first IBM logo was created in 1924, when the Computing-Tabulating-Recording Company changed its name to International Business Machines Corporation. As part of their transformation, the creators of the company decided to replace the previous ornate, rococo letters of the "CTR" logo into more modern wording of "Business Machines" in sans-serif font. The 1924 IBM logo was given a globe shape girded by the word "International" to suggest the company's worldwide expansion.

The globe shape IBM logo failed to accomplish the friendly and caring image of the company as it was faceless, bureaucratic, and cold. Thus, the company made a change to its IBM logo, the first in the company's 22 years of business profile. The new logo appeared on the masthead of the January 1, 1947 issue of Business Machines with surprisingly little fanfare. The previously designed globe was altered to the simple lettering of "IBM" in a typeface called Beton Bold.

In May 1956, Tom Watson Jr. took over the company as the new Chief Executive after his father passed away. In steps to exemplify the new management and technological era, the company endured subtle changes in its IBM logo to communicate that any change would come within an overall continuity. Created by noted graphic designer Paul Rand, the new logotype replaced the former one with City Medium, as the letters "IBM" took on a more solid, grounded and balanced appearance. In 1972, a new version of IBM logo was introduced, again designed by Paul Rand. The solid letters were replaced by horizontal stripes, suggesting speed and dynamism.

Now IBM has one of the world's most recognizable logos. It is simple yet very appealing and a prefect visual representation of the multinational. If observed closely, the 8-bar blue IBM logo, also known as "Big Blue", generates a message of "Equality". The Big Blue IBM logo, with its lower right parallel lines, highlights in the shape of an "equals" sign. Furthermore, the term "BIG" in the Big Blue IBM logo refers to the company's size in the market share, whereas, the "BLUE" is the official color of the eight-bar IBM logo.

1. What is the passage mainly about?

    A. Paul Rand and IBM logos.

    B. The graphic evolution of IBM logos.

    C. The typography of IBM logos.

    D. The power of IBM logos.

2. Which of the following is NOT true of the first IBM logo?

    A. It was made in sans-serif font.

    B. It had a globe shape encircled by the word "International".

    C. It helped to establish the friendly and caring image of the company.

    D. It lasted about 22 years before it was replaced by a new design.

3. Which of the following is NOT true of the 1956 IBM logo?

    A. It was totally different from the 1947 IBM logo.

    B. It was used to signify a new management and technological era.

    C. It conveyed a message that any change would come within an overall continuity.

    D. It had a more solid, grounded and balanced look than the previous one.

4. Which of the following IBM logo was NOT designed by Paul Rand?

    A. "IBM" in a typeface called Beton Bold.

    B. "IBM" in a typeface called City Medium.

    C. The 1972 version of IBM logo.

    D. "IBM" with horizontal stripes.

5. A sense of "Equality" suggested by the Big Blue IBM logo can be attributed to its _____.

    A. horizontal stripes

    B. blue color

    C. lower parallel lines

    D. big letters

Interactive Tasks

Role-play

13 **Role-play the following situation with your partner.**
Situation:
　　Li Ming and his American friend David are walking around in the downtown area when David catches a glimpse of the Starbucks.
You may begin like this:
David: Look, the Starbucks! Shall we go and have a cup of coffee there?
Li: Sure. Starbucks is easy to recognize among so many shops here. Look around, and you find it quickly.
David: The Starbucks logo shows a green band with two stars and a crowned Siren in the center of the logo. It's simple yet very attractive.
Li: I like its green and white color and the image of the girl, especially her wavy hair.

Group Work

14 **Work in groups to work out your own short drama.**
1. Form groups of four or five students;
2. Each group chooses a topic concerning graphic design, e.g.
   A study of graphic works at home or abroad;
   An introduction to a designer and his works.
3. Members of each group collect materials from library and the Internet to work out their PPT slides;
4. Based on the PPT slides, each member of the group gives oral presentation of his part.

Follow-up Task

Writing

15 **Directions**: For this part, you are going to write a composition on the topic: **Posters in Modern life**. You should write at least 120 words following the outline given below in Chinese:
1. 随处可见的海报与现代生活密切相关；
2. 海报一般分为商业海报、公益广告及艺术海报三大类；
3. 好的海报应该有以下特点……

Unit 6　Landscaping

Highlight

Topic area	Communication	Skills
Some best-known gardens in the world; French formal gardens; English landscape gardens; Traditional Chinese gardens.	hold a central place in rarely equaled in at regular intervals conform to Just as...so.... prone to	Knowing some best-known gardens in the world; Knowing the French formal garden; Describing and discussing gardens.

Starting-out Task

1 Look at these pictures and discuss the following questions with your partner.

1. The following pictures show some best-known gardens in the world. Can you tell their names and locations?

Unit 6 Landscaping

2. What else, such as the time of construction and the styles, do you know about these gardens?
3. How do you like the styles of these gardens?

Listening Tasks

Micro Listening Skills

2 Listen to the following passage and try to fill in the missing words.

Informal gardens are 1. _____ by flowing curves, non-symmetrical arrangements of 2. _____ and spaces and plants that are allowed to grow into their natural shapes. The lines are softer and more 3. _____ and the planting is less rigid than formal gardens. 4. _____, gardens have always had their most formal areas near the house, 5. _____ becoming more informal as they get further away and this is still a good 6. _____ today. In the informal garden, the 7. _____ framework is almost entirely 8. _____ by planting and the garden should look as though it has grown up naturally. Informal gardens are harder to design than formal ones as they are ruled by 9. _____ and natural looking planting. A site that isn't a 10. _____ shape can be a good basis for an informal garden.

Passage

Central Park

Central Park, Wollman Rink

Aerial view of Central Park

Words & Phrases

Frederick Law Olmsted /ˈfredrɪk lɔːˈɒlmsted/	弗雷德里克·劳·奥姆斯特德
Calvert Vaux /ˈkælvɜːt vɒks/	卡尔弗特·沃克斯
wetland /ˈwetlænd/ n.	湿地
reshape /riːˈʃeɪp/ v.	改造
rink /ˈrɪŋk/ n.	溜冰场
carousel /ˌkærəˈsel/ n.	旋转木马
reverently /ˈrevərəntlɪ/ adv.	恭敬地
foresight /ˈfɔːsaɪt/ n.	远见

3 Listen to the passage and decide whether the following statements are true (T) or false (F).

1. ____ Central Park was the first city park in the United States.
2. ____ Olmsted and Vaux were influenced by French garden style.
3. ____ The natural environment in Central Park is almost entirely landscaped.
4. ____ Central Park contains several natural hills and lakes.
5. ____ Some people call Central Park the heart of New York.

4 Listen to the passage again and complete the following sentences with the information you have heard.

1. The park was first opened in _____ on _____ acres of land.
2. The area now occupied by Central Park was mostly _____.
3. Central Park has a theater to present _____ each summer.
4. Today landscape architects still praise Olmsted for his _____ and _____.

Reading Tasks

Focus Reading

Pre-reading Questions

1. Do you know any famous gardens of France?
2. Have you ever heard of the Sun King and Versailles?
3. What makes the Gardens of Versailles so famous?

French Formal Gardens in the 17th Century[①]

Gardens held a central place in the history of seventeenth European art and architecture. In this century, geometric layouts—defined as French formal or Baroque gardens—were designed according to exact mathematical rules and strict symmetry and planted with artificially trimmed plants and trees. This style is based on the principle of imposing order over nature. It reached its apogee with the creation of the Gardens of Versailles and was widely copied by other courts of Europe.

The French formal garden evolved from the Italian Renaissance garden, a style imported into France at the beginning of the 16th century. The Italian Renaissance style, typified by the Boboli Gardens in Florence and the Villa Medici in Fiesole, was characterized by a geometric arrangement of planting beds or parterres laid out in symmetrical patterns; the use of fountains and cascades to animate the garden; stairways and ramps to unite different levels of the garden; grottos, labyrinths, and statuary on mythological themes. The gardens were designed to represent harmony and order, the ideals of the Renaissance, and to recall the virtues of Ancient Rome.

The sixteenth-century Italian garden with its monumental terraces, sculptures, and waterworks was much admired and imitated in Northern Europe, particularly in France. Beginning in 1528, King Francis I of France created new gardens at the Chateau de Fontainebleau, which featured fountains, parterres, a forest of pine trees brought from Provence and the first artificial grotto in France. In 1546 the architect Philibert de l'Orme designed the gardens of the Château d'Anet following the Italian rules of proportion. The carefully prepared harmony of Anet, with its parterres and surfaces of water integrated with sections of greenery, became one of the earliest and most influential examples of the classic French garden.

While the gardens of the French Renaissance were much different in their spirit and appearance from those of the Middle Ages, they were still not integrated with the architecture of the chateaux, and were usually enclosed by walls. The different parts of the gardens were not harmoniously joined together, and were often placed on difficult sites chosen for terrain

---

[①]This text is adapted from *The French Formal Garden* from http://en.wikipedia.org

easily to defend. All this was to change in the middle of the 17th century with the development of the first French formal garden.

The first important French formal garden was at the Chateau of Vaux-le-Vicomte, 55 km southeast of Paris. Built from 1658 to 1661 for Nicolas Fouquet, the superintendent of finances of Louis XIV, it was an important influence on much of the architecture that followed. One of the radical innovations at Vaux-le-Vicomte was that the building, the gardens, and the interior, were all planned together as one ensemble. The architect Louis le Vau, the interior designer Charles le Brun and the landscape architect André le Notre worked closely together on a large-scale project for the first time. Their collaboration marked the beginning of a new order: the magnificent manner that is associated with the "Louis XIV style".

The Gardens of Vaux-le-Vicomte

At Vaux, for the first time, the garden and the chateau were perfectly integrated. A grand perspective of 1,500 meters extended from the entrance gate of the chateau to the furthest statue of the Hercules; and the space was filled with parterres of evergreen shrubs in ornamental patterns, and the alleys were decorated at regular intervals by statues, basins, fountains, and carefully sculpted topiaries.

The organization of the landscape—the building, the garden, and the art—roughly conformed to the model described by André Mollet, ordered symmetrically around a central axis. The symmetry attained at Vaux achieved a degree of perfection and unity rarely equalled in the art of classic gardens. The remarkable use of laws of perspective and optical illusion gave the observer the pleasant sensation of being able to "embrace" the gardens at a glance.

The chateau was at the center of the strict spatial organization and dominated from whatever distance it was seen. Undoubtedly, such a "reigning" position over such a large area symbolized the power and success of the master of the house. Unfortunately, the magnificence of the gardens and their opening festivities inspired the envy and anger of Louis XIV, who at the time boasted only a modest little hunting lodge in the grounds of Versailles. Fifteen days later Fouquet was thrown into prison, where he was to remain until he died.

Shortly after Fouquet's arrest, Louis XIV decided to expand on the palace and park at Versailles. He employed the same trio of designers as Fouquet had at Vaux le Vicomte. In 1661, Louis XIV commissioned André Le Nôtre with the design and lay-out of the gardens of Versailles which, in his view, were just as important as the Château.

The garden was basically conceived in terms of three areas which had the castle as their point of reference. From the center alleys radiated outward like a fan into the surrounding space, where they branched out in multiple forms, thereby defining more and more new sections of the garden. The works were undertaken at the same time as those for the palace and took forty years to complete. In the beginning the site of Versailles was marshy land prone to water accumulation in large amounts. Ultimately the designed landscape of it became the focus of a new town.

The Gardens of Versailles

The Gardens of Versailles were the greatest achievement of the French garden style. They were the largest gardens in Europe—with an area of 6,000 hectares, and were laid out on an east-west axis followed the course of the sun. The central symbol of the Gardens was the sun, the emblem of Louis XIV, best illustrated by the statue of Apollo in the central fountain of the garden. In contrast with the grand perspectives, reaching to the horizon, the gardens were full of surprises. They had meticulously manicured lawns, abundant blooming flowers, valuable statues and sculptures, impressive water fountains and a grand canal.

The creation of the gardens of Vaux Le Vicomte and Versailles, together with numerous others, defined a whole new style and scale of landscape design. What distinguished the new formal garden from the earlier Renaissance garden tradition, even though it consisted largely of the same elements, was the concentration on dynamic spatial features and splendor. Typical is the French formal garden's enormous scale, complexity of composition, richness of ornamentation, and sweeping vistas. The gardens not only had an important representative purpose, but also became ideal meeting places, functioning as centers for a host of social activities, from open-air dining with musical and theatrical performances, to sports and games.

The French formal garden is directly associated with Andre Le Notre, the most well-known of all French landscape gardeners. The basic elements of Le Nôtre's design consisted of a strongly unified composition, carefully balanced and proportioned for optimal visual effect. Centering on the palace and its dominating axis, a broad vista over the whole layout was offered, showing a hierarchical arrangement of parterres and waterworks within a grid plan, strictly lined by hedges and bosquets.

Le Nôtre's works not only perfectly mirrored the social relationships of the period but also provided the dramatic settings for numerous festivities, artistic performances, entertainments and social gatherings. By the time of his death in 1700, Le Nôtre had raised the field of landscape architecture to a new level of maturity and his ideas and approach to landscape architecture had spread across the whole of Europe.

Andre Le Notre

Architecture played a dominant role in the French formal garden. The designers saw their work as a branch of architecture, which simply extended the space of the building to the space outside the walls. Gardens were designed like buildings, with a succession of "rooms" which a visitor could pass through following an established route. The designers used the language of architecture in their plans. The spaces were referred to as *salles* and *théâtres* of greenery. The "walls" were composed of hedges. Just as architects installed systems of water into the chateaux so the designers of the French garden laid out elaborate hydraulic systems to supply the fountains and basins of the garden.

After Le Nôtre's death in 1700, his ideas continued to dominate the design of gardens in France. Nonetheless, a few variations in the strict geometry of the garden began to appear. Elaborate parterres were replaced by parterres which were easier to maintain. Circles became ovals and irregular octagon shapes appeared. Gardens began to follow the natural landscape, rather than moving earth to shape the ground into artificial terraces.

In the middle of the 18th century, the influence of the English landscape garden, and the popularity of the Chinese style, a style which rejected symmetry in favor of nature and rustic scenes, brought an end to the reign of the French formal garden.

(1,463 words)

Vocabulary

impose /ɪmˈpəʊz/ *vt.* force the acceptance of 强加
apogee /ˈæpədʒiː/ *n.* the highest point of power or success 顶点,极点
typify /ˈtɪpɪfaɪ/ *vt.* represent in a typical manner 代表,象征
parterre /pɑːˈteə/ *n.* 花坛,花圃
symmetrical /sɪˈmetrɪkl/ *adj.* having both sides exactly alike 对称的
cascade /kæsˈkeɪd/ *n.* 小瀑布
animate /ˈænɪmət/ *vt.* give life to 使有生命
stairway /ˈsteəweɪ/ *n.* 楼梯
ramp /ræmp/ *n.* an inclined surface connecting two levels 斜坡;坡道
grotto /ˈgrɒtəʊ/ *n.* small cave 洞穴,岩穴
labyrinth /ˈlæbəˌrɪnθ/ *n.* 迷宫
statuary /ˈstætʃʊərɪ/ *n.* (总称)雕塑,塑像
mythological /ˌmɪθəˈlɒdʒɪkəl/ *adj.* 神话的;虚构的
monumental /ˌmɒnjuˈmentəl/ *adj.* very large, needing much work 巨大的
terrace /ˈterəs/ *n.* flat level area cut from a slope 平台;梯田
waterworks /ˈwɒtəwɒks/ *n.* 水务工程;喷水装置
proportion /prəˈpɔːʃən/ *n.* harmonious arrangement or relation of parts or elements within a whole 均衡;相称,协调
chateau /ˈtʃætəʊ/ *n.* 〈法〉城堡
integrate /ˈɪntɪgreɪt/ *vt.* make into a whole or make part of a whole 使一体化;使结合
greenery /ˈgriːnərɪ/ *n.* 绿色植物
terrain /teˈreɪn/ *n.* piece of ground having specific characteristics 地形,地面
superintendent /ˌsjuːpərɪnˈtendənt/ *n.* person who directs and manages an organization 监管
radical /ˈrædɪkəl/ *adj.* thorough and complete 根本的,彻底的
interior /ɪnˈtɪərɪə/ *n.* the part which is inside 内部;室内
shrub /ʃrʌb/ *n.* low bush with several woody stems 灌木
ornamental /ˌɔːnəˈmentəl/ *adj.* adding ornament 装饰的

alley /ˈælɪ/ *n.* path in a garden or park 小径；园道
at regular intervals 每隔一定间隔
basin /ˈbeɪsən/ *n.* hollow place containing water 水池
sculpt /skʌlpt/ *vt.* shape (a material like stone or wood) by whittling away at it 雕刻；造型
conform to 遵守，依照
optical /ˈɒptɪkəl/ *adj.* relating to or using sight 视力的；光学的
illusion /ɪˈluːʃən/ *n.* something seen wrongly, not as it really is 错觉，幻觉
sensation /senˈseɪʃən/ *n.* direct feeling coming from the senses 感觉，感受
embrace /ɪmˈbreɪs/ *vt.* take and hold in the arms 拥抱
festivity /feˈstɪvɪtɪ/ *n.* a festive event 庆祝活动；庆典
lodge /lɒdʒ/ *n.* a small house for hunters 小舍
trio /ˈtriːəʊ/ *n.* any group of three people or things 三人小组
commission /kəˈmɪʃən/ *vt.* charge with a task 委任，委托
conceive /kənˈsiːv/ *vt.* have the idea for 构想，设想
radiate /ˈreɪdɪeɪt/ *vi.* extend or spread outward from a center 射出，向四周伸出
branch out 拓展；扩张
marshy /ˈmɑːʃɪ/ *adj.* (of soil) soft and watery 沼泽的；湿地的
prone to 易于；有……倾向的
emblem /ˈembləm/ *n.* a visible symbol representing an abstract idea 象征；标记
meticulously /mɪˈtɪkjʊslɪ/ *adv.* in a meticulous manner 细致地；一丝不苟地
manicure /ˈmænɪˌkjʊə/ *vt.* trim carefully and neatly 修剪
spatial /ˈspeɪʃəl/ *adj.* involving or having the nature of space 空间的
splendor /ˈsplendə/ *n.* the quality of being magnificent or splendid or grand 壮观；华丽
representative /ˌreprɪˈzentətɪv/ *adj.* serving to represent or typify 表现的
unified /ˈjuːnɪfaɪd/ *adj.* operating as a unit 统一的，一元化的
optimal /ˈɒptəməl/ *adj.* most desirable possible under a restriction expressed or implied 最佳的，优化的
hierarchical /ˌhaɪəˈrɑːkɪkəl/ *adj.* classified according to various criteria into successive levels or layers 分等级的；分层的
grid /ɡrɪd/ *n.* a network of horizontal and vertical lines that provide coordinates for locating points on an image 格栏，网格
bosquet /ˈbɒskeɪt/ *n.* 丛林，矮林
succession /səkˈseʃən/ *n.* a group of people or things arranged or following in order 连续不断的人或事物
salle /sɑːl/ *n.* 〈法〉大室，厅
elaborate /ɪˈlæbəreɪt/ *adj.* carefully worked out and with a large number of parts 精致复杂的
hydraulic /haɪˈdrɒlɪk/ *adj.* concerning or moved by the pressure of water or other liquids 水压的；液压的

oval /ˈəʊvəl/ *n.* anything which is egg-shaped 卵形的；椭圆形的
octagon /ˈɒktəgən/ *n.* a flat figure with eight sides and eight angles 八边形；八角形
rustic /ˈrʌstɪk/ *n.* connected with or suitable for the country 乡村式的；质朴的

Proper Names

the Boboli Gardens	波波里花园（意大利）
Florence /ˈflɔːrəns/	佛罗伦萨（意大利地名）
the Villa Medici /ˈvilə medɪtʃiː/	美第奇庄园（意大利）
Fiesole	费埃索（意大利地名）
King Francis Ⅰ /ˈfrænsɪs/	弗朗西斯一世（法国国王）
Fontainebleau /ˈfɒntɪnbləu/	枫丹白露（法国地名）
Philibert de l'Orme	菲利贝·德·洛梅（法国建筑师）
the Château d'Anet	阿内府城堡（法国）
the Chateau of Vaux-le-Vicomte	沃子爵府城堡（法国）
Nicolas Fouquet	尼古拉斯·富凯（路易十四财政大臣）
Versailles /veəˈsail/	凡尔赛（宫）
Louis XIV	路易十四
Louis le Vau	路易·勒沃（法国建筑师）
Charles le Brun	夏尔勒·布伦（法国画家）
André le Notre	安德烈·勒诺特尔（法国造园师）
the Hercules /hɜːkjuliːz/	赫拉克勒斯（希腊神话中的大力士）
André Mollet	安德烈·莫莱（法国造园师）
Apollo /əˈpɒləu/	阿波罗（希腊神话中的太阳神）

Text Exploration

5 Choose the best answer to each question with the information from the text.

1. The seventeenth-century French gardens were constructed in a style that _____.
   A. became the model for 18th European garden design
   B. showed the respect for nature
   C. emphasized the control and manipulation of nature
   D. presented an idealized view of nature

2. What does the Italian Renaissance garden emphasize?
   A. human domination over nature
   B. harmony and order
   C. mythological themes
   D. natural landscape

3. Which of the following is true of the gardens of Château d'Anet?
   A. It was created by Andre Le Notre.
   B. It was a great example of the French formal garden.
   C. It was a perfectly symmetrical garden.

D. It was largely inspired by the Italian Renaissance garden.
4. Which of the following is true of the Italian Renaissance gardens?
   A. They were usually built in the open areas.
   B. They had grand perspectives.
   C. They were once favored and copied in Northern Europe.
   D. Each section of the gardens was well integrated.
5. Which of the following was/were located at the center of the landscape at Vaux?
   A. The statue of the Hercules.
   B. Some parterres.
   C. Some topiary.
   D. The building.
6. Which of the following words best describes the "Louis XIV style"?
   A. exquisite
   B. natural
   C. splendid
   D. wild
7. Which of the following is NOT true of the Gardens of Versailles?
   A. It was expanded from a lodge used for royal hunts.
   B. It contained a grand canal.
   C. It marks the climax of the French formal garden.
   D. It took fifty years to complete the vast enterprise.
8. Which of the following is NOT true of Le Notre?
   A. He invented the model of geometric layouts.
   B. He made use of perspective spatial knowledge in the design.
   C. He set the style for European gardens in the seventeenth century.
   D. He designed the elaborate Versailles gardens.
9. The French garden designers draw their inspiration from _____.
   A. literature
   B. painting
   C. architecture
   D. philosophy
10. Which of the following does not account for the decline of the French garden style in the 18th century?
    A. The arrival of the English landscape park.
    B. The death of André Le Nôtre.
    C. The introduction of the Chinese style.
    D. The considerable work required to build and maintain the garden.

Unit 6 Landscaping

6 Complete the following chart with the information from the text.

Paragraphs	Aspects	Details
2—4	The Italian influence	The French formal style has origins in _____ which was brought to France at _____; The Italian garden with its _____ was much admired and imitated in France.
5—8	The Gardens of Vaux-le-Vicomte	For the first time, the garden and the chateau were _____; The symmetry achieved a _____ rarely equaled in the art of classic gardens.
9—11	The Gardens of Versailles	The Gardens were _____ of the French formal style. The Gardens occupied _____, and were laid out on _____ followed the course of the sun.
13—14	André Le Nôtre	His design consisted of a _____ composition, carefully _____ for optimal visual effect. His works not only reflected _____ of the period but also provided the _____ for numerous social activities.
16—17	The decline	In the middle of the 18th century, the style of the French garden began to wane in favor of _____ gardens under the influence of _____ and _____.

7 Discuss the following questions with the information from the text.

1. What is the French formal garden?

2. How is the typical French formal garden different from the earlier Renaissance garden?

3. What are André Le Nôtre's great achievements in landscape design?

4. How was the French formal garden related to the philosophical ideas in the 17th century?

5. Which garden style do you prefer, the French garden or the Chinese garden?

Vocabulary Expansion

8 Fill in the blanks with the right words given below. Change the form where necessary.

apogee	typify	animate	proportion	ensemble
sculpt	conceive	splendor	radiate	elaborate

1. The drawings of young children usually lack _____; they make arms and legs look like sticks.
2. Printed accessories paired with printed wardrobe equal the perfect summer _____.
3. The king was _____ by the artist over a period of a few weeks.
4. Asteroids absorb heat from the sun and then _____ it away into space.
5. The idea for that poster was the _____ of my career.
6. The desert is like a line drawing waiting to be _____ with color.
7. Abraham Lincoln _____ the politician who rises from humble origins to a position of power and influence.
8. The dam project was _____ in 1977 by a group of scientists.
9. The wells are dressed with large framed panels decorated with _____ mosaic-like pictures made of flower petals, grasses, leaves, berries and moss.
10. The _____ of the ancient monument awed us into silence.

9 Choose the word or phrase that best keeps the meaning of the sentence if it is substituted for the underlined word or phrase.

1. The decision was theirs and was not imposed on them by others.
   A. taxed   B. forced
   C. put   D. assessed
2. The artist spent years on his monumental painting which covered the whole roof of the church.
   A. impressive   B. excellent
   C. large   D. innovative
3. The car's design successfully integrates art and technology.
   A. applies   B. coordinates
   C. adds   D. absorbs
4. Years of logging had left the mountains in this area prone to mudslides.
   A. totally destroyed by B. frequently hit by
   C. rarely exposed to   D. more likely to suffer from
5. They commissioned an architect to manage the building project.
   A. authorized   B. introduced
   C. employed   D. sent
6. The changes were introduced to conform to the international classification.
   A. contribute to   B. adapt to
   C. fit with   D. comply with
7. The hotel was run by a trio of brothers.
   A. a pair of   B. a group of three
   C. a team of four   D. a couple of
8. He could see through the windows a vista of green fields.
   A. mental view   B. visual effect

C. great vision D. distant view
9. The transatlantic balloonists <u>laid out</u> a backup plan in case of an emergency.
   A. worked out B. found out
   C. came out D. made out
10. The company began by specializing in radios but has now decided to <u>branch out</u> into computers.
    A. reach B. enter
    C. expand D. join

10 Translate the Chinese sentences into English by simulating the sentences chosen from the text.

Chosen Sentences	Simulated Translations	Chinese Sentences
Gardens **held a central place in** the history of seventeenth European art and architecture.		城市河流在城市的自然景观和集体记忆中占有重要位置。(**collective memory**)
The sixteenth-century Italian garden with its monumental terraces, sculptures, and waterworks was **much admired and imitated** in France.		这位英国设计师的古怪风格受到了全球各地粉丝们的广泛推崇和效仿。(**quirky**)
The alleys were decorated **at regular intervals** by statues, basins, fountains, and carefully sculpted topiaries.		城里的主要街道上每隔一段距离就会有路灯。
The symmetry attained at Vaux achieved a degree of perfection and unity **rarely equalled** in the art of classic gardens.		任何人都可以在比利牛斯山找到自己最好的休养之地,它景观的多样性在欧洲鲜有能比者。(**retreat, Pyrenees, diversity**)
Just as architects installed systems of water into the chateux, **so** the designers of the French garden laid out elaborate hydraulic systems to supply the fountains and basins of the garden.		要为一首音乐找到正确的节拍,同样,你也要找到适合自己生活的节拍。(**pulse, rhythm**)

Supplementary Readings

11 Passage One

Before the 18th century, English gardens tended to follow French and Dutch fashions, employing garden designers from these nations. During the latter half of the 17th century, English gardens were formal, as almost all European gardens had been for over a thousand years.

The desire for more "natural" gardens was first expressed by writers. William Temple praised Chinese garden design in an essay published in 1692, which helped to open European minds to the possibility of creating non-traditional gardens. Alexander Pope also urged a return to the simplicity of nature in place of the formal garden. Indeed, English gardens had been losing some of their formality during the late 17th century. The following era saw the birth of the English Landscape movement.

William Kent was one of the originators of the English landscape garden. Yet he was no horticulturalist. His gardens were often dotted with classical temples replete with philosophical associations. In 1729, Kent designed an influential garden for Lord Burlington at Chiswick House. He replaced the formality of the existing formal garden with a freer design. Lines were no longer straight, paths curve and wander, and parterres are replaced by grass. Trees were planted in clusters rather than in straight lines, and rounded lakes replaced the rectangular ponds of the earlier style. The garden became open, a park joining the house to the outside world rather than a carefully nurtured refuge from it.

The most important of the early English landscape gardens was at Stowe, where Lancelot "Capability" Brown was hired as head gardener in charge of executing Kent's designs. Brown's curious nickname came from his habit of telling prospective clients that their gardens showed "great capabilities". His gardens dominated the gardening style from the 1750s to the 1780s. His style involved bringing the sweeping landscape right up to, and surrounding the house and most of his gardens were idealized visions of the English countryside.

Humphrey Repton became a landscape gardener in 1778 and began to take the lead in Britain. His work was a sort of stepping stone between a "natural" landscape and the return to the formal style. He modified Brown's ideas by introducing a formal layout of decorative plants near the house. He reintroduced flowerbeds with terraces directly outside the house that could be used to enjoy the flowers. Repton, who replaced Capability Brown as head gardener at Hampton Court, is considered to be the first person to use the phrase "Landscape Gardener".

1. Which of the following is true of Temple's essay?
    A. It helped landscapers to create traditional Chinese gardens.
    B. It provided inspiration for new type landscape gardens.
    C. It expressed a negative opinion of Chinese gardens.
    D. It was first published in the early 18th century.
2. What of the following is NOT true of William Kent?
    A. He knew much about plants.
    B. He considered the landscape as a classical painting.
    C. His gardens included classic temples.
    D. He designed gardens at Stowe.
3. Which of the following is NOT an element in English landscape garden?
    A. Winding paths.
    B. Trees planted in clusters.

Unit 6 Landscaping

  C. Rectangular ponds.
  D. Rounded lakes.
4. What accounted for the origin of Brown's nickname "Capability" Brown?
  A. His great capabilities in garden design.
  B. His great success in executing gardens at Stowe.
  C. His fondness for speaking about gardens having potentials for improvement.
  D. His fame as a leading gardener from the 1750s to the 1780s.
5. What can you learn about Humphrey Repton from the last paragraph?
  A. He used stepping stones in his design.
  B. He added flowerbeds into the garden design.
  C. He returned to the formal garden style.
  D. He was the first head gardener at Hampton Court.

12 Passage Two

  Chinese Garden building saw its heyday during the Ming and Qing dynasties. Different from the classical European gardens, in which geometric patterns dominate, Chinese gardens are made to resemble natural landscapes on a smaller scale. Traditional Chinese gardens fall into three categories: imperial, private, and landscape gardens.

  Imperial gardens are massive in scale. They were usually created out of natural landscape, with man-made structures added to them to bring out the grandeur of the imperial family. Most imperial gardens have three sections which serve administrative, residential, and recreational purposes. In large imperial gardens, the main buildings are connected by an imaginary line in the middle of the garden on a north-south axis. Other buildings scattered among hills and waters are linked by subordinate lines, forming a well-designed symmetry. Imperial gardens are also characterized by colored paintings, man-made hills and lakes.

  Suzhou, known as the home of the gardens, displays the most and the best Chinese traditional private gardens. These gardens are complex and exquisite landscapes imitating natural scenery. The designs were especially adapted to the small space available in private gardens.

  Private gardens were mostly built at one side or the back of the residential houses. In almost every garden, there is a large space set in a landscape of artistically arranged rockeries, ponds, pavilions, bridges, trees, and flowers. Surrounding the beautiful scene are small open areas partitioned by corridors or walls with latticed windows or beautifully shaped doors. Buildings in the garden were used for receiving guests, holding banquets, reading, or writing poetry. They are open on all sides and are often situated near the water. The winding corridors connect various buildings and also provide a covered veranda as shelter from the rain and shade from the sun.

  Landscape gardens are places for public recreation. The landscape garden mainly contains natural scenes with abundant greenery and sources of water, so it looks more natural than artificial. Good examples include the ten West Lake scenes in Hangzhou, the twenty-four Slim West Lake scenes in Yangzhou and the eight Da Ming Lake scenes in Jinan.

Many famous poets and painters contributed greatly to the development of landscape gardens. They either left poetic inscriptions for those gardens, or designed many of the gardens themselves. In order to commemorate those poets and painters, later generations had their poems and inscriptions engraved on tablets, pavilions, or pagodas, thus enriching and inspiring visitors.

1. What is the passage mainly about?
    A. The history of Chinese classical gardens.
    B. The types of Chinese classical gardens.
    C. The characteristics of private gardens.
    D. The development of imperial gardens.
2. Which of the following is true of imperial gardens?
    A. They were places for public recreation.
    B. The main buildings are connected by an east-west axis.
    C. They were built at the back of the main buildings.
    D. They occupy large areas.
3. Which of the following element is NOT mentioned in paragraph 3?
    A. Water.   B. Rocks.
    C. Arts.   D. Buildings.
4. Which of the following is NOT true of private gardens?
    A. They are usually combined with dwellings.
    B. They are characterized by large ponds.
    C. Waterside buildings in them have no walls.
    D. The areas around the scene are separated by corridors or gates.
5. What are landscape gardens characterized by?
    A. Elegant style.
    B. Exquisite construction.
    C. Natural scenes.
    D. Grandeur looks.

Interactive Tasks

Role-play

13 **Role-play the following situation with your partner.**
Situation:

Li Ming and his American friend David are walking around in Yuyuan Garden, an ancient garden in the city. It is the first time that David visits a traditional Chinese garden, so they start a conversation about the features and elements of the Chinese garden.

You may begin like this:

David: What a beautiful garden! It's so different from the western garden style.

Li: Yes, Chinese gardens have special features of its own. There are some key elements. Just look around, and you'll find them.

David: These strange rocks are interesting. Do they represent something?

Li: Rocks are important in a Chinese garden. They are considered to possess strong and male characteristics.

Group Work

14 Work in groups to work out your own short drama.

1. Form groups of four or five students;
2. Each group chooses a topic concerning landscape design, e.g.
   A study of gardens and parks at home or abroad;
   An introduction to a landscape designer and his works.
3. Members of each group collect materials from library and the Internet to work out their PPT slides;
4. Based on the PPT slides, each member of the group gives oral presentation of his part.

Follow-up Task

Writing

15 Directions: For this part, you are going to write a composition on the topic: **Classical Chinese Gardens**. You should write at least 120 words following the outline given below in Chinese:

1. 园林是中国文化的重要组成部分之一;
2. 中国古典园林造园的四大要素;
3. 中国古典园林对其他国家也产生了影响。

Unit 7 Photography

Highlight

Topic area	Communication	Skills
Some best-known photographs in the world; War photograph; What makes a good photographer?	stir up have no idea about work out be willing to The point of …is…	Knowing some best-known photographs in the world; Knowing the qualities of a good photographer.

Starting-out Task

1 **Look at these pictures and discuss the following questions with your partner**.
1. The following are some world famous pictures. Do you know anything about them?

Unit 7 Photography

2. What else, such as the time of creation and the names of the photographers, do you know about these pictures?
3. How do you like these pictures?

Listening Tasks

Micro Listening Skills

2 **Listen to the following passage and try to fill in the missing words.**

   War photography changed how people 1. _____ war and how news publications reported armed 2. _____. While people may not fully understand the grim reality of war by reading a news 3. _____, they often immediately grasp it by viewing graphic pictures of war.

War photography has always been 4. _____, both in terms of the explicit nature of combat photography and 5. _____ military censorship of images. The American Civil War marked the first time a team of photographers took pictures of war. The resulting photos of battle and death 6. _____ the public, who were used to seeing war 7. _____ as a romantic, noble endeavor.

While combat photography had been around for over a century before World War Ⅰ, not many pictures were taken during this war due to 8. _____ military censorship. Combat photography during World War Ⅱ, especially those 9. _____ pictures of the Nazi concentration camps prompted both 10. _____ and public outrage.

Dialogue

Taking Pictures

Words & Phrases

refresh /rɪˈfreʃ/ v.	使精神振作
stunning /ˈstʌnɪŋ/ adj.	极好的
ritual /ˈrɪtjuə/ n.	仪式
underexpose /ˈʌndərɪkˈspəuz/ v.	(底片)曝光不足
manipulate /məˈnɪpjuleɪt/ v.	(熟练地)操作

3 Listen to the dialogue and decide whether the following statements are true (T) or false (F).

1. ____ Jack looked very energetic after his journey to India.
2. ____ India is a place Jack loves because of its long history.
3. ____ The best opportunity to take pictures in weddings in India is when the bride is being decorated.
4. ____ Taj Mahal is the most visited and most photographed place in India because it is a symbol of India.
5. ____ Rose can't recognize what's in the picture taken by Jack because she has never been to India.

Unit 7 Photography

4 **Listen to the dialogue again and complete the following sentences with the information you have heard.**

1. India is such a _____ place because of the stunning colors of her people, the history of her great _____, the rich street life and the _____ weddings.
2. Most Indian families do not mind a _____ photographer at the wedding and they usually co-operate with _____.
3. Proper _____ is very important in photography. The more light within the scene, the more the film will be exposed. Conversely, the less light a scene has, the less the film will be exposed.
4. Many photographers _____ a light meter. It's a tool that _____.

Reading Tasks

Focus Reading

Pre-reading Questions

1. What is a good photograph in your eyes? Give reasons for your answer.
2. How can a person become a good photographer?
3. Ken Rockwell said that "Photography is the power of observation, not the application of technology." To what extent do you agree with this sentence?

How to Become a Great Photographer?

Photographs are amazing. Photographs bridge the gap between cultures, landscapes and generations. Through photographs, we preserve history—our child's first steps, a decaying civilization, or rare and endangered animals. Through photographs, we recall the first steps on the moon, the inauguration of a new president and the lifting of a flag on a far-away hill during war. So many mothers laboriously decorate large scrapbooks just to protect their precious sweet memories. Photographs evoke the essence of places we have not been to, we perhaps will not return to and should never forget.

Photographs are not about technique. Many people still mistakenly think that mastering simple issues like shutter speeds and depth of field is all there is to know about photography. Photographs communicate something, be it an idea, concept, feeling, thought or whatever, to a total stranger.

A good photograph stirs up emotions. From a good laugh at a silly kitten tangled in thread to a feeling of horror over an image of war, photographs should make the viewer feel something strongly. So before you release your shutter, ask yourself what emotion you want your image to evoke. Awe at the beauty before you? Hope when your viewer sees someone helping a homeless person? Identify the feeling before you shoot and your photographs will likely improve.

A good photograph always tells a story. A photograph of landscape tells a story about the land; it shows the viewer whether the land is tranquil or in upheaval, whether it is resting quietly in winter or bursting with activity in spring. Just like you should know the feeling you want to evoke, know the story you want to tell.

A good photograph tells the viewer something more than just how something looks. They show more than the subject you are photographing. A truly good photograph says something about life itself. It makes the viewer stop and think. We've all seen many cute animal pictures which have enormous appeal because they tell us that life can be playful, that it is still full of fun and innocence. Photographs of the Grand Canyon are no more than pretty pictures unless the viewer can also see more than the rocks themselves. A cliff says that life can be dangerous. Rocks caught in early morning light show that even something as solid as a rock also has a gentle quality. Use your photographs to communicate things you know about life.

What then makes someone into a truly great photographer? Is it their equipment, their repertoire of images, their vast travels? These are only by-products of the craft. "Greatness" is obtained through the character of the photographer. "Great" photographers are every-day, ordinary people.

Humility

First, let's level the playing field. All of us are in the same standing where photography is concerned. I can create great photographs. You can create great photographs. In reverse, I can also create bad photographs as you can. No one of us is better at this than the other.

Part of achieving any status comes from showing true humility. To put it frankly, you must know that you do not know and in not knowing, know to ask someone who does. This statement may seem a bit quirky, but the truth of it is so simple. Photography is about making right decisions. A "great" photographer then is someone who sees they lack the ability sometimes to make a decision and has the courage to ask for help.

There are three types of photographers. There is the technical photographer. He is all about the equipment and the formulas. He can give you millimeters and focal lengths. There is the subject photographer. He takes photographs to study the object itself. He knows breeding habits, plumage differences, longitude and latitude. Then there is the artist. The artist has no idea what he just photographed or how he photographed it, yet somehow creates the most pleasing pictures.

Each type of photographer has its place in the field of photography. Each type also often lacks the skills of the other two. The technician spends so much time obtaining equipment that he never grasps the fundamentals of composition. Subject photographers become single-minded in their pursuit of the next sighting and forget that other people do not have their unique understanding. Artists take amazing pictures, but label them all "bird", "car" or "church".

Great photographers will ask questions of those who have knowledge they do not have, and the kindness to in return answer questions from those who need to know.

Patience

If you want to be a great photographer, it's nearly impossible without patience. Amazing photographic moments do not often just drop into our lap. They are obtained because you walked that extra mile in the desert sun, because you sat ten more minutes waiting for the creature to emerge, because you rose up early to catch the best light. Without patience, you have the opportunity for great shots through luck. But you have little opportunity for true greatness in general.

Photographing animals and children are two perfect examples. Neither subject will stay still for very long. It takes time on the photographer's part to capture behavioral shots. What makes Little Johnny most remind his parents of who he is? Usually it is the things he does when he thinks you are not watching, and capturing those will take patience.

Patience also takes organization. Make a list of whatever you need to take along with you for your photo shoot. Discover what time of day animals are most active. Find out when the light will fall at the proper angle for that shot. Remember any filters or other equipment you might need. For studio shots, plan out your props. Part of being able to wait comes from not having to do other things that should have been done in advance. Nothing else can be more disturbing.

Perseverance

What is closely related to patience is perseverance.

Photography, when practiced at the highest levels, is a pursuit that is full of amazing highs and terrible lows. There's so much that can go wrong in a photograph that you may usually feel stunned when it works out. If you're just happily shooting snapshots and documenting life around you, there's little chance you've encountered these wild highs and lows. But if you pursue photographic greatness, then they are no stranger to you. In today's world we may face various kinds of counter influences, opposition or discouragement. In today's world there's the war, global recession, huge competition, bad light, bad backgrounds, crowds, gear failure, bad weather, etc. These are the forces which work against making the truly great image and only those who stick it out despite those forces massing against them, can be great.

Perseverance means that you might have to return to that location and try again. If the first set of photographs is not what you wanted, be willing to admit it and be dedicated enough for a second take. Many photographers have the experience to photograph the same objects over and over and over again to get exactly what they have in their minds. Landscape photographer Ansel Adams referred to this as visualization. It is said he would develop the same images many times until he had the print he desired. We should all be just as committed to our results as that!

Observation

Great photographers become great by developing their power of observation. It is always a good suggestion that photographers (of all skill levels) take a photo trip and at first leave their camera in the car. The point of the trip is to develop an ability to "see" scenes as photographs. Ask yourself questions and observe what scenarios you can create.

"Could I stand there and frame the castle with this tree?"

"If I lowered my camera perspective, would that be a more pleasing angle?"

"Should the family stand this direction by the fountain instead?"

Observation is really about finding the answers to such questions, and in finding the answers, making the process of observing a habit. You begin to notice things you used to pass by, and you're always examining your surroundings for possible photographs. You spot two toddlers sharing a toy in the park as their mothers look on and ask yourself how you would capture that moment. The shadows of clouds sweeping across a rolling meadow generate images in your mind.

A photographer who cannot visualize photographs will never advance as a photographer. Every photographer feels he is up against a wall at some point in time, but you break out of these moments again through the power of observation. You recognize you do the things necessary to re-spark your imagination.

What truly makes someone a "great" photographer is not the money or the fame. It's not the equipment, the experiences or the stories. It is that they have achieved the goals they set out for themselves, created photographs they are pleased with and had fun along the way.

(1,499 words)

Vocabulary

inauguration /ɪˌnɔːgjʊˈreɪʃən/ *n.* formal induction into office 就职典礼
evoke /ɪˈvəʊk/ *v.* to call forth 唤起
scrapbook /ˈskræpbʊk/ *n.* a book with blank pages used for the mounting and preserving of pictures, clippings or other mementos 剪贴簿
shutter /ˈʃʌtə/ *n.* a mechanical device of a camera that controls the duration of a photographic exposure 快门
tangle /ˈtæŋgl/ *v.* to involve in awkward complications 处于混乱状态
awe /ɔː/ *v.* to inspire with awe 敬畏
tranquil /ˈtræŋkwɪl/ *adj.* free from disturbance 安静的
upheaval /ʌpˈhiːvəl/ *n.* a sudden, violent disruption 剧变
repertoire /ˈrepətwɑː/ *n.* the range of skills of a particular person 某人的全部技能
humility /hjuːˈmɪnɪtɪ/ *n.* the quality of being humble 谦卑
reverse /rɪˈvɜːs/ *v.* the opposite or contrary 相反
quirky /ˈkwɜːkɪ/ *adj.* strikingly unconventional 离奇的
millimeter /ˈmɪniːmɪtə/ *n.* one thousandth of a meter 微米
plumage /ˈpluːmɪdʒ/ *n.* the covering of feathers on a bird 鸟类羽毛
fundamental /ˌfʌndəˈmentl/ *adj.* of or relating to the foundation or base 基础的
pursuit /pəˈsjuːt/ *n.* the act of striving 追求
filter /ˈfɪltə/ *n.* an optical devices used to reject signals, vibrations, or radiations of certain frequencies while passing others 滤光器
stun /stʌn/ *v.* to daze 使晕眩
perseverance /ˌpɜːsɪˈvɪərəns/ *n.* steady persistence in adhering to a course 坚持不懈
recession /rɪˈseʃən/ *n.* an extended decline in general business activity 衰退
gear /gɪə/ *n.* equipment used for a particular activity 设备
visualize /ˈvɪʒuəlaɪz/ *v.* to form a mental image of 使……形象化
scenario /sɪˈnɑːrɪəʊ/ *n.* a setting for a work of art 艺术品的背景

Proper Names

Ansel Adams   安塞尔·亚当斯

Text Exploration

5 Choose the best answer to each question with the information from the text.

1. What is the main idea of the first paragraph?
   A. The functions of photographs.
   B. The subjects of photographs.
   C. The characteristics of photographs.
   D. The significance of photographs.

2. What message is conveyed by a cute animal picture?
   A. The animal world is full of mysteries.
   B. Life is full of fun and innocence.
   C. The beauty of life is there for people to explore.
   D. Human being should live harmoniously with animals in the world.
3. What does it mean by "humility" in this passage?
   A. Be willing to learn from others.
   B. Be modest about one's achievements.
   C. Knowing one's limitations and working on them to improve.
   D. Knowing one's limitations and be brave to ask for help.
4. In what way do photographing animals and children differ from photographing other things?
   A. It asks for more patience.
   B. It asks for more complex photographing skills.
   C. It asks for more communicative skills.
   D. It asks for cameras of higher levels.
5. How can we achieve more patience in photographing?
   A. Learn to accept failure.
   B. Don't expect too much about the outcome.
   C. Make good preparations for photographing.
   D. Acquire necessary skills to make progress.
6. According to the passage, what is the most disturbing thing for a photographer?
   A. Not knowing how to respark your imagination.
   B. Not being able to develop the ability of observation.
   C. Having to wait patiently to capture a proper moment to shoot a picture.
   D. Having to do things that should have been done in advance.
7. If you practice photograph at high level, _____.
   A. It will be more demanding in terms of photographing skills.
   B. It will help you have a better understanding of the art of photography.
   C. It will be a painful process with lots of happiness and frustrations.
   D. It will be more demanding in terms of physical strength.
8. What can we learn from Ansel Adams?
   A. Be willing to accept failure.
   B. Trying to accumulate experience as a photographer.
   C. Be committed to our results.
   D. Knowing the importance of observation.
9. Why is taking a photo trip and leaving your camera in the car at first is a good suggestion for photographers?
   A. It can help photographers develop an ability to see scenes as photographs.
   B. It can help photographers develop an ability to imagine the final results of their

pictures.

C. It can help photographers focus more on their subjects instead of cameras.

D. It can help photographers be more observant with their surroundings.

10. What does the underlined sentence "Every photographer feels he is up against a wall at some point in time" mean?

A. It means that you reach a time of great trouble.

B. It means that you reach a level that is hard to exceed.

C. It means that you come across great challenges.

D. It means that you reach a time that is hard to succeed further.

6 **Complete the following chart with the information from the text.**

Parts	Main idea	Details
Part One	_____ of good photographs	Good photographs _____ emotions. Good photographs always _____. Good photographs tell something more than just _____.
Part Two	What _____ great photographer?	1) Humility: If you see you lack that ability to _____, do not be ashamed to ask for help. 2) Patience: It's essential for a photographer to be patient when you take pictures of _____. Part of being able to wait comes from _____ other things that should have been done in advance. 3) _____: It means that you might have to return to location and try again. 4) Observation: Great photographers become great by _____ their power of observation.

7 **Discuss the following questions with the information from the text.**

1. Based on the passage, why are photographs amazing?

2. What is the difference between technical photographer and subject photographer?

3. Why is it very important for a photographer to develop the ability to observe?

4. In your opinion, what qualities are important for good photographers?

5. What should we pay attention to if we want to shoot good pictures?

Unit 7 Photography

Vocabulary Expansion

8 Fill in the blanks with the right words given below. Change the form where necessary.

patient	awe	humiliate	recession	generation
capture	innocence	emerge	evoke	pursue

1. We will be extremely happy if our efforts _____ your enthusiasm.
2. We looked with a sense of _____ at the enormous ancient buildings.
3. I stand on this rostrum with a sense of deep _____ and great pride.
4. We can _____ electric power by splitting atoms.
5. Can you provide any evidence that he was _____ of the crime?
6. Asia may well _____ as the world's largest producer as well as the world's largest consumer market.
7. He pushed his son to _____ a musical career.
8. By providing more services it is more likely for you to _____ a larger market.
9. He walked so slowly that his brother lost _____ with him.
10. Bankruptcy is a common phenomenon in an economic _____.

9 Choose the word or phrase that best keeps the meaning of the sentence if it is substituted for the underlined word or phrase.

1. Diversity is of fundamental importance to all ecosystems and all economies.
   A. irreplaceable   B. indispensable
   C. essential   D. great
2. The agreement preserved our right to limit trade in endangered species.
   A. retained   B. emphasized
   C. advocated   D. denied
3. There have been enormous increases in agricultural productivity.
   A. magnificent   B. terrific
   C. glorious   D. tremendous
4. News of the disaster stunned people throughout the world.
   A. shocked   B. terrified
   C. touched   D. bewildered
5. The photographs published in the newspaper stirred up some painful memories.
   A. raised   B. evoked
   C. irritated   D. showed
6. The pursuit of wealth was the main reason for the changes for those enterprises.
   A. quest for   B. craze for
   C. interest in   D. motive of
7. The Home Secretary described the latest crime figures as disturbing.
   A. terrifying   B. worrying

    C. depressing   D. disgusting

8. The <u>capture</u> of the city is still remote and major military decisions must be taken.

    A. destruction   B. defeat

    C. destroy   D. occupation

9. It is not surprising that she always <u>sticks out</u> in a crowd.

    A. stood out   B. vanished

    C. faded   D. disappeared

10. If you travel across the country, you may quickly know that each town has a <u>character</u> all its own.

    A. fame   B. feature

    C. quality   D. reputation

10 Translate the Chinese sentences into English by simulating the sentences chosen from the text.

Chosen Sentences	Simulated Translations	Chinese Sentences
Photographs **bridge the gap** between cultures, landscapes and generations.		学习外语有助于缩小不同文化间的差距。
A good photograph **stirs up** emotions.		反对派们正竭力在选民中激起不满情绪。(**opposition, voter**)
…only those who **stick it out** despite those forces massing against them, can be great		被告一口咬定说他是无辜的。(**innocent**)
If the first set of photographs is not what you wanted, **be willing to** admit it and be dedicated enough for a second take.		一个人要有所进步,就必须努力工作,而且甘愿做出某些牺牲。
The point of the trip is to develop an ability to "see" scenes as photographs.		关键是:我们卷入了这场斗争。(**involve**)

Supplementary Readings

11 Passage One

    Tourism pre-dates photography but today the two practices are closely intertwined, each shaping and stimulating the other. Photography serves tourism as advertisement, commodity and memento and tourism serves photography as vehicle, justification and structuring activity.

    Photographs promote tourism when they appear in newspaper and magazine advertisements, on billboards and in television commercials. They are usually idealized and reduced to a few widely recognized signifiers, such as a palm-fringed beach, Big Ben, the Taj Mahal or a sombrero. Often, as in the cases of Niagara Falls, Yellowstone, the Scottish Highlands and the Alps, these images drew on pre-photographic visual conventions to identify, define and legitimize new tourist destinations.

Tourists buy photographs before, during and after their travels. Differing in use from advertisements and brochures, these images are commodities in their own right, functioning as means of instruction, gifts or mementoes. As early as the 1850s tourists could buy individual prints or albums depicting popular sites from hotels, booksellers and street vendors. Today, postcards, posters, souvenir publications, photo-decorated T-shirts, plates and ashtrays are on sale wherever tourists gather. Some images offer tips on local codes of behavior, or incorporate brief information on the sites they depict. In general, images marketed to tourists are limited to those of instantly recognizable iconic subjects.

Amateurs travelled with cameras long before photography was easy or accepted, but the invention of roll-film made it much simpler, cheaper and more commonplace. Early tourist snapshots often resembled the professional "view scraps" long available for sale, but the shift from buying photographs to making them gradually made photography a major component of the tourist today.

In the early 21st century, against the background of mass tourism's vast expansion since 1945, photographers are often given signposts to the best point for a successful picture; film cartons litter popular sites; and organizers of photographic workshops in scenic locations advertise photograph taking as the rationale for the trip.

When tourists return home, their photographs become evidence of a journey which can be sorted, shared and organized into an idealized narrative. The social or sharing aspect of tourist photography remains significant. The conventions of tourist seeing are thus deeply established in society, replicated and passed on as expectations to future vacationers.

1. The main idea of the first paragraph is _____.
   A. the interrelationship between tourism and photograph
   B. the role that photography plays in tourism
   C. the function of photography as advertisement, commodity and memento
   D. the increasing popularity of photography with tourists
2. When did mass tourism begin expanding vastly?
   A. As early as 1850s.
   B. Since 1945.
   C. In the early 21st century.
   D. Not mentioned.
3. Which of the following statements is NOT true according to the passage?
   A. The history of tourism is longer than that of photography.
   B. One function of photography in tourism is promoting tourism.
   C. Usually the images aimed for tourists are the most advertised ones in mass media.
   D. Photographs serve as evidence of their journey for tourists.
4. How did the early amateurs take pictures during their journey?
   A. They imitated those pictures taken by professional photographers.

B. They took pictures in their own ways.

C. They took pictures in the way they had been taught from books.

D. They took very original pictures of their own.

5. What do those organizers of photographic workshops do with photographing in the early 21st century?

A. They use it as a means to develop the local economy.

B. They use it as a feature of some scenic locations.

C. They use it as a useful means to make profit.

D. They use it as a reason to attract tourists to begin a trip.

Passage Two

How the lighting of a scene affects the exposure of the film is one of the most basic photography concepts. The more light within the scene, the more the film will be exposed. Conversely, the less light a scene has, the less the film will be exposed. While overexposed film turns out pictures that are too bright, underexposed film will be too dark, appearing "blacked-out." Understanding how to manipulate lighting will help a photographer properly expose his film.

Another basic principle of photography is composition, or the technique of setting up the subject within the camera's frame. The proper composition of a shot is directly related to the angle at which the photographer takes the picture. With a particular camera angle and a planned composition, a photo can draw in the viewer's eye, add meaning to the image or add a sense of movement and dynamism to the scene.

If the photographer wants his viewer to focus on a certain aspect of the shot, he can place the subject in a certain area of the frame. For example, putting the subject higher in the frame gives the subject an imposing presence on the viewer. On the other hand, placing the image lower tends to make the subject more submissive and possibly more mysterious to the critical viewer's eye.

By drawing the viewer's eye to a particular part of a picture, the photographer also invests a particular meaning of feeling to his shot. Depending on the subject photographed, its placement within the frame can make it appear more mysterious, forceful, compliant or intriguing.

Another set of basic photography concepts involves the skills used by a photographer to make an image appear dynamic. For instance, a shot with the subject framed directly in the middle can make the viewer feel as though he is falling into the subject.

An example of this would be a picture of a person looking through a hollow log while the photographer is at the other end of the log snapping a picture of the person's face. In this shot, the viewer's vision moves through this tunnel, shooting immediately towards the person's face. While not as overtly dynamic as action shots, this sort of compositional concept adds a subtle sense of movement to the picture.

1. What will happen if the film is overexposed?
   A. The picture will be blacked-out.
   B. The picture will be too bright.
   C. The subject in the picture will be unable to identify.
   D. The film will become useless.
2. In what way is composition important to photography?
   A. Proper composition makes the picture more eye-pleasing.
   B. Proper composition helps the photographer have a more balanced color.
   C. Proper composition determines the angle at which the photographer takes the picture.
   D. Proper composition helps emphasize the subject in the picture.
3. What should you do if you want to make the subject subordinate?
   A. Put it in the middle of the frame.
   B. Put it higher in the frame.
   C. Put it at the corner of the frame.
   D. Put it lower in the frame.
4. If you want to make an image dynamic, you should _____.
   A. put it in the middle of the frame.
   B. put it on the top of the frame.
   C. put it at the bottom of the frame.
   D. put it around the corner of the frame.
5. How many basic concepts are discussed in this passage?
   A. 2.   B. 3.   C. 4.   D. 5.

Interactive Tasks

Role-play

13 **Role-play the following situation with your partner.**
Situation:
  Two students are talking about how to take good photos. They exchange their ideas about the basic concepts of photography.
You may begin like this:
David: Are these all taken by yourself? They are really wonderful pictures.
Lucy: Thank you. They are taken in Yunnan last summer holiday.
David: Seems that you are an expert in photography. I am still a green hand in this field. I always have blacked-out pictures.
Lucy: Aha, that's because the film has been underexposed.

Group Work

14 **Work in groups to do an oral presentation about photography.**
1. Form groups of four or five students;
2. Each group chooses a topic concerning photograph, e. g.
   A research of photographs taken by famous photographers;
   An introduction to a photographer and his photos.
3. Members of each group collect materials from library and the Internet to work out their PPT slides;
4. Based on the PPT slides, each member of the group gives oral presentation of his part.

Follow-up Task

Writing

15 **Directions**: For this part, you are going to write a composition on the topic: **Taking good photographs**. You should write at least 120 words following the outline given below in Chinese:
1. 摄影一种非常有用的技能;
2. 什么样的摄影是好的摄影作品;
3. 如何拍摄好的摄影作品。

Unit 8 Chinese Traditional Folk Arts

Highlight

Topic area	Communication	Skills
The four famous embroideries in China; The characteristics of the four famous embroideries in China; An understanding of other types of traditional folk arts in China, such as the shadow show and puppet show as well as the knife and sword.	inseparable from give rise to well known for to a new level in addition to	Knowing the four famous embroideries in China and their respective characteristics; Knowing how to distinguish one embroidery from the others; Comments on the famous embroideries.

Starting-out Task

1 Look at these pictures and discuss the following questions with your partner.

1. What are the four famous embroideries according to the geographical locations?
2. In addition to the four famous embroideries, what other types can you think of? Please give two or three examples.
3. The following pictures show the embroideries of different types. Which one do you like best? And can you tell their differences?

艺术类研究生英语教程

Listening Tasks

Micro Listening Skills

2 Listen to the following passage and try to fill in the missing words.

Embroidery is the 1. _____ cloth art that involves the use of needles and thread. Embroidery was originally done 2. _____, or in other words, by hand. It is basically done for 3. _____ purposes by sewing various types of materials into a layer of cloth or fabric to create patterns and designs that are usually a 4. _____ of the beauty of nature.

Embroidery, a folk art with a long tradition, 5. _____ an important position in the history of Chinese traditional arts and crafts. It is, in its long development, 6. _____ from silkworm-raising and silk-reeling and 7._____. Today, silk embroidery is practiced nearly all over China. As far as the Chinese embroidery is 8._____, the best commercial products, it is generally agreed, come from four provinces: Jiangsu (notably Suzhou), Hunan, Sichuan and Guangdong, each with its 9._____ features. Each has its own characteristics, namely, the 10._____ subject, technique and material, so on and so forth.

Dialogue

Traditional Chinese Folk Arts

Benjamin is a foreigner who desires to buy some traditional Chinese arts and crafts for his friends in his own country. When he is choosing the presents for his friends, he has a lively chat with the shop assistant.

Words & Phrases

folk /fəʊk/ adj.	民间的
craft /krɑːft/ n.	工艺
paper-cut	剪纸
miracle /ˈmɪrəkl/ n.	奇迹
wholesale /ˈhəʊlseɪl/ n.	批发

3 Listen to the dialogue and choose the best answer to the following questions.

1. What was Benjamin's purpose of entering the crafts shop?
   A. To have a look at the crafts.
   B. To choose some presents for his friends.
   C. To kill his leisure time.
   D. To conduct a special survey.

2. Why did the shop assistant say "You are Neally an expert on it" when Benjamin asked the price of the wood carving?
   A. Because it is very expensive and few people can afford it.
   B. Because it looks excellent and the craft is very refined.
   C. Because it is very rare.
   D. Because his girl friend must be interested in it.

3. Why did the shop assistant recommend Benjamin to buy some paper-cuts for his foreign friends?
   A. Because it is very cheap.
   B. Because it can be kept for a long time and is not easily broken.
   C. Because the color is red and it is the symbol of good luck.
   D. Because it is easy to carry and many foreign people are fond of it.

4. What was Benjamin's response when he heard that the shop assistant had collected all the paper-cuts herself?
   A. Admired.   B. Astonished.   C. Angry.   D. Cheerful.

4 **Listen to the dialogue again and complete the following sentences with the information you have heard.**

1. The paper-cut is suitable because it is easy to _____ and foreign friends are also interested in it. They think that is a _____.
2. The shop assistant _____ that Benjamin might consider buying some _____.
3. The shop assistant opens the shop because she is _____ in arts and she has even spent a lot of time doing _____ on the _____ arts of China.

Reading Tasks

Focus Reading

Pre-reading Questions

1. Can you name some famous types of traditional Chinese embroideries?
2. Do you know the cities that are famous for embroidery in China?
3. In your opinion, what are the purposes of the embroidery?

Chinese Traditional Folk Art—Embroidery[①]

Embroidery, a folk art with a long tradition, has an important position in the history of Chinese arts and crafts. In its long development embroidery has been inseparable from silkworm raising, silk reeling and weaving. Embroidery is the art or handicraft of decorating fabric or other materials with designs stitched in strands of thread or yarn by means of a needle. Embroidery may also use other materials such as metal strips, pearls, beads, quills, and sequins. Sewing machines can be used to create machine embroidery.

China was the first country in the world to weave silk. Silkworms were domesticated as early as some 5,000 years ago. The production of silk threads and fabrics gave rise to the art of embroidery. In 1958, a piece of silk embroidered with a dragon and phoenix was discovered in a state of Chu tomb of the Warring Sates Period (475—221B.C.). More than 2,000 years old, it is the earliest piece of Chinese embroidery ever unearthed. Dated from Zhou Dynasty as one folk handicraft arts, Chinese embroidery became widespread during the Han Dynasty (206B.C.—A.D.220) and many embroidered pieces discovered date back to that period. Chinese hand embroidery is famous for silk embroidery as a traditional art form passed from generation to generation. Today, silk embroidery is practiced nearly all over China. The Four Famous Embroideries of China refer to the Xiang embroidery in central China's Hunan Province, Shu embroidery in western China's Sichuan Province, Yue embroidery in southern China's Guangdong Province and Su embroidery in eastern China's Jiangsu Province.

Suzhou embroidery

Suzhou embroidery, also known as Su embroidery, or "su xiu", has a history of more

---

①This text is taken and adapted from "Embroidery Arts & The Four Traditional Chinese Embroidery Styles" at http://blog. ffcrafts. com/post/Suzhou_embroidery_Xiang_embroidery_Yue_embroidery_Shu_embroidery_Folk_Arts. html than 2,000 years.

Su embroidery is the general name for embroidery products in areas around Suzhou, Jiangsu Province. Well known for its smoothness and delicateness, Su embroidery won Suzhou the title City of Embroidery in the Qing Dynasty. In the mid and late Qing, Su embroidery experienced further developments involving works of double-sided embroidering. There were 65 embroidery stores in Suzhou City. During the Republic of China period (1912—1949), the Su embroidery industry was in decline due to frequent wars and it was restored and regenerated after the founding of new China. In 1950, the central government set up research centers for Su embroidery and launched training courses for the study of embroidery. Weaving methods have climbed from 18 to the present 40.

Suzhou artists are able to use more than 40 needlework and a 1,000 different types of threads to make flowers, birds, animals and even gardens on a piece of cloth. The Suzhou embroidery is refined and exquisite, its best-known work being an embroidered cat with bright eyes and fluffy hair looking vivid and lifelike. The main theme of Suzhou embroidery is nature and the environment.

Suzhou embroidery features a strong, folk flavor and its weaving techniques are characterized by the following: the product surface must be flat, the rim must be neat, the needle must be thin, the lines must be dense, the color must be harmonious and bright and the picture must be even. Su embroidery products fall into three major categories: costumes, decorations for halls and crafts for daily use, which integrate decorative and practical values. Double-sided embroidery is an excellent representative of Su embroidery.

Xiang embroidery

Xiang embroidery with the excellent technique and unique style is a well-known handicraft created by Hunan people, and one of the four famous embroideries.

Xiang embroidery of long standing is originated from the folk embroidery in Hunan Province. From the excavated embroidery sample of the Chu grave in Changsha area in 1958, embroidery in Hunan had a definite development in Spring and Autumn Period around 2500 years ago. Also, from the forty excavated embroidery clothes in Mawang pile of Changsha area in 1972, the embroidery in Hunan had developed in a higher lever around 2100 years ago of West Han Dynasty. After this, during the endless development, the elegant art style had formed gradually.

In its later development, Xiang Embroidery absorbed the characteristics of traditional Chinese paintings and formed its own unique characteristics. Xiang embroidery experienced its heyday at the end of the Qing Dynasty (1644—1911) and in the early Republic of China (early 20th century), even surpassing Su embroidery. After the founding of the People's Republic of China, Xiang embroidery was further improved and developed to a new level.

The magnificent vigor of the far view and the lifelike art effect, are the unique Xiang embroidery well known around China and overseas. Xiang embroidery has the hard damask, soft damask, transparent glass gauze, and nylon as the fine artworks. Embroidery articles have not only the rare enjoyed artworks, but also handsome and practical commodities, including the screen, picture, bedcover, pillowslip, bedspread, cushion, table cloth, handkerchief and all kinds of embroidery cloth, etc.

Yue embroidery

Also called Guang embroidery, Yue embroidery is a general name for embroidery products of the regions of Guangzhou, Shantou, Zhongshan, Panyu and Shunde in Guangdong province.

According to historical records, in the first year of Yongzhen's reign (805) during the Tang Dynasty (618—907), a girl named Lu Meiniang embroidered the seventh volume of the *Fahua Buddhist Scripture* on a piece of thin silk 30 cm long. And so, Yue embroidery became famous around the country. The prosperous Guangzhou Port of the Song Dynasty promoted the development of Yue embroidery, which began to be exported at that time. During the Qing Dynasty, people regarded animal hair as the raw material for Yue embroidery, which made the works more vivid. During Qianlong's reign (1736—1796) of the Qing Dynasty, an industrial organization was established in Guangzhou. At that time, a large number of craftsmen devoted themselves to the craft, inciting further improvements to the weaving technique. Since 1915, the work of Yue embroidery garnered several awards at the Panama Expo.

Influenced by national folk art, Yue embroidery formed its own unique characteristics. The embroidered pictures are mainly of dragons and phoenixes, and flowers and birds, with neat designs and strong, contrasting colors. Floss, thread and gold-and-silk thread embroidery are used to produce costumes, decorations for halls and crafts for daily use.

Shu embroidery

Shu Embroidery, also called Chuan embroidery, is the general name for embroidery products in areas around Chengdu, Sichuan Province.

Shu embroidery enjoys a long history. As early as the Han Dynasty, Shu embroidery was already famous. The central government even designated an office in this area for its administration. During the Five Dynasties and Ten States Periods (907—960), a peaceful society and large demand provided advanced conditions for the rapid development of the Shu Embroidery industry. Shu embroidery experienced its peak development in the Song Dynasty (960—1279), ranking first in both production and excellence. In the mid-Qing Dynasty, the Shu embroidery industry was formed. After the founding of the People's Republic of China, Shu embroidery factories were set up and the craft entered a new phase of development, using innovative techniques and a large variety of forms.

Originating among the folk people in the west of Sichuan Province, Shu embroidery formed its own unique characteristics: smooth, bright, neat and influenced by the geographical environment, customs and cultures. The works incorporated flowers, leaves, animals, mountains, rivers and human figures as their themes. Altogether, there are 122 approaches in 12 categories for weaving. The craftsmanship of Shu embroidery involves a combination of fine arts, aesthetics and practical uses.

Unit 8 Chinese Traditional Folk Arts

In addition to the four major embroidery styles there are Ou embroidery of Wenzhou, Zhejiang Province; Bian embroidery of Kaifeng, Henan Province and Han embroidery of Wuhan, Hubei Province.

Organic development and accumulation over centuries has made embroidery a complete art of rich patterns and malleable forms that evoke intense aesthetic pleasure. Works fall naturally into different series according to the subject matter and the technique. They include oil painting, traditional Chinese painting, water towns, flowers, so on and so forth. Examples of practical-use embroidered articles are garments, handkerchiefs, scarves and so on.

(1,337 words)

Vocabulary

embroidery /ɪmˈbrɔɪdərɪ/ *n.* patterns that are sewn onto fabrics using threads of various colors; fabrics that is decorated in this way 刺绣;绣花;绣品

inseparable /ɪnˈsepərəbl/ *adj.* not able to be separated 不能分离的

weave /wiːv/ *vi.* to make sth. by crossing threads or strips across, over and under each other by hand or on a machine called a LOOM 编织;纺织

decorate /ˈdekəreɪt/ *vt.* to make something look more beautiful by putting things on it 装饰;点缀

stitch /stɪtʃ/ *n.* one of the small lines of thread that you can see on a piece of fabric after it has been sewn; the action that produces this 缝针;缝线

yarn /jɑːn/ *n.* thread that has been spun, used for knitting, weaving, etc. 纺纱;纺线

quill /kwɪl/ *n.* a large feather from the wing or tail of a bird 翎羽;鹅毛笔

sequin /ˈsiːkwɪn/ *n.* a small circular shiny disc sewn onto clothing as decoration(作服饰用的)圆形闪光金属片

domesticate /dəˈmestɪkeɪt/ *vt.* to make a wild animal used to living with or working for humans 驯养动物

phoenix /ˈfiːnɪks/ *n.* a magic bird that lives for several hundred years before burning itself

and then being born again form its ashes 凤凰
unearth /ʌnˈəːθ/ *vt.* to find something in the ground by digging 发掘；出土
delicate /ˈdelɪkət/ *adj.* small and having a beautiful shape or appearance 精美的
refined /rɪˈfaɪnd/ *adj.* made pure by having other substances taken out of it 精妙的
exquisite /ɪkˈskwɪzɪt/ *adj.* extremely beautiful or carefully made 精致的
fluffy /ˈflʌfɪ/ *adj.* like fluff; looking as if it is soft and light 蓬松的；松软的；毛茸茸的
rim /rɪm/ *n.* the edge of something that is circular 边缘；轮缘
excavate /ˈekskəveɪt/ *vt.* to dig in the ground to look for old buildings or objects that have been buried for a long time; to find something by digging in this way 挖掘；发掘
surpass /səˈpɑːs/ *vt.* to do or to be better than sth./sb. 超越；超过；凌驾
magnificent /mægˈnɪfɪsnt/ *adj.* extremely attractive and impressive; deserving praise 壮丽的；极好的；宏伟的
damask /ˈdæməsk/ *adj.* & *n.* a thick fabric, usually made from silk or linen, with a pattern that is visible on both sides 缎子的；锦缎
transparent /trænsˈpærənt/ *adj.* allowing you to see through it; allowing you to see the truth easily 透明的；易懂的
gauze /gɔːz/ *n.* a light transparent fabric, usually made of cotton or silk 薄纱
nylon /ˈnaɪlɒn/ *n.* a very strong artificial material, used for making clothes, rope, brushes, etc. 尼龙；聚酯氨纤维
prosperous /ˈprɒspərəs/ *adj.* rich and successful 繁荣的；兴旺的
incorporate /ɪnˈkɔːpəreɪt/ *vt.* & *vi.* to include something so that it forms a part of something 把……合并；混合
malleable /ˈmælɪəbl/ *adj.* easily influenced or changed 可锻的；可塑的
aesthetic /iːsˈθetɪk/ *adj.* concerned with beauty and art and the understanding of beautiful things 美的；美学的；审美的
garment /ˈgɑːmənt/ *n.* a piece of clothing 衣服

Proper Names

Su Embroidery	苏绣
Xiang Embroidery	湘绣
Yue Embroidery	粤绣
Shu Embroidery	蜀绣
Buddhist Scripture	佛经
Ou Embroidery	瓯绣
Bian Embroidery	汴绣
Han Embroidery	汉绣

Unit 8 Chinese Traditional Folk Arts

Text Exploration

5 **Choose the best answer to each question with the information from the text.**

1. The development of embroidery is closely related with some things. Which of the following is NOT true?
   A. Silk reeling.
   B. Weaving.
   C. Knitting.
   D. Silkworm raising.
2. When did the Chinese Embroidery become widespread?
   A. During the Zhou Dynasty.
   B. During the Han Dynasty.
   C. During the Tang Dynasty.
   D. During the Qing Dynasty.
3. Which of the following does not belong to the Four Famous Embroideries in China?
   A. Su Embroidery.
   B. Yue Embroidery.
   C. Han Embroidery.
   D. Xiang Embroidery.
4. Su embroidery won Suzhou the title City of Embroidery in the Qing Dynasty for _____?
   A. its delicateness
   B. its smoothness
   C. its uniqueness
   D. both A and B
5. Which of the following is/are the characteristic(s) of the Su Embroidery?
   A. The rim must be neat.
   B. The surface must be flat.
   C. The lines must be dense.
   D. All of the above ones.
6. Which of the following about the Xiang Embroidery is NOT true?
   A. It even surpassed the Su Embroidery in the early Republic of China.
   B. It experienced its heyday at the end of the Ming Dynasty.
   C. In its later development, it absorbed the characteristics of traditional Chinese paintings.
   D. Xiang embroidery has the hard damask, soft damask, transparent glass gauze, and nylon as the fine artworks.
7. During the Qing Dynasty, people regarded _____ as the raw material for Yue embroidery, which made the works more vivid.
   A. animal hair
   B. damask
   C. nylon
   D. silk
8. According to the text, which of the following is NOT the frequent object of the Yue Embroidery?
   A. Dragons.
   B. Phoenixes.
   C. Birds.
   D. Human images.
9. _____ experienced its peak development in the Song Dynasty (960—1279), ranking first in both production and excellence.

A. Shu Embroidery.   B. Yue Embroidery.
C. Xiang Embroidery.   D. Su Embroidery.

10. According to the text, Shu Embroidery combines three elements together. Which of the following is NOT true?
   A. Fine arts.   B. Aesthetics.
   C. Practical uses.   D. Academic value.

6 Complete the following chart with the information from the text.

Embroidery	Geographical Location	Characteristics
Su Embroidery	Su embroidery is the general name for embroidery products in areas around _____, _____ Province.	The product surface must be _____, the rim must be _____, the needle must be _____, the lines must be _____, the color must be _____ and bright and the picture must be _____.
Shu Embroidery	The general name for embroidery products in areas around _____, _____ Province.	Shu embroidery formed its own unique characteristics: _____, bright, neat and influenced by the _____, customs and _____.
Xiang Embroidery	Xiang embroidery of long standing is originated from the folk embroidery in _____ Province.	The magnificent vigor of the _____ view and the _____ art effect, are the unique Xiang embroidery well known around China and overseas. Xiang embroidery has the hard damask, soft damask, _____ glass gauze, and _____ as the fine artworks.

7 Discuss the following questions with the information from the text.

1. What is the main theme of Suzhou Embroidery? And what are the main themes of Shu Embroidery?

2. What is the most famous work of Suzhou Embroidery?

3. Give some examples of the practical commodities of Xiang Embroidery.

4. According to your own understanding, as to the aesthetic and practical use of embroideries, which one is more important or more valuable?

5. If you had an access to embroidery studying, which type of embroideries would you like to choose?

Vocabulary Expansion

8 Fill in the blanks with the right words given below. Change the form where necessary.

| delicate | domesticate | magnificent | surpass | transparent |
| prosperous | incorporate | malleable | inseparable | decorate |

1. There is no denying that his success is _____ from his hard work.
2. Once he _____ his opponent, but to our regret, he was taken over at the last minute.
3. As the glass is _____, people can see from the inside what happens in the outside world.
4. She is fond of buying some small articles to _____ her bedroom.
5. The Chinese society in the Tang Dynasty was so _____ that it aroused the world's attention.
6. As the teenagers are _____, teachers should pay attention to their psychological development.
7. The _____ of the two companies will make more profit in the future.
8. Women were treated as _____ flowers needing special treatment.
9. The _____ of silkworms was very universal in China.
10. The Taj Mahal is a _____ building, which impresses tourists all over the world.

9 Choose the word or phrase that best keeps the meaning of the sentence if it is substituted for the underlined word or phrase.

1. The production of silk threads and fabrics <u>gave rise to</u> the art of embroidery.
   A. made...come into being   B. made it rise
   C. raised   D. prompted
2. Silkworms were <u>domesticated</u> as early as some 5,000 years ago.
   A. kept at home   B. kept in one's own country
   C. raised (animals) at home   D. kept in foreign countries
3. The star <u>refers to</u> items which are intended for the advanced learner.
   A. belongs to   B. connects to
   C. describes   D. involves with
4. Industry in Britain has <u>been in decline</u> sine the 1970s.
   A. decreased   B. increased
   C. raised   D. risen
5. Her wedding dress was absolutely <u>exquisite</u>.
   A. beautiful and carefully made   B. expensive
   C. of high quality   D. suitable
6. They worked very <u>harmoniously</u> together.
   A. peacefully and without any disagreement   B. pleasantly
   C. earnestly   D. conscientiously

7. These programs will <u>integrate</u> with your existing software.
   A. co-work   B. combine
   C. compound   D. form a partnership
8. This area has been <u>designated</u> as a National Park.
   A. referred to   B. declared officially
   C. described   D. chosen
9. There will be a prize for the most <u>innovative</u> design.
   A. creative   B. studious
   C. laborious   D. irregular
10. In its <u>heyday</u>, the company ran trains every fifteen minutes.
    A. most powerful period   B. beginning period
    C. least successful period   D. central period

10 Translate the Chinese sentences into English by simulating the sentences chosen from the text.

Chosen Sentences	Simulated Translations	Chinese Sentences
In its long development embroidery has been ***inseparable from*** silkworm raising, silk reeling and weaving.		这个项目的成功和创新的设计有着密切的关系。(**project**)
The production of silk threads and fabrics ***gave rise to*** the art of embroidery.		这部小说的成功带来了一系列的续篇。(**sequels**)
Well known for its smoothness and delicateness, Su embroidery won Suzhou the title City of Embroidery in the Qing Dynasty.		这个景点以其众多古迹而闻名于世。(**historical site**)
After the founding of the People's Republic of China, Xiang embroidery was further improved and developed ***to a new level***.		改革开放后，中国的经济发展进入了一个全新的层次。(**Reform and Open to the outside**)
In addition to the four major embroidery styles there are Ou embroidery of Wenzhou, Zhejiang Province; Bian embroidery of Kaifeng, Henan Province and Han embroidery of Wuhan, Hubei Province.		除了这些安排以外，另增救护车值班至午夜。(**extra ambulances**)

Unit 8 Chinese Traditional Folk Arts

Supplementary Readings

Passage One
A Miracle Impressed the World: Suzhou Embroidery[①]

Su embroidery—*The Region South of the Yangtze*

It is worldly acknowledged that there are four types of worldly renowned local embroidery in China, namely, the Suzhou Embroidery, the Xiang Embroidery, the Yue Embroidery as well as the Shu Embroidery. All the four kinds of traditional Chinese embroidery have their own features. Some people hold the opinion that Suzhou embroidery is the most famous one among them because of its combination of the great wisdom, delicacy and the patience as well.

It has been rated by UNESCO as the state-list non-material cultural heritage in 2006. Suzhou embroidery has identified its distinct artistic style as early as in Ming Dynasty after centuries of improvement since its origination. Many factors have their roles to play in its development and prosperity, such as geographical convenience, good humane atmosphere as well as the wisdom of local people in Suzhou.

Suzhou embroidery is featured by some characteristics, for instance, fineness, elegance as well as pureness. Embroidery needle is the symbol of fineness. It is a miracle to fulfill the whole work with just a thin, plain stitch. Elegance and pureness are embodiment of features of Suzhou embroidery. Elegance is the comment of the whole picture, showing an air of nobleness, neither fussy nor petty. Pureness refers to the cleanness of the whole piece.

---

①This article is adapted from "*Suzhou Embroidery—a Miracle from a Needle*" at the website: http://www.tianjinwe.com/rollnews/201012/t20101211_2807009.html.

Fineness, elegance and pureness are due to profound influence of Wu culture, which nurtures delicate, smart, tender and careful Suzhou lady, who exerts magic on threads and needles, knitting splendid artworks one by one.

Su embroidery—*Butterflies*

Su embroidery—*Belle Paintings*

Embroiders applied many different needling methods to express features and themes of pictures. Most of the artworks embody richness and inner beauty of Suzhou culture. From 1970s to 1980s, the double-sided embroidery *Cat* was well-known around the world. But embroiders with high ambition and fine skills were not satisfied with the recovering and development of traditional Suzhou embroidery, they created double-faced embroidery with varied colors, making disparity in color, pattern and stitching method in two sides.

  We consistently enrich the expressiveness of embroidery. As for the themes, we inherit our traditional culture and absorb foreign essence. As for the methods of stitches, we use the stitches in a diverse and full way. As for the material of thread, we use shinier one. We promote Suzhou embroidery in an all around way.

  The old embroiders diligently work on their favorite field. They not only make the birds or flowers as their favorite themes, but also combine the understanding of culture, pursuit of pureness as well as the affection for Suzhou. In this sense, this embroidery is both material and spiritual.

1. Some people hold the opinion that Suzhou embroidery is the most famous one among them because of its combination of some elements. Which of the following is NOT true?
   A. Wisdom.   B. Economy.
   C. Patience.   D. Delicacy.
2. Suzhou embroidery has identified its distinct artistic style as early as in _____ after centuries of improvement since its origination.
   A. Ming Dynasty   B. Qing Dynasty
   C. Han Dynasty   D. Yuan Dynasty
3. Which of the following information about Suzhou Embroidery is NOT true according to the text?
   A. Suzhou embroidery is featured by some characteristics, for instance, fineness, elegance as well as pureness.
   B. It has been rated by UNESCO as the state-list non-material cultural heritage in 2005.
   C. Many factors work in the development and flourishing of it, such as geographical convenience, good humane atmosphere as well as the wisdom of local people in Suzhou.
   D. From 1970s to 1980s, the double-sided embroidery *Cat* was well-known around the world.
4. _____ is the comment of the whole picture, showing an air of nobleness, neither fussy nor petty.
   A. Elegance.   B. Delicacy.
   C. Smoothness.   D. Pureness.
5. How do embroiders enrich the expressiveness of embroidery?
   A. In terms of the themes, we inherit our traditional culture and absorb foreign essence.
   B. As for the methods of stitches, we use the stitches in a diverse and full way.
   C. When it comes to the material of thread, we use shinier one.
   D. All of the above.

Passage Two

Yue Embroidery[①]

Yue embroidery, as one of the four most famous traditional embroidery in China, occupies an important place in the field of Chinese embroidery. This kind of embroidery has its production center in Guangzhou, Guangdong Province.

Yue embroidery—*Prosperity Brought by the Dragon and the Phoenix*

Yue embroidery is said to be created by the minorities, and form its own style in the middle and late Ming Dynasty. It's marked by the following five features. Firstly, various kinds of threads are applied: besides silk threads and velvet threads, peacock feather and horse tail fur are also twined into velvet as threads. Secondly, it's strong in contrast, particular about magnificent effect. Thirdly, golden threads are mostly used to embroider the outline of patterns. Fourthly, decorative patterns are over-elaborate, fashionable and lively. Topics with local characteristics are applied, such as "Birds pay homage to the king", marine fish & shrimps, bergamot & fruits. Fifthly, most embroidery workers are male. It is available of rich varieties of products, including quilt covers, pillowcases, bed-sheets, shawls, scarves, table curtains, embroidered clothes, footwear and head-wear, and costumes, as well as mirror screens, hanging scrolls, and banners.

---

①This paper is adapted from "*Yue Embroidery*" at the website: http://www.suxiu.gov.cn.

Unit 8 Chinese Traditional Folk Arts

Yue embroidery—*Still Life*

During the years of Zhengde (A. D. 1506—1521), Ming Dynasty, Yue embroideries were exported to Portugal, England, France via European vessels, becoming favorite ornaments among the palace, imperial household, and nobles. According to "Records of Silk Embroidery of Cunsu Workshop", in the palace of Qing Dynasty, there used to be collection of 8 pieces of Yue embroideries of Ming Dynasty, such as "Bo Gu Scrolls", embroidered with up to 95 pieces of ancient pots, wares and jade-wares, "Stitching is thinner than hair, stitch with care propriety", some "outlines are embroidered with threads made of horse tails", in neat design, "Needles holes are hidden well, seamless", sully representing the excellent craftsmanship of Yue embroidery of Ming Dynasty. It also adopted the exported peacock feathers to make silk threads for embroidery of clothes and daily necessities, brilliant and luxuriant. In the 22nd year of Qianlong period, Qing Dynasty (A. D. 1757), Kao-tsung ordered that the western vessels should have access to Guangzhou Port only, which enhanced the development of Yue embroidery and made it become famous around the world.

As early as in the 1915 Panama International Exposition and 1923 London Exposition, Yue embroidery was already highly appreciated. Nowadays, big pieces of hand-made embroidery articles such as quilt covers, screens, small pieces like pouches, fan covers, embroidered shoes, sleeves and skirts for women, the background is bestrewed with flowers, with thin velvet flatly stuck to the silk surface; some may only embroidered in color green blue in unique style. In a word, Yue embroidery, with strong local characteristics, won great popularity in Hong Kong, Macao and overseas compatriots.

1. Yue embroidery is said to be created by the minorities, and form its own style in _____.
   A. the middle and late Ming Dynasty
   B. the late Ming and early Qing Dynasty
   C. the middle and late Qing Dynasty
   D. the Middle Qing Dynasty

2. Which of the following is not the feature of Yue Embroidery, according to the text information?
   A. Various kinds of threads are applied: besides silk threads and velvet threads, peacock feather and horse tail fur are also twined into velvet as threads.
   B. Golden threads are mostly used to embroider the inner parts of patterns.
   C. Decorative patterns are over-elaborate, fashionable and lively.
   D. Most embroidery workers are male.

3. During the years of Zhengde (A.D.1506—1521), Ming Dynasty, Yue embroideries were exported to some foreign countries. Which of the following is NOT true?
   A. Portugal.
   B. America.
   C. England.
   D. France.

4. In the _____ year of Qianlong period, Qing Dynasty (A.D. 1757), Kao-tsung ordered that the western vessels should have access to Guangzhou Port only, which enhanced the development of Yue embroidery and made it become famous around the world.
   A. 22nd
   B. 21st
   C. 23rd
   D. 14th

5. What's the author's attitude toward the Yue embroidery?
   A. Positive.
   B. Negative.
   C. Indifferent.
   D. Feverish.

Interactive Tasks

Role-play

13 Role-play the following situation with your partner.

Situation:

Han Lei, a Chinese student, invited his foreign friend John to visit a museum which exhibits the Chinese embroidery. After visiting the museum, they have a heated discussion about the traditional Chinese folk arts.

You may begin like this:

John: Wonderful! It is one of the most wonderful art and craft that I have ever seen in the world!

Han: I am impressed by the fine craftsmanship of the embroidery as well. It is hard to image how they stitch the lifelike objects on the small and thin cloth.

John: It seems that they can stitch whatever they want. Are there many different types of embroidery in China?

Han: Of course. According to the different geographical locations, there are the famous four embroideries and some others of minor importance.

Group Work

14 **Work in groups to work out your own presentation**.

1. Form groups of four or five students;
2. Each group chooses a topic concerning Chinese embroidery, e.g.
   A study of the famous four Chinese embroideries;
   An introduction to one of the embroideries and its uniqueness.
3. Members of each group collect materials from library and the Internet to work out their PPT slides;
4. Based on the PPt slides, each member of the group gives oral presentation of his part.

Follow-up Task

Writing

15 **Directions**: For this part, you are going to write a composition on the topic: **The Value of the Traditional Chinese Embroidery**. You should write at least 120 words following the outline given below in Chinese:

1. 中国传统刺绣根据地域可以分为若干种类,尤以四大刺绣闻名于世;
2. 刺绣可以起到装饰和美化的作用;
3. 刺绣作品还有很强的实用性,很多生活用品都是刺绣作品。

Key and Script

Unit 1 Chinese Painting

Starting-out Task

1 **Look at these pictures and discuss the following questions with your partner.**

1. Classical Chinese paintings can be divided into three categories: landscape, figure, and bird & flower.
2. They are: *Dwelling in the Fuchun Mountains*《富春山居图》, *Hibiscus Flowers and Golden Pheasant*《芙蓉锦鸡图》and *Han Xizai's Party*《韩熙载夜宴图》.
3. *Dwelling in the Fuchun Mountains* was painted by Huang Gongwang(黄公望) of Yuan Dynasty. It's a landscape painting. *Hibiscus Flowers and Golden Pheasant* was painted by Zhao Ji(赵佶), an emperor of North Song Dynasty. It's a bird & flower painting. *Han Xizai's Party* was painted by Gu Hongzhong(顾闳中) of Five Dynasties. It's a figure painting.

Listening Tasks

2 **Listen to the following passage and try to fill in the missing words.**

1. techniques 2. exaggerated 3. detail 4. calligraphy 5. contours 6. curved 7. running
8. unique 9. combination 10. decorative

3 **Listen to the dialogue and choose the best answer to the following questions.**

1. C 2. A 3. D 4. B

4 **Listen to the dialogue again and complete the following sentences with the information you have heard.**

1. texture; strokes 2. poets; calligraphers 3. poetry; calligraphy; seal cutting

Reading Tasks

Text Exploration

5 **Choose the best answer to each question with the information from the text.**

1. D 2. A 3. B 4. C 5. D 6. A 7. D 8. C 9. B 10. A

6 **Complete the following chart with the information from the text.**

Paintings	Painters	Details
Night-Shining White	Han Gan Tang Dynasty (618—907)	"Night-Shining White" was the <u>favorite steed</u> of an emperor who led his dynasty to <u>the height of its glory</u> but who, tethered by his infatuation with a <u>concubine</u>, neglected his charge and eventually <u>lost his throne</u>.
Groom and Horse	Zhao Mengfu, Yuan Dynasty (1206—1368)	Zhao's portrait of the horse and groom may be read as an admonition to those in power to <u>heed the abilities of those in their command</u> and to conscientiously employ their talents in <u>the governance of their people</u>.
Twin Pines, Level Distance	Zhao Mengfu, Yuan Dynasty (1206—1368)	The pine tree is a symbol of <u>survival</u> and an emblem of <u>the princely gentleman</u>. Zhao Mengfu's pines may reflect the artist's determination to preserve his <u>political integrity</u>.

Key and Script

7 Discuss the following questions with the information from the text.

1. The aim of the traditional Chinese painter is to capture not only the outer appearance of a subject but its inner essence as well—its energy, life force and spirit.
2. The scholar-official paintings could be drawn using the same kind of brush skills required for calligraphy; expressive calligraphic brush lines were the chief means employed to animate their subjects. Whereas professional artisans preferred a colorful, realistic style of painting; their paintings were drawn through the highly illusionistic use of mineral pigments.
3. Because in so doing, he underscored not only its basis in calligraphy but also the fact that painting was not merely about representation.
4. Open-ended.
5. Open-ended.

Vocabulary Expansion

8 Fill in the blanks with the right words given below. Change the form where necessary.

1. resigned   2. elite   3. expertise   4. calligraphy   5. paradigm   6. emblem   7. banished   8. distilled
9. regime   10. manuscript

9 Choose the word or phrase that best keeps the meaning of the sentence if it is substituted for the underlined word or phrase.

1. C   2. A   3. B   4. D   5. A   6. C   7. D   8. B   9. C   10. D

10 Translate the Chinese sentences into English by simulating the sentences chosen from the text.

1. Every night, more often than not, you'd find Wood at the local pub.
2. Queen Victoria led the British Empire to the height of its glory in the 18th century.
3. The course took the form of seminars and lectures.
4. Technology has had an immense impact on society.
5. Both men and women watch football games, but often to very different ends.

11 Passage One

1. D   2. A   3. B   4. C   5. B

12 Passage Two

1. D   2. B   3. C   4. A   5. D

Unit 2   Sculpture

Starting-out Task

1 Look at these pictures and discuss the following questions with your partner.

1. They are the *Winged Victory of Samothrace*, *the Thinker*, the *Rebellious Slave*, and the *Statue of Liberty*.
2. The *Winged Victory of Samothrace* was made of marble by a sculptor of Ancient Greece around 190 BC; *the Thinker* was made of bronze by Auguste Rodin in 1880; the *Rebellious Slave* was made of marble by Michelangelo in 1513; the *Statue of Liberty* was made of bronze by joint work of French sculptor Bartholdi and French engineer Gustave Eiffel.
3. Open-ended.

Listening Tasks

2 Listen to the following passage and try to fill in the missing words.

1. dimensional   2. resources   3. suntanned   4. divinities   5. religious   6. kingship   7. sacred
8. altar   9. contemporary   10. thematic

3 Listen to the dialogue and decide whether the following statements are true(T) or false(F).
1. T 2. T 3. T 4. F 5. F

4 Listen to the dialogue again and complete the following sentences with the information you have heard.
1. shrines; temples 2. 1,000 3. fired 4. wisdom

Reading Tasks

Text Exploration

5 Choose the best answer to each question with the information from the text.
1. B 2. C 3. D 4. A 5. C 6. D 7. A 8. B 9. B 10. C

6 Complete the following chart with the information from the text.

Period	Time Span	Details
Mycenaean Art	1550—1200 BC	During this period there were two separate civilizations on the mainland: <u>the Greeks and the Mycenaeans</u>; The Greeks learned <u>how to build gates and tombs</u> and <u>how to use different metals in art</u>.
Sub-Mycenaean or Dark Age	1200—1025 BC	The few items that have been found show <u>no new methods or innovation</u>.
Proto-Geometric Art	1025—900 BC	This time period was the Greeks' first expression of <u>reviving their civilization</u>.
Geometric Art	900—700 BC	This time period led to the establishment of primary Greek institutions such as <u>the Greek city state</u> and <u>the Greek alphabet</u>; Large temples and sanctuaries were built in tribute to <u>the gods</u> and were furnished with precious <u>statues</u>.
Archaic Age	700—450 BC	We begin to see an amalgamation of <u>Greek and oriental art</u>; The Archaic age was best known for the emergence of <u>stone statues of humans</u>.
Classical Art	480—323 BC	It was during this age that sculptors had mastered <u>marble</u> and began creating statues that showed <u>joyous freedom of movement and expression</u>, while celebrating mankind as <u>an independent entity</u>.
Hellenistic Era	323—31 BC	The artists of this period did not stick to <u>classical conventions and rules</u> but turned to <u>a more experimental movement and a sense of freedom</u>; One of the largest and most magnificent statues in human endeavor, the <u>Colossus of Rhodes</u> was built during this period.

7 Discuss the following questions with the information from the text.
1. Greek sculpture has had a profound effect throughout the ages. Many of the styles have been reproduced and copied by some of the finest artists to have ever lived e.g. Michelangelo. Actually, all of western art stem from ancient Greek sculpture.
2. First, the former was made of limestone while the latter was sculpted from marble; second, the former came across as rigid and unnatural while the latter showed joyous freedom of movement.
3. This was because the Greeks believed that suppression of the emotions was a noble characteristic of all civilized men, while the public display of human emotion was a sign of barbarism.
4. Open-ended.
5. Open-ended.

Vocabulary Expansion

8 **Fill in the blanks with the right words given below. Change the form where necessary.**

1. exquisite   2. silhouetted   3. cripple   4. revive   5. downfall   6. endeavor   7. prominence
8. counterpart   9. assimilate   10. dominate

9 **Choose the word or phrase that best keeps the meaning of the sentence if it is substituted for the underlined word or phrase.**

1. C   2. A   3. B   4. A   5. D   6. B   7. C   8. A   9. D   10. B

10 **Translate the Chinese sentences into English by simulating the sentences chosen from the text.**

1. Rodin is one of the most famous sculptors to have ever lived.
2. People are more inclined to sleep in spring.
3. The Jews had been scattered around the world from the time they were exiled in the 6th century BC right up until the establishment of Israel in 1948.
4. 2008 saw the first time the Olympic Games were held in China.
5. Man differs from animal in that the former can speak whereas the latter can't.

11 Passage One

1. B   2. C   3. A   4. D   5. C

12 Passage Two

1. B   2. A   3. D   4. C   5. B

Unit 3   Theatre

Starting-out Task

1 **Look at these pictures and discuss the following questions with your partner.**

1. The Sydney Opera House is a multi-venue performing arts centre in the Australian city of Sydney. It was conceived and largely built by Danish architect Jørn Utzon, finally opening in 1973 after a long gestation starting with his competition-winning design in 1957. The Sydney Opera House is administered by the Sydney Opera House Trust, under the New South Wales Ministry of the Arts.

2. Broadway theatre, commonly called simply Broadway, refers to theatrical performances presented in one of the 40 large professional theatres with 500 seats or more located in the Theatre District and in Lincoln Center, in Manhattan in New York City. Along with London's West End theatre, Broadway theatre is widely considered to represent the highest level of commercial theatre in the English-speaking world. The Broadway theatre district is also a popular tourist attraction in New York.

3. Beijing Opera was born when the "Four Great Anhui Troupes" brought Anhui Opera, or what is now called *Huiju*, to Beijing in 1790, for the birthday of the Qianlong Emperor. Beijing Opera was originally staged for the court and came into the public later. In 1828, some famous Hubei troupes came to Beijing. They often jointly performed in the stage with Anhui troupes. The combination gradually formed Beijing Opera's main melodies. The form grew in popularity throughout the 19th century and the Anhui troupes reached their peak of excellence. Beginning in 1884, the Empress Dowager Cixi became a regular patron of Beijing Opera. Beijing Opera was initially an exclusively male pursuit. The Qianlong Emperor had banned all female performers in Beijing in 1772. The appearance of women on the stage began unofficially during the 1870s. By 1894, the first commercial venue showcasing female performance troupes appeared in Shanghai.

Listening Tasks

2 Listen to the following passage and try to fill in the missing words.

1. exclusively 2. illusion 3. derives 4. elements 5. costumes 6. properties 7. borrows
8. characters 9. defines 10. expressions

3 Listen to the passage and decide whether the following statements are true (T) or false (F).

1. F 2. F 3. T 4. T 5. T

4 Listen to the passage again and complete the following sentences with the information you have heard.

1. accompanied by an orchestra
2. a golden age of opera
3. in central and eastern Europe
4. many experiments with modern styles

Reading Tasks

Text Exploration

5 Choose the best answer to each question with the information from the text.

1. C 2. D 3. D 4. C 5. C 6. B 7. D 8. A 9. D 10. A

6 Complete the following chart with the information from the text.

Time	Details
1977	Sir Andrew Lloyd Weber began setting music to T. S. Elliot's "*Old Possum's Book of Practical Cats*" to see if he could write music around lyrics.
1980	1. Elliot's wife gave Weber some of her husband's unfinished verse which inspired him to work with director Trevor Nunn to explore Elliot's works deeper, discovering many further references to *Cats*. 2. Inspired by a rough draft of yet another poem given to the team by Elliot's wife, Weber and Nunn wrote the opening piece "*Jellicle Cats*".
1981	*Cats* premiered in the West End at the New London Theatre on 11 May.
1982	*Cats* made its debut on Broadway on 8 October.
1998	A video version of *Cats* was produced based upon the stage version.
2000	*Cats* closed on Broadway on 10 September 2000, after a total of 7,485 performances.
2002	*Cats* had played a total of 8,949 performances in London when its final performance in London's West End was on its 21st birthday, 11 May 2002.

7 Discuss the following questions with the information from the text.

1. *Cats* held the record as London's longest running musical until 8 October 2006. It also remains Broadway's second longest-running show in history.
2. She began with studying her own cats to get a sense of their movement. Trying to capture the agility, sensuality, and mysterious emotions of cats, she put her dancers through strenuous exercises which eventually led to the physical capabilities she hoped for. When previews began, she stayed late night after night refining the show.
3. Morrison demanded that every costume in the production would be handmade, from the figure-hugging unitards to the striking yak hair wigs.
4. Open-ended.
5. Open-ended.

Key and Script

Vocabulary Expansion

8 Fill in the blanks with the right words given below. Change the form where necessary.

1. inventory   2. rehearsal   3. inception   4. associate   5. phenomenal   6. sensuality   7. gorgeous
8. glamour   9. privilege   10. vigorous

9 Choose the word or phrase that best keeps the meaning of the sentence if it is substituted for the underlined word or phrase.

1. B   2. C   3. B   4. D   5. A   6. B   7. A   8. D   9. C   10. B

10 Translate the Chinese sentences into English by simulating the sentences chosen from the text.

1. They were trapped at the top of the mountain until the dawn of 12th, when the rescue team arrived.
2. Convinced by Richard that it's the best time to purchase a house, he has decided to apply to bank for a mortgage.
3. The survival of these refugees would not be possible without the timely humanitarian aid.
4. He strongly opposed this plan since its inception, claiming that it's completely impractical.
5. Fu Lei is more than a prominent translator, he is an outstanding esthetician.

11 Passage One

1. D   2. C   3. B   4. D   5. B

12 Passage Two

1. C   2. A   3. B   4. D   5. C

Unit 4   Western Classical Music

Starting-out Task

1 Look at these pictures and discuss the following questions with your partner.

1. 1) piano; the famous pianists: Franz Liszt, Frédéric Chopin;
   2) violin; the famous violinists: Nicolò Paganini
   3) orchestra; the famous musician: Ludwig van Beethoven
   You may give other examples and more types of classical music.
2. They are guitar, piano, pedal harp and bassoon.
3. Open-ended.

Listening Tasks

2 Listen to the following passage and try to fill in the missing words.

1. featured   2. release   3. blind   4. compositions   5. co-written   6. avoided   7. electronics
8. necessarily   9. peak   10. leaned

3 Listen to the passage and choose the best answer to the following questions.

1. B   2. D   3. B   4. D   5. A

4 Listen to the passage again and complete the following sentences with the information you have heard.

1. perfected; Italy   2. versatility; struck; head   3. delicate; orchestral; brilliance

Reading Tasks

Text Exploration

5 Choose the best answer to each question with the information from the text.

1. C   2. D   3. C   4. D   5. B   6. A   7. D   8. C   9. C   10. C

6 Complete the following chart with the information from the text.

Musical Instruments or Musical forms	Representative Musicians	Details
Violin	A famous violinist: (1782—1840) Name: Nicolò Paganini	He preferred the larger and <u>louder</u> violins like those by Antonio Stradivari or Guarneri del Gesù
Piano	A famous pianist: (1811—1886) Name: Franz Liszt	He and Paganini dazzled audiences throughout Europe with their performances, elevating the status of the musician from <u>servant</u> to <u>demi-god</u>.
Opera buffa	Name: Wolfgang Amadeus Mozart	His opere buffa such as *Così fan tutte* were popular with the general public

7 Discuss the following questions with the information from the text.

1. It is the middle class that pushed the development of classical music.
2. According to the venues or places for playing music, the classical music is divided into theater music and parlor music.
3. The "bigger is better" mentality led to some new musical forms, such as the tone poem and large-scale symphonic and operatic works.
4. Open-ended.
5. Open-ended.

Vocabulary Expansion

8 Fill in the blanks with the right words given below. Change the form where necessary.

1. access 2. espouse(d) 3. financially 4. comprehensively 5. symmetrical 6. virtuosity
7. rebellion 8. entertaining 9. consequence 10. preservation

9 Choose the word or phrase that best keeps the meaning of the sentence if it is substituted for the underlined word or phrase.

1. A 2. A 3. D 4. A 5. A 6. A 7. B 8. A 9. A 10. B

10 Translate the Chinese sentences into English by simulating the sentences chosen from the text.

1. The teacher asked students to ponder over the implication of the proverbs in this paragraph.
2. The disparity between the rich and the poor is the root cause of this strike.
3. Most of the fieldwork consisted of making tape recorders.
4. With the rise of various vocational schools, young people have more access to professional education.
5. All the existing models will be eventually replaced by the new design.

11 Passage One

1. D 2. D 3. B 4. A 5. C

12 Passage Two

1. C 2. A 3. C 4. B 5. D

Unit 5 Graphic Designing

Starting-out Task

1 Look at these pictures and discuss the following questions with your partner.

1. They are poster for the 13th Vienna Secession exhibition, designed by Austrian artist Koloman Moser,

1902; Plakatstil poster for Priester matches, designed by German designer Lucian Bernhard, 1905; logo for AEG (a German company) designed by German architect Peter Behrens, 1907; army recruiting poster featuring "Uncle Sam," designed by American artist James Montgomery Flagg, 1917.

2. Open-ended.
3. Open-ended.

Listening Tasks

2 Listen to the following passage and try to fill in the missing words.

1. combines 2. convey 3. particular 4. computer-generated 5. make up 6. screens 7. organize 8. humble 9. billboards 10. stimulates

3 Listen to the passage and decide whether the following statements are true (T) or false (F).

1. F 2. F 3. F 4. F 5. T

4 Listen to the passage again and complete the following sentences with the information you have heard.

1. recognizable; memorable
2. simple geometric; powerful message
3. film industry; poster design
4. identities; still exist today

Reading Tasks

Text Exploration

5 Choose the best answer for each of the following questions.

1. C 2. B 3. B 4. B 5. C 6. D 7. A 8. C 9. B 10. C

6 Complete the following chart with the information from the text.

Paragraphs	Aspects	Details
1	The Industrial Revolution	The Industrial Revolution has changed <u>the agricultural and handicraft economies</u> of the West into <u>industrial manufacturing economies</u>; It also changed the <u>ways to use graphic designs</u> and provided <u>new technologies to produce them</u>.
2—4	Poster as a popular medium	Posters were used widely to <u>advertise new modes of transportation, entertainment, and manufactured goods</u>; The poster became a popular medium for graphic designing, partly due to <u>the development of larger sizes of types</u> and <u>innovation of new typefaces</u>; It became even more popular as a result of <u>advances in lithography</u> and the <u>use of color lithographs</u>.
5—8	William Morris and the private-press movement	Morris believed that a return to <u>the craftsmanship and spiritual values of the Gothic period</u> could restore balance to modern life; Morris' Kelmscott Press recaptured <u>the beauty and high standards</u> of incunabula, and the book again became <u>an art form</u>; The Kelmscott Press had a great impact on <u>the rise of the private-press movement</u>.
9—14	Art Nouveau	Art Nouveau was an <u>international design movement</u> that touched all of the design arts; Its graphic designs were inspired by <u>Japanese ukiyo-e woodblock prints</u> and characterized by <u>sinuous curvilinear lines</u>; It became a transitional movement <u>from Victorian design</u> to the <u>modern art movements of the early 20th century</u>.

7 Discuss the following questions with the information from the text.

1. One is the invention of the router that enabled the economical manufacture of abundant quantities of wooden types. The other is the advances in lithography, by which designers could create increasingly colorful posters.
2. Morris's concept of the well-designed page, his beautiful typefaces, and his sense of design unity inspired a new generation of graphic designers; his rediscovery of earlier type styles also triggered a redesign process which led to a great improvement in the quality and variety of fonts; many designers directly imitated the style of the Kelmscott Press; more commercial areas of graphic design were similarly revitalized by the success of Morris.
3. Art Nouveau was an international design movement that emerged and touched all of the design arts during the 1890s and the early 20th century. Its defining characteristic was a sinuous curvilinear line.
4. Open-ended.
5. Open-ended.

Vocabulary Expansion

8 Fill in the blanks with the right words given below. Change the form where necessary.

1. momentum   2. abstract   3. revitalized   4. upgrade   5. vibrant   6. craftsmanship   7. rhythmic
8. practitioner   9. signify   10. publicize

9 Choose the word or phrase that best keeps the meaning of the sentence if it is substituted for the underlined word or phrase.

1. D   2. C   3. A   4. C   5. C   6. D   7. C   8. A   9. D   10. B

10 Translate the Chinese sentences into English by simulating the sentences chosen from the text.

1. The Internet makes it possible for freelance designers to reach a wider audience than ever before.
2. It is reported that the planned high-speed train system will cost less than half as much as building more freeway lanes and airport runways.
3. Some meteorologists fear the drought could last well into 2012.
4. She was actively involved in HR practices and handled approximately 200 employees of the organization.
5. Deeply concerned with the earthquake, most people have turned the disaster into a torch relay of love.

11 Passage One

1. C   2. B   3. B   4. C   5. A

12 Passage Two

1. B   2. C   3. A   4. A   5. C

Unit 6   Landscaping

Starting-out Task

1 Look at these pictures and discuss the following questions with your partner.

1. They are the Villa d'Este(千泉宫) at Tivoli, Italy; the gardens at Versailles(凡尔赛宫), France; Stourhead Garden(斯图海德园), Wiltshire, England; the Master-of-Nets Garden(网师园), Suzhou, China.
2. The Villa d'Este is an Italian Renaissance garden, created in 1572. The gardens at Versailles are typical of French formal style, and were created in the 17th century. Stourhead Garden is an English landscape garden, created in the 1740s. The Master-of-Nets Garden is a classical garden, designed during the Song

Key and Script

dynasty (A. D. 960—1270).

3. Open-ended.

Listening Tasks

2 Listen to the following passage and try to fill in the missing words.

1. characterized   2. features   3. fluid   4. Traditionally   5. gradually   6. philosophy   7. underlying
8. disguised   9. irregularity   10. geometric

3 Listen to the passage and decide whether the following statements are true (T) or false (F).

1. F   2. F   3. T   4. F   5. T

4 Listen to the passage again and complete the following sentences with the information you have heard.

1. 1857; 770   2. wetlands with no trees   3. plays and musical concerts   4. genius; foresight

Reading Tasks

Text Exploration

5 Choose the best answer to each question with the information from the text.

1. C   2. B   3. D   4. C   5. D   6. C   7. D   8. A   9. C   10. B

6 Complete the following chart with the information from the text.

Paragraphs	Aspects	Details
2—4	The Italian influence	The French formal style has origins in <u>Italian Renaissance gardens</u> which was brought to France at <u>the beginning of the 16th century</u>; The Italian garden with its <u>monumental terraces, sculptures, and waterworks</u> was much admired and imitated in France.
5—8	The Gardens of Vaux-le-Vicomte	For the first time, the garden and the chateau were <u>perfectly integrated</u>; The symmetry achieved a <u>degree of perfection and unity</u> rarely equaled in the art of classic gardens.
9—11	The Gardens of Versailles	The Gardens were <u>the greatest achievement</u> of the French formal style. The Gardens occupied <u>an area of 6,000 hectares</u>, and were laid out on <u>an east-west axis</u> followed the course of the sun.
13—14	André Le Nôtre	His design consisted of a <u>strongly unified</u> composition, carefully <u>balanced and proportioned</u> for optimal visual effect. His works not only reflected <u>the social relationships</u> of the period but also provided the <u>dramatic settings</u> for numerous social activities.
16—17	The decline	In the middle of the 18th century, the style of the French garden began to wane in favor of <u>more natural and rustic</u> gardens under the influence of <u>the English landscape garden</u> and <u>the Chinese style</u>.

7 Discuss the following questions with the information from the text.

1. It is a style of garden based on symmetry and the principle of imposing order over nature.
2. It is different from the latter in its enormous scale, complexity of composition, richness of ornamentation, and sweeping vistas.
3. He created the parks and gardens of Vaux Le Vicomte and Versailles, raised the field of landscape architecture to a new level of maturity and set the style for European gardens until the arrival of the English

landscape park.

4. Open-ended.
5. Open-ended.

Vocabulary Expansion

8 Fill in the blanks with the right words given below. Change the form where necessary.

1. proportion   2. ensemble   3. sculpted   4. radiate   5. apogee   6. animated   7. typifies
8. conceived   9. elaborate   10. splendor

9 Choose the word or phrase that best keeps the meaning of the sentence if it is substituted for the underlined word or phrase.

1. B   2. C   3. B   4. D   5. A   6. D   7. B   8. D   9. A   10. C

10 Translate the Chinese sentences into English by simulating the sentences chosen from the text.

1. Urban rivers hold a central place in the physical landscape and collective memory of cities.
2. The quirky style of this British designer is much admired and imitated by fans all over the globe.
3. There are street lights at regular intervals on the main street of the town.
4. Anyone can find their perfect retreat in the Pyrenees, as it has a diversity of landscapes rarely equaled in Europe.
5. Just as it is important to find the right pulse for a piece of music, so you must find the right rhythm by which to live your life.

11 Passage One
1. B   2. A   3. C   4. C   5. B

12 Passage Two
1. B   2. D   3. C   4. B   5. C

Unit 7   Photography

Starting-out Task

1 Look at these pictures and discuss the following questions with your partner.

1. They are: *V-J Day in Times Square*《时代广场的胜利日》, *Suffering of the Eyes*《苦难的眼睛》and *Sudan in Hunger*《饥饿的苏丹》.

2. *V-J Day in Times Square* is a photograph by Alfred Eisenstaedt that portrays an American sailor kissing a young nurse in a white dress on V-J Day in Times Square on August 14, 1945. It became a cultural icon overnight.

   Suffering of the Eyes was taken by Henri Cartier Bresson when he visited Nanjing in 1948. This anxious look of the boy photo was taken when people buying rice in a long queue. The pictures show the Chinese people's misery and suffering.

   Sudan in Hunger was taken by Kevin Carter in 1993 during the Sudan famine. It depicts a famine stricken child crawling towards a United Nations food camp, located a kilometer away. The vulture is waiting for the child to die so that it can eat it. The picture shocked the whole world and it was awarded Pulitzer Prize in 1994. Kevin Carter was criticized for not helping the child and two months after he won the prize, he committed suicide.

3. Open-ended.

Key and Script

Listening Tasks

2 **Listen to the following passage and try to fill in the missing words.**

1. perceived 2. conflict 3. article 4. controversial 5. potential 6. shocked 7. portrayed
8. extensive 9. horrific 10. patriotism

3 **Listen to the dialogue and decide whether the following statements are true(T) or false(F).**

1. T 2. F 3. T 4. F 5. F

4 **Listen to the dialogue again and complete the following sentences with the information you have heard.**

1. fascinating; monuments; grand 2. volunteer; poses 3. lighting and exposure 4. purchase; measures the amount of light in a scene

Reading Tasks

Text Exploration

5 **Choose the best answer to each question with the information from the text.**

1. A 2. B 3. D 4. A 5. C 6. D 7. C 8. C 9. A 10. B

6 **Complete the following chart with the information from the text.**

Parts	Main idea	Details
Part One	characteristics of good photographs	Good photographs <u>stir up</u> emotions. Good photographs always <u>tell a story</u>. Good photographs tell something more than just <u>how something looks</u>.
Part Two	What <u>makes</u> great photographer?	1) Humility: If you see you lack that ability to <u>make right decisions</u>, do not be ashamed to ask for help. 2) Patience: it's essential for a photographer to be patient when you take pictures of <u>animals and children</u>. Part of being able to wait comes from <u>not having to do</u> other things that should have been done in advance. 3) <u>Perseverance</u>: It means that you might have to return to location and try again. 4) Observation: Great photographers become great by <u>developing</u> their power of observation.

7 **Discuss the following questions with the information from the text.**

1. Photographs bridge the gap between cultures, landscapes and generations. Through photographs, we can preserve history.
2. The technical photographer is all about the equipment and the formulas while the subject photographers take photographs to study the object itself.
3. With observational ability, you will begin to notice things you used to pass by and you will have a habit of always examining your surroundings for possible photographs.
4. Open-ended.
5. Open-ended.

Vocabulary Expansion

8 **Fill in the blanks with the right words given below. Change the form where necessary.**

1. evoke 2. awe 3. humility 4. generate 5. innocent 6. emerge 7. pursue 8. capture
9. patience 10. recession

9 Choose the word or phrase that best keeps the meaning of the sentence if it is substituted for the underlined word or phrase.

1. C   2. A   3. D   4. A   5. B   6. A   7. B   8. D   9. A   10. C

10 Translate the Chinese sentences into English by simulating the sentences chosen from the text.

1. Learning a foreign language helps us bridge the gap between two different cultures.
2. The opposition is trying to stir up feelings of dissatisfaction among the voters.
3. The accused person stuck out that he was innocent of the crime.
4. To get ahead, one must work hard and be willing to make certain sacrifices.
5. The point of all this is that we are involved in this struggle.

11 Passage One

1. A   2. B   3. C   4. A   5. D

12 Passage Two

1. B   2. C   3. D   4. A   5. B

Unit 8 Chinese Traditional Folk Arts

Starting-out Task

1 Look at these pictures and discuss the following questions with your partner.

1. The four most famous Chinese embroideries are: Su embroidery, Yue embroidery, Xiang embroidery and Shu embroidery.
2. You may give answers like Ou embroidery of Wenzhou, Zhejiang Province; Bian embroidery of Kaifeng, Henan Province and Han embroidery of Wuhan, Hubei Province.
3. Open-ended.
   You can tell the differences between them from the following aspects: the subject or theme of the embroideries, the technique and the color and so on.

Listening Tasks

2 Listen to the following passage and try to fill in the missing words.

1. fascinating   2. manually   3. decorative   4. reflection   5. occupies   6. indispensible   7. weaving
8. concerned   9. distinctive   10. respective

3 Listen to the dialogue and choose the best answer to the following questions.

1. B   2. C   3. D   4. B

4 Listen to the dialogue again and complete the following sentences with the information you have heard.

1. carry; miracle   2. recommended; paper-cuts   3. interested; research; folk

Reading Tasks

Text Exploration

5 Choose the best answer to each question with the information from the text.

1. C   2. B   3. C   4. D   5. D   6. B   7. A   8. D   9. A   10. D

Key and Script

6 Complete the following chart with the information from the text.

Embroidery	Geographical Location	Characteristics
Su Embroidery	Su embroidery is the general name for embroidery products in areas around <u>Suzhou</u>, <u>Jiangsu</u> Province.	The product surface must be <u>flat</u>, the rim must be <u>neat</u>, the needle must be <u>thin</u>, the lines must be <u>dense</u>, the color must be <u>harmonious</u> and bright and the picture must be <u>even</u>.
Shu Embroidery	The general name for embroidery products in areas around <u>Chengdu</u>, <u>Sichuan</u> Province.	Shu embroidery formed its own unique characteristics: <u>smooth</u>, bright, neat and influenced by the <u>geographical environment</u>, customs and <u>cultures</u>.
Xiang Embroidery	Xiang embroidery of long standing is originated from the folk embroidery in <u>Hunan</u> Province.	The magnificent vigor of the <u>far</u> view and the <u>lifelike</u> art effect, are the unique Xiang embroidery well known around China and overseas. Xiang embroidery has the hard damask, soft damask, <u>transparent</u> glass gauze, and <u>nylon</u> as the fine artworks.

7 Discuss the following questions with the information from the text.

1. The main theme of Suzhou embroidery: nature and the environment.
   The main theme of Shu embroidery: flowers, leaves, animals, mountains, rivers and human figures.
2. The most famous work of Suzhou Embroidery is an embroidered cat with bright eyes and fluffy hair looking vivid and lifelike.
3. The practical commodities of Xiang Embroidery: the screen, picture, bedcover, pillowslip, bedspread, cushion, table cloth, handkerchief and all kinds of embroidery cloth, etc.
4. Open-ended. But you should give your own reasons.
5. Open-ended.

Vocabulary Expansion

8 Fill in the blanks with the right words given below. Change the form where necessary.

1. inseparable   2. surpassed   3. transparent   4. decorate   5. prosperous   6. malleable
7. incorporation   8. delicate   9. domestication   10. magnificent

9 Choose the word or phrase that best keeps the meaning of the sentence if it is substituted for the underlined word or phrase.

1. A   2. C   3. B   4. A   5. A   6. A   7. B   8. B   9. A   10. A

10 Translate the Chinese sentences into English by simulating the sentences chosen from the text.

1. The success of this project is inseparable from its innovative design.
2. The popularity of this novel gave rise to a series of sequels.
3. This scenic spot is well known for its historical sites.
4. After the policy of "Open and Reform to the Outside", the economy of China has developed to a new level.
5. In addition to these arrangements, extra ambulances will be on duty till the mid-night.

11 Passage One
1. B   2. A   3. B   4. A   5. D

12 Passage Two
1. A   2. B   3. B   4. A   5. A

Unit 1　Chinese Painting

Listening Tasks

Micro Listening Skills

Chinese traditional painting is highly regarded throughout the world for its expression and techniques. According to the means of expression, Chinese painting can be divided into two categories: the *xieyi* school and the *gongbi* school. The *xieyi* school is marked by exaggerated forms and freehand brush work. The *gongbi* school is characterized by close attention to detail and fine brush work.

Chinese painting and Chinese calligraphy are closely related because lines are used in both. Lines are used not only to draw contours but to express the artist's concepts and feelings. For different subjects and different purposes a variety of lines are used. They may be straight or curved, hard or soft, thick or thin, pale or dark, and the ink may be dry or running. The use of lines and strokes is one of the elements that give Chinese painting its unique qualities.

Traditional Chinese painting is a combination of the arts of poetry, calligraphy, painting, and seal engraving. In ancient times most artists were poets and calligraphers. Inscriptions and seal impressions help to explain the painter's ideas and sentiments and also add decorative beauty to the painting.

Dialogue

Chinese Painting

Susan is an international student in China. She just visited an exhibition of classical Chinese paintings. Then she had a talk with her Chinese friend Ni Jin, who is fond of Chinese paintings.

S: Ni, I just attended an exhibition of classical Chinese paintings. I quite enjoyed it. But I need to know more to further appreciate them.

Ni: Let's see whether I can be of any help.

S: What's the paper used by painters?

Ni: It's *Xuan* paper. That's what makes classical Chinese painting different from western art.

S: No wonder they look quite special.

Ni: And you may feel surprised that many early Chinese paintings were on silk, not on papers.

S: So why? Isn't it true that silk is more expensive than paper?

Ni: That's simply because the invention of silk is earlier than that of paper by a long historical period.

S: But is it better to paint on paper?

Ni: Of course. It is believed that the texture of *Xuan* paper is most suitable for Chinese painting. It allows the writing brush wet with Chinese ink, making strokes varying from dark to light.

S: I found some paintings are very similar in their contents.

Ni: Right. Classical Chinese paintings can be divided into three categories: landscape, figure, and bird & flower.

S: I like those of sceneries best.

Ni: Landscapes and bird & flower paintings demonstrate the central place of nature in Chinese thought. Very often bird & flower paintings reflect painters own ideals and characters.

S: What are the most popular figures of those figure paintings?

Ni: The images of emperors, philosophers and court ladies provide role models.

S: I also found there are poems on many paintings.

Ni: Yes. You know many Chinese painters were at the same time poets and calligraphers. They will often add a poem on the painting, and there will always be a seal.

S: That really makes a painting more unique.

Ni: So many people say that classical Chinese painting is an art combining four Chinese arts: poetry, calligraphy, painting and seal cutting.

Unit 2 Sculpture

Listening Tasks

Micro Listening Skills

Humans have created three dimensional, sculptural objects throughout their history. A wide range of materials and techniques have been and continue to be used which reflect local practices and the resources available. Classical sculptors worked in both bronze and marble, but bronze was popular because its shiny gold color imitated oiled, suntanned skin. Sculpture is produced for numerous reasons and functions in a range of different ways. Many peoples produce sculptures that depict divinities or cultural heroes in human or animal form which would have been used in a religious or ritual context. Other types of sculpture celebrate kingship and power, commemorate ancestors or relate to beliefs about death and afterlife. Sculpture is found in a wide variety of contexts, both sacred and secular. A work might be placed on an altar located in the landscape or it could be applied to architecture. The works of contemporary sculptors can be found in both public and private contexts and explore a range of issues, both formal and thematic.

Dialogue

Sculptures in the British Museum

Jane and Richard are looking around in the British Museum.

Jane: What a large collection of sculptures here!

Richard: The collection of sculptures here has inspired artists for hundreds of years and is a rich source of ideas.

Jane: Oh, yeah! Here is a cool bronze statue. Who does it represent?

Richard: Well, it probably represents Hermes, the messenger of the gods.

Jane: But why is it nude?

Richard: Because in ancient Greece, the nude embodied classical culture's idealized conception of human figure.

Jane: How was the statue used in ancient Greece?

Richard: It is not known, but it might have decorated household shrines or gardens or been given as offering to temples.

Jane: I see. Greek sculptures are marvelous. How about sculptures in other parts of the world?

Richard: Let me show you a statue of ancient China which was made more than one thousand years ago. It's a Luohan, a follower of Buddha.

Jane: Really? How could the colors remain so strong and so bright over such a long period of time?

Richard: Well, the colors survive particularly well because the glaze does not rub off once fired.

Jane: His ears are much longer than people of today. Did people in ancient China have long ears?

Richard: Of course not. Probably, long ears indicated wisdom in ancient China.

Jane: Where did ancient Chinese people place such statue?

Richard: Such Luohan figures were usually placed along the walls of a temple entrance, or grouped in pairs on either side of the main Buddha sculpture. But this one was discovered in an ancient tomb in northern China.

Jane: Both eastern and western sculptures show their unique artistic charms. It's really hard to say which is more beautiful.

Richard: Actually each is beautiful in its own way.

Unit 3   Theatre

Listening Tasks

Micro Listening Skills

Theatre is a branch of the performing arts. Any performance may be considered theatre; however, as a performing art, theatre focuses almost exclusively on live performers enacting a self-contained drama before an audience. A performance qualifies as dramatic by creating a representational illusion. The word "theatre" derives from the Ancient Greek word *theatron* meaning "a place for viewing." A theatrical performance may include music, dance and various elements of stagecraft such as costumes, sets, lights, stage properties and sound engineering, among others.

Modern Western theatre derives in large measure from ancient Greek drama, from which it borrows technical terminology, classification into genres, and many of its themes, stock characters, and plot elements. Theatre scholar Patrice Pavis defines theatricality, theatrical language, stage writing, and the specificity of theatre as synonymous expressions that differentiate theatre from the other performing arts, literature, and the arts in general.

Passage

The Evolution of Opera

Opera is an art form in which singers and musicians perform a dramatic work combining text and musical score. Opera is part of the Western classical music tradition. Opera incorporates many of the elements of spoken theatre, such as acting, scenery, and costumes and sometimes includes dance. The performance is typically given in an opera house, accompanied by an orchestra.

Opera started in Italy at the end of the 16th century and soon spread through the rest of Europe. In the 18th century, Italian opera continued to dominate most of Europe, except France, attracting foreign composers such as Handel. Opera seria was the most prestigious form of Italian opera, until Gluck reacted against its artificiality with his reformed operas in the 1760s. Today the most renowned figure of late 18th century opera is Mozart, who began with opera seria but is most famous for his Italian comic operas. The first third of the 19th century saw the advent of grand opera typified by the works of Meyerbeer. The mid-to-late 19th century was a golden age of opera, led and dominated by Wagner in Germany and Verdi in Italy. The popularity of opera continued through the verismo era in Italy and contemporary French opera through to Puccini and Strauss in the early 20th century. During the 19th century, parallel operatic traditions emerged in central and eastern Europe, particularly in Russia. The 20th century saw many experiments with modern styles. With the rise of recording technology, singers such as Enrico Caruso became known to audiences beyond the circle of opera fans. Operas were also performed on radio and television.

Unit 4 Western Classical Music

Listening Tasks

Micro Listening Skills

George Shearing appeared on the American jazz scene in the early 1940s with a series of successful recordings that featured a fine-tuned rhythm section of guitar, bass, drums and vibraphone. He was already quite famous in England, but after the release of his hit song *September in the Rain*, his quintet rose to new heights.

Shearing was born blind in London on August 13, 1919. He began playing piano at age three and soon fell in love with the music of Earl Hines, Fats Waller, and Art Tatum. At 19, he performed jazz accordion in Claude Bampton's all-blind band and got his first real taste of show business. Shearing won over American audiences with his own style of boogie-woogie, blues and jazz swing. One of his best-known compositions is the jazz standard *Lullaby of Broadway*, co-written with lyricist George David Weiss.

Shearing avoided the trappings of jazz fusion, synthesizers and electronics that arrived late in his career. He believed that more volume didn't necessarily mean better music. At the peak of his career, George Shearing was immortalized in Jack Kerouac's 1957 novel *On the Road*. Upon seeing Shearing in a Chicago nightclub, Kerouac wrote, "as always he leaned his blind head on his pale hand, all ears opened like the ears of an elephant, listening to the American sounds and mastering them for his own English summer-night's use."

Passage

Piano

The ancestry of the piano can be traced to the early keyboard instruments of the fifteenth and sixteenth centuries—the spinet, the dulcimer, and the virginal. In the seventeenth century the organ, the clavichord, and the harpsichord became the chief instruments of the keyboard group, a supremacy they maintained until the piano supplanted them at the end of the eighteenth century. The clavichord's tone was metallic and never powerful; nevertheless, because of the variety of tone possible to it, many composers found the clavichord a sympathetic instrument for intimate chamber music. The harpsichord with its bright, vigorous tone was the favorite instrument for supporting the bass of the small orchestra of the period and for concert use, but the character of the tone could not be varied save by mechanical or structural devices.

The piano was perfected in the early eighteenth century by a harpsichord maker in Italy. This instrument was called a piano e forte, to indicate its dynamic versatility; its strings were struck by a recoiling hammer with a felt-padded head. The wires were much heavier in the earlier instruments. A series of mechanical improvements continuing well into the nineteenth century, including the introduction of pedals to sustain tone or to soften it, the perfection of a metal frame, and steel wire of the finest quality, finally produced an instrument capable of myriad tonal effects from the most delicate harmonies to an almost orchestral fullness of sound, from a liquid, singing tone to a sharp, percussive brilliance.

Unit 5 Graphic Designing

Listening Tasks

Micro Listening Skills

Graphic design is a creative process that combines art and technology to communicate ideas. Graphic designers work with a variety of communication tools in order to convey a message from a client to a particular audience. They handle drawn, painted, photographed, or computer-generated images, but they also design the letterforms that make up various typefaces found in books, menus, movie credits and even on computer screens. They create or choose these elements—the typography, images, and the so-called "white space"—and then organize them into one piece of artwork. Graphic design is a part of your daily life. From humble things like gum wrappers to huge things like billboards to the T-shirt you're wearing, graphic design informs, persuades, stimulates, attracts attention and provides pleasure.

Passage

American Designer Saul Bass

Saul Bass was an American graphic designer, best known for his work in film and classic logo design. He studied designing in New York as a teenager and developed a unique style that is both recognizable and memorable.

Bass is famous for his use of simple geometric shapes and their symbolism. Often, a single dominant image stands alone to deliver a powerful message. These shapes were often hand drawn by Bass to create a casual appearance. His ability to create such a powerful message with basic shapes makes the work even more impressive.

Bass is best known for his work in film. He started out in the industry doing poster design, first hired by director and producer Otto Preminger. Bass had an uncanny ability to capture the mood of a film with simple shapes and images, much like his other work. He went on to work with other directors such as Alfred Hitchcock and Stanley Kubrick, designing classic posters for movies such as *Vertigo* and *The Shining*.

From poster design, Bass moved on to creating impressive title sequences for many films. These opening credits felt like animated graphic design, maintaining Bass's print style for a consistent branding of a film. This work continued late into Bass's career. To top off his involvement in the film world, Bass won an Oscar in 1968 for his short film *Why Man Creates*.

Bass was also responsible for creating memorable logos, many of which still exist today. Through his freelance work and with his firm Saul Bass & Associates, he created identities for companies such as AT&T, Bell and Warner Communications. In addition, Bass designed the posters for the 1984 Los Angeles Olympic Games and several Academy Awards shows.

Unit 6 Landscaping

Listening Tasks

Micro Listening Skills

Informal gardens are characterized by flowing curves, non-symmetrical arrangements of features and spaces and plants that are allowed to grow into their natural shapes. The lines are softer and more fluid and the planting is less rigid than formal gardens. Traditionally, gardens have always had their most formal areas near the house, gradually becoming more informal as they get further away and this is still a good philosophy today. In the informal garden, the underlying framework is almost entirely disguised by planting and the garden should look as though it has grown up naturally. Informal gardens are harder to design than formal ones as they are ruled by irregularity and natural looking planting. A site that isn't a geometric shape can be a good basis for an informal garden.

Key and Script

Passage

Central Park

Central Park was the first major city park in the United States. It still is the most famous. The park draws more than 20 million visits a year, making it one of New York City's most popular attractions.

The park was first opened in 1857 on 770 acres of land. In 1858, Frederick Law Olmsted and Calvert Vaux won a design competition to improve and expand the park. Influenced by 18th-century English landscape design, they aimed to make a beautiful natural environment with lakes, woods and open areas for all the people of New York to enjoy.

The huge manmade landscape cost $14 million to build. The area was mostly wetlands with no trees. The park builders reshaped the land with tons of soil and rock and millions of trees and plants. They created hills and lakes. They designed bridges, roads and paths. They added more than fifty statues, monuments and fountains of water. They completed their work in 1878. Later, playgrounds, baseball fields and an ice skating rink were built in the park. Today, Central Park also has a zoo, a carousel ride for children and a theater where plays and musical concerts are presented each summer.

Millions of people who live in New York love Central Park as a place to escape from their small apartments in high-rise buildings. Central Park is a place of peace, quiet and natural beauty that is surrounded by tall buildings and the noisy, crowded streets of New York. Some people call it the heart of the biggest city in America.

What exists today is essentially Olmsted and Vaux's plan, with more trees, buildings and roads. Landscape architects still speak reverently of Olmsted's genius and foresight, and the sensitive visitor can see the effects he sought.

Unit 7 Photography

Listening Tasks

Micro Listening Skills

War photography changed how people perceived war and how news publications reported armed conflict. While people may not fully understand the grim reality of war by reading a news article, they often immediately grasp it by viewing graphic pictures of war.

War photography has always been controversial, both in terms of the explicit nature of combat photography and potential military censorship of images. The American Civil War marked the first time a team of photographers took pictures of war. The resulting photos of battle and death shocked the public, who were used to seeing war portrayed as a romantic, noble endeavor.

While combat photography had been around for over a century before World War I, not many pictures were taken during this war due to extensive military censorship. Combat photography during World War II, especially those horrific pictures of the Nazi concentration camps prompted both patriotism and public outrage.

Dialogue

Taking pictures

Jack has just returned from a journey to India and he is enjoying the pictures he took there with Rose.

Rose: Hey, you look totally refreshed! How about you journey to India?
Jack: Wow, it's amazing. India is a photographer's dream.
Rose: Oh, why is that?

Jack: It's such a fascinating place because of the stunning colors of her people, the history of her great monuments, the rich street life and the grand weddings.

Rose: Wait, how can you participate in the weddings there as a tourist?

Jack: Well, this is one of the reasons why I love India. Most Indian families do not mind a volunteer photographer at the wedding and they usually co-operate with poses. I found that the best opportunities for the weddings occur behind the scenes when the bride is being decorated and during the rituals.

Rose: That must be very interesting.

Jack: Sure, you can take a look at the pictures taken there.

Rose: Aha, good pictures. Is this Taj Mahal?

Jack: Yes, it is synonymous with India. Its beauty makes it the most visited and most photographed in India.

Rose: That's for sure. What happened to this picture? I can't recognize what's in it.

Jack: Ah, this one is underexposed so it's too dark.

Rose: I don't know much about taking pictures. What do you mean?

Jack: You know proper lighting and exposure is very important in photography. The more light within the scene, the more the film will be exposed. Conversely, the less light a scene has, the less the film will be exposed.

Rose: Oh, I see your point. Overexposed film turns out pictures that are too bright and underexposed film will be too dark, appearing "blacked-out".

Jack: That's it. For a photographer, how to manipulate the lighting or film speed to ensure the adequate level of exposure is of great importance.

Rose: Seems rather demanding. I think it's too hard for me.

Jack: Not that difficult. You can use some tools to do that.

Rose: Really?

Jack: Many photographers purchase a light meter. It's a tool that measures the amount of light in a scene.

Rose: You mean, with that light meter, you can choose the appropriate film speed?

Jack: That's right.

Unit 8   Chinese Traditional Folk Arts

Listening Tasks

Micro Listening Skills

Embroidery is the fascinating cloth art that involves the use of needles and thread. Embroidery was originally done manually, or in other words, by hand. It is basically done for decorative purposes by sewing various types of materials into a layer of cloth or fabric to create patterns and designs that are usually a reflection of the beauty of nature.

Embroidery, a folk art with a long tradition, occupies an important position in the history of Chinese traditional arts and crafts. It is, in its long development, indispensible from silkworm-raising and silk-reeling and weaving. Today, silk embroidery is practiced nearly all over China. As far as the Chinese embroidery is concerned, the best commercial products, it is generally agreed, come from four provinces: Jiangsu (notably Suzhou), Hunan, Sichuan and Guangdong, each with its distinctive features. Each has its own characteristics, namely, the respective subject, technique and material, so on and so forth.

Key and Script

Dialogue

Traditional Chinese Folk Arts

Benjamin is a foreigner who desires to buy some traditional Chinese arts and crafts for his friends in his own country. When he is choosing the presents for his friends, he has a lively chat with the shop assistant.

Translation of the Texts

Unit 1 Chinese Painting

"阅读"中国画

中国的赏画方式可用两个字表达:"读画",即:阅读画。那么如何来阅读画呢?

以韩干《照夜白》图为例,该图画的是一匹马。最初,仅有1英尺多见方,其后千百年间不断有人增加题跋和印章,现已装裱成为一幅长达20英尺的长卷。画上的马四周满是热情洋溢的溢美之词。令人称奇的是,透过众多题跋和印章,马的精气神脱颖而出,跃然纸上。此马如此神骏是因为画家仔细观察了真实的马和前人对马的描绘,汲取两者精华,创作了形神兼备的"龙驹"形象。画家达到如此效果,所用的手段却无比简练:纸上笔墨而已。

这就是传统中国画家的宗旨:不仅表现事物的外在形态,更表现其内在精髓——能量、活力和精神。为达此目标,中国画家多半拒绝使用色彩,正如喜欢黑白两色的摄影师,中国画家视色彩为干扰。他还拒绝利用光影的多变特性来产生立体感,也不用厚重的涂色来掩盖瑕疵。反而,他所仰仗的唯有线条——无法修改的笔墨痕迹。

这种技能所需的训练源于书法实践。传统上,每一个中国读书人自幼年学写字开始就要临摹汉字的标准写法。学生逐渐接触不同的汉字书写风格,临摹大书法家亲笔题写的碑文,这些碑文刻在石头上,便于拓印。久而久之,习练者逐渐形成自己的个人风格,即对前人范本的提炼和重新诠释。

4世纪时,王羲之对书法实践进行了革新,使之成为一门高等艺术。到了11世纪,要想通过科举考试进入政府工作,除熟读历史文学经典外,好书法是重要标准。于是,科举登第者往往自认为是新型精英群体,是"文人官员",负有建立和维护道德及审美标准的责任。他们用自己掌握的历史知识来影响时事。他们对历史的诠释对帝王产生约束。他们的诗歌、日记和评论成为后人评价统治者的依据。

正是这些人在《照夜白》上写满了题跋,盖满了印章。他们凭借自己的艺术知识判断出图上所画的是一匹御马,归8世纪的一名统治者所有。他们还认识到,马不仅象征着中国的军事力量,推而广之,还象征着中国本身。他们能读懂马的辛酸与无奈。"照夜白"本是一位功业显赫的皇帝的心爱坐骑,可这位皇帝后来因迷恋一个宠妃,荒废朝政,最终失去皇位。

这位皇帝未能让他的宝马纵横驰骋,后人以此喻指统治者不能正确认识下属官员的才干。无疑,600年后,退职的文人官员赵孟頫在他所绘的马中表达的就是这个意思。长久以来,相马之术喻指慧眼识才的能力。赵孟頫所绘马和马夫画像可解读为对当权者的劝诫,劝说当权者留意手下人的才干,认真将他们的才干用于统治人民的目的。

假如帝王无视臣下的建议,不公正或不道德,文人官员往往辞官隐退。这种举动历来被理解为他们不愿辅佐帝王,是他们在面对无法容忍的环境时作出的无声的抗议。改朝换代的年代尤其令人忧伤,忠于前朝者往往拒绝服务于新朝。还有,文人官员有时因介入当权者的朋党之争而被罢官。这些情况下,失意者会借助书画艺术来表达自己的信念。由于这些人代表了社会的道德良知,他们的艺术影响力极大。

文人官员画家在多数情况下用墨在纸上作画,所画之物无非是竹、枯树、山石之类,绘画这类物体所用技法与书法的运笔技法无异。这使得他们的艺术有别于宫廷画师和专业画家所用的色彩多样、写实的绘画风格。他们对自己业余画家的身份颇为得意,创造了新的、个性独特的绘画形式,以富有表现力的毛笔书法线条作为主要手段,让所画之物变得栩栩如生。

　　赵孟頫是新派业余文人画家的典范。他不仅是一名训练有素的文人官员,还是一名杰出的书法家,一名将毛笔技法运用于绘画的书法家。为将自己的文人绘画和专业画师的绘画区别开,他用"写"而非"画"来定义他的艺术。这样一来,他不仅强调绘画需要书法基础,还强调绘画不只是表现事物本身——这一点他在《双松平远图》的题跋中予以强调。赵是追求完美的文人,他所选的绘画对象和格调都是经过深思熟虑的。由于松树在冬季也能保持绿色,它被视为生命的象征。又因为松树延展的枝条庇护了林中其他小树,它成了君子的象征。赵不久前刚辞去蒙元政权的官职,他一定是刻意通过"写"松来表达对一位朋友的深情厚谊。这幅画可被解读为描写两个人物形象——他本人和那位朋友。

　　由于文人画家运用象征、格调和书法技法来表达信念和情感,他们把追求外形相似的绘画技巧留给职业画师。这些画师或许擅长于将人的外貌描绘得栩栩如生,但他们绝不可能表现出人性方面更深层次的涵义。

　　文人画家第一次在同一件作品中使用了书法、题诗、绘画三种表现手法,融"三绝"于一体。在这样的画作中,题诗和图画的意象和富有灵性的书法线条前后贯穿,表达了画家的思想和感情。一旦题跋诗成为一件作品中必不可少的组成部分,后世的藏家和赏画者会经常增加题跋以"和"前人。所以,画家搁笔之日并不是一幅画最终完成之时,随着后世藏家和赏画者增加题跋和印章,这幅画还在不断完善。多数题跋以题记的形式写在画的四边、手轴或册页的附页;还有一些可能直接题写在画上。《照夜白》以这种方式留下了一千多年的传承记录,这也为该画增色不少。

　　作为历史和美学价值观的裁定者,文人对艺术品位影响巨大。甚至连帝王都逐渐接受了文人的理念。虽然一些帝王成为了才华横溢的书法家,但他们更愿意起用那些为他们的统治歌功颂德的画家。专业宫廷画师和业余文人画家都使用象征主义,但两者的目的常常不同。赵孟頫的松能反映画家在政治上保持忠直的决心,而一幅宫廷画师的山水画则可解读为对帝国良好秩序的颂扬。文人画家所画的水仙花可反映出画家以此花的纯洁芬芳来象征自己的高洁,而宫廷画师笔下葱翠的兰花则更多意在诱发后宫嫔妃的感官愉悦。

　　"阅读"中国画就是和过去进行对话。展开一幅卷轴、翻看一本画册页,可让人和作品进行深入的、实实在在的沟通。千百年来人们一直在分享和重复人与画的这种亲密关系。读画可一人独享或与友人共享。不论何种形式,正是透过这样的阅读,画的涵义变得越发清晰了。

Unit 2　Sculpture

希腊雕塑的七个阶段

　　希腊雕塑在历史上有着深远的影响。其许多风格被一些有史以来最杰出的艺术家,如米开朗基罗,所效仿。事实上,所有的西方艺术都起源于古希腊雕塑。希腊人将许多材料用于雕塑,包括青铜、大理石和石灰石,因为这些材料在希腊储量丰富。其他的材料,比如黏土,也用于雕塑。但由于这些材料质地易碎,做出来的雕塑作品几乎没有存世的。希腊雕塑之所以重要还因为这些作品讲述了神、英雄、事件、神兽的故事,反映了希腊的文化。希腊雕塑主要可分为七个阶段:迈锡尼艺术时期、后迈锡尼或黑暗时期、原始几何风格时期、几何艺术时期、古风时期、古典时期和希腊化时期。

　　迈锡尼艺术时期是现存希腊艺术品所能追溯到的最早时期。这一时期的地点是在希腊本土,时间大约从公元前1550年到公元前1200年。这一时期在希腊本土有两种不同的文明:希腊文明和迈锡尼文明。当时迈锡尼的技术比希腊先进,希腊文明从迈锡尼文明那里学到很多东西。希腊学会如何建筑大门和陵墓(如阿伽门农之墓)以及如何使用迈锡尼的技术将不同的金属用于艺术。狮子门前著

349

名的迈锡尼巨型城墙就是他们石工技艺的典范。

由于特洛伊的陷落，公元前1200年前后，迈锡尼艺术走向衰落。这时期被称为后迈锡尼或黑暗时期，时间上大约从公元前1200年到公元前1025年。这一时期保留下来的雕塑作品为数极少，也没表现出什么新的技法和创新。这或许是因为那个时期频繁的战乱严重破坏了文明的发展。

下一个时期（公元前1025—900）被称为原始几何风格时期，我们逐渐发现陶制品开始用简单的图案、曲线和黑色条纹来修饰。现代人认为，这一时期的希腊人第一次表现出对文明的复兴。据信随着快速陶轮的发明，他们开始了对陶器的艺术尝试。这一时期作品的显著特征是在器物的颈部和腹部有水平的宽条纹，还有同心圆和许多刷痕。这些图案主要表现一些抽象的元素。

几何艺术时期大致从公元前900年到公元前700年，比起以前的时期是一个突变，这一突变还造就了希腊的主要制度和习俗，如希腊城邦、希腊字母。此时雕塑和雕刻的功能是表现各城邦的英雄和过去的传奇故事，其中既有人的故事，也有动物的故事。新的贸易线路和殖民机会的增加使希腊艺术进入了繁荣时期。人们修建了巨大的神庙和圣殿来供奉神明，里面用贵重的雕像来装饰。全副武装的战士、两轮马车还有战马是几何艺术时期最常见的象征物。

随着地中海东部和尼罗河三角洲新商路的开辟，我们逐渐看到了希腊艺术和东方艺术的融合。古风时期（公元前700—450）随之而来。这一时期表现了更加自然主义的艺术风格，反映了来自近东地区和埃及的重要影响。许多希腊艺术家逐渐吸收东方艺术家的思想，开始在作品中使用棕榈叶和莲花纹样，狩猎图案和一些混合怪兽的画像，如：狮身鹫首的怪兽（一半是鸟，一半是狮子），斯芬克斯（一半是女人，一半是长翅膀的狮子），还有女妖塞壬（一半是女人，一半是鸟）。希腊本土的艺术家和殖民地的艺术家互相竞争，看谁能创造出最伟大、最新颖的奇迹。爱琴海诸岛，特别是纳克索斯岛和萨摩斯岛的雕塑家们，用大理石雕刻了巨大雕像；罗德岛的金匠专攻精巧的珠宝工艺；克里特岛的青铜工匠用华美的浮雕来装饰盔甲和匾额。希腊本土的一些杰出的艺术中心，如斯巴达、科林斯和雅典，也展现了各自重要的地域差别。斯巴达和邻近的拉科尼亚生产的象牙雕刻和青铜制品无与伦比；科林斯的陶艺工匠发明了一种技法，在器物上饰以小型动植物的侧面轮廓，其图案如同壁毯一般。相比之下，雅典的画师更倾向于在花瓶上绘制表现神话场面的图案。古风时代最有名的就是出现了石质人物雕像，比如石灰石制作的 kouros（男性）和 kore（女性）雕像。

这些新的雕像表现了裸体的年轻人，他们脸上总是带着微笑。尽管这些雕像的主要目的是体现人体的完美，但多数的雕像还是给人留下拘谨而僵硬的印象。虽然有种种缺陷，但希腊人还是这一时期最早发明自由站立的雕像的民族。

古典艺术时期（公元前480—323）创建于"黄金时代"，即从希腊的崛起与扩张到亚历山大大帝的去世。古典时期可被视为艺术的转折点，这一时期创造了大量迄今为人们所称道的精美雕塑。这一时期雕塑家掌握了大理石的雕刻，开始创造一些体现欢快的自由活动的作品，同时他们把人作为独立的实体来歌颂了。

展现自由活动的最佳作品是米隆的《掷铁饼者》，这也是这一时期最重要的希腊古典雕塑之一。这一时期，人们第一次认可了人体解剖结构在雕塑中的价值，并用石头和青铜使之永恒。过去那些静止、僵化的人体姿态已被新式的、"快照式"的立体动作所取代，这样人们就可以欣赏到人体之美。普通人第一次被视为与神明相像，这意味着人体第一次成为研究对象并获得了应有的重视。古典时期的希腊雕像脸上是没有表情的，而"野蛮人"则表现出夸张的表情。这是因为希腊人认为对感情的压抑是文明人的高贵品质，而公开表露感情则是野蛮的标志。即使在最戏剧性的情况下，也要用逻辑性和理性来控制情感。

这个时代最伟大的雕像是奥林匹亚山的宙斯像和帕特农神庙的雅典娜像。这两件作品都是菲迪亚斯设计的。这两尊雕像的复制小样迄今尚存，但不幸的是，原作品早已付之一炬。希腊雕塑在表现纯粹的自由、自醒和自主方面，超过了其他任何艺术形式。这些价值观激发古希腊人打败了强大的波斯,并使他们发展出一种保障每个人尊严的社会模式。

希腊化时期(公元前323—31)大约始于亚历山大大帝之死,终结于公元前31年的亚克兴战役。希腊化时期的逻辑思维相比从前有巨大的变化。这一时期的艺术家不再拘泥于古典时期的惯例和规则,而是在作品中试验新的动作,尝试自由的感觉,这使得艺术家能从独特的角度发掘作品的主题。

要了解两者区别,只需比较一下《德尔斐的驭手》和《男孩赛马》这两尊雕像。前者是古典时期的作品,表现了尊贵与谦恭,而后者是希腊化时期的作品,极度表现能量与活力。技术和材料上的巨大进步让人们有条件建造了有史以来最宏大、最辉煌的雕像:《罗德岛太阳神巨像》。不幸的是,频繁的劫略和地震毁掉了这尊据传有纽约《自由女神像》那么高的雕像。希腊化时期最著名的雕塑有:《垂死的高卢人》、《米洛的维纳斯》、《萨莫色雷斯的胜利女神》。这些作品描写古典英雄,但是融入了希腊化的艺术风格,使得这些作品充满激情,也更具美感。

Unit 3　Theatre

美妙的视觉盛宴

《猫》于1981年5月11日在伦敦西区的新伦敦剧院首演。开始时并非一切顺利,剧中的演员之一,朱迪·丹契,在伦敦公演之前的排练中拉伤了筋腱。随后这一角色由伊莲·佩姬接替。这个角色为佩姬做了强化并且由佩姬来演唱歌曲《回忆》。这部音乐剧由特雷弗·纳恩担任导演,吉莉安·林恩担任副导演和编舞。《猫》一共在伦敦演出了8 949场。《猫》最后一次在伦敦西区的演出恰逢它的21岁生日,2002年5月11日,演出还在科文特公园的大屏幕上转播以满足没有能够买到最后一场演出门票的该剧的粉丝们。《猫》一直保持着在伦敦演出时间最长的音乐剧纪录,该纪录直到2006年10月8日才被《悲惨世界》打破。

《猫》在百老汇的初次亮相是1982年10月8日,在冬园剧院由同样的制作团队演出。1997年6月19日,《猫》成为百老汇历史上演出时间最长的音乐剧,共演出了6 138场。在演出了共计7 485场次之后,《猫》于2000年9月10日停止了公演。它在百老汇的演出纪录直到2006年1月9日才被《歌剧魅影》打破。现在其仍然保持着百老汇历史上公演时间第二长的纪录。

1998年,以舞台版本的《猫》为基础制作了一个视频版本,包括伊莲·佩姬、肯·佩吉、约翰爵士在内的许多来自不同舞台剧制作的舞蹈演员和歌手都参与了演出。该版本由戴维·马利特导演,由该剧最初的、受人尊敬的设计师吉莉安·林恩以伦敦的亚德菲剧院为背景负责编舞和舞台设计,通过录像带和DVD的形式发售,并且在世界各地的电视台播放。

安德鲁·劳伊德·韦伯爵士在1977年开始为T.S.艾略特的诗《老鼠讲讲世上的猫》配乐。对于韦伯来说,这些歌曲实际上是一种尝试,他想试一试自己是否能为诗歌谱曲。1980年,在一场音乐会中表演了这些歌曲之后,艾略特的妻子瓦拉里·艾略特将她丈夫的一些未完成的诗稿交给了韦伯,主要是《格瑞泽贝拉:魅力猫》。这些诗启发他去找导演特雷弗·纳恩一起探讨艾略特著作的深层内涵,并发现其中还有更多涉及猫的部分。在瓦拉里送来的另一份诗的草稿的启发下,两人创作了该剧开场的这一段《洁里柯的猫》。

83岁的林恩,该剧最初的舞蹈设计者,对于那些早期的日子仍然历历在目。当时正在筹备音乐剧《俄克拉荷马》的她接到了英国制作人卡梅伦·麦金托什的电话,让她去见见韦伯,后者刚刚从美国回来,为了给他的制作寻找经费,但是毫无收获。

她说:"他直接带我去了他家,倒上两杯白葡萄酒并且直接切入主题。我听了他的介绍后非常激动和兴奋,以至于我一直在说,而他也是一直滔滔不绝,所以我觉得我们两个人谁也没有听清另一个人说了什么。"

在被韦伯说服以艾略特的诗为基础制作一个大型的音乐剧是个好主意之后,纳恩开始构思舞台设计,林恩开始编排舞蹈。纳恩觉得该剧的设计应该展示猫的视角、猫的标准以及它们眼中人类古怪的行为。就这样,垃圾场的流浪猫世界诞生了。林恩在正式彩排之前花了一个月来设计舞蹈,所有设计都利用了她在西区剧院音乐剧中的舞蹈表演经验并得到了一位法国哑剧艺术家的帮助。她从研究自己的猫开始,来了解猫的行为。她努力去捕捉猫的敏捷、感受以及它们的神秘情感,她要求舞蹈演员勤加练习以达到她所希望的水准。在她看来舞蹈应该"述说每首歌里的故事,而不是随意地表现。"

预演开始之后,林恩不分昼夜地改进表演。"这是与众不同的表演,因为稍不留神就会让它看上去非常幼稚",她说,"《猫》最为突出的地方是它带来了异乎寻常的感官刺激和精神上的冲击。当这两者与哑剧表演、舞蹈、疯狂和速度糅合在一起的时候,它是绝妙的。"

然而,除了舞蹈设计和舞台设计,如果没有才华横溢的道具设计监督罗恩·莫里森和假发制作师沙伦·凯斯的鼎力相助,这些穿戴着莱卡夹层假发的猫科动物也无法如此光彩四溢、充满魅力。莫里森要求每一套演出服都由手工制作,从连体紧身衣到叹为观止的牦牛毛假发。由于表演者跳舞时往往伴随大幅度的运动,莫里森说,表演服每6~9个月就需要更换。曾经参与《骇客帝国》《芝加哥》以及《泰坦尼克号》等制作的凯斯认为,假发是演员重要的一个部分,不是随随便便戴到头上的,一次表演前当她正将假发"粘"到舞蹈演员头上的时候她说,能回来帮忙演出"对我来说就像一种荣幸,它包含了太多东西,每次都有新鲜感"。她接着补充道,"许多人非常热爱这出剧,许多第一次感受它的人在内心深处都对它叹为观止。"在《猫》的道具清单中大约有60顶假发,每一套价值大约4 000美金。

自从在百老汇演出之后,《猫》在全世界各个地方公演。15年前,它曾经让悉尼的观众赞不绝口,而现在它再度回归。最新的澳大利亚制作版本的《猫》在阿得雷德首映,创造了1 400万的票房纪录。导演乔-安妮·罗宾逊在该剧的筹备初期就参与到其中,并帮助原来的舞蹈编排吉莉安·林恩创作猫的舞步来配合安德鲁·劳伊德·韦伯创作的歌曲。"这是一整个团队的工作。我们觉得'这要么完全是一场灾难,要么是非凡的成功。'"罗宾逊说道,"该剧第一次公演,大家的反应就超乎寻常,我们自己也激动万分。"罗宾逊说从1981年首演到现在,《猫》是"从未有过的新鲜、美妙的视觉盛宴"。谁能想到这样一个温驯的小动物能成为最受欢迎的舞台剧的灵感?

在澳大利亚,来自昆士兰17岁的卡莱布·巴特罗,成为最年轻的出演《猫》的演员。巴特罗在2008年的《你认为你可以跳舞》中崭露头角。在《猫》的排练当中,他发现跟上舞蹈的步伐极具挑战性。"虽然只是舞步而已,但是作为猫来表现是完全不同的一回事。"他说,"要想做到像猫一样舞动是非常难的。每个人开始跳起来只是像一个舞者,但是我们逐渐了解了猫的生理结构,它们如何移动,它们的生理结构如何帮助它们做到不同的事情。我们需要时刻将此表现出来,所以有许多躬背和其他的背部动作。"年轻的演员就像他们的前辈一样为《猫》带来了活力和爱。他们为能够将葛丽兹贝拉、罗腾塔格、麦卡维弟和众多朋友们介绍给年轻一代的粉丝而感到自豪,他们共同合作一起抓住了众多观众的心。

伦敦首映30年之后,《猫》已经不再只是一部音乐剧。它超越了猫有九条命的传说成为了一个毛茸茸、生气勃勃的现象。如果你热爱音乐剧并且还没有看过这部剧的专业演出,不要让任何事情成为你不去观看该剧的理由。设法在尽可能靠前的地方找个座,尽情体验这些美妙的、毛茸茸的小家伙给你带来的完美的舞台感受。

Unit 4　Western Classical Music

聆听19世纪古典音乐

你一定听说过"古典音乐"一词吧。你的脑海中有无曾思考过这些问题:什么叫做古典音乐?如何来欣赏古典音乐？这里我们将共同走进19世纪古典音乐的世界,相信你会对这个特殊的音乐有更加全面的了解。

19世纪的西方社会经历了巨变。民主思想和工业革命席卷了整个欧洲,并改变了各个阶层的人们的生活。新旧世界秩序的冲突是从拿破仑战役到美国内战期间冲突的根源所在。世界的各个角落都在不断变化,纽约如此,伦敦也是这样,维也纳也不例外,甚至到今天人们仍然可以感觉到这种变化。

音乐家、作曲家和乐器制造商的生活都深受这种社会变革的影响。在此之前,音乐家通常被教堂或者宫廷雇佣演奏,他们仅仅是这些贵族的仆人。作曲家作曲是为了给贵族表演使用,而乐器制造商制造的乐器都是为了给那些富有的赞助商或他们雇佣的音乐家使用。然而在19世纪,由于作曲家和演奏家可以经济独立,音乐组织逐渐脱离了赞助商的统治。

一个全新的艺术美学运动——浪漫主义——取代了18世纪末那些古典主义者所鼓吹的秩序主义、对称主义和形式主义。浪漫主义者反其道而行之,他们重视自然界,把普通人的生活理想化,反对社会陈旧传统,强调情感在艺术中的重要性。在音乐领域,伴随着那些音乐家或作曲家谋生的新机会,浪漫主义者开辟了两块看起来完全相反的场所进行音乐演奏——大剧院和会客厅。

剧场乐

工业革命的其中一个结果就是中产阶级的产生。与之前存在的阶层相比,这个新的经济阶层由众多收入不菲、业余时间宽裕的人组成。随着中产阶级的兴起,更多的普通人想演奏音乐和学习音乐。整个西欧大陆逐渐扩大的中产阶级队伍对音乐的狂热激发了负责音乐表演、教育和传承的音乐组织的形成。一些音乐家和作曲家之所以声名显赫,就是因为众多追捧音乐演奏会的人的狂热。从贝多芬开始,作曲家们开始举办大型的演奏会,以此来向公众推出他们的作品。随着听众的要求逐渐增高,作曲家们开始创作大型的音乐剧,而这必然要求更多的演奏者和乐器。

这种所谓的"越大型越好"的想法导致了一些新的音乐类型,例如交响诗(取材于文学的音乐)、大型的交响乐和歌剧作品。管弦音乐开始发展,包括一些更大型的弦乐部分,它们拥有充足的木管弦乐、铜管弦乐和更多的打击乐器。更易操作和精确演奏的新型管弦乐器和铜管乐器也加入进来。交响乐形成了一种独特的音乐形式,而协奏曲则发展成了音乐家们展示演奏技巧的形式。交响乐团不再依赖大键琴(在巴洛克风格中它是传统低音的一部分),通常由一流的小提琴演奏家引领。歌剧也不甘落后,形成了以地域为特色的意大利、法国和德语国家等多种风格。作为喜歌剧的一种,意大利喜歌剧迅速流行起来。纵横19世纪,作曲家们不断地推进和打破音乐形式、表演者、乐器和演奏场地的界限,比如埃克托·柏辽兹、约翰内斯·勃拉姆斯和理查德·瓦格纳等。

那些依靠自己的精湛技巧使得听众为之沉醉和目眩的音乐家成了音乐界的第一批超级明星。19世纪两个最著名的例子就是小提琴家尼科洛·帕格尼尼(1782—1840)和钢琴家弗朗茨·李斯特(1811—1886)。他们两个都依靠自己的演奏使得全欧洲的听众为之迷醉,同时也提高了音乐家的地位:从地位卑微的仆人变成了神一般的巨人。他们的名声远扬整个欧洲,而他们的相似性也用很多视觉艺术形式被记录了下来。

为了承担起独奏者那些精湛的、激昂的演奏和为大型音乐会演奏提供所需要的大量乐器,演奏者们需要更加有力的乐器。帕格尼尼所使用的安东尼奥·斯特拉迪瓦里小提琴和瓜奈里大提琴(1698—1744)更大,声音更加洪亮,取代了之前那些更轻细的顶级乐器,如约克伯·史戴纳小提琴和阿玛蒂家族。以弗朗茨·李斯特为代表的钢琴家们的要求促使钢琴的制造和设计朝着大型乐器的方向发展,最终取代了18世纪那种木质结构的钢琴,它们有着钢铁铸造的框架,可以承受数千磅的压力。

室内乐

与上面所讲的情况相反,19世纪的音乐在令人亲近的会客厅受到了广泛的欢迎。那个时候,家庭生活的中心是客厅和会客厅，孩子们在那里在大人的监督和指导下学习和游戏，家庭成员也在那里招待亲友同伴。为小型人群演奏的音乐表演流行了起来，而且一些作曲家和演奏家完全可以通过在这些小型场所的演奏并以此吸引富裕的赞助人做到经济上自给自足，其中最著名的就是弗雷德里克·肖邦（1810—1849）。

与在音乐会大厅里演奏的音乐相比，在会客厅演奏的音乐完全是不同的形式。独奏表演和室内音乐十分流行，几乎包含了所有的音乐种类，从歌剧和管弦乐录音到伤感的爱情歌曲和歌谣。在美国，斯蒂芬·福斯特作曲的赞歌和民歌补充和完善了欧洲的音乐种类。

随着客厅成为家庭生活的中心，音乐教育也变得越来越重要。孩子通常都会去学习演奏乐器，这也成了全面教育的一部分；对于女孩子来说，会演奏乐器比读书还要重要。当客人或者可能的求婚者到家中拜访的时候，孩子们和少年就会演奏最新流行乐曲来招待他们。

家庭演奏会使用各式各样的乐器，尤其以吉他、竖琴、六角手风琴和班卓琴最为流行。但是，在家庭音乐演奏中最重要的乐器还是钢琴，因为不管是对于独奏来说，还是一队歌唱家和乐器演奏家的伴奏来说，钢琴都显得尤为重要。为了适应家庭演奏的需要，出现了很多小型的钢琴，从开始时的方形钢琴到后来竖直的钢琴。小型钢琴占地面积小，尽管它们比不上大型钢琴的力量，但是却便宜很多。随着工业革命带来的科技进步，乐器开始批量生产——尤其是钢琴——给美国和欧洲巨大的需求市场提供了看起来源源不断的乐器。钢琴一直都是家庭生活的中心要素，直到被20世纪出现的留声机、收音机和电视取代。

在对19世纪的古典音乐有了大致的了解之后，我们可以看出，古典音乐的发展，尤其是19世纪这两种特殊的古典音乐形式，和社会的变革有着不可分割的关系。此前的古典音乐一直被认为是高雅的，代表贵族的某些特征，并非面向工人阶级。然而，那些认为只有上流社会才能欣赏古典音乐，或者古典音乐代表上流社会的想法都是不正确的，因为在美国许多古典音乐家本身就是工人阶级，而且许多去音乐会的人和买音乐碟片的人并非都是上层社会的人。在古典音乐时期，一个典型的例子就是莫扎特的喜歌剧大受普通民众的喜爱，如《女人心》。从这个角度看，文化不同方面的发展和社会的变革不无关联。

Unit 5　Graphic Designing

19世纪的平面设计

工业革命是一个动态过程，它开始于18世纪后期，并一直持续到19世纪。西方农业和手工业经济逐渐演变成靠蒸汽机、电力和内燃机提供动力的工业制造经济。人类活动的许多方面发生了不可逆转的改变。社会发现了平面设计的新用途，开发了新的生产技术。工业技术降低了印刷和纸张的成本，从而使设计师的作品能到达比以往任何时候都更广泛的受众手中。

海报对于平面设计师来说是一种较为流行的媒介。在整个19世纪中，木刻活版字海报被广泛应用于新的交通工具、娱乐、商品的广告宣传。造成这种情形的部分原因在于，字体的创造者们开发了更大尺寸的字体，引入了包括无衬线字体和装饰设计的新字体。一位从事印刷的美国人达留斯·威尔斯发明了木版切割机，使得大批量制作大型木刻活版字更加经济，其成本不到大型金属版的一半。

海报变得更受欢迎还得益于平版印刷技术的进展，这项技术由巴伐利亚的阿罗斯·塞菲尔德于1798年发明。在这个发明的基础上，彩色平版印刷被广泛应用于19世纪下半叶。设计师创造了越来越多的彩色海报，装点着城市的墙壁，为各种重大活动、娱乐节目和家用产品作宣传。使用彩色印刷术的设计师们将文本和图像整合成为一件艺术品。由于摆脱了凸版印刷的技术束缚，他们可以自由地创造别具一格的装饰品和字体风格。

这场海报设计运动起势于法国,海报设计师儒勒·舍雷是这场运动的先驱。从1867年开始他创造了大型平版印刷海报,鲜明的色彩、生动的人物、带纹理的平坦形状,捕捉到了处于世纪之交的巴黎的"美好年代"。在整个职业生涯中,舍雷设计了上千种广告海报。

19世纪工业化的副产品之一是书籍装帧设计和生产质量的下降。当时流行的是便宜的薄纸、劣质的印刷、单调的灰色油墨、乏味的字体。19世纪末兴起的图书设计复兴活动是英国工艺美术运动的直接结果。运动的领导者威廉·莫里斯是设计发展史上的一个重要人物。自19世纪60年代到90年代,莫里斯积极从事着家具、彩绘玻璃、纺织品、壁纸、挂毯的设计活动。莫里斯对工业化和工厂制度的问题极为关切。他认为,向哥特式时期的工艺水平和精神价值的回归,可以让现代生活恢复平衡。他排斥没有品位大量生产的工业品和粗制滥造的制作,推崇他所设计的制作精良的美丽物件。

1888年莫里斯决定成立一个出版社以恢复早前几十年的书籍印刷质量。他的凯尔姆斯科特出版社于1891年开始出版书籍,采用的是老式手动操作印刷机、丰厚的油墨及手工纸品。它重新获取了古版书籍之美和高标准,书籍再次成为一种艺术表达形式。凯尔姆斯科特出版社的杰作是556页、耗时4年制作的《杰弗里·乔叟作品集》。

威廉·莫里斯和凯尔姆斯科特出版社对平面设计有着巨大的影响。莫里斯的设计观——精心设计的页面、漂亮的字体以及设计的整体感启发了新一代平面设计师。莫里斯对早期字体风格的探求和重新审视也引发了一个充满活力的重新设计过程,使得设计、印刷的字体品种质量和数量都大为改善;许多设计师直接模仿了凯尔姆斯科特出版社的镶边、首字母缩写和字体样式。莫里斯的成功还振兴了更多平面设计的商用领域,如印刷及广告工作。

同样受到了工艺美术运动启发的还有美国图书设计师布鲁斯·罗杰斯,他在提升书籍设计质量方面起着重要的作用。他将精美书籍的设计理想带入了商业化的生产中,为20世纪初设计精良的书籍制订了标准。罗杰斯具有出色的视觉比例感。他还将设计视为一个决策过程,认为整体的和谐统一是结合了边距、纸张、字体样式和大小、空间位置的微妙选择去创造的。

新艺术运动出现于19世纪90年代至20世纪初,是一个国际性的设计运动,涉及了所有的设计艺术。蜿蜒的曲线是其主要特点。新艺术运动的设计往往采用风格化抽象的图形、轮廓线和平坦的画面,其灵感来自日本的浮世绘版画。在日本风格的基础上,新艺术运动设计师们将颜色,而非色调造型,作为其图形的主要视觉特点。

最具创新性的新艺术运动海报之一是亨利·德·图卢兹·罗特列克于1891年为舞者拉·古留所作的海报,当时拉·古留在红磨坊表演。图卢兹·罗特列克将意象简化成简单的平面形状来表现舞蹈和环境氛围。图卢兹·罗特列克只创作了三十几幅海报,但他早期对浮世绘技巧的应用,推动了平面设计向意象还原发展。他对文字和图形元素通常作同样处理,都采用了自然随意的笔触,使之巧妙搭配。

在巴黎工作的捷克年轻艺术家阿尔丰斯·穆夏被广泛认为是将新艺术风格推向视觉表达极致的一位平面设计师。他的设计创造始于19世纪90年代,他的画面常常有青春美貌的女性,其服饰和发型曲线流畅富有韵律,达到了理想化的完美形象。他将华丽的装饰性元素、风格化的字体和曲线玲珑的女性形体融入紧凑的构图中。像当时许多其他设计师一样,穆夏最初成名于海报设计,但也收到了杂志封面、产品包装、书籍设计、宣传品,甚至邮票的设计委托。这样,整个期间平面设计活动的作用和范围不断扩大。

威尔·布拉德利,一位自学成才的美国设计师,是另一位新艺术运动的早期实践者。他的杂志封面、字体风格和海报展示了广泛全面的技巧和设计方法。布拉德利从欧洲新艺术运动和工艺美术运动获取了灵感,将它们融入了自己对视觉意象的个性处理中去。到19世纪90年代时,照相制版流程已经得到完善。这使得艺术品原作的复制比手工雕版准确得多。布拉德利的作品将文字和图形有机结合成富有活力的整体,它们的印刷制版就采用了这种新技术。

新艺术运动拒绝历史主义,强调艺术形式的发明,因此它成为维多利亚时代的设计向20世纪初现代艺术运动的过渡阶段。比利时艺术家和设计师亨利·凡德·威尔德的作品就明显体现出这种过渡感。在19世纪90年代从后印象派绘画转向家具和平面设计后,他利用了灵感源于自然界的线条和形状,将它们抽象提取为"纯粹的形式",也就是说,它们表现为设计师发明的抽象形式,而不是来自大自然的形式。如他为Tropon浓缩食品(1899年)所作的海报,起伏的直线运动,有机统一的形状和温暖色调的颜色,结合成一个抽象的图形表达。虽然这张海报被解释为分离蛋黄和蛋白的过程,一般的观看者仍将它视为纯粹的图形。

建筑师查尔斯·雷尼·麦金托什、赫伯特·麦克内尔同样探索了形式问题,他们和艺术家玛格丽特和弗朗西斯·麦克唐纳(姐妹)合作,从19世纪90年代开始,进入了艺术创新时期。这个格拉斯哥四人团开发出一种直线型的结构,结合了花卉和曲线元素的几何组成。他们作品中使用了大胆、简洁的线条来定义颜色平面。他们将矩形结构和浪漫、宗教意象结合起来,应用在非正统的家具、工艺品、平面设计中。例如,在为格拉斯哥美术学院创作的海报中,他们对垂直构图的强调是显而易见的。

Unit 6　Landscaping

17世纪法国规则式园林

园林艺术在17世纪欧洲艺术和建筑史上占有重要的地位。这个世纪出现了被定义为法国规则式或巴洛克式园林的几何布局样式。它依照精确的数学规则和严格的对称性进行设计,用人工修剪的植物和树木造型。这种风格以中轴对称为基础,体现了"强迫自然接受匀称"的法则。凡尔赛园林的出现标志着此种园林艺术达到了空前辉煌,欧洲其他宫廷纷纷效仿。

法国规则式园林由意大利文艺复兴时期园林演变而来,后者于16世纪初传入法国。意大利文艺复兴时期园林的代表作有佛罗伦萨的波波里花园和费埃索的美第奇庄园,此种风格将几何状花圃或刺绣式花坛对称排列,以瀑布和喷泉增添园中景物的生动,用台阶和坡道连接不同层次的花园,并布置了神话主题的洞穴、迷宫和雕像。花园设计旨在表现文艺复兴时期的理想——和谐与秩序,追忆古罗马的美德。

16世纪的意大利园林因其巨大的台地、雕塑、水景造型,在欧洲北部地区,特别是法国得到了推崇和效仿。1528年,法国国王弗朗西斯一世开始在枫丹白露城堡建造新花园,内有喷泉、花坛、从普罗旺斯移植过来的松树林,以及法国第一个人造洞窟。1546年建筑师菲利贝·德·洛梅按照意大利园林的比例规则设计了阿内府邸花园。园内花坛和水景与绿地部分有机整合,呈现出精心打造的和谐氛围,由此阿内府邸花园成为法国经典园林中最早、最有影响的范例之一。

虽然法国文艺复兴时期园林在内涵和外观上与中世纪园林相比有很大不同,但园林与城堡建筑之间缺乏关联,而且通常都被围墙封闭起来。园林各部分往往建在容易防守的特殊地形之上,彼此之间没有和谐地整合起来。17世纪中叶法国第一个规则式园林的出现则改变了这一切。

位于巴黎东南55千米处的沃子爵府邸花园是第一个重要的法国规则式园林。它建于1658~1661年,为路易十四的财政大臣尼古拉斯·富凯打造,对后世许多建筑产生了重要的影响。它的重大创新之一在于,将建筑、花园以及内部装饰作为一个整体进行了规划。建筑师路易·勒沃,室内设计师夏尔勒·布伦和造园师安德烈·勒诺特尔三人在这个大型项目上首度密切合作。他们的合作标志着一个新秩序即"路易十四式"宏伟风格的开端。

在沃子爵花园,园林和城堡第一次有了完美的结合。1 500米的辽阔景致从城堡大门一直延伸到最远处的大力士雕像;其间布置着排成图案状的常绿灌木花坛,园路上每隔一定距离就会安排雕像、水池、喷泉和精心修剪的园林小品作为装饰。

所有景观(建筑、园林、艺术品)的布局大致遵循了安德烈·莫莱所描述的模式,围绕一个中心轴进行对称排列。沃子爵花园的对称手法所达到完美和统一,在古典园林艺术中鲜有能比者。透视法和光学幻象的出色应用,给观者带来一种能将花园"一目了然于心中"的愉悦。

城堡位于这种严谨空间布局的中心,无论从多远看都处于制高点。无疑,这种居于辽阔之地的"统治"位置象征了城堡主人的权力和成功。不幸的是,宏伟壮丽的园景和开幕庆祝活动引起了国王路易十四的嫉妒和愤怒,当时路易十四能引以为豪的只有位于凡尔赛不起眼的狩猎行宫。15天后富凯被投入监狱,终身监禁。

逮捕富凯后不久,路易十四决定扩大凡尔赛的城堡和林园。他雇用了富凯在沃子爵府邸所用的3人设计团队。1661年,路易十四委任安德烈·勒诺特尔进行凡尔赛宫花园的设计和布置工作,在他看来,花园和城堡同样重要。

花园的设计构思基本上以城堡为基准点,按照三个区域进行规划。园道自中心呈扇状向外辐射到周围空间,然后以多种形式展开,从而划定了更多新的区域。这项工程与宫殿工程同期开工,工期持续了四十多年。凡尔赛最初处于容易大量积水的沼泽地带。而最后,它所建成的景观变成了新城镇的亮点。

凡尔赛宫苑代表了法式园林最高成就。它们是欧洲最大的园林,占地面积6 000公顷,东西向主轴的布局象征着太阳的运行轨迹。它以路易十四的标记——太阳作为花园的重要象征,花园中央喷泉的阿波罗雕像即为最好的说明。凡尔赛园林有着宏大壮观的风景线,一望无际,相比之下,花园本身也让人惊叹。有精心修整的草坪,大批盛开的鲜花,珍贵的雕像和雕塑,令人难忘的喷泉和大运河。

沃子爵府邸花园和凡尔赛宫苑以及大批其他园林的完工,确立了一种全新的景观设计风格和空间尺度。这种新的规则式园林风格包含着与早期文艺复兴时期园林传统大致相同的成分元素,但与后者有区别的是其强烈的空间特征和壮丽辉煌之景。法式园林最典型的特点是规模宏大、构图复杂、装饰丰富、景色辽阔。花园的重要目的不仅在于展示,它还成为理想的聚会场所,多种社交活动的中心,可举办有音乐和戏剧表演的露天宴会、体育运动和游戏活动。

法国规则式园林与法国最著名的造园师安德烈·勒诺特尔密切相关。勒诺特尔基本的设计要素中包含了一个高度统一的构图,通过仔细平衡配比来达到最佳视觉效果。围绕着宫殿和主轴线,一片辽阔的景致呈现在整个布局之上,花坛和水景被有序地安排在其中的几何形格网中,并以树篱和小树丛精确地隔开。

勒诺特尔的作品不仅准确地反映了这一时期的社会关系,还为众多的庆祝活动、文艺演出、娱乐和社交聚会提供了出色的空间场所。勒诺特尔于1700年去世,此时他已将景观建筑提升到了一个新的高度,他的园林建筑思想和方法传遍了整个欧洲。

建筑在法式园林中起到了主导作用。造园师们将自己的工作视为建筑的分支——不过是建筑空间向墙壁外的延伸。设计园林犹如设计建筑物,游览者可以通过既定路线走过一个又一个的"房间"。设计者在设计方案中,会使用建筑语言,空间被称为"室"和"绿化剧院","墙"是由绿篱构成的。建筑师在城堡里安装供水系统,同样,造园师也设计了复杂的液压系统为喷泉和花园的水池供水。

1700年勒诺特尔去世以后,他的造园理念继续统治着法国的园林设计。然而,在严谨的几何式园林中有一些变化开始出现。复杂精美的花坛,被更易于养护的花坛所取代。正圆变成了椭圆,还出现了不规则的八角形。花园开始遵循自然景观样式,而不是搬运泥土去建造人工台地。

18世纪中叶,由于英国景观园林的影响以及排斥对称、主张自然质朴的中国风格的流行,法国规则式园林的统治地位宣告结束。

Unit 7　Photography

如何成为一个伟大的摄影家

照片是神奇的。它是不同文化、不同地貌、不同代人之间的一座桥梁。有了照片,我们可以保存历史——孩子迈出的第一步、正在衰落的文明或是珍奇而又濒危的动物。有了照片,我们可以重温人类踩在月球上的第一步、新总统的就职以及遥远的战场上插在山头上的旗帜。那么多的妈妈们费劲地装饰大大的剪贴本就是为了留住那些甜蜜的回忆。有些地方我们还不曾去过,有些地方我们或许不会重游,有些地方我们永远都不应该忘记,而照片能帮我们铭记所有的一切。

摄影与技巧并无必然的联系。许多人仍然错误地认为掌握了简单的诸如快门速度、景深等知识就了解了关于摄影的全部。摄影是与陌生人交流的工具,无论所要交流的是一个观点、概念、感觉,想法或是其他种种。

一张好的照片能激发人的情感。无论是看到一个傻乎乎小猫咪被线缠住时的善意的微笑还是面对一幅关于战争的照片时产生的恐惧,照片总能让观众强烈地感觉到什么。因此,在你按快门之前,问问自己你希望这张照片激发起怎样的情感。是面对美丽的事物时的敬畏还是希望你的读者看到一个人在帮助无家可归的人?在拍照前先确定这种情感,你拍的照片可能会有进步。

一张好的照片总能讲述一个故事。一张风景照会诉说关于土地的故事;它展现给读者这片土地是安静的还是正在经历剧变,是安静地矗立在冬天里还是在春意里骤然苏醒。就像你应该了解想要激发的情感一样,你也应该了解你想表达的故事。

一张好的照片告诉读者的不止是某个东西是什么样子的。他们能讲述比摄影对象更多的内容。一张真正好的照片讲述生活。它让读者停下来思考。我们看过了很多可爱的动物图片,它们之所以吸引人是因为这些图片让我们知道生活可以是这样好玩的,生活依然充满了乐趣和天真。那些大峡谷的图片如果你看到的仅仅是岩石的话那它们充其量不过是一些好看的图片而已,除非观众能看到岩石外的东西。悬崖告诉我们生活可能是危险的。曙光中的岩石则告诉我们即便是坚硬如岩石的东西也有一种温柔的特质。用你的照片去与人交流你所了解的生活吧。

那么,如何造就一个真正伟大的摄影家呢?是他们的设备,是他们对影像的掌握还是他们的远行?这些只是摄影艺术的副产品而已。伟大只能通过摄影家的品质来获得。伟大的摄影家其实是平凡的普通人。

谦卑

首先,让我们置身于同一条起跑线上。说到摄影,我们每一个的起点都一样。我可以拍出好的作品,你也可以。同样的,我也会和你一样,拍出失败的作品。谁都不比谁强。

要想在这一行得到别人的认可你得表现出真正的谦卑。说得直白一点吧,不知为不知,当你不懂的时候要去向懂的人请教。这句话听起来有些别扭,但事实就是这么简单。摄影关乎如何作出正确的决定。"伟大"的摄影家是指有时候缺乏作出正确决定的能力但有勇气去向别人请教的人。

有三种摄影师。技术型摄影师关注设备和规则,他懂得微米和焦距等知识;主题型摄影师拍照就是为了研究某个主题的。他懂繁殖习性、鸟类羽毛的差异、经度和纬度等。还有一种是摄影艺术家,他们并不知道自己刚才拍的是什么,也不清楚自己是如何拍出来的,但是往往就是他们能拍出最为赏心悦目的照片来。

Translation of the Texts

在摄影领域,这三种摄影师都占有一席之地,每一个类型都缺乏另两类所具备的技能。懂技术的花了太多时间去购置设备以至于他们从未真正掌握构图的基本原理;关注于主题的摄影师一门心思地追寻下一个主题目标,完全想不到其他人并没有他们那样对某个事物的独特理解;摄影艺术家们将他们拍摄的令人惊异的照片标注上"鸟"、"车"或是"教堂"。

伟大的摄影师会就自己不懂的问题向懂行的人提问,并且也会善意地解答别人提出的问题。

耐心

如果你想成为一个伟大的摄影师,没有耐心是几乎不可能实现的。精彩的摄影作品并不是从天上掉下来的。为了拍到它们,你得为此在沙漠的烈日里比别人多走一英里的路,你得为了等动物出现而多坐十多分钟,为了捕捉最佳的光线你得一大早起来。没有耐心,你偶尔因为运气仍然可能拍出好作品,但是你几乎很难有机会成为真正杰出的摄影师。

给动物和孩子拍照就是最好不过的例子了,他们绝对不会老老实实待上很久。摄影师需要耐心地捕捉拍摄的时机。小约翰尼通常是如何提醒他的父母他的存在的?通常是当他认为你没在看他的时候他所做的事情,而捕捉这样的瞬间是需要耐心的。

耐心还需要有条不紊的组织。拍照时记得列一个你需要所有东西的清单,搞清楚一天之中的什么时候动物们最活跃以及什么时候光线会照射到适合拍照的角度。记得带上你可能会用得上的滤光器或其他的设备。如果在工作室拍照,布置好小的道具。只有提前做好其他的事情你才有可能耐心地等待。再没有比未能提前做好该做的事情更让人烦恼的了。

坚持不懈

与耐心直接相关的是坚持不懈。

最高境界的摄影是一条充满了成功的喜悦和失败的痛苦的道路。在摄影过程中有太多的方面可能会出错,以至于真的出现这样的问题时往往让人瞠目结舌。如果你只是开开心心地拍些快照来记录自己身边生活的话,那么你不太可能体验那种极致的快乐或是忧伤。不过如果你的追求是成为真正伟大的摄影师,那你就不会对这样的情绪感到陌生了。在这个世界上,我们时常会面对各种各样的负面影响,来自他人的反对或劝阻。在这个世界上,有战争、全球性的经济衰退,巨大的竞争,糟糕的光线、背景、人群,还有诸如设备故障,恶劣的天气,等等。所有这些都会阻碍我们拍出真正伟大的影像来,而只有那些坚持到底的人才能成就不朽。

坚持不懈意味着你可能不得不返回拍摄地再试一次。假如你的第一组照片达不到你想要的效果,老老实实地承认这一点并且专注地再来一次。许多摄影师都有过这样的经历,要经过一次又一次的尝试最终才能拍出他们脑海中的画面。风景摄影师安塞尔·亚当斯将之称之为可视化。据说他会将同一张底片洗印很多张,直到最终得到他想要的影像为止。我们也应该像他一样忠于我们想要的效果直至最终完成。

观察力

观察力的培养能成就一个伟大的摄影家。对无论哪种级别的摄影师,来一次摄影之旅,并且在一开始将相机扔在车上都不失为一个好的建议。重要的是要培养将画面"看"成照片的能力。给自己提问题,观察你能创造出什么样的背景。

"我能站在那儿,将城堡和那棵树都取进镜头里吗?"

"如果我将相机放低,角度是否会更好?"

"这家人是不是应该沿这个方向站在泉边呢?"

通过观察可以找到上述问题的答案,在求解的过程中,让观察成为一种习惯。你会开始注意到以前忽视的事情,你也会一直审视周围寻找可以拍摄的对象。你看到两个蹒跚学步的孩子在分享一个玩具,他们的妈妈在旁边看着。问问自己怎样才能捕捉这样的瞬间。掠过起伏的牧场的云影也会在

359

你的脑海里形成影像。

一个无法将照片形象化的摄影师永远都无法进步。在某个时候每一个摄影师都会感觉遇到瓶颈，通过观察你可以打破这样的瓶颈。你意识到你在做必要的事情来重新激发你的想象力。

无论是钱还是名望都无法造就一个伟大的摄影师，设备、经历或是故事也不行。只有当他们达到了自己设定的目标，创造出让自己喜欢的作品，并且在整个过程中找到了乐趣，他们才能成为真正伟大的摄影师。

Unit 8　Chinese Traditional Folk Arts

中国传统民俗艺术——刺绣

作为历史悠久的民俗艺术，刺绣在中国艺术界占有重要的地位。在其漫长的发展过程中，刺绣和养蚕、抽丝摇纱、编织有着不可分割的联系。刺绣是一种可以装饰织布或其他的材料，即用针来把设计的图案用丝线绣出来的艺术或手工艺。刺绣还可以使用其他材料来完成，如金属条、珍珠、珠子、翎毛和圆形闪光的金属片，还可以用缝纫机来完成机器刺绣。

中国首创抽蚕丝编织。早在5 000年前中国人就开始养蚕。丝线和丝织物的生产推进了刺绣艺术的产生。1958年，在战国时期(475—221BC)的楚墓中出土了一件绣有龙凤图案的绣品，这件绣品拥有2 000多年的历史，是出土的中国刺绣中最早的一件。作为民俗艺术，刺绣可以追溯到周代，在汉代(206BC—AD220)得到广泛流传，很多出土的绣品都是那个时期的作品。作为世代相传的传统工艺，中国手工刺绣以丝织品刺绣而闻名。在今天的中国，丝织品刺绣几乎在中国的各个地方得以发展。中国的四大名绣指的是产自中国中部地区湖南省的湘绣、中国西部地区四川省的蜀绣、中国南部地区广东省的粤绣和中国东部地区江苏省的苏绣。

苏绣

苏州刺绣，又叫苏绣，有着两千多年的悠久历史。

苏绣是对产自江苏苏州地区的绣品的总称。苏绣以其绣品光滑精妙著称，在清代为苏州赢得了"丝绸之府"的美称。在清代的中后期，苏绣得到了进一步的发展，出现了双面刺绣的作品。当时的苏州拥有65间刺绣作坊。在中华民国(1912—1949)时期，由于频繁战乱，苏绣走向了衰退。新中国对苏绣进行了修复，中央政府于1950年设立了苏绣研究中心，还为苏绣学习开设了苏绣培训课程。与此同时，编织的手法也从18种跃升到了现在的40种。

苏绣的工艺者们可以使用40多种缝纫技法和1 000种不同的丝线在绣布上绣出花、鸟、甚至花园的图案。苏绣做工精妙，尤以一幅猫咪图案而出名，绣图中的猫咪眼睛炯炯有神，毛发蓬松，栩栩如生。苏绣的主要主题就是大自然和生活环境。

苏绣以浓厚的民间风味为特色。它的编织技巧主要有以下特征：绣品的表面必须平整、边缘要整齐、针要细、线要紧、颜色要协调明亮、整张画面要自成一体。苏绣作品主要有三类：戏服、廊厅装饰和日常工艺品，这使得苏绣融合了装饰作用和实用价值。双面绣作品是苏绣中出类拔萃的代表。

湘绣

四大名绣之一的湘绣，有着美妙绝伦的技艺和独特的风格，是湖南人民创造上的一项著名的手工艺。

历史悠久的湘绣起源于湖南省的民间刺绣。从1958年长沙地区的楚墓中出土的刺绣作品来看，湖南的刺绣在约2 500年前的春秋时期得到了很大的发展。还从1972年长沙地区的马王堆中出土的40件刺绣服装中，可以看出，湖南的刺绣在2100年前的西汉时代发展到了更高的层次。此后，在漫长的发展中,湘绣雅致的艺术风格逐渐得以形成。

在后来的发展中,湘绣汲取了中国传统绘画的特点,形成了自己的独特风格。湘绣在清代末期(1644—1911)进入了其发展的鼎盛时期,在20世纪初期的民国初期甚至还超越了苏绣。新中国成立后,湘绣得到了进一步的完善,达到了全新的水平。

海内外闻名的湘绣作品的独特之处在于其远景的巨大能量和栩栩如生的艺术效果。湘绣以质坚的绸缎、柔软的绸缎、透明的薄纱和尼龙作为刺绣材料。刺绣作品不仅拥有着艺术欣赏的珍贵价值,还是好看实用的物品,包括屏风、画、被面、靠垫、床罩、垫子、桌布、手帕和所有的刺绣服装等等。

粤绣

粤绣又叫广绣,是对广东省广州、汕头、中山、番禺和顺德地区绣品的总称。

根据历史记录,唐代(618—907)的永贞元年(805),一个名叫卢眉娘的女孩在不到一尺长的丝绢上绣出了《法华经》七卷。粤绣也因此在国内广为人知。宋代时期繁荣的广州港口因开始出口绣品而促进了粤绣的发展。清代时期,人们开始利用动物的毛发作为粤绣的原材料,这使得绣品更加生动真实。在清代乾隆年间(1736—1796),广州设立了一个生产绣品的工业组织。那时,不计其数的工匠艺人都潜心钻研这门技艺,促进了编织技术的进一步发展。从1915年开始,粤绣在巴拿马世博会上获得了多项荣誉。

受我国民俗艺术的影响,粤绣形成了自己的独特风格。绣品的图案多以龙凤、花鸟为主,同时绣品有着整齐划一的设计,颜色对比鲜明。丝线、棉线和金丝线刺绣被用于做戏服、廊厅装饰和日常工艺品等。

蜀绣

蜀绣,也叫做川绣,是对四川省成都地区的刺绣作品的总称。

蜀绣源远流长。早在汉代,蜀绣就已经闻名遐迩。中央政府还曾经在这个地方专为此设立了一个管理办公室。在五代十国时期(907—960),和平的社会环境和庞大的需求量为蜀绣事业的迅速发展提供了优越的条件。蜀绣在宋代(960—1279)达到了发展的顶峰,在生产和做工精细方面都位居第一。在清代中期形成了蜀绣产业。新中国成立后,设立了许多蜀绣加工厂,开始使用创新的技艺和更加丰富的形式,使得蜀绣的发展迈进了一个全新的阶段。

源于四川省西部民间的蜀绣逐渐形成了自己的独特风格:平滑、明亮、整齐,而且受其地理环境、风俗习惯和文化传统的影响。蜀绣绣品把花、叶、动物、山、河和人物作为创作主题。对于编织工艺来说,共有12种类122种方法。蜀绣的技艺包含了优美的艺术、美学价值和实用价值。

除了这四种主要的刺绣外,还有浙江省温州的瓯绣、河南省开封的汴绣和湖北省武汉市的汉绣。

有机的发展和岁月的积累使得刺绣成为一个样式丰富、形式可塑的艺术门类,激发了强烈的美学乐趣。因主题和技法的迥异,绣品自然形成了不同的类别。它们包含了油画、传统中国画、水乡、花卉等等。有实用价值的绣品有服装、手帕、围巾等等。